Trade
and the
American Dream

T0204423

Trade
and the
American Dream

A Social History of
Postwar Trade Policy

Susan Ariel Aaronson

Forewords by Senator William V. Roth Jr.
and Congressman Robert T. Matsui

THE UNIVERSITY PRESS OF KENTUCKY

Scholarly publisher for the Commonwealth,
serving Bellarmine College, Berea College, Centre
College of Kentucky, Eastern Kentucky University,
The Filson Club, Georgetown College, Kentucky
Historical Society, Kentucky State University,
Morehead State University, Murray State University,
Northern Kentucky University, Transylvania University,
University of Kentucky, University of Louisville,
and Western Kentucky University.

Editorial and Sales Offices:
The University Press of Kentucky
663 South Limestone Street, Lexington, Kentucky 40508-4008

Library of Congress Cataloging-in-Progress Data

Aaronson, Susan A.
    Trade and the American dream : a social history of postwar trade
policy / Susan Ariel Aaronson.
        p.   cm.
    Includes bibliographical references and index.
    ISBN 0-8131-1955-3 (cloth : alk. paper). —ISBN 0-8131-0874-8
(pbk. : alk. paper)
    1. United States—Commercial policy—History—20th century.
2. United States—Economic conditions—1945-   3. International
economic relations.   I. Title.
HF1455.A593   1996
382'.3'0973—dc20   95-51058

Manufactured in the United States of America

Contents

Illustrations

Tables and Figures

Tables

Figure

Foreword
Senator William V. Roth Jr.

Two of the most significant achievements of the 103rd Congress were the passage of legislation to approve and implement the North American Free Trade Agreement (NAFTA) and the Uruguay Round—the eighth round of multilateral trade negotiations under the General Agreement on Tariffs and Trade (GATT). These historic trade agreements were the subject of extensive and, at times, very polarized and divisive debate, and their final approval remained in doubt until the last few days of Congressional consideration. Ultimately, bipartisan support and strong leadership prevailed in support of both agreements.

The NAFTA debate centered primarily on the impact on jobs of free trade with a developing, lower wage country, while the Uruguay Round debate focused largely on the sovereign powers of the United States and the ability to control its own economic destiny. These were not new concerns, but they have been part of the congressional debate on agreements to liberalize trade for more than half a century, particularly in relation to the efforts of the U.S. to create the first multilateral trade organization and tariff reduction agreement—the International Trade Organization (ITO) and the GATT.

These historic undertakings are just a few of the fascinating events readably documented in Susan Aaronson's comparison of U.S. trade policymaking during 1939-1951 and 1980-1995. In *Trade and the American Dream*, Aaronson's portrayal of the executive branch's legislative strategy, the congressional debate, and the public's role surrounding the achievement—or the lack of achievement—of the major trade agreements during these time periods brings to light not only the similarities, but also the major differences in the policy process between these two periods.

While the passage of NAFTA and the Uruguay Round, and ongoing recent intiatives to expand trade liberalization, such as Chile's accession to NAFTA and broader free trade and investment initiatives throughout Asia and the western hemisphere, portend that there is no turning back U.S. active engagement in an open, rule-based world economy, Aaronson underscores why we cannot afford to be complacent about the inevitability of this trend. Although trade has never been more important to U.S. economic prosperity than it is now, it has also become more controversial and divisive among both opinion leaders and the public. Likewise, it is increasingly the subject of presidential political campaigns and antitrade activist groups. These developments are helping to break down several decades of solid bipartisan support for major trade initiatives.

In some respects, we have come full circle. One of the most striking similarities between the post-World War II period and the post-Cold War period pertains to the roots of, and traditional struggle for, power and authority over the direction of U.S. trade policy between the executive and legislative branches of the government. In particular, the Truman administration's battle to gain an extension of the Reciprocal Trade Agreements Act (RTAA) tariff negotiating authority has some very familiar rings to it when compared to the current debate in Congress over the extension of expired "fast-track" authority, which is today's version of special procedures delegated to the President for the completion of major trade agreements. The RTAA renewal efforts in 1948 took place during a Republican-controlled Congress at a time when American priorities had shifted to the domestic realm. These efforts raised serious questions about the administration's trade policy objectives, including the general appropriateness of using the RTAA for a broad-based new multilateral trade organization such as the ITO. We are now on the threshold of a similar debate about the nature and purpose of future fast-track authority, including whether it should be used for much broader objectives than those for which it was originally designed. It may be an arcane subject to many, but it is of fundamental importance to the future direction of U.S. trade policy and role in the world economy.

There are at least three lessons to be learned from *Trade and the American Dream*. Above all, it is essential that there be fuller public understanding of how trade affects the average American and the economy as a whole, particularly with respect to how trade can help Americans achieve the American dream. It is important, however, to recognize that international trade is not without its costs, such as those most poignantly felt by workers who lose their jobs from increased international competition. We should also acknowledge that agreeing to binding trade rules and principles requires a willingness on our part to abide by them, even though they may place certain constraints on our ability to act in contravention of such rules and principles. Nevertheless, our trade with other nations is ultimately not about destroying the American dream, but about building it, and absent greater understanding of the true benefits and costs of trade to the economy, the increasingly vocal voices against trade agreements—agreements which open markets and establish common trade rules and principles—will seriously hamper our ability to move forward with major new trade initiatives.

The second key lesson that is relevant to future trade initiatives is that Congress and the President must exert strong leadership in support of them. The third lesson is that there must be a cooperative, bipartisan process between the Congress and the executive branch in the development and execution of such initiatives; Congress has strong constitutional grounds for expecting to be fully informed and involved in any major trade negotiation led by the executive branch. The lack of these key elements during the negotiation and consideration of the ITO led to its ultimate downfall. The fact that there was little public understanding of the agreement was one more reason for inaction.

Trade and the American Dream is a history that policymakers, students of trade policy, and trade practitioners alike should read for the insights it provides and the lessons that can be learned. It is an informative, revealing, and very timely book.

Foreword
Congressman Robert T. Matsui

As an elected Representative for the people of Sacramento for well over a decade, I have made the expansion of trade a top priority. Trade has had great benefits in terms of economic opportunity not only for the people of California, but for the country as a whole. Expansion of trade through agreements such as the North American Free Trade Agreement (NAFTA) and the General Agreement on Tariffs and Trade (GATT) is crucial for the continued economic growth of the United States.

Our country has a mature economy and an aging population. The U.S. population growth rate is less than one half that of the rates in some of the fastest growing countries in Asia and Latin America. That means that the largest concentration of young workers and potential consumers will be in these developing countries. The so-called Big Emerging Markets including China, Indonesia, India, South Korea, Mexico, Argentina, Brazil, South Africa, Poland, and Turkey make up 49 percent of the world's population. It is interesting to note that the share of the population under the age of 15 is 25.1 percent in Korea, 35.8 percent in Indonesia, and 38.6 percent in Malaysia. Increasingly, we will look to the economies of Asia and Latin America for future growth.

In the last five years, growth in exports accounted for about 50 percent of total U.S. economic growth. The U.S. recently regained its status as the most efficient economy in the world and is the world's largest exporter. We need markets in which to sell the tremendous work product of this economy. Our economic well-being is already linked with our ability to trade, with approximately 27 percent of our economy dependant upon trade. The jobs of over 11 million workers in this country are dependant on exports, and these jobs on average are paying higher wages than non-trade-related jobs.

Trade and the American Dream: A Social History of Postwar Trade Policy develops an interesting and detailed account of the development and ultimate failure of the International Trade Organization (ITO) and applies the lessons gleaned from that initiative to more recent debate over the NAFTA, the GATT, and particularly the World Trade Organization (WTO). Additionally, Susan Aaronson makes some important comments with regard to the future for trade policy. The author's primary observation—that trade policy suffers when limited to a closed, elitist process which prevents the participation and comprehension of complex trade agreement by the public—is right on target.

During the debate on the NAFTA and the GATT, I worked with the administration and with business and interest groups to facilitate a convincing discourse on these agreements to the American people. For example, on the issue of sovereignty (which Aaronson correctly notes was a focal point of the debate over the GATT), I emphasized a number of key facts. The implementing bill specified that U.S. laws prevails if it is in conflict with any provision of the agreement. Also, under the implementing language, an extensive federal-state consultation process was established regarding any matters arising under the agreements that may affect the states. Further, the implementing bill established extensive consultations with congressional committees and the private sector regarding compliance with any dispute settlement finding that is adverse to the U.S., including implementation of any change in U.S. statutes, regulations, or practices which are subject to the adverse finding. Finally, annual reports to the Congress describing the activities of the WTO were required under the implementing language of the GATT agreement. Nonetheless, more educational and outreach efforts must be undertaken.

There are two disturbing trends in our nation today which must be addressed, or they will undermine efforts to expand trade and the resulting increased economic opportunities. The first and most pressing is the growing disparity between rich and poor. Even in the past several years in which we have enjoyed economic growth, wages have remained stagnant and have even eroded for the working poor. We were making progress on this front in the past, and, in fact, from 1929 to 1969 the equality gap was narrowed. However, that dynamic began to change in the 1980s. By 1992 the top 20 percent of American households received 11 times as much income as the bottom 20 percent of households. Further, there is some evidence to suggest that mobility from poverty is decreasing. This lack of equitable distribution will fuel the mistaken perception that free trade impoverishes rather than strengthens us. It is true that trade increases competition and that, in turn, will increase pressure on low-skill jobs. The answer, however, is not to close our doors. The answer is to continue to invest in our people through education and to support working families and their children.

The second trend is that of increasing deficits with our trading partners. We have already undertaken a number of initiatives to open markets for increased exports. However, as we have learned, it takes more than just a good agreement to ensure that our autos can compete abroad and that our high value intellectual property such as movies and CDs are given adequate protection abroad. I am hopeful that the WTO, rather than being seen as a threat to our sovereignty, will instead be a means by which the barriers to our exports will be removed.

Finally, my appreciation goes out to the author for her effort to increase the awareness of the history of trade issues. I know that future readers will benefit, as have I, from seeing recent debates over the NAFTA and the GATT in a larger historical context. Hopefully, armed with increased understanding, we can all better contribute to the ongoing and vital discussion of the interface between trade policy and our domestic policy objectives.

Acknowledgments

I received a lot of help in researching and writing this book. Professor Louis Galambos criticized my arguments and helped me find new and better ways to communicate my ideas. This study could not have been completed without the encouragement and love of my husband. He lived with this book for over four years, and it wasn't always a good roommate. He is terrific. My parents, Professors Sheldon and Shirley Aaronson proofread the book and watched my son. They steadfastly supported me in every way.

The ideas presented in this book were also improved by discussions with many of the former postwar planners, including William Diebold, Ray Vernon, John and Margaret Leddy, J. Robert Schaetzel, Willis Armstrong, Willard Thorp, and Leonard Weiss; with Dan Gardner of the Department of Commerce; and with scholars at the Brookings Institution. The librarians at the Brookings Institution patiently helped me obtain many hard-to-locate documents. Mary Alexander, Professor Bill Becker, Susan Carter, Joe Cobb, Kim Elliot, Patti Goldman, Professor I.M. Destler, Congressman Bill Frenzel, Debbie Lamb, Cynthia Johnson, Mary Irace, Mark Ritchie, Lori Wallace, Professor Ron Walters, and Professor Tim Zeiler read chapters or drafts and improved them. This work is dedicated to all of these generous people, but especially to Imogen and J. Robert Schaetzel. It is also dedicated to Ethan Aaron Wham, who will inherit our policies.

Introduction

Harry S Truman was a small *d* Democrat; he believed that enlightened public policy derived from the people. In 1949, he told the Shriners, "Foreign policy is not made by the decisions of the few. It is a result of the democratic process. The major decisions in our foreign policy . . . have been made on the basis of an informed public opinion and overwhelming public support."[1] But Truman's words to that quintessential American group did not reflect Truman administration trade policies—policies that had undergone radical change during his presidency.

In 1947, the United States led global efforts to reduce trade barriers with the oddly named General Agreement on Tariffs and Trade (GATT). For some fifty years, the GATT sponsored trade negotiations that dramatically reduced world trade barriers, from tariffs to procurement laws, and spurred global economic growth. The American people benefited from that success for a long time—in rising wages, a broad supply of competitively priced goods and services, increased economic opportunities, and relative international economic stability.

GATT's record of success did not inspire overwhelming public support. Five decades later most Americans still understood little of U.S. trade policy. They did not know how the United States depends on trade, why we trade, or what GATT does.[2] Public understanding of trade policy was not commensurate with the importance of trade to domestic and international economic health.[3]

Public awareness of trade policies increased in the 1970s and 1980s. As the American economy was battered by inflation, recession, high interest rates, a rise in the value of the dollar, and growing trade deficits, the American people struggled with longer work weeks, declining job security, wage stagnation, and increasing wage inequality. They often blamed American trade policy for these problems. As President William Jefferson Clinton

> # GATT= Jobs,
> # Economic Growth,
> # Tax Cuts
> # And Leadership.

Ad, Merrill Lynch, Government Relations Office, published in *Roll Call*, December 1, 1994.

> # If President Bush thinks Americans back his trade agenda at GATT, he's wrong.
>
> **A TIMELY WARNING TO GATT DIRECTOR GENERAL ARTHUR DUNKEL**
>
> **AMERICAN CITIZENS AND THE U.S. CONGRESS WILL NOT ACCEPT A GATTASTROPHE.**

Ad, The Citizen Trade Watch Campaign and the Fair Trade Campaign, published in *Roll Call*.

acknowledged in 1994, one reason for these problems was the globalization of the U.S. economy and "intense competition in our own markets . . .
from people who work for wages our folks couldn't live on." Growing
numbers of Americans concluded that freer trade policies and mechanisms actually hampered the ability of hardworking citizens to achieve
the "American dream"—to equal or to exceed the income of their parents.[4]

From the historian's vantage point, this conclusion is both sad and
ironic. These policies were developed by a small group of U.S. policymakers during the Great Depression, who had seen expanded foreign markets for U.S. manufactured goods as the only way to keep the American
dream alive for American workers. These men and women developed both
an international organization and rules to govern trade. But they (and the
policymakers who followed them) did not explain to working Americans
why the United States was encouraging greater trade, why an international organization to govern world trade was necessary, and how such
policies would benefit the man and the woman on the street.

This book examines both how proponents communicated and how
the public understood freer trade policies. It focuses on the development
and debate over three very different international organizations designed to
govern world trade: the International Trade Organization (ITO), the General Agreement on Tariffs and Trade (GATT), and the World Trade Organization (WTO). The debates over these innovations were opportunities
to educate the American people about global economic interdependence.

The GATT was simply a temporary multilateral agreement designed
to provide a framework of rules and a forum to negotiate trade barrier reductions among nations. It was built on 1934 legislation (the Reciprocal
Trade Agreements Act—RTAA) that allowed the Executive Branch to negotiate trade agreements. The ITO, in contrast, set up a code of world
trade principles and a formal international institution. The ITO's charter
was truly revolutionary: it broke new ground by attempting to harmonize
a wide swath of foreign and domestic policies that can affect trade flows.
The ITO's architects were greatly influenced by Lord John Maynard Keynes,
the British economist. The ITO represented an internationalization of the
view that governments could play a positive role in encouraging international economic growth. But Congress never voted on the ITO, and consequently the provisional GATT (which was not a formal international
organization) governed world trade from 1947 until 1994.

Almost fifty years after the United States announced plans to develop an international organization to govern trade, this "club" finally
became a formal international institution in 1994. A week after Congress
approved the eighth round of the GATT, the Uruguay Round, President
Clinton signed the implementing legislation. This round created a new

World Trade Organization (WTO) to replace the GATT. The WTO will provide a permanent arena for member governments to address international trade issues, and it will oversee the implementation of the trade agreements negotiated in the Uruguay Round.[5]

Although policymakers described the WTO as an evolution of the GATT, the WTO was not simply the GATT with a makeover or a reincarnation of the ITO. As the eminent legal scholar John H. Jackson noted, the WTO is "a mini-Charter." As under the GATT, panels would weigh trade disputes, but these panels would have to adhere to a strict time schedule. Moreover, in contrast with GATT procedure, no country could veto or delay panel decisions. If U.S. laws protecting the environment (such as laws requiring gas mileage standards) were found to be de facto trade impediments, the United States would have to change its law, face retaliation, or compensate the other party.[6] As a result, some Americans saw the WTO as a threat to U.S. sovereignty—the ability of the American people to determine their own laws and regulations.

From ITO to GATT

During the ITO debate some fifty years earlier, some Americans had also worried about the power of an international trade organization to force changes in U.S. laws and practices. Their concern was understandable. The American people had not called for such an organization and did not comprehend its implications. And policymakers did little to further their understanding of these policies.

During the 1930s and 1940s, such policymakers as Cordell Hull, Harry Hawkins, Dean Acheson, Will Clayton, Clair Wilcox, Winthrop Brown, and William Fowler steered the executive and legislative branches toward freer trade policies and mechanisms.[7] They were assisted by academics and internationalist business leaders who joined the federal government during the war years.[8] Working with their Allied government counterparts, these men and women determined that the only way to prevent a third world war was to develop a lasting international structure to ensure peaceful cooperation. An international trade organization was central to these plans. But the ITO required years of negotiation; it was drafted three times over four years before the final charter was signed by fifty-four nations in March 1948.[9] Thus, the ITO missed the flurry of support for internationalism that accompanied the end of the war.

The final charter for the ITO was the most comprehensive international agreement ever negotiated; it had provisions setting rules of behavior for the use of import quotas, exchange controls, state trading, and commodity agreements; policies to achieve full employment; and rules to regulate investment and economic development. The ITO also included a secretariat with the power to arbitrate trade disputes and limited enforcement authority. Its signatories hoped that the ITO would lead to trade barrier reduction and spur international economic growth. The ITO's architects believed American businesses and American workers could prosper in a world of planned economies because all economies would "play by the rules" as they sought to achieve growth.[10]

Most Americans, however, had little interest in U.S. trade policy. The war and the Depression had made them more insular, rather than more internationalist, and frequently less receptive, rather than more open, to economic policy innovation. Although the United States emerged from World War II the richest, strongest, and most powerful nation in the world, most Americans did not feel rich and powerful. They were sick of the war, tired of international problems, and ready to return to more local or insular concerns. Polls revealed that the public was confused by the nation's new responsibilities as well as by the ever-increasing alphabet soup of agencies and policies designed to meet them.[11]

Moreover, creation of a new international organization to govern trade was not a top priority for President Harry S Truman or the U.S. Congress. Because 1948 was a presidential election year, Truman waited until April 1949 to present the final charter to Congress.[12] Congress was preoccupied with world events, such as the invasion of Korea.[13] Although the House held hearings, the Senate never scheduled a hearing date. The busy senators and their constituents were focusing on the battle between "the American assembly line and the Communist party line."[14] In November 1950, the president decided not to resubmit the ITO to the Congress.

Many factors collectively contributed to the ITO's demise: they include changing international circumstances, party politics, special-interest opposition, and Truman administration ambivalence. This book focuses on the legislative and public relations strategy of senior Roosevelt and Truman administration officials.[15] In November 1947, as policymakers were negotiating the ITO final charter, senior Truman administration officials in Washington began to distance themselves from the last of the proposed international organizations. These officials, who saw communism on the march, thought the ITO's comprehensive approach to trade seemed ill-fitted to a world plagued by economic and political instability. Moreover, they were reluctant to use the administration's limited political capital to defend the ITO, since the administration had not developed a broad-based constituency in support of radical change to the nation's trade policies. They recognized that voters were focused on other more immediate issues, such as affordable housing and jobs for veterans. Finally, senior policymakers had an alternative mechanism to liberalize world trade, one which would not require direct Congressional approval or popular approval. Ever so gradually, they put their efforts into the supposedly provisional GATT. And soon thereafter, because of its more limited purview, the GATT developed a coterie of support.

From GATT to WTO

In 1954, the Eisenhower administration tried to create an international organization to govern world trade. But Congress never voted on the proposed Organization for Trade Cooperation.[16] For the next thirty years, the GATT proved an adequate, albeit informal, means of achieving global trade barrier reduction. And it developed a core constituency of opinion leaders who supported American leadership of economic internationalism.

By the 1980s, however, policymakers and business leaders in the U.S. and abroad agreed that the GATT's infrastructure would have to be strengthened to encourage global trade barrier reduction.[17] The Omnibus Trade and Competitiveness Act of 1988 explicitly called for "more effective and expeditious dispute settlement mechanisms." Creation of a firmer foundation for the GATT became an important objective of the eighth round of world trade talks, the Uruguay Round. This objective was endorsed by Presidents Ronald Reagan and George Bush. Again, however, they did little to involve or inform the American people as to why an international organization to govern world trade was necessary.[18]

The Debate Over Multilateral Trade Policy

There are two major differences between the debate over trade policy in the post–World War II period and that of the 1990s. As "the American Century" comes to a close, opinion leaders are divided as to the proper course of trade policies. At the same time, growing numbers of Americans are concerned about trade policy and are organizing to effect its direction.[19]

In the postwar period, opinion leaders (journalists, academics, and business, community, agriculture, and labor leaders) of the Right and the Left gradually recognized that international economic growth, spurred by the United States, could unite the world against communism. These "elites" came to accept freer trade through the GATT in the belief that it would encourage both democracy and economic growth in the United States and around the world. Republican and Democratic administrations worked with Congress to produce trade bills that expanded the purview of GATT while protecting specific sectors.[20]

Most Americans, however, remained apathetic about trade.[21] After all, international trade was a relatively small percentage of GNP, and the bulk of our goods and services were "made in the U.S.A." A small but growing minority of Americans understood that American firms must import in order to export.[22] But this understanding did not translate into popular support of multilateral trade liberalization measures or the specific mechanisms of the ITO or GATT.

In the first decade following World War II, U.S. leadership of global efforts to free trade was not a hot political, social, or economic issue. Americans were intent on maintaining the higher standard of living they had attained during World War II and with buying some of the consumer goods that had been in limited supply. Few could see a connection between the ITO, the GATT, and more jobs or cheaper, more plentiful goods. And policymakers did little to help them make that connection.[23] Most Americans knew the rewards that sector-specific protection had provided for over a hundred years, but they could point to few concrete benefits of freer trade. They feared that lower tariffs would create unemployment. Proponents of freer trade such as economists, business or civic leaders, or government officials acknowledged that jobs were lost as a result of trade. But they did little to show how the world economy could create high-paying jobs for Americans. It is not surprising that polls reported public confusion and ambivalence about the comprehensive nature of the ITO and the GATT and the policy shift that they presented.[24] Most Americans had little understanding of the effects of America's growing economic interdependence on their jobs, their investments, their standard of living, and upon American democracy.[25]

Ever so gradually, public concern about trade policy grew. By the 1970s, international trade was a much larger percentage of the nation's output. The trade deficit seemed to increase every year. Korea, Singapore, and China, once poor, seemed increasingly adept at producing the high-tech goods that the United States had once dominated, from aircraft and cars to computers. As trade scholar I.M. Destler noted, "the diminished relative position of the United States . . . discredited, to a degree, arguments for a continuing commitment to open trade."[26]

Although the public seemed to favor free markets in principle, they continued to believe that jobs, industries, and U.S. sovereignty needed to be protected by U.S. economic policy. The American people became increasingly disillusioned with the perceived failure of trade policy to protect these interests.[27]

America's leadership of efforts to free trade did not provide the

Table 1. United States Total Trade as a Percentage of Gross National Product*

Year	Total Trade	GNP	% of GNP
1940	$ 72	$ 773	9.3
1945	$ 89	$1,355	6.6
1950	$114	$1,204	9.5
1955	$154	$1,495	10.3

*in billions of 1982 dollars

Source: Council of Economic Advisers, *Economic Report of the President: Transmitted to the Congress, February 1986* (Washington, D.C.: GPO, 1986), 254-55.

Table 2. United States Total Trade as a Percentage of Gross Domestic Product*

Year	Total Trade	GDP	% of GDP
1960	$ 48.1	$ 513.0	9.3
1965	$ 66.9	$ 702.7	9.5
1970	$ 112.8	$1,010.7	11.1
1975	$ 259.0	$1,585.9	16.3
1980	$ 573.1	$2,708.0	21.2
1985	$ 719.7	$4,038.7	17.8
1987	$ 871.0	$4,539.9	19.2
1990	$1,186.0	$5,546.1	21.4
1992	$1,311.0	$6,038.0	21.7
1993	$1,385.9	$6,374.0	21.7

*in billions of 1993 dollars

Source: Council of Economic Advisers, *Economic Report of the President: Transmitted to the Congress, February 1994* (Washington, D.C.: GPO, 1994) 268-69.

prosperity and job security that the "experts"—economists, business leaders, and government officials—had promised.[28] In the twenty-five years following the war, the real wage of average American workers more than doubled, but from 1973 to 1991, real compensation of average workers was only 6 percent higher. The real wages of blue-collar workers actually fell in this period.[29]

Some of these same experts began to wonder whether U.S. trade policy (or other factors) hurt the very people—American workers—that it had been designed to assist.

In business, labor, agriculture, and government, many of these experts began to debate the future of U.S. trade policy. America's trade policy leaders agreed that "relatively free trade within a world system of common rules should continue to serve as the guiding star of U.S. policy," but they disagreed as to how to get there.[30] Some academics, lobbyists, and policymakers called for an activist industrial policy.[31] Some labor, agriculture, and business leaders argued that threats of new U.S. restrictions would help achieve a more level playing field, even if the net result led to greater global protection. Still others called for a greater emphasis on punishing the unfair trade practices of America's trading partners. They eventually succeeded at developing changes to U.S. trade law that would make it easier to allege that foreign competitors had dumped or subsidized their goods. Finally, some called for deemphasizing multilateral approaches to trade and focusing U.S. efforts on bilateral trade negotiations. All of these ideas were heard on Capitol Hill and reflected in legislation—some of which passed.[32]

This debate was not only about economics. Some intellectuals began to suggest that America's social stability was threatened by economic interdependence. Moreover, during the 1970s, the purview of the GATT grew to include rules governing the use of nontariff trade barriers, such as health and safety standards. Representatives of agriculture, consumer, and environmental organizations worried that domestic laws designed to protect the environment or the public health could be challenged as illegal trade barriers.[33] They organized to educate the public about trade and reoriented the debate to consider how globalization could affect American democracy.[34]

Concerns about sovereignty, however, were not limited to the Left. Influenced by such economic nationalists as Pat Buchanan and business leader H. Ross Perot, growing numbers of prominent Republicans including Senator Robert Dole and Representative Newt Gingrich questioned how multilateral trade policies might affect U.S. sovereignty. Many leaders also expressed concern that with the end of the cold war, the United States was paying too high a price (financially, economically, and politically) for its leadership of international organizations. Their concerns signaled growing fears that America was losing control over its destiny. This debate also revealed deep division within the Republican party over whether support for free markets should stop at the border.[35]

Thus, the debate on trade had come full circle. A history of the ITO, GATT, and the WTO may provide new insights about U.S. trade policy. It will show that concerns about the impact of trade—on the American democracy and attainment of the American dream—are not new. I hope it will also illuminate ways that policymakers can improve the dialogue about trade policy with the American people.

Methodology

Policymakers argue that an informed citizenry is a requisite for democracy. Yet as the history of the ITO, GATT, and WTO will reveal, policymakers did little to involve or educate the American people about trade policy. Trade policy was the turf of experts: in business, labor, agriculture, academia, and government.

Students of trade policy, like policymakers, have not been concerned with public opinion on trade. When they write books about trade, economists, historians, and political scientists focus on the tug-of-war between government officials, members of Congress, and representatives of special interests—groups of citizens organized to protect their economic or political interests.[36] As economist Mancur Olson noted, interest groups are organized precisely because members of these groups believe they have a stake in any changes to the American system. In contrast, the mass public remains unorganized because they do not believe such changes will affect them or because the effects of these changes are too minor to motivate them to act politically.[37] So, these authors ignore general public opinion.

For example, E.E. Schattsneider's 1935 work on the Smoot-Hawley tariff remains the premier study of interest group politics. Although Schattsneider recognized that these pressure groups can't substitute for the public, he does not include public opinion in the index, and he notes the views of consumers only in a footnote.[38] Writing about trade policy in the 1960s historian Thomas Zeiler believes the state leads interest groups into accepting eventual policy decisions.[39] The public is irrelevant. Other political scientists and historians focus on congressional–executive branch politicking, but still ignore the unorganized public.[40] In an essay describing political scientists' efforts to develop a synthesis on trade, political economist John Odell never mentions public opinion.[41]

Just as policymakers should not presume that public silence equals acquiescence, analysts of trade policy should not assume that the general public does not matter in shaping trade policy. Although elites "make" policy, it is debated, discarded, supported, or ignored by non-"movers and shakers" in the public arena.[42] The public can affect trade policy as members of groups (the organized public) or as members of the unorganized/general public. We need to understand how the *unorganized* as well as the organized (concerned public) perceived these innovations.[43] Moreover, the clout of the organized public may be declining. Americans are simply not joining groups or associations they way they used to. This is especially true for labor unions, a group that is particularly concerned about trade policy.[44]

Today the unorganized public can have a major impact on public policy through new mediums of technology such as fax machines and interactive television. Growing numbers of Americans develop and express their views by listening to radio or television talk shows, watching Congress on C-Span, or participating in discussion groups on the Internet. Policymakers are increasingly aware of the power of these technologies to connect the unorganized public and influence policymakers. They would play an important role in the debate over the WTO.[45]

In the 1980s and 1990s, the views of the unorganized public had a growing impact on policy. Political candidates had long relied on polls (data summarizing the views of the unorganized public) to determine public views about their leadership. In this period, however, public opinion polls became front-page news. Some policymakers relied on polls to determine their positions on public policy.[46] In these instances, the dialogue about policy was reversed.

I have relied on a wide range of sources to convey the dialogue between the public and policymakers on trade. To convey the depth and diversity of opinion, I have analyzed archival data, government documents, editorials, magazines, journals, newspapers, transcripts of talk shows, interviews, and congressional testimony. I have interviewed trade policy officials, lobbyists, economists, citizen activists, and reporters. These sources provided a good overview of organized public opinion. I have relied on polls to convey general public opinion. Through the Roper Center, an archive for polls, I reviewed every poll on trade policy from 1936 to 1951. Using America Online, I examined every poll on trade policy in 1994 (as Congress considered the WTO).

Polling, however, is an art and not a science. Polls are only as good as the wording of questions, the order of questions, and the ability of the questioner to keep bias out of the data. To get around these problems, I have relied on nonpolitical, well-respected sources of polling data, focusing specifically on those polls that asked the same or closely related questions over a number of years.[47] Rosita Thomas and Mike Kolakowski of the Library of Congress and Andrew Kohut of the Times Mirror Center for the People and the Press helped me better understand polling data. With the help of the reference librarians at the Brookings Institution, I also examined public, congressional, and special-interest opinion on a broad range of issues, such as internationalism, European recovery, NAFTA, and U.S. economic policies. This helped me place the dialogue on trade policy in the context of a broader debate on the government's role in the economy.

Organization of the Book

The history of the ITO, GATT, and WTO begins in chapter 1, which traces the development of American tariff policy and shows how policies to liberalize trade were patched onto policies to protect specific sectors of the economy. Chapter 2 focuses on the initial process of planning and examines the linkage of trade and employment, as well as Keynesian and classical economics, in the postwar plans. Chapter 3 outlines the early legislative strategy adopted by the trade policy planners and its implications for public understanding and for congressional support of their efforts. It shows how policymakers devised a two-track structure for the ITO and the GATT. Chapter 4 examines changes in public opinion and the postwar planning structure in 1943-46. Chapter 5 discusses the public response to the ITO at several hearings around the nation. Chapter 6 presents the negotiation of the GATT and the final charter for the ITO as well as the 80th Congress's response to these mechanisms. Chapter 7 looks at how the public and the 81st Congress, again under Democratic control, viewed trade policies in the context of continued economic disarray. Chapter 8 discusses how the Truman administration abandoned the ITO. I also examine the development of a constituency in support of the GATT.

The last chapters will discuss the dialogue about trade policy in the 1980s and 1990s. In Chapter 9, I examine how trends in the U.S. economy affected support for multilateral trade liberalization. Using the debate over the North American Free Trade Agreement (NAFTA), I examine the role of new interest groups, including consumer and environmental groups, as well as new mediums for dialogue in the debate about trade and the achievement of other policy goals. Chapter 10 focuses on policymakers' efforts to communicate the Uruguay Round of the GATT and the proposed World Trade Organization to the general public and to Congress. In my conclusion, I compare the dialogue about the ITO/GATT in the postwar period and the GATT/WTO in the 1990s. Given the importance of trade to the health of the U.S. economy today, I suggest ways to further public understanding about trade policy.

1
The Roots of
Multilateral Trade Policy

Tennessean Cordell Hull was a "good old boy," a respected member of Congress, and chairman of the national Democratic party. Like many of his southern colleagues, Hull believed high tariffs were an abomination. But Hull went further. He linked trade barriers (such as tariffs and preferences) with war, whereas "unhampered trade dovetailed with peace." This good old boy's disdain for high tariffs spurred him to action during his many years in Congress.[1]

Hull deserves credit as one of the fathers of the GATT, but his obsession with trade was not shared by most of his fellow Americans. As early as 1916, Congressman Hull called for an international economic conference to promote fair and friendly trade relations. At such a conference, America would reduce its tariffs in response to reciprocal trade barrier reduction by other nations. But his ideas gained little support in the prosperous twenties. In 1929, he warned his congressional colleagues, "Our neglect to develop foreign markets for surpluses is the one outstanding cause of unemployment." But his warnings fell on deaf ears.[2]

Hull achieved his dream of freer trade policies as Franklin D. Roosevelt's secretary of state. In 1934, Congress passed the Reciprocal Trade Agreements Act (RTAA), ostensibly to increase exports. Hidden in this path-breaking legislation was a growing belief that American jobs and the American standard of living were linked to open world trade. The legislation implied that the health of the U.S. economy could not be divorced from that of the world at large.[3]

The legislation also broke tradition in another important way—by shifting some of the responsibility for determining trade policy from the legislature to the executive branch.[4] This transfer of responsibility to the executive branch began the process of "internationalizing trade policy;" a process that would culminate in the ITO and the GATT. But the Reciprocal Trade Agreements Act also created a system of governmental experts to decide trade policies. The initiative for trade policy was thus placed in the hands of people not directly accountable to the public.[5] It also allowed protectionists to argue that freer trade policies were not democratically determined.

This chapter briefly describes the development of U.S. trade policy.[6] I focus on the 1934 reforms, which made bilateral and ultimately multilateral trade liberalization possible. Supporters of freer trade policy rooted these reforms in American economic conditions; they argued that tariff reduction would create jobs. For all his political skills, however, Hull did little to convince Americans that freer trade policies would be in their economic interest. Although the public was receptive to new economic policies to mitigate the Depression, most Americans still believed that tariffs protected jobs and their ability to achieve the American dream. This perception would make it difficult to build a constituency in support of radical change to U.S. trade policies. To understand opposition to the development of multilateral trade policies, we must begin with America's long history of protection.

A Brief History of U.S. Trade Policy

America's founding fathers were trade policy realists. The memory of years of "taxation without representation" underscored the dangers of protection as well as the need to encourage new markets for America's fledgling economy. The Constitution delegated responsibility for trade policy "to regulate commerce with foreign nations" and to "lay and collect . . . duties" to the Congress.[7]

Policymakers utilized tariffs to protect specific sectors of the economy, but they also signed treaties of navigation and commerce and emphasized a reciprocity policy on shipping. They directed their efforts toward developing America's vast and rich internal resources.[8] However, some Americans (notably Alexander Hamilton and eastern industrialists) began to see tariffs as a tool to stimulate U.S. economic development. The notion of using tariffs to protect America's infant industries gained ground as the country struggled to develop. By raising the price of imports, tariffs served as an incentive to buy domestical goods. Government officials liked the selective nature of tariffs as well as the fact that the Treasury captured tariff revenue.[9] Support for this "Hamiltonian" approach grew after the War of 1812. A "new nationalism" provided the ideology for protecting America's burgeoning manufacturing and textile industries.[10]

Protecting the domestic market remained the focus of American trade policies in the years 1820-70, when modern corporate institutions had yet to become a significant factor in shaping policy. The federal government rarely intervened to encourage exports, although the United States relied on foreign capital and had a growing international trade.[11] Nevertheless, although general tariff levels remained moderate, tariff protection spread to many sectors. Legislators learned it was simpler to compensate those injured by tariffs by protecting them too rather than to reduce the protection given to the first party. Any one interest, once granted protection, tended to regard that level of protection as its prerogative. But America's growing recourse to tariffs was not universally supported; in fact, the spread of tariffs stimulated heated and divisive debate.[12]

Policymakers' focus on the domestic market and their growing use of tariffs was understandable. America's growing population, abundant resources, and expanding industry contained ample opportunity. Some businessmen began to build a nationwide market for their products. As Alfred Chandler delineated, large firms prospered when they achieved cost advantages from economies of scale and scope. Soon these efficiencies enabled some firms to move into foreign markets.[13]

By the early twentieth century, growing numbers of American producers sought foreign markets to counteract downturns in U.S. demand or to gain further economies of scale. Trade statistics reflect this growing internationalization: in 1890, the United States had a relatively small share of world trade, 3.9 percent, but by 1913, the United States had 11 percent. By the end of World War I, America had become a large producer and exporter of manufactured goods. Some segments of U.S. industry and agriculture were now dependent on overseas markets.

Yet American policy did not keep pace with America's growing trade; the United States continued to rely on relatively high tariffs. A lower U.S. tariff would have facilitated foreign sales by making it easier for foreigners to earn dollars to purchase U.S. exports and service debts to U.S. creditors.[14] Business and labor leaders as well as members of Congress still believed that the nation needed high tariffs to prosper, even though growing numbers of workers, farmers, and producers depended on exports.[15]

By the turn of the century, policymakers and business leaders did develop new mechanisms and institutions to reshape trade policy. The Department of State as well as the Department of Commerce and Labor developed closer relationships with businessmen and nurtured a constituency supportive of increasing American exports.[16]

At the same time, some reformers proposed radical changes to the nation's economic policy. They believed that American consumers had long paid high hidden taxes when they purchased imports and that tariffs were the "mother of trusts." They called for a two-pronged solution: the income tax would replace the tariff as the principal source of government revenue, and "experts," rather than Congress, would "scientifically determine" tariff rates.

Some business leaders joined these reform efforts. These leaders were not free traders—they wanted tariffs to be maintained—but they regarded tariff fluctuation as the greater evil and therefore accepted modest revisions in the hope of achieving tariff certainty. Without the traditional vociferous opposition, in 1913 Congress passed the Underwood Tariff, a significant tariff reduction, and the income tax, which reduced government reliance on tariffs to fund government. In 1916, Congress established the Tariff Commission.[17] As historian Robert Wiebe noted, these reforms signaled a stronger voice for more internationally oriented business in business associations and a new governmental emphasis on stimulating exports as well as providing protection. But they did not moderate or end America's broad system of protection. Trade policy continued to lag America's economic position.[18] Moreover, these reforms did little to alert Americans to the nation's economic interdependence or to the costs of protection.

However, these reforms did signal that members of Congress felt increasingly overwhelmed by pressure to provide protection to these interests. According to political scientist I.M. Destler, members began to "channel that pressure elsewhere, pushing product-specific trade decisions out of the committees of Congress and off the House and Senate floors to other governmental institutions."[19]

U.S. protectionism actually increased in the 1920s. Because of the problems of postwar adjustment, Congress imposed high duties on about forty agricultural products in 1921. In 1922, manufacturers joined in a growing stampede for protection. Americans wanted it all—open markets for their products, a reasonable amount of imports, a protected home market, and "economic self-sufficiency."[20] The gap between American trade policies and America's growing dependence on trade was growing wider.

Between 1922 and 1933, neither the country's policymakers nor business and community leaders acknowledged the linkage between America's economic health and that of other nations. American multi-nationals and American investment spurred U.S. and global economic growth. By 1922, American companies held 16.9 percent of total world exports and 12.9 percent of total world imports, and American business increasingly relied on imports for the raw materials for its manufactured goods.[21] Nevertheless, Americans clung to protection as the basic tenet for trade policy while subsidizing the merchant marine and agriculture and exempting agricultural products from the nation's traditional trade principles. Although some representatives of business, labor, academic, and civic groups worried about growing protectionism in the U.S. and overseas, they could do little to change American trade policy. Most Americans had little insight into America's growing economic interdependence.[22]

Trade, Employment, and International Economic Interdependence

By 1930, with the Great Depression under way, a growing number of business, agricultural, labor, and governmental leaders began to see trade policy, and tariffs specifically, in a different light. Some of these individuals were internationalists, who recognized that there was a fundamental imbalance between the international accounts of the United States and the rest of the world. Others concluded that the only way out of the Great Depression was to create larger (foreign) markets for American goods. Others were traditional freer traders who thought that lowered trade barriers were in the national interest. All of these groups recognized that access to foreign markets could create jobs for Americans. The most direct way to gain such markets would be to reduce reciprocal trade barriers between America and its trading partners. Nonetheless, most policymakers continued to support protectionist measures. The potential to create jobs through lower trade barriers and increased trade seemed riskier than preserving jobs through the proven tool of protection.[23]

Some analysts believe the scope and level of tariffs reached a high water mark in 1930, during the presidency of Herbert Hoover. The Smoot-Hawley Tariff Act of 1930 raised rates on many items, even products the United States did not produce. Many members of Congress thought higher tariffs would protect them from the political fallout from jobs lost in their communities and help their chances for reelection. In addition, some politicians continued to believe that tariffs were a domestic policy tool not subject to international negotiations.[24]

As the Great Depression deepened, the United States and world economies faltered. American exports fell from $5.157 billion in 1929 to $1.576 billion in 1932. World markets for U.S. agricultural products shrank dramatically. America's trading partners adopted a wide range of trade restrictions, including exchange controls, bilateral trading arrangements, and quantitative limits on imports. As they lost their jobs or livelihoods, growing numbers of Americans now understood that there was a linkage between trade policies, employment, and economic growth.[25] But they were a distinct minority. Although the Great Depression broke the public view that high tariffs created and maintained the nation's economic growth, support for maintaining sector-specific tariffs endured.

However, the Great Depression transformed public opinion about the proper role of government in the domestic economy. In 1933, everyone knew someone who had lost his or her job or had no prospects for advancement. With unemployment as high as one-fourth of the workforce, many Americans were less certain that market forces would "correct" the unemployment problem.[26] They turned to government for a solution, convinced that the federal government should, as President Franklin D. Roosevelt stated, "protect the economic welfare of all the people."[27]

Many government officials and academic economists shared the new notion of governmental responsibility for employment. They too were concerned by the large numbers of unemployed or underemployed men and women. Officials working on international economic policy faced the daunting task of reconciling the new imperative to combat unemployment with their long-term efforts to encourage freer trade.[28] This task was difficult because trade liberalization can have contradictory economic effects: over the long run, freer trade can create jobs, but in the short term it can also create unemployment.[29] Moreover, in 1933, no economic ideology indicated to government officials how to create jobs and achieve freer trade. Finally, although Cordell Hull had inserted a strong tariff reduction position in the 1932 Democratic party platform, candidate Franklin D. Roosevelt was ambivalent, fearing that "the introduction of so controversial a subject into Congress might derail other important legislation."[30] As a result, the United States moved slowly and incompletely from using protection as a rationale for job maintenance to using trade liberalization as a rationale for job creation.

At the London Economic Conference in 1933, Secretary of State Cordell Hull hoped to encourage participating nations to reduce trade barriers. Participants achieved a compromise where each nation would take steps to stabilize exchange and trade relations. The very compromise suggested that the health of the economies were linked. As Hull negotiated, however, Congress increased tariffs on several agricultural commodities. Roosevelt's priorities were domestic recovery; for a variety of reasons (including disinterest) he rejected the compromises achieved in London.[31]

Hull and his aides (who included Francis Sayre, Herbert Feis, and Harry Hawkins) debated how they could best gain congressional and executive branch support for a radical change to U.S. trade policy. They recognized that if they wanted to change America's foreign economic policies, the executive branch (read State Department) would have to wrestle greater control over trade policymaking from the Congress. Moreover, if any new instrument interfered with an existing program such as the New

Deal's program of aid to farmers, it would not get the president's support.[32]

The efforts of these internationalists were bolstered by growing public recognition of the consequences of international economic disorder. According to trade policy historian John M. Dobson, "As warehouses overflowed and factories closed down, cries for greater Government efforts to create foreign markets arose."[33] Roosevelt heard these pleas. Ever the experimentalist, he decided to give Hull's ideas a chance. On March 2, 1934, President Roosevelt requested authority to negotiate commercial agreements with foreign countries, and the chairman of the House Ways and Means Committee, Robert L. Doughton, introduced an administration bill designed to authorize such agreements. Supporters of the bill argued that "national and international economic conditions made broad executive discretionary powers imperative." To Hull, this approach would "lift the economic level of the world without interfering with domestic measures."[34]

Congress debated the legislation for some four months. Although some members opposed the legislation for protectionist reasons, many members had difficulty reconciling this new approach with America's democratic tradition of determining trade policy. They objected to what they saw as an unconstitutional delegation of legislative power. These members alleged that the act infringed Article I, section 8, and Article II of the Constitution.[35] Moreover, they worried that "the vesting of authority in one man, who would have to rely mainly upon the advice of others, was unwise. . . . Without any provision for public notice and hearings . . . an element of instability was injected into an already maladjusted situation."[36] Some opponents feared that Congress was being forced to give advance approval for any agreements into which the president might enter.[37] Finally, some members wondered if the trade agreements were in fact treaties, which required ratification by two-thirds of the Senate.

These concerns about the new approach were on target; State Department officials were not very interested in obtaining public input in the negotiations. Both Francis B. Sayre, assistant secretary of state, and Cordell Hull opposed provisions in the legislation for a public hearing. Hull told the Senate Finance Committee, "Nothing is more impossible than to go through the equivalent of a long judicial procedure, hearings here and hearings there." According to Sayre, "If the people of the country cannot trust their own president with all the instrumentalities they have for bringing pressure to bear on him . . . we might as well abdicate and close up shop." But members of Congress redesigned the act to include public notification and hearings. A Committee on Reciprocity Information would sponsor hearings where interested parties could present their views on potential tariff reductions.[38]

The legislation directed the President to seek information and advice from other agencies in deciding which countries to negotiate with and which products to negotiate tariff reductions for. The Department of State created the Trade Agreements Committee to monitor the program. This interdepartmental committee was composed of officials from the Departments of State, Treasury, War, Labor, Commerce, and Agriculture, and from the Tariff Commission. The names of these committee members were made public, and members were supposed to represent their departments' perspectives, not their own opinions.[39]

Hull also opposed publishing a preliminary list of items being considered for concession, fearing such a procedure "would give away to foreign nations our ammunition." But the legislation required that the secretary of state must issue a public notice of intention to negotiate, along with a list of products on which the United States will consider granting concessions. After public hearings on these potential concessions, the Trade Agreements Committee debates lists of those products on which the United States will request concessions and of those products on which we should consider granting concessions. The Trade Agreements Committee, the secretary of state, and the president must then approve the suggested bargaining schedules and recommendations.[40]

Although Congress was able to ensure some public notification and involvement, congressional concerns about democracy would continue to haunt the Reciprocal Trade Agreements Act. Even supporters recognized that the process was designed to facilitate interests sophisticated in influencing trade policy and did little to involve the general public.[41] However, this was not a key concern for Cordell Hull and his lieutenants.

Implications of the New Approach to Trade Policy

The Reciprocal Trade Act was not a free trade measure; it passed as an amendment to the Smoot-Hawley Tariff Act. The RTAA was pragmatic legislation, designed first to improve America's economic position in world markets and only in the long run to advance freer trade. Hull and other proponents of the act believed that the incentive of reduced U.S. tariffs could induce other nations to agree to open their markets.

Moreover, the RTAA did not radically change previous trade policies. As before, tariffs could only be reduced selectively, on a product-specific basis. The RTAA continued long-standing policies of reciprocity, nondiscrimination, and the allocation of authority to the president to negotiate tariffs.[42] Special interests retained much of their ability (and their expertise) to influence trade policy considerations. As State Department officials noted, tariff concessions were granted "only after exhaustive study shows that they will not result in material injury to any group of American producers." Thus, the RTAA built freer trade upon sector-specific protection.[43]

Congress retained much of its ability to set the parameters of trade policy. The act granted authority to the executive only for three years, forcing the executive to return to Congress to obtain renewed authority as well as feedback on the agreements it had made. This reliance on Congress ensured that the State Department would be responsive to the needs of specific sectors and would work "to reconcile . . . export promotion with import protection."[44]

But the RTAA certainly changed the procedures and players involved in making trade policy. The RTAA made trade liberalization (which many perceived as radical change) possible. The act gave the executive branch greater authority to negotiate trade agreements concerning a wide range of commodities. According to Professor Stephan Haggard, by delegating authority to the executive, Congress allowed new organizational interests and government officials to develop competence on trade issues. Such officials would be less likely to kowtow to special interests and might take a more internationalist approach to trade. In the hearings on tariff levels and in the bilateral negotiations to achieve trade agreements, executive branch officials had to weigh tariff reductions from the standpoint of the national interest rather than from the perspectives of those protected by specific tariffs.[45]

The RTAA helped create a public constituency in support of trade liberalization. But the constituency for freer trade was small compared to the numbers of Americans who supported protection. The idea that protectionism preserved U.S. jobs was so embedded in the American polity that the government had to portray the Reciprocal Trade Agreements Act as a temporary measure that would increase employment.[46] In his message to Congress asking for the RTAA, the president argued that it was necessary because the decline in world trade "has meant idle hands, still machines, despairing farm households, and hungry industrial families."[47]

Policymakers had finally developed a trade policy that acknowledged the effect of U.S. tariff policies on U.S. and global economic conditions. No longer could policymakers describe tariff policies as nonnegotiable, strictly domestic policies. But the United States had not ended its addiction to tariffs. Moreover, freer trade policies did not inspire public enthusiasm. Most Americans understood neither the process of reciprocity nor the implications of U.S. tariff policy. In a February 1938 American Institute of Public Opinion (AIPO) poll, only 49 percent of those polled had heard of "Secretary Hull's efforts to make trade treaties with other countries." Some 73 percent of them approved of his efforts.[48] But a January

1940 poll by AIPO found that only 10 percent of those polled could correctly define the term "reciprocal trade treaties," while 53 percent of those polled admitted they did not know what the term meant.[49] Other polls revealed equal confusion about the implications of freer trade. An AIPO poll on January 30, 1940 reported that 64 percent disapproved of letting "South America sell more farm products here" in order to sell more manufactured goods to South America.[50] Although the RTAA permanently altered the dialogue between the American people and their government on trade, American opinion had not caught up to the reality of America's economic role in the world or the importance of trade to the U.S. economy.[51] To most Americans, trade had nothing to do with their attainment of the American dream.

U.S. policymakers were moving faster than public opinion. With the coming of war in the 1940s, American policymakers would have an opportunity to develop plans for the peace. Much of their attention would be directed toward finding ways to encourage freer trade while expanding both trade and employment. They hoped it might attract public support.[52]

2

Linking Jobs to Trade Policy, 1939–1942

By 1939, advocates of freer trade policies could point to the trade agreements program as a modest success. The United States had increased its trade with some twenty countries without causing serious injury to any American industry. But bilateral trade agreements could not induce the rest of the world to dismantle their myriad forms of trade protection. More importantly, these agreements had little impact on the nation's economic growth. Firms continued to fail in record numbers. Unemployment remained relatively high.[1]

Given continued economic stagnation, some State Department officials hoped to develop a more comprehensive approach to economic policy, one that would stimulate global employment as well as global economic growth. But there was no public constituency calling for such change. Moreover, President Roosevelt, Secretary of State Cordell Hull, and Treasury Secretary Henry Morgenthau were focused on more immediate issues, including the spread of war throughout Europe.

Ironically, the war provided government officials with an opportunity to experiment. Harley Notter, a State Department official, suggested "establishing a group of officers" to formulate a program of action to restore peace in the future.[2] Notter's recommendation was echoed by private citizens. Although many Americans wanted to avoid entanglement in another foreign war, they recognized the need to prepare for the war's aftermath. The Council on Foreign Relations, the National Association of Manufacturers, and the Federal Council of Churches were among many groups that offered the government their assistance in developing plans for the peace.[3]

On September 16, 1939, Secretary of State Hull appointed Leo Pasvolsky as his special assistant to work on problems of the peace. Pasvolsky, a noted international economist and experienced State Department hand, was told to devise international economic and political "arrangements." Pasvolsky tackled economic problems first.[4]

But Pasvolsky was frequently frustrated as he tried to develop economic plans for the future peace. From 1939 to 1941, postwar planning was not a top priority, and Pasvolsky was not given the resources he needed.[5] It was not until late in 1940, with the assistance of Harry Hawkins and the staff of the Division of Trade Agreements, that the planners developed an effective way to gain bureaucratic support for the economic plans.

Out of their efforts was born an innovative approach to global trade liberalization designed to expand global trade and employment. The postwar planners hoped it would convince the public that freer trade would lead to greater prosperity as well as more jobs and prosperous U.S. businesses.[6] However, this trade policy had little relation to the dreams of most Americans.

The Slow Development of the Trade Policy Plans

On February 3, 1941, Secretary Hull established a small staff of eight, the Division of Special Research, under Pasvolsky, and directed them to develop new approaches to achieve multilateral trade liberalization.[7] But Pasvolsky's group soon stepped onto the administrative turf of other State Department divisions, including Harry Hawkins's Division of Trade Agreements, which had responsibility for trade policy and the specific mechanism of the RTAA. Hawkins, who had a long and successful working relationship on trade with Secretary Hull, could have easily frustrated the work of Pasvolsky's group. However, Hawkins saw opportunity in collaborating with Pasvolsky. As noted above, he yearned for a more comprehensive approach to free trade. Hawkins also recognized that the spread of the war would make bilateral trade agreements relatively unimportant.[8] He directed his staff to work in tandem with the Division of Special Research.[9] Despite the collaborative efforts of Pasvolsky, Hawkins, and their staffs, the planning process soon stalled.

In an attempt to move the process forward, Secretary Hull established (in December) a departmental committee, the Advisory Committee on Problems of Foreign Relations, to study problems of peace and reconstruction and to advise the planners. But the meager staffing of the State Department and the crush of world events forced the Advisory Committee to focus on current policy.[10] In 1940, Hull tried to broaden the postwar planning process by involving officials from other agencies in the Interdepartmental Group to Consider Post-War International Economic

Problems and Policies. This informal group included high-level staff from key agencies such as the Executive Office of the president, the Tariff Commission, the Federal Reserve Board, and the War Department. However, these officials were also overwhelmed with work on daily crises. As a result, the Interdepartmental Group also made little progress in planning for the postwar era.[11]

In its fourth attempt, the State Department finally developed an effective approach to gaining bureaucratic support for the postwar planning process. As the war spread throughout Europe and Asia, government officials began to look for ways to cooperate with British officials on shaping the peace as well as the war effort. Understanding that Great Britain's agreement would be a sine qua non to the success of any economic plan, they determined to use the United States–British relationship to achieve their long-term objectives. A new tool, lend-lease, would serve as leverage.[12]

Lend-lease and the Postwar Economic Plans

Lend-lease was implemented after the signing of the tripartite pact between Germany, Italy, and Japan on September 27, 1940. The Axis alliance gave Roosevelt and his advisors an opportunity to reshape America's overall foreign policy.[13] The Treasury Department drafted legislation allowing the U.S. government to provide materials that friendly nations needed in return for specific actions "in defense of freedom." With lend-lease, the United States assisted nations that, by defending themselves, were reducing the danger of war spreading to the United States. Congress approved lend-lease legislation on March 11, 1941, as a German invasion of Great Britain appeared imminent.[14]

Lend-lease was a shrewd policy mechanism: it supported the defense efforts of our lend-lease partners while facilitating the work of the commercial policy planners. Trade policy goals were to be achieved through its Article VII. This article was vaguely written; some State Department staff would spend hours analyzing its intent.[15] But it was clear that the United States and its lend-lease partners were committed to begin conversations on policies and mechanisms to establish "acceptance of the basic commercial principles which were indispensable to the establishment of a sound economic order in the post-war world."[16] Thus, lend-lease would couple the immediate objective of winning the war with the long-term economic goal of winning the peace.[17]

State Department officials used Article VII to justify an expansion of the postwar planning staff.[18] Under a grant from the Rockefeller Foundation, the Council on Foreign Relations lent the department several members of its staff. These men, who included William Diebold and Courtney Brown, worked with the division to prepare a series of issue papers on international problems. They would make major contributions to the economic postwar plans.[19] With this additional staffing, the postwar planners were able to maintain the State Department's control over the commercial policy plans and broaden their perspective without adding to the department's budget. The planning effort gained legitimacy, because the Council was respected by both business leaders and academics. Nonetheless, the planning process remained relatively insular, as the Council staff basically agreed with the State Department's trade ideology.[20]

As postwar planning gained in influence and in administrative support, the first of several interagency turf battles arose. On July 30, 1941, President Roosevelt appointed Vice President Henry A. Wallace to head a new Economic Defense Board. This board was designated to advise the president on postwar economic reconstruction and on specific steps to expedite the establishment of peacetime economic relationships.[21] This created a dilemma for State Department officials. They did not want to interfere with the new agency's actions in service to the war effort. However, they also did not want to "resign to a new and inexperienced organization" State's responsibility for postwar planning and foreign policy. State Department officials may have also feared that Wallace's left–New Deal stance would lead to unrealistic plans for future foreign economic policies. From his writing, they may have believed he was not ardently committed to expanded world trade.[22] Assistant Secretary of State Dean Acheson and his staff determined to reestablish State's control by diversifying participation in the planning committees under the department's aegis. They worked out an elaborate program for liaison with other agencies and private organizations, an accommodation that enabled State to stay in charge of all areas of foreign economic policy (except monetary and agricultural policies).[23] Over the next two years, the State Department managed interagency policymaking well, despite continued threats to its purview by war-related as well as permanent government agencies.[24]

As the battles over policies and turf waged on, Hull decided he must build an external constituency for the postwar planning process, especially if and when the United States entered the war.[25] Hull and the president took several steps to gather this support. In his lend-lease address to Congress, President Roosevelt stated, "We look forward to a world founded upon four essential human freedoms." One of these, "freedom from want," became the basis of Hull's efforts to convince the American public that there could be no secure peace without "economic understanding" and stability.[26] But Hull did not direct his staff to be any more specific. The planners still did not view public understanding as a high priority of the planning process.

Senior postwar planners such as Acheson, Pasvolsky, and Hawkins, as well as Hull and Roosevelt, gave speeches and testimony to bolster public support for the planners' efforts.[27] They endured numerous chicken and pea dinners on the Council of Foreign Relations' and League of Women Voters' lecture circuit. In America's cities and heartland, they found that internationalist sentiment as well as public support for U.S. governmental responsibility for economic growth and stability were growing. They decided that Americans were coming to accept the idea that government actions could help secure full employment and economic stability.[28] Surveys by the State Department revealed that many Americans recognized the close relationship between expanding world trade and high U.S. income and employment. Polls also reported increased support for international trade liberalization.[29] These polls, however, did not show understanding that specific tariffs would have to be reduced to achieve multilateral trade liberalization.

In 1940, Hull and Roosevelt formally linked the Reciprocal Trade Agreements Act to the postwar planning process. In statements to the Congress urging another three-year renewal, both men described the RTAA as more than an emergency measure to expand exports and create jobs. It was also an essential tool for achieving world peace. A congressional report stated: "The choice before us is whether we shall lead the way toward the slough of economic despair . . . or towards the heights of economic progress, sustained prosperity, and enduring peace . . . for the world."[30]

But this new expanded rationale did not create bipartisan support. In the Minority Report, Republican representatives Daniel A. Reed, Harold Knutson, Bertrand W. Gearhart, and Frank Carlson, among others, described the RTAA as dangerous to the nation's economic and political health. According to the Minority, the act was not only "back-handed and unconstitutional," but it "places in the hands of one individual the absolute power of life and death over every branch of domestic agriculture and industry dependent upon tariff protection." The report argued that the result was "bureaucratic tariff making" by self-anointed "experts," who undemocratically assert that "they are capable of doing a better job of tariff making than the Congress." The "only way in which American agriculture, industry and labor can be assured of the protection of their rights and careful consideration of . . . the interests of the whole Nation is through approval of the trade treaties by Congress."[31]

Republicans were not the only opponents of the RTAA. Some fourteen Democratic senators (from western states representing cattle, farming, and mining interests) joined their Republican counterparts in an effort to defeat the 1940 Trade Act Extension. The extension resolution passed the House 218–168; in the Senate the margin was a tight 42–37.[32]

This close call did not inspire the postwar planners to involve or educate the public in the relationship of trade liberalization to its planning activities.[33] In 1941, one official warned that the United States would pay a price for that failure, because "solutions must evolve from the people." He advised senior postwar planners that as the executive branch came to monopolize foreign policy, Americans would become frustrated by their inability "to affect that policy." But the planners, concerned with control and secrecy, continued to exclude the people and their representatives from the commercial policy planning process.[34]

Meanwhile, the postwar planners began bilateral consultations with Great Britain in the summer of 1941. President Roosevelt and Prime Minister Winston Churchill (and their staffs) agreed that a declaration of common principles would facilitate cooperation and postwar planning.[35] As the negotiations evolved, however, they brought to the surface broad differences in how the two nations viewed governmental responsibility for trade and employment.

The British negotiators were reluctant to delineate their future trade policies. Many Britons feared that the adoption of the nondiscriminatory (most-favored-nation) approach to trade would force Britain to abandon the system of Imperial Preference, which allowed Britain to grant preferences to its colonies and dominions and to maintain strong ties between the Great Britain and Commonwealth nations. Some of the American negotiators, however, especially Undersecretary of State Sumner Welles, were determined that the "vital principle" of nondiscrimination be embodied in all the statements and actions on international trade.[36] These differences dashed American hopes for a strong common statement on trade liberalization.[37]

Roosevelt, who was not sympathetic to Britain's preferences, nevertheless understood the domestic political pulls on his friend Churchill. Ever the politician, Roosevelt accepted a broad statement to the effect that nondiscriminatory trade relations would be the guiding principle for international trade, but that existing obligations (that is, preferences) would be respected (and therefore continued). In addition, he assured Churchill that Point Four of the Atlantic Charter would commit the British only to discuss preferences in the upcoming Article VII discussions.[38]

With this understanding, the two allies jointly released the Atlantic Charter on August 14, 1941.[39] Although Anglo-American cooperation seemed to have taken a giant step forward, to many postwar planners the process had moved two steps backward. They feared the Atlantic Charter raised more problems and questions about future trade policies than it resolved.[40]

After December 7, 1941, when Japan attacked Pearl Harbor, the United States joined Britain as a belligerent. Now the United States had to mobilize and plan for war as well as for peace. Hull hoped the two efforts would not compete. His plans for the peace were bolstered when on January 1, 1942, twenty-six nations signed the Declaration of the United Nations. The Allies were now apparently united in their aims for war and peace, having subscribed to the goals of the Atlantic Charter.[41]

By 1942, the United States had come a long way in developing the postwar plans for multilateral trade liberalization. It had committed itself to a twofold international economic program: international cooperation directed toward economic welfare ("freedom from want") and "collaboration between all nations in the economic field with the object of securing economic advancement and social security."[42] However, the State Department had not yet involved the public in the planning process: only a small, handpicked group of nongovernmental advisers and government officials had participated in developing the plans for freer trade. The first test of whether the American people supported these objectives would be the Anglo-American negotiations under Article VII.

The U.S./British Negotiations on Full Employment and Trade

With a firm declaration of Allied goals for the war and the peace in hand, the postwar planners returned to their efforts to forge a consensual trade policy with Great Britain. Article VII committed the signatories to discussions of their longterm economic objectives for the peace. Harry Hawkins's staff soon took control of these discussions and provided "the initiative and planning" for the Department's strategy for implementing Article VII.[43] These officials turned to the Reciprocal Trade Agreements Act for legislative justification for their work, although they knew it was not explicitly designed to implement freer trade on a multilateral basis.[44]

State Department officials also knew that it would be extremely difficult to forge a consensus with British officials on future trade policies. As the Atlantic Charter discussions revealed, many British negotiators did not see eye to eye with the State Department on the benefits of nondiscriminatory trade.[45] Most British citizens seem to have opposed any attempts to modify the system of preferences.[46] Moreover, many advocates of government intervention to protect employment, such as Lord John Maynard Keynes, did not support American efforts to liberalize trade.[47] Although neither the British public nor the war cabinet were united behind Keynesian concepts, the American negotiators seemed intimidated by Keynes. He had great influence in the United States and abroad.[48]

The U.S. postwar planners struggled to understand and to reconcile Lord Keynes's views with their aspirations.[49] They knew his primary concern was Britain's economic health and its long-term ability to create jobs for its people. Keynes feared that Britain could become too attached to the boom/bust cycle of the American economy; he did not trust American macroeconomic management. Britain, he believed, would be better off managing its balance of payments among the "sterling area" nations in the commonwealth.[50] The planners concluded that Keynes was "preoccupied with the problems of unemployment," problems that led him to support "bilateral commercial and economic arrangements," which allowed "a close control of international trade and payments."[51]

Keynes was no protectionist. He recognized "that the advantages of an international division of labor are real and substantial" and that immoderate protection "may lead to a senseless international competition which injures all alike." Thus, as early as 1936, Keynes had argued for the "simultaneous pursuit" of high domestic employment "by all countries together."[52] Nonetheless, Keynes believed nondiscriminatory policies would no longer work. He had concluded, "We must be free to work out new and better arrangements" that would accommodate national employment objectives.[53]

Despite their differences with Keynes, many postwar planners in the State Department, including Harry Hawkins and Dean Acheson, hoped to find common ground on his "new and better" approach. They shared Keynes's desire to reconcile trade and employment objectives but differed on the means to that end. Most feared bilateralism would only make the situation worse.[54] They determined to build something "new and better" by relying on expansionary trade policies, thinking that all economies would grow under such policies and that employment would, too. This, they believed, would allow them to harmonize Keynesian and classical economic views on trade. Welles, Hawkins, and other State Department officials resolved "to make our position clear"—that is, to convince Keynes and other British officials to support their plans.[55]

Keynes, Acheson, and the U.S. ambassador to Great Britain, John Gilbert Winant, found common ground in two broad linkages for the Article VII discussions.[56] The first coupled British actions on preferences to American action on tariffs, and the second linked action on trade policy to actions promoting economic expansion.[57] But the new draft did not convince the British Cabinet.[58] Throughout 1941, neither Ambassador Winant nor Secretary Hull could convince Prime Minister Churchill to sign a lend-lease agreement containing the compromises.

Meanwhile, the postwar planners were having problems on another front. Some U.S. government officials were insisting that the British buy wheat in fixed proportions from the United States, Canada, Australia, and Argentina rather than from the cheapest source. This recommendation infuriated British policymakers, as Britain was incurring heavy physical, psychological, and financial losses in the war.[59] Although the wheat issue was resolved, American credibility was damaged.[60] The Americans had delivered two conflicting messages on trade: first, that the U.S. government was divided on the appropriate policies to achieve trade liberalization; and second, that the United States was willing to abandon its vision of freer trade to benefit certain sectors of its own economy (such as agriculture).

Hull recognized that these divergent strategies would jeopardize America's immediate and postwar objectives. He called on the president to discuss future trade policies directly with Churchill, but the president understandably favored the nation's political and military goals over longer-term trade policies. Roosevelt, in two communications, provided "a definite assurance that we were no more committed to the abolition of Imperial Preference than the American Government were committed to the abolition of their high protective tariffs." The British Cabinet was "won over," and the revised draft of Article VII was signed on February 23, 1942.[61]

Problems with the Article VII Compromise on Trade and Employment

The new draft of Article VII led to some confusion concerning how to proceed with future commercial policy planning.[62] Under the resolution, the planners would rely on two methods to achieve the Atlantic Charter and Article VII objectives: liberalization of international trade and financial policies and "maintenance of domestic purchasing power by fiscal methods." But was the approach workable under U.S. law? The planners recognized that "these two methods" were "often advocated as rival philosophies."[63] Moreover, Article VII appeared to link British elimination of preferences to American reduction of tariffs and lend-lease aid, a congressional prerogative.[64] Under the authority of the RTAA, tariff cuts were selective and were granted in return for equivalent concessions by other nations. Flat across-the-board cuts were never made.[65] As the planners knew, Congress was unlikely to approve any broad horizontal reduction under the RTAA or to devise a new legislative mechanism to give the president this authority.[66]

Congressional opposition was not the only potential problem; the political future of the postwar plans was shaky because Secretary Hull and the planners had not yet built a constituency of support. Hull was well aware of the need to involve representatives of the public in the planning process.[67] Yet it was not until 1942 that he set up an "Advisory Committee." This committee was designed to bring the planners together with members of Congress and representatives of special interests. The full Advisory Committee only met four times because of wartime concerns about secrecy. The opportunity for a broad exchange between government officials and concerned citizens was thus lost, and the potential for misunderstanding and opposition from individuals left out of the process was increased.

The Advisory Committee contributed to its own isolation. Following the normal course of committee evolution, it divided up into functional subcommittees to facilitate an in-depth examination of particular problems. These subcommittees, which did the bulk of the postwar planning in 1942, were dominated by State Department officials.[68]

The Subcommittee on Economic Policy, chaired by Assistant Secretary of State Acheson, was responsible for postwar trade policy. This committee included governmental and nongovernmental members.[69] In the initial drafting phase, Acheson and Pasvolsky hoped that members would speak as experts, rather than as agency or private-sector representatives, and that they would think creatively about long-standing problems.[70] Thus, Hull, Acheson, and their colleagues knew that they needed to develop grassroots, labor, and business support for their proposals. However, they did not include members of Congress or representatives of protectionist interests that might be threatened by efforts to liberalize trade.[71] In early 1943, Hull again reorganized the planning process, but this attempt also failed.[72] Foreign service officers and civil servants gained greater control over the planning strategy, and outsiders were even less likely to be heard by the commercial policy planners.

Hull knew from his experience on Capitol Hill how lobbyists and special interests could sabotage new policies. He hoped to deploy public support for freer trade against the special interests that might oppose the department's postwar plans. Yet the senior postwar planners had done little to create such public support or public understanding either directly through public forums or indirectly through Congress. Hull said that the postwar planning was "a task not for governments alone, but for parents, and teachers."[73] But from 1939 to 1942, he did nothing to see that ordinary Americans such as parents and teachers were consulted for their views on trade and employment issues, either directly or indirectly through Congress.[74]

By 1942, the postwar planners had built a paper foundation to accommodate two very different policy goals: trade liberalization and full employment.[75] But this trade policy, born of the Great Depression and the war, soon developed an identity crisis. Although it resembled classical economics on trade, to some observers it looked less a child of Adam Smith than one of Keynes.[76]

In fact, the trade policy was a child of both theories, and as a policy half-breed it faced an uncertain future. Neither the public nor their elected representatives were involved in its early development and nurturing. By not granting adequate voice to the views of Congress and the private sector, the trade policy planners risked creating future problems for their strategy on Capitol Hill.[77] Many members of Congress were already concerned about ceding congressional authority on postwar planning and on trade policy.

The planners believed they could build a constituency for their plans by linking war and peace, future jobs and trade. However, as Cordell Hull noted, the public and Congress would need to see a connection between the plans devised by the State Department and each American's future well-being.[78]

3

Gaining Congressional Approval for Multilateral Trade Liberalization, 1943–1945

I n 1943, the postwar planners were optimistic about the postwar plans. Although the war was not going well for the Allies, support for international cooperation seemed to be growing among elites. The Republicans issued the "Mackinac" resolution, urging the United States to play its proper role in postwar international cooperation.[1] It looked like Congress would extend the authority of the president under the Reciprocal Trade Agreements Act. And U.S. and British negotiators had reached agreement on the broad outlines of their plans to expand world trade

However, by 1945, as the war moved to a close, the fervor for creating new international institutions began to evaporate among senior Roosevelt administration officials. As the famous columnist Walter Lippman noted, the New Dealers "are now a set of tired middle-aged men," less committed to policy innovation. Even once ardent supporters of a new approach to ordering the world economy such as Cordell Hull and Leo Pasvolsky were increasingly cautious about the limits of public support for internationalist initiatives. They recognized there was no wellspring of public support for radical change to the nation's foreign economic policies.[2] In spite of these hurdles, the postwar planners continued to move forward with their ambitious plans for trade.

The Legislative Basis for the Proposed ITO

On September 12, 1943, Secretary of State Cordell Hull took to the airwaves to explain how America's economic postwar plans would meet the national interest. Hull's speech was deliberately general, emphasizing the need for international economic, social, and political collaboration "to create conditions in which . . . each nation will have enhanced opportunities to develop and progress in ways of its own choosing."[3] Hull provided little information about how the economic postwar plans might affect the interests of Americans in their multiple roles as voters, workers, consumers, and shareholders, and he said nothing about a proposed international organization to further global economic growth.

But the postwar planners had already become quite specific. They believed trade must be expanded on a nondiscriminatory basis, and policies should be directed toward keeping that trade in the hands of private enterprise. An international trade organization would facilitate achievement of these objectives.[4]

Most of the background work for the proposed international trade organization was developed by government officials who met as the Special Committee on the Relaxation of Trade Barriers.[5] The Special Committee members disagreed on how best to reconcile foreign and domestic economic growth, but they shared a belief that the time was right to gain support for global trade liberalization in the United States. A Special Committee report noted that U.S. unemployment was virtually nonexistent, American industry was less dependent on protection than in the 1930s, and the global economy would soon be adjusting to peacetime needs.[6]

As the postwar planners recognized, however, three factors could thwart the achievement of freer trade. The first was the timing of their efforts. They knew any program for trade liberalization would "encounter opposition from special interest groups and their spokesmen," but the "opposition is in a weaker position now than it has been in the past or will be . . . after the war." The time to face that opposition "is already upon us."[7] Timing might affect their success in a second way. The planners recognized "the extent to which one country may be willing to go towards the relaxation of a type of trade barrier . . . might depend on the extent to which other types of trade barriers . . . are also relaxed." They concluded that the only feasible approach to multilateral trade liberalization was to address all trade barriers simultaneously.[8]

Current trade law presented a third and final obstacle to simultaneous trade barrier reduction. The RTAA did not authorize simultaneous trade barrier reduction, but only the selective reduction of tariffs on specific products. Moreover, the legislation was directed toward bilateral negotiations and said nothing about multilateral negotiations. Thus, under the RTAA, the United States could not facilitate the reduction of a wide range of trade barriers (such as preferences or exchange controls) between many nations. Moreover, international discussions about trade liberalization had moved forward on the premise of sweeping, mutual trade barrier reductions, although the trade policy planners had no legal authority to achieve a multilateral and horizontal negotiation.[9] Although these officials recognized the gap between their objectives and their authority, it did not spur them to develop new, more appropriate legislation or to educate the public and Congress about their strategy and objectives.

The planners were soon reminded that trade policies were also domestic policies. The Reciprocal Trade Agreements Act was not popular with the American people or the Congress; most Americans had never heard of the act and didn't understand its objectives. The RTAA had long engendered congressional hostility because it was perceived as a challenge to legislative control of the nation's economic policies. Some members of Congress saw the act as a New Deal program, and a growing conservative coalition of Republicans and Southern Democrats felt the New Deal deserved dismantling.

The House Hearings on the third renewal of the RTAA should have given the trade policy planners pause.[10] The hearings, in April and May 1943, revealed the strength of special-interest opposition to freer trade even in a time of supposedly bipartisan foreign policy. Twenty-nine witnesses testified for and sixteen witnesses against the RTAA; fifteen briefs were submitted in its favor and seventeen against its continuation. Labor, business, and farm groups as well as members of Congress testified on both sides of the issue.[11] Farmers, workers, business leaders, and members of Congress feared that trade liberalization could undermine America's standard of living by forcing U.S. workers to compete with cheap labor.[12] Some witnesses and members of Congress stressed that the United States was fighting the war to restore the American economic and political systems, not to change them or "export the New Deal." They determined to ensure that the planners could not do so.[13] Moreover, witnesses and members of Congress expressed concerns about executive branch control of trade policies. Workers, congressmen, and some business leaders complained that the process for determining tariff reduction was secretive and did not include representatives from the people or affected interests.[14] They claimed the process for reducing tariffs was undemocratic and even "totalitarian," because representatives of the people delegated their power to the executive branch to determine the nation's tax policy.[15] To regain control over the trade policy process, these opponents recommended House or Senate approval of trade agreements.[16]

Although the RTAA was extended with greater legislative support than in previous renewals, the hearings should have warned the planners not to ignore congressional concerns. Congress was clearly worried about future foreign economic policies; members wanted more information and more control over the policy development process. Several members of Congress as well as outside witnesses expressed concern about the unclear linkages between Article VII of lend-lease and the trade policy plans, but

Table 3. Some Prominent Proponents and Opponents of 1943 Renewal of the
Reciprocal Trade Agreements Act

Some Proponents:	Some Opponents:
Agriculture: American Farm Bureau Federation	*Agriculture:* National Grange, National Cooperative Milk Producers Conference
Labor: International Ladies Garment Workers Union, Brotherhood of Railway Steamship Clerks, National Women's Trade Union League	*Labor:* American Wage Earners Protective Conference
Business: National Foreign Trade Council	*Business:* American Tariff League
	Prominent Opponents: George Peek
Prominent Republicans: Charles P. Taft, William Allen White, Henry Stimson	
Newspapers: Baltimore Sun, Christian Science Monitor, Emporia Gazette, New York Times, St. Louis Post Dispatch	

Source: House Committee on Ways and Means, *Hearings on H.J. Res. 111: Extension of Reciprocal Trade Agreements Act,* 78th Cong., 1st sess., Apr. 12-23, 1943.

the planners made no special effort to explain how lend-lease agreements had served to induce American allies to participate in trade negotiations.[17] Some members of an increasingly assertive Congress charged that the administration "had indicated its intention to keep peacemaking out of Congressional hands"; they used the hearings to show their determination to be viewed as partners in policy development.[18] Furthermore, the hearings revealed that special interests (including protectionists) had certainly not lost their influence on Capitol Hill. Congress responded to the hearings with a two-year extension of presidential authority to negotiate trade agreements rather than the three years originally requested by the State Department.[19] Congress clearly intended to keep the planners on a short leash.

In 1943-44, Congress sent other signals to the postwar planners. Both the House and Senate set up postwar planning committees and passed several resolutions on their goals for peace. In addition, Senate Foreign Relations Committee members stressed that the lend-lease master agreements were to be used to achieve wartime goals only.[20] But these actions did not motivate the planners to explain how they would use Article VII to develop the plans. The planners seemed more concerned with meeting international demands for dramatic tariff reduction than with answering congressional pleas for inclusion and control.

The 1943 hearings may, however, have been a wake up call to senior officials at the State Department about the strength of the opposition to policies linking trade and employment. Both British and American observers noted that Cordell Hull appeared to recognize the political costs of attempting to build an international trade organization and that he now seemed to view it as less of a priority. Other important officials, including Henry Wallace, the vice president, and Undersecretary Sumner Welles, were never overly enthusiastic.[21] Nonetheless, discussions with the British on a coordinated approach to international economic policies began in the fall of 1943.

As the planners focused on the international means of achieving their goals, British officials were also firming up their approach to an international trade organization. In conjunction with British officials in the Board of Trade, James Meade of the war cabinet drafted a plan called the Commercial Union. Meade had written his plan in response to Keynes's proposal for a clearing union. It included a convention to reduce tariffs and provided for a secretariat to to settle disputes. Meade was delighted when the Americans welcomed his plans.[22]

The British and American plans became the focus of Anglo-American discussions held in Washington in September and October 1943, under the aegis of Article VII discussions. British participants on commercial policy issues were Sir Percivale Liesching of the Board of Trade, James Meade representing the Board of Trade, and Lionel Robbins of the war cabinet. On the U.S. side, key participants included Myron C. Taylor, the head of the Special Committee; Assistant Secretary of State Dean Acheson; Assistant Secretary of Commerce William L. Clayton; Leo Pasvolsky; and Harry Hawkins and his able assistants Don Fuqua, John Leddy, and Leroy Stinebower.[23]

The American and British negotiators found both common ground and significant areas of disagreement in their wide-ranging discussion. They agreed the plans needed to link trade and employment objectives through economic expansion and to establish some system for the free convertibility of currencies. Both groups of negotiators stressed that "the problems to be faced after the war would be so great, so urgent, . . . that . . . action on multilateral lines" was required.[24] But they disagreed on the specifics and timing of trade barrier reductions. The British reiterated that changes in preferences had to be linked to substantial tariff reduction as part of a nexus of concessions.[25]

America's postwar planners were better at reading and responding to international developments than at attending to political realities at home. International signals came in loud and clear. British officials repeatedly stressed that bilateral negotiations were not "an adequate means for reducing trade barriers immediately and tariff reductions under bilateral trade agreements would not be accepted as a full discharge of the obligation of Article VII to reduce trade barriers." American diplomats in Britain frequently warned that the U.S. government would have to reduce tariffs substantially to "buy" changes in preferences. The Canadians echoed this view, insisting on simultaneous multilateral negotiations during Article VII discussions in January and February 1944.[26]

The U.S. planners were in a bind. To be internationally successful they had to gain British support, but the British (and the Canadians) demanded multilateral, simultaneous reduction of trade barriers. The RTAA, as then constituted, would not allow enough concessions to achieve international agreement. Many of the senior planners recognized one way to escape this bind: to build public and congressional opinion in support of multilateral trade liberalization based on an understanding of the economic position of America's allies, especially Great Britain.[27] This approach might have allowed the planners to draft new legislation and to make a case for it with Congress. However, after a further round of discussions, senior State Department officials decided not to follow that course.[28]

As early as 1943, support at the top for a multilateral approach to trade liberalization and for linking trade and employment seemed to be weakening. British economist Lionel Robbins described a conversation with the special assistant to the U.S. Ambassador in London, E.F. Penrose. Penrose "more than hinted at a vast struggle in the State Department" between advocates of freer trade and those who supported control of commodities (such as the Wheat Agreement).[29] Don Fuqua told James Meade that Harry Hawkins "was running a terrific risk . . . in taking the grand line . . . in favor of a multilateral approach to Commercial Policy because the Secretary of State is an ultra-cautious man. The implication of this was . . . that Hull is still extremely unconvinced of the multilateral approach."[30]

State Department officials became increasingly assertive about the economic postwar plans with America's allies. A comprehensive memorandum, prepared for British, Soviet, and American concurrence at the Moscow Conference, outlined eight objectives for international economic cooperation, including an expansion of international trade on a nondiscriminatory basis, the regulation and ultimate elimination of arrangements to restrict production and trade in individual commodities, and the establishment of stable foreign exchange rates.[31] Harry Hawkins and his staff in the Trade Agreements Division (formerly the Division of Commercial Policy) recommended that the United States "push forward vigorously the discussions" with the United Kingdom and other countries to reach tentative agreement "on the substance of a general multilateral convention on commercial policy."[32] They hoped international backing along

these lines would inspire greater public support, they but did little to foster that support.

Secretary of State Hull continued to keep the public in the dark
about the trade policy plans. In a November 11 speech to Congress on the
Moscow Conference, he focused on general political and international cooperation and did not mention specific U.S. objectives or mechanisms.[33]
Other than through that speech, the general public was not notified of the
planners' aspirations. In 1944, some government officials urged a new approach built on popular support and rooted in new trade legislation, but
the majority of the senior postwar planners ignored that advice.[34] As a
result, few Americans even knew that the U.S. government was planning
an international organization on trade.

The Development of a Constituency for the United Nations and the Bretton Woods Institutions

As the planners deliberated in 1944, other international organizations
were moving closer to becoming a reality. Ironically, many of the planners
believed an international trade organization "must succeed or there will
be so serious a gap in the international relations structure as to bring ev-
erything down in ruins."[35] Yet the ITO had barely been designed when
the planners started to erect the other international institutions. Unfortunately, the planners failed to incorporate lessons from their construction
in the plans for an international trade organization.

The efforts to develop the United Nations (UN) and the Bretton
Woods institutions (the World Bank and the International Monetary
Fund) were characterized by greater public involvement than the effort
to develop an ITO. In establishing the UN, an international organization
to spur global cooperation and develop peaceful solutions to international
disputes, the planners were able to build on strong public support. Many
Americans, who regretted the U.S. failure to join the League of Nations
after World War I, concluded that an international security organization
might have fostered international cooperation. Although membership in
the United Nations entailed a major shift in U.S. foreign policy, it was a
change that the American public saw as necessary.

Public opinion muted the traditional Republican opposition to internationalism. Many Republican leaders seemed to acknowledge that
they would have to shed their isolationist image to survive in the postwar
world, given the United States' clear responsibility for world order.[36] Consequently, Roosevelt administration officials were able to emphasize publicly the nonpartisan development and negotiation of the United Nations.

Many UN planners recognized that public opinion would provide a framework for their objectives and strategy for achieving a world security organization. Throughout 1944, they worked hard to build and sustain public support.[37] Senior officials cautiously courted Congress and involved representatives of the public and Congress developing proposals for the proposed organization, while working to obtain international assent to their plans. Their well-publicized efforts to involve Congress neutralized congressional and especially Republican opposition.[38] The negotiating process also included members of special interests: forty-two national organizations were invited to serve as consultants to the American delegation at the San Francisco Conference. Finally, the nation's leaders consistently emphasized the importance of the UN. Both President Franklin D. Roosevelt and President Harry S Truman frequently noted that the proposed United Nations would meet the public interest. At the same time, respected business, government, civic, and religious leaders emphasized their support for this policy innovation.[39] Because a broad cross section of people participated in its development, many Americans perceived the UN as designed for them and in their interest.

The Senate debate on the United Nations Charter revealed the depth of support for this radical change to America's foreign policies. According to Ruth Russell, who wrote an extensive history of U.S. involvement in the UN's development, witnesses who thought the charter was too strong (a superstate) were counterbalanced by those who thought it too weak. After five days of debate, the Senate approved the UN by an overwhelming vote of 89-2 (with five Senators absent).[40]

The history of the Bretton Woods Institutions (BWI) is also characterized by the appearance of public involvement, although representatives of banks and internationalist organizations played the largest role. Unlike the UN, the BWI initially aroused little public interest and support. Few Americans understood the need for international financial rules and institutions, stable exchange rates, and financial support for development. But the BWI planners focused on conveying the benefits of these institutions to the American people and Congress, with Treasury Secretary Henry Morgenthau Jr. and his deputy Harry Dexter White spearheading the difficult efforts. Morgenthau stressed, "Our job isn't done until it is sold."[41] It would not be an easy sell.

The BWI planners mounted a wide-ranging public relations campaign. They made sure the delegation to Bretton Woods included representatives from Congress, the financial community, and academia. White held daily press conferences at Bretton Woods and encouraged public discussion of the two proposed institutions. To build a constituency in support of the BWI, Treasury hired a public relations firm; invited academics, business leaders, ministers, and bankers to discuss the proposals; and tried to portray the institutions in simple terms appealing to the general public. So effective was his campaign that Senator Robert A. Taft complained that Morgenthau had used tax dollars to fund one of "the most . . . organized . . . propaganda efforts which this country has ever seen." These marketing efforts paid off in July 1945, when Congress passed the Bretton Woods Agreements Act.[42]

Both the UN and the BWI benefitted from Republican reluctance to oppose internationalist initiatives in 1945. (According to Dean Acheson, the Republicans "couldn't afford to be against every international measure, so they flocked to a man to vote for Bretton Woods.") But these institutions were also tributes to effective leadership and the appearance of consensual decision making. Roosevelt, Truman, and their secretaries of state consistently emphasized the importance of the UN; Morgenthau and White were devoted to establishing the BWI. Executive branch, congressional, special interest, and community leaders working together were able to forge a consensual approach to erecting these institutions.[43]

The ITO was a far different story. No ground swell of public support spurred Congress to work with the ITO's architects. Moreover, the much-touted congressional/executive consensus on foreign policy did not extend to trade policy. It was quite possible to favor internationalist initiatives and oppose the administration's approach to multilateral trade liberalization. Finally, although Hull once saw an international trade organization as essential to his postwar plans, his commitment appeared to be wavering. He did not attend the conferences with the British that developed these plans. There is no evidence to show that President Roosevelt supported these plans. Although the president said he viewed establishment of rules for international trade as essential, his lack of involvement may have conveyed the implicit message that an international trade organization was not crucial.

Tailoring the Proposed ITO to Existing Legislation, the RTAA

While the UN and BWI planners gained support for their plans, the trade policy planners argued over the proper legislative strategy to achieve their international objectives. Throughout 1944, the postwar planners were unable to agree whether to build on the RTAA or to devise a new legislative vehicle for the ITO.[44] By the end of 1944, State Department staff had weighed the benefits and detriments of five different approaches, which they called Proposals A through E. Three had serious detriments, so the planners focused on Proposals A and E.[45]

Proposal A, which U.S. and British negotiators had discussed since 1943, called for horizontal tariff reduction. It would maximize U.S. bargaining power but force the planners to abandon the RTAA and develop a legislative alternative. Proposal A reflected the planners' growing concerns about congressional and protectionist backlash. It included an escape clause that could be invoked if rising imports damaged a particular industry or commodity. The planners hoped the escape clause would mollify the fears of Congress and special interests about the economic impact of freer trade. Nonetheless, Proposal A would have radically changed America's longstanding approach to tariff policy.[46]

In contrast, Proposal E built upon current policy. Under this approach, as nations negotiated bilateral tariff reductions, a multilateral group of conferees would also discuss the reduction of nontariff barriers, cartels, and commodity issues. This proposal had several advantages: it would "assure the general extent of tariff reduction and would provide tariff reduction simultaneous with the relaxation of non-tariff barriers. It would be highly selective and . . . possible under the Trade Agreements Act." Proposal E would also achieve multilateral freer trade through bilateral negotiations, but this strategy presented serious negotiating problems. Although Proposal E was more politically feasible, most of the trade policy planners preferred Proposal A.[47] They wanted to build the ITO on new legislation.

Although they had narrowed their options, the trade policy planners seemed unable to reach a consensus on their legislative strategy. On February 8, 1945, William A. Fowler of the State Department drafted a resolution aimed at increasing and extending the trade agreements policy, gaining the blessing of Congress for the broad multilateral plans, and concentrating "public and Congressional support behind a single measure." Fowler noted that the highest priority was to gain increased authority for tariff reduction, and he recommended that the State Department request its traditional three-year extension. He thought the planners could obtain increased authority, a horizontal reduction, and the three-year extension, but worried that the multilateral proposals might split public support and jeopardize the increased authority the planners needed to continue their international discussions to create an ITO.[48]

Not even Fowler's draft could move the process forward. Some of Fowler's more politically astute colleagues, unsure whether Congress would let them achieve all three goals in 1945, concluded that they had to use the multilateral-bilateral approach to obtain congressional support simply to gain renewed authority. They believed that more members of Congress would support the multilateral-bilateral approach because it was "a selective method which [had] worked in the past."[49]

At the last minute, the planners tried to ascertain whether they could use public support to convince Congress of the benefits of a horizontal tariff reduction. On the one hand, they believed growing support for the general concept of trade liberalization might foster greater public support for a new approach to trade policy. Its benefits would be abundantly clear to many producers and traders; they "would have something concrete to fight for." On the other hand, because the multilateral-bilateral approach would yield fewer benefits, it would be difficult to rally these same groups in its support. The planners concluded that Proposal A might "capture the popular imagination as a far reaching step toward international economic progress," helping its chances in Congress.[50]

But it was already too late to use public opinion to shape congressional behavior. The planners had lost the opportunity to use public support for the UN and the BWI to build support for an international trade organization. Nor had they taken advantage of the few public statements in favor of trade liberalization to build a consensus for their plans.[51]

As the plans for an international trade conference reveal, public approval was not a high priority for the planners. One planner wrote, around July 1, that the United States "should make up an agenda for the conference and recommend the position the United States should take on each subject on it. . . . Our proposals should then be sent to all governments with a statement . . . that their comments would be welcome." At the same time it should be "made public . . . to allow opportunity for the public and Congress to become familiar with them and to get their reactions."[52] This passive strategy might have been successful if a consensus already existed; it would surely not work where the public was confused about or uninterested in the issue.

On November 30, 1944, Assistant Secretary of State Dean Acheson made the first public announcement of the plans for a world trade conference. In testimony before the House Special Committee on Post-War Economic Policy and Planning, he declared the department's intention "to seek an early understanding with the leading trading nations, indeed with as many nations as possible, for the . . . reduction of all . . . barriers to trade" at the earliest possible date. "This agreement would of course be submitted to the Congress for its consideration." But he did not invite Congress or the public to participate in its design. Acheson and the other planners kept the specifics of their work under wraps.[53]

Several key planners, including Harry Hawkins, challenged Acheson's approach. Hawkins, now economic advisor to the U.S. ambassador in

London, called for a strategy that would emphasize both public and international support equally and simultaneously. Because early congressional approval of the multinational approach was needed to get international backing, he recommended that the planners get legislative authority for horizontal cuts, even if doing so required abandoning the RTAA. The secretary's staff committee agreed with Hawkins. "Advantage should be taken of the public interest in, and support of the San Francisco Conference and . . . it would be very desirable to advance proposals for the economic side of the peace at the same time. On this basis we might be ready to make a detailed public statement of our program in two or three months."[54] After a preliminary sounding of congressional sentiment, Assistant Secretaries Acheson and Clayton concluded that Congress would never approve further authority for explicit multilateral negotiations.[55]

Events soon forced the planners to stop vacillating and choose an alternative on which to build their legislative strategy for an international trade organization. The president's authority under the RTAA would soon expire, and the planners feared losing even its limited authority for trade liberalization. The planners finally decided not to develop new legislation and to put their efforts behind the selective approach that had characterized the RTAA since 1934. The RTAA became their priority.

The RTAA hearings, held in April through June 1945, forced the planners to confront the power of Congress and special interests to affect the postwar plans.[56] The Senate hearing was particularly antagonistic. Fifteen witnesses testified in favor of the legislation, and eight additional groups submitted positive briefs; thirty-three witnesses testified against the bill, and twenty submitted negative briefs. At the House Hearings, sixteen witnesses testified against and nine for the legislation. As in 1943, labor, business, and farm groups, as well as government officials, testified on both sides of the issue.[57]

Opponents of trade liberalization presented both traditional and new arguments against the RTAA. Echoing the RTAA hearings in 1943, farmers, workers, business leaders, and members of Congress expressed their concern that freer trade would undermine America's standard of living. Representatives of business, labor, and Congress argued that the Department of State could not be trusted to develop economic policies in the interest of the American people.[58] Representatives of business, labor, and Congress again stressed that for Congress to delegate its authority to determine tariff policy would make trade policy undemocratic.[59]

Opponents of freer trade also added some new twists, linking jobs and trade to oppose both the extension of the RTAA and any change to trade policies. Some argued that the United States must first achieve full employment and only then move toward freer trade. Others maintained

Table 4. Some Prominent Proponents and Opponents of 1945 Renewal of the Trade Agreements Act

Some Proponents:	Some Opponents:
Agriculture: American Farm Bureau Federation, National Farmers Union	*Agriculture:* National Grange, National Cooperative Milk Producers Conference, Southern Commissioners of Agriculture, National Association of Commissioners, Secretaries, and Directors of Agriculture
Labor: International Ladies Garment Workers Union, Brotherhood of Railway Steamship Clerks, National Women's Trade Union League, Congress of Industrial Organizations, Textile Workers Union, International Union of Mine, Mill and Smelter Workers	*Labor:* American Wage Earners Protective Conference, American Watchmakers Union
Business: National Foreign Trade Council, Committee for Economic Development, Commerce and Industry Association of New York	*Business:* American Tariff League, American Glassware Association, Bicycle Institute of America, Toy Manufacturers, American Mining Congress, Independent Petroleum Association
Prominent Republicans: Charles P. Taft, William Allen White, Henry Stimson	*Prominent Opponents:* George Peek, Senator John Thomas
Newspapers: Baltimore Sun, Christian Science Monitor, Emporia Gazette, New York Times, St. Louis Post Dispatch	
Civic Groups: League of Women Voters, General Federation of Women's Clubs, American Association of University Women	

Source: House Committee on Ways and Means, *Foreign Trade Agreements: Report to Accompany H.R. 3240,* 79th Cong., 1st sess., May 18, 1945, and *Hearings on H.R.* 3240: An Act to Extend the Authority of the President under Section 350 of the *Tariff Act of 1930, as Amended,* 79th Cong., 1st sess., May 30-June 5, 1945.

that lowering the tariff would effectively increase immigration, because the American worker would have to compete with lower-priced labor.[60] The use of a jobs rationale to argue against renewed presidential authority for trade liberalization should have motivated the planners to clarify their intentions.

However, the planners did not use the hearings to explain how they would utilize expanded authority to foster multilateral trade liberalization. The officials who testified never discussed the proposed ITO, even though Congress reminded them of the public's right to know. The House Report, in calling for the approval of the legislation, noted, "The economic future of this country will depend upon the ability of the American people to see their real interests clearly. . . . The Committee is confident they will not be misled in this matter."[61] Instead of heeding this warning, the planners chose to keep the American people in the dark.

The minority report on the RTAA took a different tack by linking freer trade to "regimentation." Republicans noted that "only under a socialized system of government, with industry and labor completely regimented, can we possibly hope to maintain . . . a level of imports sufficient to pay for the amount of exports which the administration contemplates." In the minority's eyes, the plans of the State Department's "world planners and globocrats" meant "the loss of a diversified economy," "the destruction of incentives to pioneer," and "the establishment of even greater and more powerful bureaucratic controls." The minority urged a more nationalistic approach. "The major effort in the post-war period . . . should be directed to the creation and maintenance of a sound domestic economy. . . . Let us ever remember that we must keep America free, strong, and prosperous if we would be the hope and salvation of the world."[62]

But supporters of freer trade ignored the linkage of their plans with socialism. Although the State Department carefully monitored congressional attitudes, the planners frequently misread congressional concerns about their objectives and strategy.[63] It is not surprising that Acheson, who was in charge of congressional relations, seemed amazed that the RTAA extension passed in 1945.[64]

A Resolution on the Plans for an International Trade Organization

Although the RTAA was extended for three years, the planners obtained little of what they needed to forge an international consensus on an international trade organization. They did not gain legislative authority for horizontal negotiations. As John Leddy wrote to his friend and boss William A. Fowler, now at the American Embassy in London, "during the hearings on the Act we have played up selectivity probably more than during any previous renewal . . . to get the authority. There is likely to be considerable opposition to any plan involving horizontal reductions."[65] Despite its limitations, it was now clear that the RTAA would have to serve as the legislative foundation for the development of the proposed ITO.

The planners soon found a way to reconcile their legislative constraints with their international objectives, but their solution would shortly jeopardize their larger foreign economic policy objectives. In April

1945, Leddy and other State Department officials devised a "nuclear" approach, whereby a few trading nations would simultaneously negotiate bilateral trade agreements and then encourage additional agreements with other groups of countries. Leddy saw the nuclear approach as "an attempt to cut the cloth of our postwar commercial policy so as to fit the legal pattern of the Trade Agreements Act and still permit bold and rapid action." At the same time, he admitted the objectives were contradictory. "Bold and rapid action, which is the only kind that will meet the urgent needs of the postwar period, simply is not possible under the Trade Agreements Act . . . . The plain truth, which should be faced now so that we can avoid delay and make progress, . . . appears to be that Congress will not delegate to the executive advance authority to do the large job that needs to be done." Leddy suggested that the planners first negotiate a multilateral agreement that "would be sold to the country and then brought back to Congress for approval." [66] Although many planners agreed with this suggestion, the planning committee now in charge of trade policies, the Executive Committee on Economic Foreign Policy, rejected it. On July 21, committee members decided to ask the British to agree to the nuclear approach. Only if the British flatly rejected it would they return to Congress to request new legislation.[67] Despite this decision, the planners debated the alternatives until November 1945, long after Congress had passed the extension of the RTAA.[68]

Meanwhile, Hawkins, Fowler, and E.F. Penrose had begun discussions with British officials to forge a consensus on general plans for an international trade organization.[69] The British were upset, but in November 1945 they accepted the nuclear approach and agreed on an outline for an international trade organization.[70] In December 1945, with British concurrence, the United States issued its "Proposals for Expansion of World Trade and Employment." The Proposals were the first published draft of American plans to link trade policies to employment policies. They were also the first public expression of U.S. intent to promote the development of an international trade organization.[71]

After two years of deliberation and dissension, the postwar planners developed a congressional strategy to achieve their international objectives. The planners hitched their plans to an ill-fitted legislative vehicle, one that could not facilitate bold (trading a wide range of trade barrier reductions for horizontal tariff reduction) or rapid action. Their incremental approach did not match their broad and innovative objectives. Moreover, the planners were unable to take advantage of what they saw as a relatively weakened opposition because of their unwillingness to directly tackle special interests and the Congress about multilateralism.

These officials were no more adept with the general and concerned public. Senior officials barely informed the public about what they were doing. It was not until 1945 that they announced their intention to negotiate an international trade organization. But the public, representatives of special interests, and members of Congress would soon affect the fate of the trade policy plans. These officials would learn that their responsibility to determine trade policies in the national interest was matched by a responsibility to make their objectives clear to the American public.

4

The Planners and the Public, 1943–1946

N ineteen forty-six was not a good year to propose a new international organization. Frustrated by the rising prices of necessities, Americans paid attention to the domestic economy. They were less supportive than during the war years of government planning in general and internationalist economic planning in particular. The ITO also made its debut at a time when events in Europe lessened the importance of longer-term mechanisms. Instead, such emergency mechanisms as food aid for Europe and financial aid to Britain became top priorities for government officials.

Changes within the government also portended problems for the proposed ITO. President Truman brought new leadership and new objectives to foreign policy. Many of his new senior officials could see little to gain from clinging to the proposed ITO.

Yet other government officials remained committed to achieving an international trade organization. They still believed in a comprehensive approach to trade policy. However, they were not concerned about public apathy. They assumed that public support would magically spring from a core constituency for internationalism and that the rationale for the ITO, the linkage of trade and employment, would resonate with the American people.

Changes to the political and economic environment, to public opinion, and to the federal bureaucracy left their marks on the proposed ITO. By 1946, ITO supporters had begun to understand that these changes did not bode well for the fate of the trade policy plans.

New Leaders, New Priorities

A core staff of experienced trade policy officials continued to work on the ITO, but key personnel changes affected the management and direction of the planning process. These changes underscore the importance of consistent leadership at the highest levels of government to successful institution building. From 1943 to 1946, America had three secretaries of state: Cordell Hull, who resigned in October 1944, Edward Stettinius, who served from November 1944 to June 1945, and James Byrnes, who served from July 1945 to September 1946.[1] These men had to shepherd a variety of mechanisms through an increasingly assertive and conservative Congress. As the ITO was neither their creation nor greatly popular, it is not surprising that it became a lower priority for the new secretaries.

The new priorities of the State Department first became evident during the hearings on the fourth extension of the Reciprocal Trade Agreements Act (RTAA), held in April through June 1945, during the last months of Stettinius's service as secretary. Stettinius was not as concerned about the links between trade policy and peace as Hull and certainly not as ardent an advocate of the RTAA. When the RTAA hearings and the San Francisco Conference on the United Nations conflicted, Stettinius went to San Francisco. He asked William Clayton, the new assistant secretary of state for international affairs, to represent him at the RTAA hearing. Traditionally, the secretary of state had presented the department's position, and some congressmen tried to use Stettinius's absence to "create the unfortunate impression" that he "has not enough confidence in the operation of the act to appear in its defense." Because Clayton was new to his position and did not receive the deference usually accorded to the secretary of state, he had a difficult time defending the RTAA.[2]

The death of Franklin D. Roosevelt on April 12, 1945, also weakened the effort to create an international trade organization. The new president, Harry S Truman brought new ideas, management, and priorities to foreign policy. Trade liberalization, and specifically an ITO, was not as high a priority for his top foreign policy team. Meanwhile, Harry Hawkins, who had led the State Department's efforts on trade policy since 1934, moved to the American embassy in London, leaving the policy in the less-experienced but equally capable hands of Clayton, Clair Wilcox, and Winthrop Brown.[3] Clayton, a wealthy cotton-broker, joined the Roosevelt administration in 1940; he was assistant secretary of commerce from 1942 until 1944, then he joined the State Department. He would become the ITO's strongest advocate in the Truman administration. Clair Wilcox taught economics at Swarthmore College and joined the State Department in 1945. Wilcox would become the principal negotiator of the final charter of the ITO. Brown, an attorney, worked on lend-lease issues in London before joining the Division of Commercial Policy. These men, however, were not well connected with the new officials at the top levels of the State Department under Stettinius and Byrnes.

Although Clayton, Willard Thorp, and Dean Acheson (who became undersecretary to Byrnes) were promoted within the State Department under its new management, their promotion did not signal an advance for the ITO in the Truman administration's priorities. The men at the top of the Department of State were preoccupied with issues such as the end of lend-lease, Europe's economic problems, Britain's financial crisis, control of atomic energy, and collaboration with the Department of the Interior on an international petroleum agreement.[4]

Changes at the top levels of the executive branch also meant new priorities and new strategies at other cabinet-level agencies. Shifts in staffing brought new blood and often less understanding than during the war years of the objectives for an international trade organization.[5] The proposed ITO may also have lost some high-level advocates in departments such as Agriculture, Commerce, Labor, and Treasury, whose support and involvement were important.

Changes at the Working Level of the Department of State

The structure for developing the plans for an international trade organization changed frequently, reflecting the new priorities for foreign economic policy that emerged as the war began to wind down. In 1943, responsibility for developing an international organization had been divided among various divisions of the State Department, including the Division of Special Research, the Office of Economic Affairs, and the Office of the Special Assistant to the Secretary (which handled other international organizations within the State Department). On January 26, 1944, the department was reorganized. The Office of Economic Affairs was abolished and replaced by the Office of Commercial Policy, directed by Bernard F. Haley, who soon returned to Stanford University to teach economics, and the Office of Financial and Development Policy, directed by Emilio Collado, an economist who served the Treasury Department and the State Department. The Office of Commercial Policy handled the bulk of work for the proposed ITO.[6]

The division of postwar planning among several offices hampered the public relations efforts of the planners. Although representatives of Leo Pasvolsky's staff continued to participate in the planning for the ITO, they focused primarily on developing the United Nations Charter. In contrast with their colleagues working on foreign economic policies, Pasvolsky's staff moved rapidly to involve internationalist outside advisors as well as government officials and, ultimately, members of Congress.[7] But because of the partition of the planning staff, the ITO's architects did not benefit from the UN planners' experience in selling the UN to the American people. The ITO's architects hoped to tie the proposed ITO to institutions such as the United Nations, but found it difficult to build public understanding of the link between the organizations already approved by 1945 and those still being planned.[8]

The reorganization also established the Executive Committee on Economic Foreign Policy (ECEFP), whose function was to examine problems affecting U.S. economic foreign policy and to formulate recommendations for the secretary of state.[9] But the ECEFP was poorly equipped to persuade the public and Congress to support the ITO: it had no outside or congressional members. The ECEFP included officials from the Departments of State, Treasury, Agriculture, Labor, Justice, War, and Commerce, as well as the Bureau of the Budget, the Federal Trade Commission, the Securities and Exchange Commission, the Foreign Economic Administration, and the Tariff Commission.[10] The committee was run by and dominated by State Department officials, who were more comfortable with international issues than with domestic issues. Without public feedback, these officials were more likely to misinterpret the implications of changing economic and political conditions for the future of their plans. It is not surprising that the planners' strategy emphasized international assent over American public approval.[11]

The ECEFP had no formal means of liaison with the American people. From 1944 to 1947, its meetings were closed to the public. The work of the ECEFP was not linked to the advisory committee directing the development of the United Nations.[12] As a result, ECEFP members, like State Department staff, could not fully profit from the lessons learned by Pasvolsky's staff.

The interagency structure of the ECEFP institutionalized a governmentwide mechanism to discuss foreign economic policy, which the State Department found particularly useful. Its subcommittees, often headed by officials from other agencies, covered the spectrum of issues that trade policies can affect.[13] State Department officials used the subcommittees to gain the cooperation of other agencies while controlling the planning process.[14] Nonetheless, many ECEFP members resented the State Department's domination of trade policy, for they perceived trade as a domestic as well as a foreign economic issue.[15]

However, because of the scope of the proposed ITO, ECEFP members spent a significant amount of time resolving turf disputes: officials argued over which agency should control the decision-making process on issues affecting trade. Among the most prominent disputes was whether commodity agreements should fall under the proposed ITO's purview or that of the Food and Agricultural Organization.[16] Although the ECEFP succeeded in developing compromises, members did not use their time, expertise, and energy to examine how the American people might see these issues, which affected so many government agencies and constituents.

The interagency planning structure did not fulfill its potential to harmonize the ITO's freer trade objectives with existing policy objectives. For example, the Proposals for the Expansion of World Trade and Employment (the first draft of the proposed ITO) suggested that nations should eliminate trade-distorting subsidies, such as agricultural export subsidies, in the interest of freer trade. Yet the Agriculture Department directly subsidized not only some agricultural products such as wool and sugar but also the exports of certain agricultural products. The Proposals also banned quantitative restrictions (import quotas). However, the Agricultural Adjustment Act authorized the president to employ import quotas when imported commodities interfered with the operation of agricultural adjustment programs.[17]

ECEFP members recognized that they could not press for freer trade and a dramatic change to the nation's farm policies at the same time. Instead, they incorporated special provisions outlining exceptions to freer trade principles in each draft of the proposed ITO, beginning with the Proposals. Yet these divergent policies came back to haunt the postwar planners. The decision to incorporate them in the ITO by codifying exceptions soon made the proposed ITO and its advocates appear hypocritical.

Implications of the Failure to Consult Outsiders

These problems were a product of the planners' rigid strategy, which can be attributed to State's domination of the planning structure.[18] As experienced trade policy staff gained greater control over the development of the ITO, international developments rather than presentation of the ITO at home remained their top priority.[19] Moreover, State Department officials were overconfident of their ability to broker between various interests to develop American trade policies. After all, the Trade Agreements Division (under Hawkins, later William Fowler) had the responsibility of recommending measures to implement Article VII of the Atlantic Charter. This, they thought, gave them alone, rather than with members of Congress or business leaders, the expertise to broker the national interest on trade policy through a multilateral trade negotiation.[20] It did not, however, absolve them of the need to consult these groups, as well as the public, to determine the national interest.

Ironically, the planners' determination to develop plans they thought were in the national interest prevented them from developing a means to include public views in the planning process. Some of the postwar planners had suggested that the State Department find ways to institutionalize a channel for including business opinion.[21] After extensive internal debate, senior State Department officials rejected this approach, concluding that as "the Department . . . has the responsibility of reconciling the conflicting interests of the various private economic groups . . . such as labor and employers, or agriculture and manufacturers, the Department should . . . avoid associating itself . . . with any one of these groups."[22] Thus, neither the general public nor the concerned public had a formal means of affecting the development of the trade policy plans. The public, however, was not acquiescent about the nation's foreign economic policies. Although some labor, business, civic, congressional, and academic study groups expressed support for the administration's objectives for an ITO, after 1946 the groups differed with the planners over the administration's timing, mechanisms, and strategy for trade liberalization.[23]

The planners were especially maladroit in dealing with business groups. Business officials who came to inquire about the postwar plans heard only generalities. The planners did meet with several business leaders and representatives of prominent business associations and incorporated some of their views on issues such as cartel and foreign investment policies into the postwar plans.[24] Nonetheless, it is surprising that they did not want to involve more deeply these members of the concerned public.

The planners also ignored the changing mood within Congress. They often testified in generalities and did not inform Congress thoroughly of the direction of their plans.[25] Perhaps they presumed that bipartisanship would continue beyond the war years and carry the ITO through to public approval. Yet many senior planners knew that this bipartisanship had never characterized trade policy before.[26]

Members of Congress as well as special interests used traditional and creative approaches to attack the ITO planning process, the objectives of trade liberalization, and the mechanism itself.[27] The hearings on lend-lease as well as on the RTAA should have alerted the planners to the fact that Congress and many special interests would try to reshape—perhaps even to reject—the postwar plans.[28] The actions of the House Special Committee on Postwar Economic Policy and Planning (the Colmer Committee) reveals the attitudinal gulf between members of Congress and the postwar planners.

At the end of 1945, the Colmer Committee went to Europe to study postwar economic conditions and found that the countries visited "were returning to . . . devices which hamper world trade." Committee members were well aware that the economic problems of these nations required American largesse. In their final report, however, they determined to grant such aid only on a quid pro quo basis.[29]

The report also included congressional recommendations for multilateral trade liberalization. Like the trade policy planners, the Colmer Committee called for an international conference to consider reduction or elimination of trade restrictions. However, the Colmer Committee recognized that such a conference could not solve all of the world's complex economic problems at once. "The aim of the conference should be simply agreement upon a general policy of reduced barriers. At the same time, a permanent economic organization should be set up to deal with the specific problems of individual countries and commodities . . . . The committee welcomes the efforts of the American negotiators . . . to set up an international trade organization."[30] Although the committee did not have high ambitions for such a conference, "high Administration officials" considered it an endorsement of the general direction the administration was taking.[31]

Support for a conference on trade liberalization was not a ringing endorsement of trade liberalization. But it was a signal that Congress recognized "our economic foreign policy is our strongest bargaining weapon in setting political policies" and that Congress would attempt to shape that weapon. "The development of trade relations and the placing of business abroad . . . needs a more aggressive policy than can normally be followed under the guidance of the Department of State alone."[32] Despite the potential for congressional intervention, State Department officials exhibited little concern for the business, public, and congressional support they would shortly need.[33]

Some of the trade policy planners did stress the need to build congressional cooperation in foreign policy. In 1944 Treasury Secretary Henry Morgenthau Jr. and some State Department officials warned the department not to ignore congressional support for an advisory commission on foreign economic policy making that would include members of Congress and the public. Morgenthau feared that rejection of the plan could set "loose an attack upon the administration charging that it fails to recognize the magnitude . . . of a sound post-war foreign economic policy."[34] The eventual advisory structure adopted for economic foreign policy, the ECEFP, did not incorporate Morgenthau's suggestions.

Senior State Department officials, including the secretary of state, gave speeches, radio addresses, and testimony, but they rarely outlined the specifics of their plans.[35] Nor did they encourage a dialogue or hearings on their objectives for trade liberalization. The ITO developmental process remained closed.

The insularity of these State Department officials may have led them to believe that the public supported their efforts. They did their own polling and in 1944 set up the Division of Public Liaison to analyze public opinion polls, editorials, congressional debates, and other indexes of popular opinion.[36] They relied on these materials, rather than on actual public input, to determine public opinion. But the polls that they monitored revealed that attitudes about planning, about the government's role in the economy, and about internationalism were changing. It is to these evolving public attitudes that we now turn.

The Views of the Public and the Selling of the ITO, 1943-1946

During much of the war, cooperation characterized the American polity. Bipartisanship substituted for party politics. Businessmen went to work for the government as dollar-a-year men and diverted their production to facilitate the war effort. Workers postponed wage requests and worked extra hours to support the defense buildup.[37] The trade policy planners hoped that the proposed ITO could be carried into fruition by this cooperative spirit.

By 1945, however, the American people were tired of their war-era sacrifices; they wanted access to the goods and services they had been denied by the Depression and the war. As the demand for goods outpaced their supply, prices rose dramatically. The patina of harmony that had characterized much of the war effort was replaced by partisan politics, strikes, work stoppages, and price gouging.[38]

With a war going on, it was politically acceptable for government officials to manage the economy: to ration goods, set standards and quotas for production, and regulate private sector activities. These efforts were not always popular, but the public understood their rationale. Americans had come to believe that the federal government had a special responsibility for the health of the economy as a whole.[39] Polls of the general public as well as of business executives showed that growing numbers of Americans supported government efforts to create jobs and smooth out business cycles.[40]

However, by December 1945, when the Proposals were first made public, many Americans had begun to reassess their beliefs regarding the role of government. According to historian Susan M. Hartmann, "The postwar period witnessed the emergence of a new middle class . . . determined to maintain their . . . economic gains . . . but unsympathetic to the needs or demands of other groups."[41] They did not want government to dictate to them what they could produce or buy. In addition, although polls revealed that many Americans feared a return of the Depression, many were less certain they wanted government to guarantee employment or economic growth.

Congress began to reflect the new public mood. As economic and political turmoil increased, bitter resentments against the Democratic party and the New Deal mounted, and Truman's authority over the Congress waned.[42] The trade policy planners soon found their strategy circumscribed.

Betwen 1943 and 1945, polls reported strong support for a government role in planning the peace and for internationalist policies.[43] Other surveys of public opinion revealed a burgeoning understanding that trade could create jobs and economic growth.[44] During the war years, an effective public education program, building on the links between trade and jobs, might have been politically salient, but the planners failed to capitalize on this situation and build a consensus in favor of their plans.[45]

By 1946, new attitudes toward the government's role in the economy revealed that the ITO's linkage of trade and employment policies might inspire opposition instead of acclaim. A State Department study noted, "Americans tend to view questions of international trade as producers not consumers; and they tend to be more conscious of the "threat" of foreign products to their jobs than of the opportunity for cheaper imports." This attitude made it difficult to portray the ITO as a vehicle for job creation; it was too indirect. Americans were not "conscious" of trade's potential to create jobs. Moreover, Truman administration officials were participating in a difficult debate over how the federal government might guarantee employment. Some Americans wanted the government to ensure jobs for all citizens who wanted to work, while other Americans feared that legitimizing government responsibility for employment would turn the United States into "a bureaucratic slave state," where capitalism was doomed.[46] In this environment, a strategy emphasizing the ITO's linkage of trade and employment might alienate and confuse rather than attract many Americans.

In 1946 as well, internationalism did not arouse public support the way it had in 1944-45. The planners hoped that linking the ITO to other international organizations would earn the ITO public support. But the planners had done little to discuss the importance of trade policy to foreign policy or to explain global economic interdependence. Polls revealed that the public was not as receptive to information about foreign affairs as they had been in the war years.[47] Consequently, the planners missed the opportunity to explain the ITO by associating it with its more popular sister institutions.

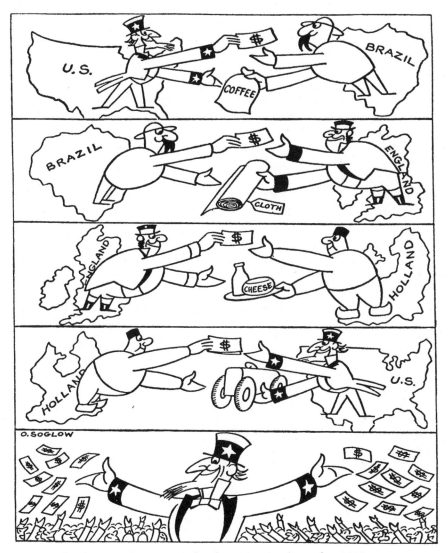

Printer's Ink, November 1946, and *Advertising Age*, December 1946

The most alarming data came from polls that asked people directly about trade. International trade policies were of little interest to most Americans, who did not understand the relationship of trade policies to the health of the American economy. Over 70 percent of the American people polled in 1946 realized the United States must buy (import) in order to sell (export).[48] According to the National Opinion Research Center

(NORC), a majority of the general public recognized that "prosperity knows no national boundaries, but that the economic welfare of the United States depended upon the prosperity of the whole world." Yet only 55 percent of those polled by the NORC thought it was very important to buy more things abroad. Moreover, NORC found that less than half had a reasonably clear idea of what tariffs are or how they work.[49] Polls also revealed that trade policies were not important issues even to those who understood the importance of trade or what tariffs do. "Knowledge of how tariffs work and fear of a business depression during the next five years seem to affect attitudes very little on the tariff issue."[50]

In the planners' defense, polls reported confusing data about trade policy and the proposed ITO. In 1946, 60 percent of those polled by NORC gave "lipservice" to the belief that a world trade organization was very important. However, NORC also noted, people were "generally far removed from the realization that foreign trade affects them personally." NORC explained this discrepancy by noting that most Americans did not feel any personal stake in the issue.[51] In contrast, those polled took a keen interest in the cost of living, an issue that affected their daily life.[52] The polls should have signaled to the planners that they must find ways to show how trade policies affected each American as they went about their daily activities as producers and consumers.

Although many of the trade policy planners were familiar with these polls, they did not take them into account. Nor did they use their understanding of the changing public mood to communicate with the public about their plans. To a great extent, they did not know how to translate understanding that "America must buy in order to sell" into support for the specific mechanism of the ITO. They carefully controlled the information they disseminated to the press and the public.[53] Both insiders and outsiders complained that the policy development process was too secretive, but the ITO's architects continued to keep the public in the dark.[54]

Between 1943 and 1945, the public was relatively receptive to international initiatives and to a program linking trade and employment. But in these years the planners kept their plans secret. By December 1945, when they finally announced their plans, the political environment and public mood had changed dramatically. The Truman administration was less committed to achieving an international organization to govern world trade. Moreover, polls revealed that the public reported little interest or understanding of trade policy. Economic conditions provided an avenue by which to educate the public about the proposed ITO, but policymakers did not take this path. As a result, by 1946 the proposed ITO was a policy without a constituency and without strong top-level support.

5

Public Response to the ITO, 1946–1947

Describing the earliest proposals for an international trade organization, Clair Wilcox wrote, "The world that is pictured in these proposals is the kind of world that Americans want."[1] But by 1946, the world pictured in these proposals was not to be. In Europe and Asia, America's allies were struggling to revive their economies. In Asia and Latin America, nations were trying to industrialize. Many of these nations wanted to restrict imports to restore their prosperity.

In recognition of global economic conditions, the ITO was changing too. The London Draft of the ITO Charter, the first of four international negotiations on the ITO, contained a plethora of exceptions and escape clauses, allowing nations to contravene trade rules of behavior.

As the ITO was being redrafted, the ITO's architects first provided details about their trade policy plans. They sponsored a series of public hearings on the ITO and GATT and revised the plans to meet some of the recommendations proposed at these hearings. For the first time, policymakers actively encouraged a dialogue with segments of the American public about multilateral freer trade policies.

The ITO's architects, however, misinterpreted the hearings. They heard them as a mandate from the people, rather than as a message from concerned special interests. Yet the public was giving a different message to the Truman administration. In November 1946, the Republicans captured the Congress and forced major changes to the design and presentation of the ITO and the GATT. Whatever the public thought about freer trade policies, they were unhappy with the president's approach to the domestic economy. Support for "one-worldism" was declining and taking on some negative associations. The world pictured by the ITO had become one accommodating "planned" and even socialist governments. It was a world many Americans wanted no part of.

The Two-Track Approach to the ITO and GATT

In 1946, the architects of the ITO adopted a new two-track approach to achieving multilateral trade liberalization.[2] The General Agreement on Tariffs and Trade (GATT) track would build on the Reciprocal Trade Agreements Act (RTAA) and be limited to achieving immediate trade barrier reductions. Therefore, it would only be a temporary instrument. The second track would link trade and employment issues and construct a new international organization (the ITO). The ITO would ultimately subsume the GATT.

To move the ITO track forward, they sent copies of the proposals to every nation in the world and invited fifteen other countries to participate in negotiations for the reduction of tariffs and other barriers to trade. Although the Soviet Union never replied, fourteen countries accepted the invitation. At the first meeting of the Economic and Social Council (ECOSOC) of the United Nations, held early in 1946, a resolution calling for an International Conference on Trade and Employment was adopted without a dissenting vote. The ECOSOC approved formation of a preparatory committee "to elaborate an annotated draft agenda" for this international conference and appointed the fifteen nations invited by the United States as well as Chile, Norway, and Lebanon to this committee.[3]

State Department staff revamped the Proposals into the format of a suggested charter for the ITO. They hoped the suggested charter would serve as a basis for the first meeting of the preparatory committee. To build an international consensus, State Department officials held discussions with other nations on their interpretation of the suggested charter and focused on the conference objectives, procedure, and staffing.

They also wrote a memorandum linking the plans for the ITO to their plans for tariff reduction. "Provisions effectuating actual tariff reductions cannot be incorporated in the Charter itself. It is proposed therefore, that to the Charter there be appended a Protocol in which each country participating in the preliminary meeting . . . would agree to reduce . . . import tariffs, or bind them against increase . . . . Tariff reductions effected in conjunction with these negotiations may stand . . . with the multilateral commitments related to other trade barriers which would be incorporated in the Charter itself. In this way each country subscribing to the relaxation of trade barriers other than tariffs . . . would also be assured that equally broad . . . action would be taken with regard to tariffs." This protocol would be the international legal basis of the GATT.[4]

The memorandum specified that each participating nation should prepare for the ITO and the GATT by formulating its positions on the principles set forth in the proposals, on what tariff reductions it could make, and on what tariff concessions it would like to receive. The memorandum also explained how the Protocol could help establish a base for the ITO. The "Protocol, consisting of the tariff schedules and of the nontariff trade barrier provisions of the draft Charter . . . should come into force, independently of the Charter."[5]

Despite this international momentum, State Department staff were worried about the success of the two-track approach. They recognized that their ability to move ahead on tariff reductions was circumscribed by the three-year authority of the RTAA. They knew the American people were increasingly distressed by national and local economic issues and less focused on global events. The upcoming congressional election would slow up progress, and the best time to negotiate international agreements would therefore be before the autumn of 1946. The planners feared that without rapid progress, international support for both the GATT and the ITO might dissipate. They determined to stay on course, pressing for international assent.[6] They did not, however, make the two-track approach public.

The Impact of the British Loan on Plans for the ITO

The momentum of the two-track approach was interrupted in midyear by the need to gain congressional approval for a loan to Great Britain, an issue with significant implications for the fate of the ITO. Britain was in terrible financial shape, unable to restore its war-ravaged economy and repay its lend-lease obligations. Growing numbers of British citizens now favored socialization of the economy to restore economic growth and stability. In response to these conditions, many U.S. government officials favored a substantial loan to Great Britain in the hopes of reviving the economy, forestalling a socialist government, and gaining support for U.S. foreign policy objectives.[7]

Although many of the ITO's architects supported the loan, they worried about its implications for the proposed ITO. Many senior planners concurred with Clair Wilcox, who said the State Department "ought to move heaven and earth" to get the loan approved in time to hold "our trade meeting." But other members of the planning staff feared that by making the loan (a short-term measure) a priority, their long-term plans for an ITO would fall by the wayside. They recognized that most Americans did not fully understand why Britain was in such a precarious economic condition. Moreover, the administration would be depleting some of its political goodwill to win the relatively unpopular British loan, rather than reserving its limited supply for the ITO.[8] Despite these costs, key trade officials including Clayton, Wilcox, and Brown redirected their energies toward passage of the loan.

Treasury and State Department officials knew that Congress wanted specific conditions attached to the loan designed to move Britain toward a less restrictive system of trading. Perceptions of what Congress would approve affected the design and amount of the loan.[9] But even this degree of attentiveness to congressional perceptions was not sufficient to ensure approval.

President Truman's Democratic majority provided no guarantee of passage. The loan quickly became entangled in the domestic politics of the postwar period. In June 1946, there was no great public support for the loan; only 38 percent of those polled approved of the loan, even with qualifications, whereas 48 percent disapproved of it.[10] Many Americans wondered why Britain should be entitled to a loan at a lower rate of interest than that charged on housing loans to returning U.S. servicemen. Some Southern Democrats, unhappy with Truman's position in favor of a Fair Employment Practices Commission, determined to punish him politically. Perceptions about international events also affected the loan. Some congressional leaders feared Britain would not keep its promises because the agreement was full of escape clauses. Others criticized the loan on the grounds that it would promote socialism. Finally, many members of Congress wondered why the United States should pour more money down the British drain in the hope of eliminating preferences. After all, they reasoned, neither lend-lease nor the World Bank had achieved multilateralism. This perspective became powerful on both sides of the aisle as well as among the public.[11]

Despite these obstacles, the debate over the loan shows how internationalist initiatives could gain congressional approval in a time of growing insularity.[12] The key factor in building support for the loan was the administration's willingness to develop new rationales for the policy based on global conditions. Loan supporters inside and outside the administration tailored their arguments to respond to congressional (especially House) concerns about the Communist menace and global political conditions, rather than relying on traditional economic rationales. In contrast, the Truman administration was far less effective in developing a rationale for the two-track approach of the GATT and the ITO and in linking them to short-term mechanisms such as the loan.

During the loan hearings, the administration relied on economic arguments to convey the relationship between the loan, the plans for an ITO, and previously adopted economic instruments such as lend-lease. However, these arguments seem frequently to have confused members of Congress. Assistant Secretary of State William Clayton was responsible for much of this confusion; his testimony on the conditionality of the loan was sometimes unrealistic and sometimes misleading.[13] He gave many congressmen the impression that if the loan were ratified, Britain would soon do away with bilateralism, the sterling bloc, and preferences.[14] Clayton's testimony contrasted with that of Assistant Secretary Dean Acheson, who emphasized the uniqueness of each policy tool and differentiated between the shorter-and longer-term utility of each measure.[15]

Many representatives pressed for further clarification of the relationship between the loan and the plans for trade liberalization. Instead of focusing on the loan's incentives to Britain to abandon preferences, they expressed fear that the loan could force the United States to lower tariffs as part of the deal. Clayton told Congress, "Whatever reductions may come in tariffs on any commodity will take place by bilateral negotiations between the United States and other countries under existing legislation." But Clayton had now left the impression that future tariff reduction would be achieved as it had been in the past, by one-on-one negotiations, one nation at a time. By the hearing's end, Representative Wolcott noted, "I am just as much confused as . . . when I started." He was not alone. Many other Americans remained confused about the relationship between the RTAA, the GATT, and the proposed ITO.[16] Although Congress approved the loan, the hearings should have warned the ITO's architects that they needed to pay more attention to congressional concerns and to involve Congress in their plans.[17]

The new director of international trade policy at the State Department, Clair Wilcox, recommended a different approach. He suggested that the department "consult with congressional leaders on the main aspects of our trade Charter before we publish it," in the belief that "prior consultation would help the cause." Wilcox also asked his boss, Will Clayton, if the department should consult with the business and labor leaders before "we go forward with the Charter?" But Clayton rejected early public and congressional involvement in the development of multilateral trade policy. "We should send such organizations copies of the Charter" shortly before publication but not consult them about the text.[18] Clayton also sent the draft Charter to other invited governments before it was published in the United States, emphasizing that the October preliminary meeting should not be postponed and that, therefore, the United Nations should immediately issue invitations to the participating governments.[19] Shortly, however, domestic developments would force him to recognize how costly this approach had been.[20]

Growing public dissatisfaction with the administration's economic policies and fear of the political implications of potential tariff cuts forced Clayton and other senior officials to give more thought to the task of maintaining public support. On April 11, Clayton wrote to Secretary Byrnes, noting that the department had originally hoped to hold the world trade conference "not later than the summer of 1946." But the negotiations had been postponed until September, and Clayton urged the secretary to ensure that the U.S. government would hold to that date. He warned, "Public opinion is prepared for action. . . . If we delay further, our friends will be discouraged . . . and we may lose their strong backing." Clayton also underscored the international costs of postponement. "If we delay now, this momentum will be lost, other countries will question our intentions . . . and we may forfeit our leadership in trade policy." The administration did delay. The negotiations were finally scheduled for April 1947.[21]

The process of developing the list of items for tariff concessions for the upcoming GATT conference also pointed out the importance of getting public opinion on the side of trade liberalization. This list was very extensive; Wilcox noted that if many of these concessions were granted, "it would, in effect, amount to a revision of the Tariff Act." He feared it would "evoke vociferous protest from vested interests, from pressure groups and opponents of the trade agreements program." Moreover, the bulky list did not conceal the magnitude of the concessions envisioned. Thus, it forced the planners to focus on how to communicate the specifics of their plans to the American public and Congress.[22]

Although based in London, the politically savvy Harry Hawkins took the lead in urging the department to develop a public strategy for publicizing the tariff negotiations. He warned that the list must be published as soon as possible so that things could "quiet down before the elections." Hawkins recognized that the Republicans would use the list as "ammunition"; thus, the executive branch must be prepared to deal with pressure groups and their congressional representatives early on. "Any commitment not to reduce certain rates can wreck the entire program. . . . There is no question but that prior to a congressional election in which most issues are local issues, with the tariff as a notorious example, there will be a tendency" for caution. Hawkins concluded that the United States must transcend that caution and move to make international negotiations a success, or lose the opportunity for trade liberalization.[23] Other officials concurred with Hawkins. One warned, "There is a tide in the affairs of men and nations. That tide now runs strongly in our favor. No one can say which way it will be running a year hence."[24] The direction of the tide would soon become obvious.[25]

Despite Hawkins's advice and Clayton's new concerns, the planners continued to favor international assent over domestic approval in 1945-46. They did not publish the Suggested Charter until September 20, 1946. In that publication, they effectively explained the relationship between the ITO and the trade agreements (GATT) negotiation.[26] But they still had not discussed ways to include congressional negotiators as participants at the GATT or ITO conferences, as the U.N. and Bretton Woods planners had done. They did, however, decide to invite experts from other government agencies to strengthen the negotiating teams.[27]

In the memo to President Truman asking for approval of their strategy, they stressed the importance of the ITO. "These negotiations must succeed, or the whole program for international economic cooperation will collapse." However, they did not ask Truman to ensure that the public recognized the urgent need for such an organization. Rather, the memo noted, "In view of the significance of these negotiations, it would be highly desirable if, when the list is issued, you could make a brief statement emphasizing the importance of the negotiations and their relationship to . . . this country's economic program."[28] Moreover, the planners did not attempt to connect the ITO or the upcoming GATT negotiations to the economic situation of average Americans. They focused on the concerns of special interests, in the belief that these interests (and not public apathy) would be the major obstacle they would encounter. In their memorandum on procedure, they asked the president to stress to his Cabinet that no commitments would be given on tariff reduction, and they recommended that the president emphasize the escape clause to allay reasonable fears of serious injury.[29]

The ITO's architects did not publicize the specifics of their tariff negotiating plans until November 9, 1946. The department issued a press release delineating its "notice of intention to conduct trade-agreement negotiations" and made public the list of products to "be considered for the possible granting of tariff concessions." The press release invited the public to submit written testimony or to appear at public hearings on the proposed tariff reductions.[30] By that time, the first international negotiations on the ITO were well under way in London (October 15-November 22, 1946).

From American Product to International Document

International negotiations transformed the plans for the ITO, changing both its scope and character. The suggested charter began as a legalistic code of rules of behavior governing international trade; it emerged from London as a more complicated and comprehensive document. The eighteen delegations refined the suggested charter's chapters on employment, commercial policy, restrictive business practices, and commodity agreements and added a new chapter on economic development.

But the London draft of the charter was a more realistic document. Many of the eighteen participating nations had emerged from the war with damaged economies; they needed a draft charter accommodative of their problems. They achieved exceptions and escapes from the ITO's rules that allowed them to contravene the objective of freer trade. The negotiations were difficult, especially regarding the relationship between trade and employment, the use and elimination of quantitative restrictions, and an old source of friction, the relationship between tariff and preference reduction. Nonetheless, the American negotiators frequently got their way; the London draft followed the suggested charter's pattern without changes of major significance.[31]

American negotiators recognized political realities and found ways to protect America's special sectors. For example, the London draft permitted domestic subsidies (such as that used under the Agriculture Adjustment Act) but banned export subsidies. But protection came at a price. As America deviated from its free trade principles, its bargaining position with its negotiating partners was weakened. The ITO became riddled with exceptions and escape clauses. These compromises also affected the credibility of the plans for the ITO. To some observers, the London draft of the ITO now codified exceptions to the rules of trade, rather than codifying the rules of trade.

The London conference clarified the relationship between the preparatory committee of the International Conference and the GATT negotiations for the participating nations. As Hawkins noted, international understanding about the relationship between the two instruments was essential: the negotiations on tariffs and the negotiations on general principles must be linked "because other countries will want to know what the U.S. is going to do about the tariff."[32] The preparatory committee recommended to the governments concerned that it sponsor tariff negotiations "in connection with, and as a part of, the Second Session of the Committee." According to William Adams Brown, a Brookings Institution scholar, "this wording was carefully chosen to indicate that the text contained in the final Act was . . . a completely independent recommendation of the representatives of governments that happened . . . to be preparing an agenda for the forthcoming Conference on Trade and Employment." This distinction "made it possible . . . to negotiate the General Agreement . . . as part of a broad effort under United Nations sponsorship . . . and at the same time to preserve the character of the General Agreement as a trade agreement between sovereign states independent of the Charter and completely outside" the ECOSOC.[33] It also enabled the United States to negotiate the GATT under the authority of the RTAA without returning to Congress for new authorization. But although international negotiators now understood how the GATT and the ITO would intersect, this approach actually created further confusion in the United States.

The Congress Weighs In

In 1946 few Americans understood why both the GATT and the ITO were necessary and what each mechanism was supposed to do. But ITO advocates did little to remedy this problem. The only argument they made to appeal to the national interest centered on the link between increased trade and peace. This argument would unfortunately prove to have decreasing political resonance. Moreover, State Department officials left Congress hanging as to how they would present the ITO to the Congress—as a joint resolution or as a treaty.[34] As a result, some congressmen perceived the plans for the ITO as an insult to congressional control over trade policy. They began to challenge the plans for the ITO and the GATT.

As noted in the previous chapter, many Americans did not believe President Truman and the Democratic Congress were doing a good job managing the nation's adjustment to peace. They were angry about housing shortages, goods shortages, and inflation. Moreover, just before the congressional election, a meat shortage forced President Truman to issue an order ending meat price controls. Voters blamed the administration for the nation's economic problems; many Americans voted Republican or simply did not vote on election day. The result was a solidly Republican Congress; the Republicans gained fifty-six seats in the House and thirteen seats in the Senate.[35]

The new Republican majority viewed the election returns as a mandate for change, a perception that would significantly affect the ITO and the GATT. Although there is no evidence that voters specifically called for any such change, some Republicans moved quickly to thwart the administration's plans for tariff reductions.[36] Representative Thomas A. Jenkins introduced a resolution to postpone further reductions in tariff duties under the RTAA and to prevent U.S. participation in the GATT talks at Geneva. Senator Arthur Vandenberg, chairman of the Senate Foreign Relations Committee, and Senator Eugene D. Millikin, chairman of the Senate Finance Committee, warned Clayton "to go easy" on the Trade Agreements Program. Senior State Department staff immediately recognized that they would have to develop compromises with Congress if the administration's foreign economic policy was to be approved. Acheson and Clayton began discussions with the two senators on potential compromises to assuage congressional concerns.[37]

Yet some Republicans were not receptive to compromise. Senator

Hugh Butler demanded that the prospective negotiations at Geneva be postponed until Congress had an opportunity to write a new foreign trade policy. He described the RTAA as a "lame-duck policy" designed to destroy America's system of tariff protection. Representatives Jenkins and Harold Knutson also persisted in their attempts to thwart movement on the GATT and the ITO. Several representatives said that the administration's plans, as well as the senators' attempts at compromise, intruded on the constitutional prerogative of the House.[38] In the face of this threat to the bipartisanship that had thus far characterized foreign policy, Senator Vandenberg and Secretaries Clayton and Acheson struggled to devise a compromise policy that would give greater control to the Republican Congress and allow the plans to proceed. House and Senate Republicans agreed to hold hearings on the operation of the RTAA and its relationship with the GATT and the ITO in 1947, while the executive branch revised the Trade Agreements Program to address Republican concerns. On February 25, 1947, the president issued Executive Order 9832, which provided an escape clause to all sectors whose tariffs might be affected by the GATT negotiations. The escape clause provided for the withdrawal or modification of concessions which caused or threatened to cause injury to a domestic industry. Although the administration had already inserted an escape clause in the RTAA beginning in 1945, it transferred the administration of the escape clause to the Tariff Commission. As Richard Garner noted, this commission was likely to be more receptive to complaints from domestic producers.[39]

The 1946 congressional election and the issuance of the Executive Order marked a turning point in the plans for the ITO. The administration was forced to admit publicly that it could not proceed without congressional approval and oversight.[40] Moreover, the British viewed the administration position as weakened and "the probability of serious attempts to obstruct the administration's ITO policy is increased."[41] From then on, the planners could not ignore the will of Congress.

Several key planners acknowledged they had paid a price for not working to obtain domestic approval at the same time that they were trying to gain international assent. They had genuine reason to be concerned.[42] They worried that the time for internationalist initiatives had come and gone and that the core constituency for trade multilateralism might be dissipating.[43] They now understood what the polls were suggesting: that "the majority of the public report little or no interest in foreign trade." Although there was "little opposition in any population group to the establishment of an international trade organization . . . the issue is not a vital one."[44] The failure to develop a supportive constituency had resulted in an indifferent public. Moreover, they now could see that Congress and special interests might well force them to make changes that could emasculate the plans for the ITO and the GATT. The changed domestic realities might mean that they would not obtain congressional approval for both the GATT and the ITO.[45]

Yet all was not lost for the planners. In return for agreeing to the escape clause, they gained congressional approval to proceed with the Geneva negotiations on both the GATT and the ITO. But they could no longer ignore the fact that they had to proceed with increased congressional oversight.

Ironically, even following the election, some of the planners still exhibited a certain arrogance toward the public and Congress. In a post-election press conference, when asked if he would involve Republican leaders in the GATT negotiations so that it would not come as a complete surprise, "Mr. Clayton explained that these agreements did not have to be ratified by Congress." Nor was Clayton willing to have congressional GATT negotiators. "Such negotiations had always been automatically a duty of the Executive Branch."[46] In early 1947, when Harley Notter tried to convince his colleagues to involve Congress and the public before it was too late, the administration simply redirected its strategy by focusing more on marketing the ITO to special interests than on working to involve the public.[47]

To their credit, the planners became more effective in responding to the concerns of special interests.[48] Although several business groups endorsed the general principles of the proposals and/or the suggested charter, they also prepared extensive criticism of specific articles.[49] The planners met with the groups and changed the suggested charter to respond to their concerns. In addition, State Department, Commerce Department, and Tariff Commission officials occasionally helped industry representatives prepare briefs for the upcoming committee on Reciprocity Information hearings, where proposed tariff reductions would be discussed.[50] The planners also arranged meetings with labor and farm leaders to discuss their plans. By actively courting these groups, the planners gained promises of support from key special interests.[51]

The efforts of the ITO's architects to meet the concerns of special interests in this period contrast with their minimal efforts to involve the public in a dialogue about the ITO and the GATT.[52] Although the planners worked hard to ascertain how best to market the two mechanisms, public communication was not their forte. At the end of 1946, administration officials studied a wide range of surveys to determine the most effective means of conveying the department's approach to trade, hoping to use the polls to develop ways to project the administration's strategy to the American people. State Department public relations staff advised the architects of the ITO that two handles would enable them to seize the mantle of the public interest: economic self interest and the general aspiration for peace. These officials stressed that associating the two would help more Americans recognize the connection between their wallets and freer trade. They also tried to link the failure of America's international economic program to the failure of its international political program. But this argument was no longer politically expedient; by that time, 57 percent of the public saw no connection between high tariffs and wars.[53]

Nor did the planners capitalize on national economic conditions to build public support for the ITO and the GATT. For example, they might have utilized public resentment against goods shortages and inflation to develop public support for cheaper and more plentiful imports through the ITO and GATT. Because the planners did not make the rationale for these mechanisms more timely, the ITO began to be perceived as less of a policy priority as other burning political and economic issues came to the fore. As a result, public discussion of the ITO continued to be "slim."[54] But that would soon change.

Live from Nine American Cities: The ITO and the GATT

The public had three opportunities in 1947 to learn about the ITO and the GATT and to debate their merit. The first hearings were sponsored by the Committee on Reciprocity Information (CRI) in Washington, D.C., and addressed only tariff issues. Under the Reciprocal Trade Agreement Act, this interagency committee was responsible for incorporating public perceptions into the final decisions on concessions to be presented at the upcoming GATT negotiations. The hearings sponsored by the executive Committee on Economic Foreign Policy (ECEFP), as well as the two sets of hearings sponsored by Congress, addressed public concerns about both the GATT and the ITO. These hearings provided insights into how the Congress, certain special interests, and some representatives of the American people felt about the two mechanisms.

The CRI hearings were an opportunity for special interests to present their views on tariff reduction. For the first few days of the hearings, the CRI sat as a unit to hear views on the general aspects of the agreements. It then split into five panels, each devoted to specific commodities. Labor, industry associations, businesses, private citizens, and others sophisticated in the ways of presenting briefs made most of the presentations to these panels.[55] The briefs did not solely protest tariff reductions; approximately 350 requested export concessions. Winthrop Brown reported that industry leaders expressed appreciation for the Panel's fairness and interest. The State Department viewed the hearings as a great success and believed that the public perceived the process as open and equitable. But the process was only open to special interests; the American people had yet to have their say on the ITO.

The most extraordinary of the hearings were those sponsored by the ECEFP in eight cities across the United States. The hearings, a wonderful example of how government can communicate with concerned (rather than grass roots) citizenry, showed that the planners indeed wanted public support at this stage of ITO development. They were also a model of intra-agency cooperation: Department of Commerce field officers made arrangements so that all interested parties could present their views.[56]

The architects of the ITO worked hard to ensure the success of the hearings. They encouraged time for audience questions and for those who had not made formal application to appear. Written briefs were also encouraged.[57] To their credit, the planners determined to utilize the hearings to develop a charter that reflected the views of a wide range of the American people, not just organized special interests.[58] But the hearings attracted few average Americans; the bulk of witnesses were only those who understood they had something at stake—representatives of special interests.

According to the ECEFP, 245 organizations and persons expressed their views on the proposed charter orally (223) or in writing (22). Of these, 208 endorsed the principles and objectives of the proposed charter; over 150 endorsed the charter almost without qualification. Forty-three persons (of whom 29 represented business and farm associations) expressed general approval of the proposed charter on behalf of their organizations but made suggestions or expressed reservations regarding certain aspects of the charter. Only sixteen witnesses opposed the charter.[59]

The ECEFP concluded that the hearings were a great success. In its final report, the committee noted that the American people had carefully studied the proposed charter and found it worthy of support, and that the public had been able to examine and criticize the charter "at this relatively early stage of its development." ECEFP members reiterated that these criticisms would be used to reevaluate the American position on the proposed charter.[60]

However, the ECEFP misinterpreted the hearings as a mandate from the American people. According to one State Department official, the hearings proved that "an overwhelming majority" approved of the ITO.[61] That conclusion does not mesh with surveys showing that most Americans were not focused on trade policies and generally did not understand them. Rather, the hearings represented the views of a wide range of

Americans concerned about trade policies. They were useful because the planners gained additional input from organizations, such as small businesses, consumer and civic groups, and private citizens, who ordinarily did not have influence on U.S. trade policy in this period. In addition, their input did not reveal strong support for the ITO.[62]

The ECEFP now had a significant amount of criticism to digest. Protectionist criticism of the ITO echoed the long-standing objection to any attempt to liberalize trade and often was voiced by sectors such as the shoe and textile industries. This brand of criticism stemmed from a fear that trade liberalization efforts were really aimed at destroying tariff protection for American industry. Protectionist opponents were most concerned about the charter's effect on specific industries and trade barriers, but the planners had anticipated this opposition and were relatively well prepared to respond to it.

But the ECEFP also had to respond to perfectionist criticism, which arose from international political and economic developments. This type of criticism was more dangerous because it was more encompassing—it addressed both the charter's impact upon global trade barriers and its effects on the domestic and global economies. William Diebold first characterized opponents holding such views as perfectionists, noting that the charter fell far short of their ideals for economic policy. Perfectionists seized upon the many ambiguities and exceptions in the suggested charter and condemned the ITO for being too wordy, complex, and consequently, "hypocritical."[63] Such arguments were used by protectionist business groups (such as the Independent Petroleum Association) as well as those who traditionally supported trade liberalization (such as the National Foreign Trade Council).

The ITO's architects found it difficult to respond to the perfectionists' arguments. They understood the sources of perfectionist frustrations: despite the competitiveness of American industry, many U.S. business and labor leaders feared foreign competition, noting that many of our trading partners and former allies had created "planned," cartelized, and even socialistic economies. The perfectionists often made no distinction between planned and communist economies.[64]

Perfectionist arguments resonated with the public. Americans did not understand why the charter was so complex and why it included escape clauses and temporary exceptions.[65] But the ITO's architects did not use this insight to explain the charter's escape clauses or to streamline their proposals for an international trade organization. Although the hearings facilitated a dialogue, they did not ensure communication.

The hearings revealed "considerable support for the Trade Agreements Program" and/or the more limited approach of the GATT. This show of support should have led the ITO's architects to weigh carefully the political implications of the two-track approach and to consider whether the American people could settle for the GATT. In addition, the planners should have noted that a large number of witnesses requested representation on the delegation to the ITO and recommended that future negotiations include experienced business negotiators. The planners should have weighed the costs of not involving those groups.[66] Their concerns, as well as the increasingly fine-tuned protests of protectionists and perfectionists, would soon be repeated on Capitol Hill.

The congressional hearings demonstrated the depth and diversity of the opposition to the administration's foreign economic policies.[67] Both the House and the Senate hearings had the ITO's architects scrambling to address questions from Congress. The questions came from Democrats and Republicans alike and reflected continued confusion about the administration's objectives and specific proposals. Although the hearings on both sides of the aisle focused on similar concerns, they differed greatly in tenor.[68]

The Senate hearings took on the air of an interrogation of Truman administration officials. Senator Millikin acted as the "good cop," attempting to gain information, and other senators, such as Albert W. Hawkes and Scott W. Lucas, acted as "bad cops," berating the administration for its trade policies. Millikin was determined that the Senate exercise greater control over foreign economic policies and that the hearing "be a factual inquiry . . . so thorough that when it is concluded, we will be able to pass . . . judgment before they go to Geneva." Moreover, the hearing was the first attempt at a "thorough sifting of an international agreement prior to its presentation to . . . Congress as a fait accompli."[69] Yet Millikin and his colleagues could not resist emphasizing their concern about the relationship between the ITO and the GATT, their confusion regarding the authority for the GATT before Congress ruled on the ITO, and their fears about the authority the ITO would have over U.S. trade law if approved. They also criticized the background of the ITO's architects, stressing that these officials were trying to create new rules for business without any real business experience.[70]

Global conditions had affected congressional perceptions, leading many senators to question not only the nation's economic policy and policymakers but the very survival of American capitalism. Senators Millikin and Owen Brewster expressed fears that, because of the balance-of-payments condition of many of America's trading partners, "we have got to plan our exports in a way so that the other fellow's exchange will not be put into disequilibrium." Some senators concluded that the only way to control balance-of-payments problems would be for creditor nations and those few nations with an export surplus to control their economies. They were understandably unwilling to alter the American economy to achieve these goals on behalf of foreign nations in disequilibrium.[71]

The hearings also unleashed special interest opposition to the administration's foreign economic policy. Old arguments about the need for protection to preserve America's standard of living were supplemented by a new argument—the escape clause would allow the negotiators to jeopardize U.S. industries without legislative restraint. Old and new variants of the perfectionist argument were also expressed: the ITO was seen as too much of a compromise; it was full of contradictions (including contradictions of U.S. law); and the many escape clauses and exceptions would make trade liberalization impossible.[72]

Despite these concerns, the Senate hearing was positive in tone compared to those held in the House. They took two months, and seventy-one witnesses appeared. Not counting administration officials, eighteen supported the administration's trade policy; thirty-nine opposed it. A wide range of labor, business, and farm groups presented testimony and briefs. Opponents of trade liberalization hoped to use the hearings to "publicize opposition to the tariff programs and . . . counteract the State Department's ITO hearings" and "serve as a go-slow warning" to the State Department at Geneva.[73] They certainly achieved their goals.

Opponents of trade liberalization condemned the State Department and expressed deep concern that its policies would jeopardize American industry. Others argued for a return to congressional control over tariffs and foreign economic policy in general.[74] The hearings also brought to the surface a new populist perspective on the need to defeat the administration's goals. In questioning ITO supporter Philip Reed of General Electric, Representative Bertrand Gearhart tried to show that trade liberalization benefited efficient high-technology industries at the expense of farmers. Other witnesses chimed in, testifying that freer trade damaged American agriculture and small business.

Perfectionist arguments were voiced by freer traders as well as protectionists; the most common complaints were that the charter was too complex and that it allowed too many exceptions.[75] Both protectionists and perfectionists argued that foreign competition was increasingly nationalized and subsidized, and many complained that other nations regimented trade. Thus, if the United States were to reduce tariffs, it would hurt U.S. industry or place trade policy above other national economic interests. Other witnesses argued that the United States would have to cartelize trade to trade with these nations.[76]

One new argument hinted ominously of a new attitude toward internationalism. Some witnesses and representatives tried to link support

Table 5. Some Prominent Proponents and Opponents of 1947 Hearings on the Operation of the Trade Agreements Act

Some Proponents:

Agriculture: American Farm Bureau Federation, National Farmers Union

Labor: International Ladies Garment Workers Union, Brotherhood of Railway Steamship Clerks, National Women's Trade Union League

Business: National Foreign Trade Council, W.R. Grace, United States Associates of the International Chamber of Commerce, National Council of American Importers, American Association of Port Authorities, Studebaker Corporation, American Bankers Association, United States Chamber of Commerce, Export Managers Club

Prominent Republicans: Charles P. Taft, Eric Johnston

Newspapers: Mobile Register, Denver Post, Chicago Sun, Miami News, Atlanta Journal, Boston Globe, Baltimore Sun, St. Louis Post Dispatch

Civic Groups: Women's Action Committee for Lasting Peace, National Association of Consumers, Americans for Democratic Action, American Veterans Committee, Federal Council of Churches of Christ, Church Peace Union

Columnists: Marquis Childs, Raymond Moley, Sylvia Porter, H.V. Kaltenborn, Raymond Swing, Gabriel Heater

Some Opponents:

Agriculture: National Grange, California Walnut Growers Association, National Cooperative Milk Producers Conference, Cultivated Mushroom Institute, United Farmers of America, National Council of Farmer Cooperatives

Labor: American Wage Earners Protective Conference, American Watch Assemblers, Amalgamated Lace Operatives of America

Business: American Tariff League, Rubber Manufacturers Association, Charles D. Ammon, president, Cushman Motor Works, Bicycle Institute of America, National Renderers Association, Maine Sardine Packers Association, Candle Manufacturers Association, Synthetic Organic Chemical Association, American Glassware Association, National Association of Wool Manufacturers

Prominent Opponents: Tom Linder, commissioner of Agriculture, State of Georgia, R.A. Trovatten, Commissioner, State of Minnesota Department of Agriculture Dairy and Food

Source: House Committee on Ways and Means, *Hearings on the Operation of the Reciprocal Trade Agreements Act and the Proposed International Trade Organization,* part 2, ii-iii, 1695-1725.

of the ITO and of internationalism with subversive groups. Such "do-gooders," they said, were recruits for communism who already supported the ITO's accommodation of planned and nationalized economies.[77] Although this allegation did not directly undermine support for the ITO and the GATT in this period, it would subtly taint many of the ITO's supporters and dissuade potential advocates from publicly supporting the ITO.

The 1946 election and the three sets of hearings held in 1947 sent a message to the ITO's architects. The foreign economic plans had finally become a subject for national and local politics, but the planners heeded only part of what they heard. They absorbed many of the criticisms and suggestions presented at the ECEFP hearings by special interests but ignored the attitudes emerging in the broader population that were reflected by members of Congress.

Public opinion and international events should have revealed to the planners that the rationale for the ITO and the GATT was becoming dated. Rapidly changing economic conditions and world events were creating new arguments both for and against the planners' goals and strategy. Although a focus on linking trade and employment remained crucial to obtaining international assent, such a focus was not particularly relevant to the concerns of the American people.[78]

Perfectionist opposition presented a new and formidable challenge. The diversity of that opposition should have convinced the planners that the ITO was too ambitious. Compromises that were necessary to meet the needs of America's trading partners appeared hypocritical to Americans who supported the objectives of multilateral trade liberalization.

The public hearings on the ITO did not deter the trade policy planners. Despite public confusion about the need for both the GATT and the ITO, they moved ahead with their plans internationally. The lack of a supportive constituency and a timely rationale, however, soon began to cause problems for their two-track strategy.

6

The ITO, the GATT, and U.S. Trade Policy, 1947–1948

When the Department of State asked its outside economic consultants for advice on how to "sell" the last of its postwar economic initiatives to the American people, economist Jacob Viner did not mince words. If the State Department wanted to gain support for the ITO and the GATT, Viner warned, it "should always be aware that it has to cater to two publics—the people whose good will we may want in the other world, and its own support in this country. It must watch both of them all the time."[1]

At first, catering to its overseas public appeared to be a successful strategy for the trade policy planners. After a troubled beginning, twenty-three nations negotiated a mutual reduction of trade barriers at the Geneva General Agreement on Tariffs and Trade (GATT) negotiations. The world had taken its first step toward achieving the trade policy planners' dream of international trade barrier reduction. The next year, when fifty-four nations agreed to the final charter of the ITO at Havana, Cuba, the last of the postwar economic institutions seemed close to becoming a reality.

But at home these international accomplishments were greeted with apathy and scorn rather than acclaim. With the spread of communism, growing numbers of Americans believed the world was dividing into two economic camps. They could not see the utility of a mechanism that would force the United States to cater to the demands of some foreign governments, whose economies seemed to fit squarely within the Communist camp.

The trade policy planners found themselves on the defensive because senior Truman administration officials were divided over the fate of the ITO. Some officials wanted the administration to continue to present the ITO as the centerpiece of its foreign economic strategy; others believed domestic and world events had passed it by. These latter officials were not opposed to the ITO, but they felt it was futile to press for its acceptance by a Republican-dominated Congress in a Presidential election year. These differences caused the Truman administration to delay a decision on *how* as well as *when* they should present the ITO to Congress.

Ironically, in this period, State Department officials became increasingly attentive to the homefront. Although they invited representatives of Congress, business, labor, and academia to advise the ITO delegation at Havana, they still did little to build a base of public support.

Domestic Repercussions for the GATT and the ITO

The architects of the ITO had two specific goals for 1947: to revise and complete the draft of the ITO charter and to prepare a detailed draft of the GATT. The "success" of the State Department-sponsored hearings reinforced their belief that they were acting in the national interest. In addition, Dean Acheson wrote to the President that his discussions with Senators Arthur Vandenberg and Eugene Millikin "appear to have assured" bipartisan congressional support.

Nonetheless, these officials were well aware that they proceeded at political risk to the administration. In a White House meeting, William Clayton, now undersecretary of state for economic affairs, warned President Harry S Truman that the proposed tariff reductions could give rise to political protests. Certain products, such as wool, might be subject to significant tariff reductions. To achieve these cuts, the administration would have to battle Congress, take on entrenched interests, and challenge long-standing policy. But the President made it clear that despite these risks, he supported the process fully. Clayton, Acheson, and Winthrop Brown left the meeting confident that they could proceed without kowtowing to special interests.[2]

The U.S. government launched negotiations on both the ITO and the GATT in Geneva on April 10, 1947. American negotiators achieved much of what they wanted in the Geneva draft of the ITO. The United States was able to minimize discrimination by countries with balance-of-payments problems and limit recourse to quantitative restrictions (import quotas) for economic development purposes.

Despite this progress, the draft charter left many issues unresolved. For example, the Geneva negotiations did not clarify whether the ITO and the GATT should withhold benefits from nonmembers; whether the ITO should allow quantitative restrictions (quotas) in certain circumstances; and whether the United States should be allowed to continue its price supports and export subsidies for certain agricultural products.[3]

This final issue became a major stumbling block to achieving multi-lateral trade liberalization. America's own house was not in order: most prominently, the United States had not reconciled its new trade policy with its long-standing agricultural programs. This inconsistency was nothing new: "Agricultural protection was the rock on which some of the best . . . interwar efforts to reduce trade barriers were wrecked." Although agriculture had not escaped the attention of the postwar planners, the Food and Agricultural Organization, established on October 16, 1945, had not been able to prevent the introduction of some creative methods of protecting U.S. agricultural interests. For example, the U.S. government guaranteed parity prices for wool and other agricultural products until December 31, 1949, to avoid economic dislocation after the war. These conflicting policy objectives resonated beyond American borders and almost unraveled the first GATT negotiations.[4]

In 1947, both the House and Senate introduced bills to address the problems of U.S. wool producers. The two bills directed the Commodity Credit Corporation to continue wool price supports (at the 1946 price) and to dispose of wool it owned at market prices. The House bill, which also included a provision intended to reduce imports by increasing the wool tariff, would not ordinarily have seemed important—wool constituted a small percentage of agricultural income. But wool protection had the potential to damage the economies of commodity exporters such as Australia, whose principal wool market was the United States. Australia had taken a leading role in organizing the support of developing nations for the charter. If the House bill became law, it would undermine America's ability to convince Australia and other developing nations that the GATT and the ITO would be in their interest.[5]

The Australians quickly pointed out the hypocrisy of the American position. In May 1947, the leader of the Australian delegation took the unusual step of writing to Clayton to request a reduction in wool duties. State Department officials recognized that if they did not meet Australia's request and reduce the wool tariff, "we will have no bargaining power" to obtain substantial elimination of preferences, tariff reductions, and adoption of the ITO charter. To move the negotiations along, America's GATT negotiators hoped to gain authorization to reduce the tariff on wool by 50 percent, effective June 1, 1948, "provided . . . that a satisfactory quid pro quo can be obtained." They noted that "the success of the whole trade program may hinge upon the President's action on the attached recommendation on wool . . . . It is more than possible that the Conference would break up."[6]

The administration enlisted Cordell Hull and Henry Stimson, two famous names, to help straighten out this conflict between the nation's foreign and domestic policy objectives. Although they wrote to members of Congress that the House bill could preclude or nullify the tariff negotiations, the House's version predominated. On June 26, Truman vetoed the bill, noting that its adoption would be "a blow to our leadership in world affairs." He urged Congress to pass the original Senate bill, which had no tariff provisions. Truman and his top lieutenants in State resolutely supported the ITO and the GATT at that moment, despite the opposition of Agricultural Department officials, wool producers, and several key members of Congress.[7]

Proponents of trade liberalization such as Clayton and Winthrop G. Brown were still concerned. They feared that even the Senate bill would not be adequate to meet Australia's concerns and salvage the GATT negotiations. Australian negotiators continued to insist that the duties on wool be reduced by 50 percent. Following the U.S. failure to offer a reduced duty on wool, Australia withdrew its tariff reduction offers and its waivers of preferential treatment with other Commonwealth countries. Soon South Africa indicated that it would take similar action. America's GATT negotiators were now convinced that "Australian dissatisfaction would probably make it impossible to get the modifications required to satisfy American business and Congressional opinion" on both the ITO and the GATT.[8]

Agriculture and State officials finally worked out a compromise that would postpone the duty reduction until June 1, 1948, and Truman approved it on August 5. Soon, the Australian and U.S. negotiators found common ground on reciprocal trade barrier reduction. However, the contradictions between America's domestic policies and trade policies could not be resolved with these stopgap measures.[9]

Although the negotiators stumbled over other products, the first round of the GATT was successfully concluded by the autumn of 1947. The GATT was brought into force provisionally under the Protocol of Provisional Application on January 1, 1948, and it awaited legislative approval to "bring the General Agreement . . . into full effect."[10] Nonetheless, after some six months of negotiations, multilateral trade liberalization had finally become a reality with the GATT, rather than the ITO.

The GATT was developed rapidly, in part because its scope was narrower than that of the ITO, and in part because of the strategy used to gain congressional approval for the two instruments. The GATT was tailored to fit the grant of legislative authority to the executive under the 1945 extension of the RTAA. The GATT did not include the ITO's articles on the maintenance of employment and on subsidies, two policy problems that could not be addressed under the RTAA. The GATT did not even include all of the commercial policy provisions covered in the ITO charter!

Moreover, because the RTAA did not authorize the executive branch to sign a treaty or build an international organization, the U.S. negotiators were very careful to portray the GATT simply as a trade agreement.[11]

The architects of the GATT paid great attention to the political implications of the language used to draft the agreement. Rather than using the term "members," which connoted affiliation with a formal organization, State Department staffer John Leddy devised the term "contracting parties" to describe GATT's signatories. Moreover, the GATT drafters developed two legal mechanisms to accept the agreement: application under the Protocol of Provisional Application (under which the United States accepted the GATT) and definitive acceptance. Under the Protocol, the provisions of the GATT are binding only insofar as they are not inconsistent with a nation's existing legislation, whereas definitive acceptance of the GATT or the ITO charter carried an obligation to change existing legislation.[12] With this clause, the United States could spur trade liberalization and contravene the rules of the GATT. Hiding behind this clause, the drafters could be certain that neither they nor the GATT could be criticized for thwarting the achievement of other U.S. policy goals.

Because the GATT's architects paid careful attention to its scope and language, hindsight has made them appear more politically agile than the ITO's architects. This is ironic, for many of the drafters of the GATT also worked on the ITO. They hoped to use the success of the GATT to build support for their long-term objective, the ITO, but their strategy backfired when senior Truman administration officials and parties outside the government began to see the GATT as an alternative to the ITO.

Success at drafting and negotiating these two agreements did not bring these officials the kudos for which they had hoped. In fact, the Geneva draft of the ITO transformed many supporters of the ITO into potential opponents and turned many of those who already questioned the ITO into vociferous opponents. Meanwhile, the bulk of Americans remained apathetic. Despite their awareness of this problem, and the continued warnings of Harley Notter and others, State Department officials did not focus on involving and informing the public.[13] In 1947, senior officials were concerned about other, more pressing issues.

The ITO Becomes Less of a Priority

Throughout the postwar period, the problems of the Old World kept redefining the priorities of the New World. In addition to the problems caused by the war, 1947 brought a winter of blizzards that brought Europe to a standstill. Although Europe was immobilized, the State Department saw communism on the march. In a meeting with members of Congress, Dean Acheson warned that "Soviet pressure on the Straits, on Iran, and on northern Greece had brought the Balkans to the point where a highly possible Soviet breakthrough might open three continents to Soviet penetration."[14] Under the guidance of the new secretary of state, General George C. Marshall, State Department officials devised several mechanisms to address Europe's political and economic difficulties as well as the spread of communism.[15] Among the most important of these tools were the Truman Doctrine, the European Recovery Program (ERP), and the North Atlantic Treaty Organization (NATO).

But the public did not share the senior officials' concerns about Europe in the first months of 1947. The Truman administration struggled to gain the public's attention and support. And their focus on Europe helped further the problems for the ITO. Although ITO proponents argued that the ITO complemented these mechanisms, it was clearly not devised to meet the short-term needs of Europe or to combat communism. As international conditions and public attitudes changed, ever so gradually, senior officials lost interest in the ITO.

But officials on the Executive Committee on Economic Foreign Policy (ECEFP) and within the State Department continued to work hard on bringing the ITO to life. They courted organized interests by inviting them to discuss the ITO. The bulk of their efforts focused on gaining the support of prominent business groups.[16]

At the State Department hearings in 1947, several prominent business leaders and government officials urged the administration to expand the proposed ITO to include a chapter regulating foreign investment. They hoped that the development of such rules would both spur increased overseas investment and protect existing investments. Some officials, such as Joseph Coppock and Woodbury Willoughby, had "serious misgivings" about such a change. Although they acknowledged that investment and trade flows were complementary, they feared that it would be impossible to achieve an international consensus on rules concerning investment.[17]

Willoughby and Coppock contended that inclusion of investment in the ITO could have negative ramifications abroad and at home. They stressed that the United States would have to use up a significant quotient of its bargaining power to get other nations to agree to include investment. In addition, they noted, this strategy might jeopardize U.S. leadership at the Havana conference because it would underscore the contradictions between American foreign economic policy and domestic policy. For example, the U.S. government would have to override state laws that restricted the ability of foreign investors to buy farmland in the United States. America could not call for international rules to govern U.S. agricultural investments overseas while the states contravened such rules at home.[18]

Coppock worried about the political price of appeasing investment interests. Like other trade policy officials, he feared the ITO would be reshaped by a parade of special interest demands. He also believed that by gratifying special interests, the ITO would lose public supporters. It might alienate "the parts of the public which do not represent special economic interests. These people . . . have . . . acquired . . . skepticism about the foreign investment . . . policy and practices of the United States . . . . Many strong supporters of ITO . . . would become suspicious."[19]

Many trade policy officials admitted that the ITO charter could not gain national approval unless it had the support of special interests and Congress. Several key business groups informed Mr. Clayton that they would "strongly support the ITO charter in toto in Congress" if investment were included in the ITO; "they will swallow all other provisions." Undersecretary Clayton took these business groups at their word and instructed his staff to draw up investment provisions. He also asked representatives of business groups to set forth their views on investment by June 1947. Although many of Clayton's subordinates continued to believe that no internationally acceptable investment provisions could be devised, they now understood that investment would be included in the final ITO charter.[20]

The Geneva negotiations on the ITO were proceeding as business representatives and State Department officials deliberated on the investment issue. Members of the U.S. delegation decided that they had to introduce investment provisions, because they feared missing the negotiating deadline. GATT negotiators proceeded with the best intentions, although they had not developed the Geneva draft positions in concert with business groups. However, business leaders felt betrayed when they heard about the Geneva draft's proposals on investment. State Department officials had invited business input but appeared to ignore business recommendations.[21] Business leaders' trust of these officials deteriorated, and their enthusiasm for the charter declined dramatically.

How can one explain this clumsy strategy? To a great extent, it reflected the continuing division within the department as to the role special interests should play in developing the ITO for the national interest. Many State Department officials were ambivalent about any degree of special interest involvement and did not want to mold the ITO to meet special interest concerns. The department's blundering was also caused by the differing perspectives of officials at Geneva and those at Washington. Officials at Geneva feared missing the negotiating deadline and did not seek permission from Washington as they forged ahead. In contrast, many of those officials in Washington now recognized that without congressional and special interest support, the ITO would go nowhere.

The question of special interest support next arose in conjunction with the ECEFP's strategy for negotiating and conveying the final charter. At the end of 1947, State Department officials debated whether to present both the ITO and the RTAA Extension to the 80th Congress or to postpone consideration of the ITO until 1949, after the Presidential election. In a letter to Clayton, Clair Wilcox stressed the need for a quick decision on these questions. Wilcox's urgency was related to the upcoming election. He recognized that during the heat of the campaign, political appointees would probably not be willing to go to bat for the ITO and warned Clayton, "The new people in key positions . . . are . . . unfamiliar with the . . . importance of the ITO." He feared that the ITO's supporters could not count on Truman administration support. At the same time, Wilcox stressed that the ITO would need special interest support if it was to gain the support of administration appointees in an election year. Citing the efforts of the Committee for the Marshall Plan, an outside group set up to gain support for the ERP, he urged Clayton to find a way to link the State Department to outside supporters of its foreign economic policies.[22]

Wilcox's concerns were on target. Many of the department's top appointees saw world problems rather differently than did many of the remaining postwar planners. Secretary of State Marshall and Undersecretary Robert Lovett did not want to dilute public support for the ERP and other priorities; they were not eager to press for long-term initiatives such as the ITO. Although the administration was still officially committed to the ITO and the GATT, they were clearly not top priorities. Because of the urgency of Europe's financial crises, these men were less concerned about failing to devise a more comprehensive solution. Clayton saw the European crisis as a catalyst for achieving freer trade, whereas many of his colleagues could see only the crisis. He tried to show them that without the ITO, "no temporary program such as the ERP could possibly have any worthwhile results."[23] But in 1947, Clayton, Wilcox, and Brown could not convince the administration of the ITO's centrality.

Preparation for the Final Charter Conference at Havana

Wilcox did, however, convince the ECEFP and top State officials that the delegation to the Havana Conference must be designed with the task of marketing the ITO to the American people in mind. Much of the planning in August and September 1947 focused on whom to include in the delegation.[24] Although these officials knew the composition of the delegation could not assure legislative and public support, careful selection of private sector and congressional delegates could help to legitimate the ITO. Choosing the members of the delegation would not be an easy task.

Senior State Department officials had an especially difficult time choosing the congressional representatives, reflecting their failure to settle on a longterm strategy to gain congressional approval for the ITO. By the end of 1947, they had not decided whether to submit the final ITO charter to Congress as a treaty (which meant the Senate would weigh it as a whole) or as a joint resolution, which required majorities in both houses of Congress. The decision was crucial to ascertaining which members to select, which congressional committees to represent, and which party representatives to send to Havana. If the ITO went to the Senate as a treaty, Senator Eugene A. Millikin's involvement would be crucial, and House Republicans could be invited merely for public relations purposes. If the ITO was presented as a joint resolution, however, then representatives from the House Foreign Affairs and Ways and Means Committees, as well as the Senate Foreign Relations and Senate Finance Committees, had to be invited. The department finally decided to invite Republican Senator Millikin and Democratic Senator Walter F. George (both of whom declined) and two members of the House Committee on Foreign Affairs, Democrat James Fulton and internationalist Republican Jacob Javits. Democratic Senator A. Willis Robertson of Virginia ultimately decided to serve as the Senate representative.[25] That only the House members were enthusiastic about making the trek to Havana should have warned departmental staffers that senators, even Democratic senators, were at best indifferent about the ITO.

The department had an equally difficult time choosing the nongovernmental advisers. Although senior State Department officials such as Clayton, Wilcox, and Francis Russell (director of public affairs) were committed to involving some special interest representatives, they were uncertain as to which organizations to select. According to Russell, the department had given such organizations "informal commitments that their interests would be represented" at Havana. But which groups should be invited, and which groups should be left out? Should the concerned interest groups decide among themselves, or should the department decide?[26]

The department had a model of how a delegation could be made representative of American interests. In 1944-45, the UN planners also had difficulty deciding which groups could serve as delegates to the United Nations Conference and which groups could participate as observers. But their approach to this problem actually created public support. Because they had long been communicating with national organizations, the UN planners were able to convince the many groups that the State Department could determine a "fair cross-section of citizen groups." The State Department selected and invited "some forty-two" groups to send representatives to San Francisco to serve as consultants to the delegation. This diversity gave the impression that the public had an impact on the design of the UN and that the mechanism was therefore both by and for the people.[27]

In contrast, the ITO's architects missed the opportunity to use the delegation to help market the ITO to the public. Ultimately, the State Department picked twelve nongovernmental advisors: five from prominent business and banking groups, three from agricultural organizations, two from labor organizations, and two from academia.[28] The department did not use their involvement to show that the ITO was crafted by as well as for the American people. Nor did they find ways to inspire the advisors to work to build support for the ITO in their churches, synagogues, workplaces, and civic groups.[29]

To their credit, the ITO's architects did include two known protectionists in the delegation. This gave them a chance to learn from protectionist concerns and to attempt to convert these opponents into advocates. But the protectionists did not become converts to the ITO's cause. One vociferous opponent, Elvin H. Kilheffer, believed he was sent to Havana as window dressing.[30]

The department held a two-day session to brief the delegates on U.S. objectives and the negotiating process.[31] This short session contrasts with the more extensive preparation of the UN delegation, in which the delegates were the chief negotiators.[32] Clayton and other senior advisors hoped to use the session to ensure that the nongovernmental advisors fully understood and supported the delegation's strategy at Havana, so they stressed the ITO's import to the administration's foreign economic policy.[33] They also hoped to use the briefing session to achieve a consensus on foreign investment, an issue that seemed to be the sticking point for many business associations.

Harry Hawkins suggested that the United States propose revising the Geneva draft and substituting an obligation on the part of each ITO member to negotiate bilateral treaties on investment at the request of any other member. This change would allow the United States to press for international agreement on investment while ensuring that America's economic clout in one-on-one negotiations could be preserved. Moreover, it would give the U.S. "commercial treaty program a big leg up." Business representatives John Abbink, Elvin Kilheffer, and H.W. Balgooyen agreed to this approach, convincing Clair Wilcox and other senior officials that they had reached a consensus. But the business representatives could not guarantee that their organizations would support this position. Moreover, this approach did not quiet the concerns of government officials who were still ambivalent about including investment in the ITO.[34]

Meanwhile, ECEFP officials were still trying to develop a governmentwide position for the Havana negotiations. Because they were aware that the ITO could not gain popular support if it challenged long-standing domestic priorities such as protection for agriculture, they focused on the exceptions that the United States would have to present at Havana. They knew other nations would use the precedent of U.S. exceptions to press for their own, and they feared that this would yield a complicated and confusing charter. They hoped, however, to limit the specific compromises and exceptions so the ITO would not appear to counteract the general objective of trade liberalization.[35]

At Havana

The majority of the U.S. delegation left Washington by train on November 18 and arrived in Havana on November 20, 1947. The delegation was in the experienced hands of Clayton and Wilcox, director of the Office of International Trade Policy. Officials from the military, the Treasury, the Departments of Commerce, Labor, and Agriculture, and the Tariff Commission made up the official delegation.[36] They hoped that this governmentwide delegation would help maintain a broad front of support for the ITO.

Some of the business advisers participated constructively in the Havana negotiations. Seymour Rubin described a good working relationship with Balgooyen, who represented the National Association of Manufacturers. Balgooyen worked with Rubin to develop the final charter's investment provisions, and he tried hard to convince his fellow business executives to support the charter.[37] In contrast, Kilheffer, who represented the U.S. Chamber of Commerce, did little to assist the delegation at Havana. His actions during the conference and after his return illustrate how difficult it was to build a solid front for the ITO and convert opponents into supporters.

Kilheffer had long been an advocate of protection for his employer, Du Pont. He used his time at Havana to develop arguments with which to oppose the policy and the policymakers. In a letter to his superiors at Du Pont, Kilheffer decried the standards of integrity of the State Department and blamed the department "for much of the economic chaos of today."

He felt the conference was a waste of time and suggested that even the U.S. government had given up on the ITO because officials had "the most important parts of the ITO charter incorporated in the Geneva General Tariff Agreement." Kilheffer believed the State Department was pulling a fast one—by using the ITO as a cover to get what it wanted through the Trade Agreements' back door with the GATT.[38] He did his best to see that the State Department failed to establish the ITO.

Kilheffer was not alone in his skepticism. Many of the representatives of the fifty-five other participating countries were also reluctant negotiators. Because most of these nations had not participated in developing earlier drafts of the ITO charter as members of the Preparatory Committee, the conference took two months longer than the ITO's planners had anticipated.[39] Almost every one of the fifty-six countries attending had national interests it wanted safeguarded and each exception greatly complicated the negotiation process. For example, the U.S. delegation worked to include an exception to ITO rules made by or for a military establishment to meet national security requirements and proposed an article permitting export subsidies, which would allow the United States to continue its approach to agricultural assistance.[40] Negotiations over these compromises took months to achieve and exhausted the limited capabilities of the delegations.[41]

The fruit of this effort was even greater opposition to the charter. ITO supporters as well as its opponents perceived the compromises as hypocritical.[42] They found most distasteful the ITO's articles on foreign investment, full employment, commodity agreements, and business practices. The drafting of the final act of the charter and its foreign investment provisions show how difficult it was for the American negotiators to draft provisions that would win international approval while conforming to the demands of Congress and special interest groups in the United States.[43]

The State Department did not fly the president or other senior officials to join Will Clayton in signing the final act of the charter. According to James Fawcett of the British delegation, the final act was deliberately designed to avoid giving "the Charter the appearance of a treaty requiring Senate approval . . . .The ITO Charter . . . will therefore be annexed to a very short instrument which will be signed by all the countries represented at the conference." Fawcett concluded that signing the act would simply "authenticate the text of the Charter."[44] The State Department clearly did not want any hoopla in Havana to stir up congressional opposition.

The charter was also designed not to alienate key U.S. business interests. The Geneva draft of the ITO included a general statement of each nation's common interest in productive economic development (Article

12). It recognized the rights of governments to transfer ownership, but only if they provided "just compensation." Many American investors considered the article unacceptable because it did not adequate-ly define "just compensation," but several influential developing countries balked at U.S. attempts to rewrite the article. As the conference stalemated on this (and many other) issues, Wilcox made a speech directed as much to executives on Wall Street as to the conferees in Havana. Chided by the eloquent Wilcox, the delegates eventually agreed to revise the investment articles to obligate members to afford adequate security to existing and future investments. These articles also provided that upon request, members could negotiate treaties to protect foreign investment. Although the charter set up the principle that foreign investors have justifiable rights, American opponents perceived the investment articles as affirming the sovereign right of governments to expropriate. Moreover, critics concluded that the charter emphasized the sovereign rights of the capital-receiving countries more than those of investing nations. Nonetheless, many U.S. government officials concurred with Willard Thorp, assistant secretary of state for economic affairs: "Any attempt at more stringent definition would have resulted in . . . so many qualifications . . . as to make the . . . provisions worse than useless."[45]

Compromises such as the articles on foreign investment, as well as those on full employment and quantitative restrictions, yielded what the department termed "a momentous achievement." But it seemed an enormous flop to many Americans, some of whom were baffled and others appalled by its many compromises. To them, the ITO seemed to sanction, as William Diebold noted, "the restriction of trade, not its liberation."[46] With this dissonant reception, it was now up to the ITO's advocates to sell it to Congress. In that task, the architects of the ITO found themselves on the defensive, discussing not just the ITO but the RTAA.

Setting Priorities: The Fate of the RTAA, the ITO, and the GATT

The American delegation had traveled to Havana with some confidence that it could quickly produce an agreement to present to the 80th Congress, but it soon became clear that this optimism was unrealistic. By the end of 1947, the congressional calendar was full; given the need to consider more popular and more urgent legislative matters, Congress was unlikely to schedule the ITO hearings.

As the Havana negotiations dragged on, Wilcox advised his colleagues that delay could jeopardize not only the ITO but also congres-

sional consideration of the RTAA, which was due to expire in June 1948.
This in turn could affect the President's authority to negotiate trade liberalization. Both the House and Senate had proposed new bills that would
alter the process of tariff determination; each authorized the Tariff Commission to study and issue recommendations to the President on the effects of proposed trade agreements. Department officials believed the bills
would give the Tariff Commission sole responsibility for determining how
far a tariff rate could be cut and extend the president's authority for only
one year, rather than the three years previously authorized over its four-
teen-year history. The administration needed this extension of authority
to continue the GATT negotiations and to bring the ITO into effect.[47]

Wilcox concluded that the department's first priority must be to
save the RTAA. Brown, chief of the Division of Commercial Policy, concurred, noting that public support had peaked. The department risked
losing that support. Renewing the RTAA would be easier than ratifying
the charter, "as the Republicans might hesitate to abolish it just previous
to elections." Wilcox recognized that approval of the act would allow
some international trade liberalization to occur with the GATT.[48]

But Wilcox and many of his colleagues were ambivalent about the
recommendation to save the RTAA. Many officials who had toiled on the
ITO, such as Brown, Wilcox, and Coppock, feared that concentrating their
efforts on the RTAA could jeopardize support for the ITO. They believed
the ITO must remain the centerpiece of the administration's foreign economic strategy and remembered how the British loan hearings had diluted
support for the Proposals. As Wilcox noted from Havana, discussion of
the RTAA would inevitably lead to discussion of the ITO, and opponents
might use the ITO to launch a flank attack on the RTAA. "The Geneva
and Havana drafts will have their first congressional consideration before
the most hostile . . . forum . . . the Committee on Ways and Means . . . . The
charter will be politically discredited before any opportunity is provided
to give it a fair hearing." To save the ITO, Wilcox and Brown stressed that
the charter should be presented to the Senate as a treaty as soon as the
conference ended. The State Department, however, did not take this suggestion. Coppock told his boss, Brown, that the department must "paint
the alternative to the ITO in such lurid colors that even the color-blind
will see the light." Doing so would prove to be a more difficult task than
Coppock and his colleagues envisioned.[49]

Wilcox, Brown, Clayton, and other key decisionmakers set out to
build congressional trust. They invited Republican Senator Arthur H.
Vandenberg and Democratic Senator Alben Barkley, as well as House
Democrats, to a meeting to discuss their strategy for winning approval for
the ITO, but the senators were so overloaded with other responsibilities

that they had no time to meet. The failure to build congressional support at an early point thus continued to create problems for the ITO's supporters.[50]

By the end of 1947, the department had still not firmed up its strategy for congressional approval of the ITO and extension of the RTAA.[51] Many of the architects of the ITO, sincerely believing they were acting in the national interest, were still uneasy working with Congress and special interests to achieve their policy goals. As a result, they acted too little and too late. Moreover, because State Department officials were still divided as to whether the ITO or the RTAA, or both, should be a priority, they wasted several months debating their strategy. As a result, they appeared confused and inept. Their indecision lessened their credibility, made it easier for their opponents to attack them, and over time undercut the likelihood of congressional approval of the ITO.

During these months, many of the same department officials were redirecting their attention to Europe's worsening economic problems and the need to craft short-term tools to spur economic recovery. They knew the ITO did not easily fit into such a toolbox. In contrast, the GATT could complement the short-term approach of the ERP, and it would not require new legislative authority. Although these more pragmatic officials recognized that the GATT could not replace the ITO, they knew it could permit them to achieve a modicum of trade liberalization without an all-out congressional fight.[52] But many advocates of the ITO both inside and outside the government did not see the GATT as a reasonable substitute. They maintained that for trade liberalization to be effective, it must be comprehensive. These officials insisted that the GATT was not broad enough to cover employment and other issues that affect trade flows. They stressed that the United States could not simply accept only the provisions that it liked and reject the rest of the charter because negotiations had not gone its way. With Clayton, they believed that the charter was "the best and most practicable agreement that can be devised at this stage of our international relations." They worried that other nations would regard failure to act on the charter "as a breach of faith," weakening the United States' position of leadership. Increasingly, however, these ITO advocates were outnumbered and outranked by officials in the Department of State who believed that the U.S. government should use other more pliable instruments to achieve free-world cooperation.[53]

The attractiveness of an alternative to the ITO can be explained by a wide range of factors. With the prominent exception of Clayton and Acheson, many of the political appointees working on foreign policy were not committed to realizing the ITO, the last of the planned postwar institutions. They had not been involved in the development of the ITO and they tied their careers to the President's election and not to a commitment to free trade or international cooperation. These men were not enamored of a long-term mechanism, identified with big government. Moreover, in a world where once-democratic Czechoslovakia had become communist Czechoslovakia, an organization designed to facilitate cooperation between communist and capitalist governments seemed a pipe dream. These appointees probably saw this kind of international initiative as a liability to the president and thus to their careers. In those years it took great political courage to advocate a long-term mechanism, one identified with big government and full employment. Their position was not politically naive. Some members of Congress were quite willing to link support of internationalism with support of world communism, so it is not surprising that many senior administration officials wanted to avoid that taint. Consequently, few high-level Truman administration officials supported the ITO and the GATT with fervor.

In discussions with the British delegation to the ITO Conference in January 1948, "Clayton admitted very frankly that he found considerable difficulty in getting United States authorities at Washington to take any . . . interest in the Charter, their attention being . . . entirely devoted to Marshall Aid." He was "most apprehensive" that the Charter would be "crowded out." Meanwhile, the Commercial Counsellor in Washington informed his superiors that the Americans doubted that the ITO "could be presented to Congress this session."[54] Although they gave speeches calling for the ITO, neither Lovett, Marshall, nor Truman had found the time to go to Havana to show the administration's strong support of the ITO program. This was probably deliberate. By 1948, Secretary of State Marshall was describing the RTAA, rather than the ITO, as "the cornerstone and keystone of our foreign policy."[55]

Over time, Truman administration officials moved toward a more pragmatic, less comprehensive approach to trade liberalization, one they thought better fit the Cold War world. They did not explicitly call for replacing the ITO with the GATT in 1948, but as Brown and Raymond Vernon noted, senior officials seemed to lose interest in the ITO. The administration was unwilling to use up its limited political capital in an election year with a Republican-controlled Congress.[56] Although not deliberately designed as an alternative, the GATT became the fallback position.

This was true in Britain as well. In October, 1947, the Board of Trade hired a group of economists to "furnish departments here with an appraisal of the alternatives to ITO." These economists wrote their report "on the assumption that the ITO would break down."[57] Like their American colleagues, the British proceeded with the ITO negotiations. They were also worried about the fate of the GATT. British officials decided to "spin out the discussions" about strengthening the GATT to ensure that it "should not collapse."[58]

Early in 1948, senior State Department officials, including Undersecretary Lovett and Counselor of the department Charles Bohlen, met with Clayton and Brown to finalize their strategy. Despite their different perspectives on the ITO, they concurred on three objectives: presidential authority for trade agreements must be preserved, Congress should be appeased, and the core constituency for trade liberalization should be maintained. They decided to concentrate on seeking renewal of the RTAA, asking for a three-year renewal but accepting one year.[59] The administration also decided to delay submission of the charter to the next session. Senior officials recognized, as J. Robert Schaetzel stated, that the charter was important legislation, "but it is not emergency legislation." In this way, although the ITO seemed unlikely to gain approval, the administration would not appear to have given up on it.[60]

Their concentration on the RTAA had significant implications for the fate of the ITO and the GATT. It preserved the negotiating authority in the executive branch while allowing the administration to press forward with its foreign economic program, and it prevented the Reciprocal Trade Agreements Act from becoming an election issue. But the strategy also made the GATT more than a provisional instrument. Twenty-two of the twenty-three signatories had put the GATT into effect by January 1948, and as one official noted, many of these nations would remain in GATT even if the charter were never approved. Moreover, GATT negotiations were continuing. Trade policy officials in the Departments of State, Agriculture, and Commerce, and in other agencies spent much of 1948 in preparation for the next round of the GATT, when eleven additional nations would work to further reduce trade barriers.[61] Gradually, the GATT emerged as an alternative to the charter, albeit a more limited one.[62]

At this crucial point, the ITO lost two of its strongest advocates. Wilcox, who had led the U.S. delegations at Geneva and Havana, resigned, pleading exhaustion. He continued to fight for the ITO by writing a book on its behalf, but he would no longer be shaping policy from within the government. Clayton resigned to return to his company and to care for his wife, but like Wilcox, he did not sever his ties to the department and the policies he so believed in. As advisor to the secretary, he presented the Marshall Plan as well as the Reciprocal Trade Agreements Extension Act and led the negotiations for the final charter. But because he was not always present to fight for the ITO at top-level meetings of government or business decisionmakers, he could not focus his considerable influence and energies on the ITO.

With these resignations, Acheson, Thorp, and Brown became the most experienced officials working for multilateral trade liberalization. However, they were also preoccupied with developing the ERP and defending the RTAA. A very qualified but less senior official, Robert Terrill, was given the responsibility of being "the focal point on ITO matters." Although Terrill had worked on the ITO since its inception, he was less connected to business, Congress, and the White House than Acheson or Clayton were.

In addition to losing the full-time expertise of these individuals, the ITO's fate was also affected by the department's growing workload. The economic bureau was understaffed and overloaded with other responsibilities, including assisting with the Marshall Plan and the Annecy Round of the GATT talks.[63] All of these factors weakened the department's efforts on behalf of the ITO.

The years 1947 and 1948 were a time of elation and despair for the architects of the ITO and the GATT. Their strategy for a comprehensive approach to international trade had yielded international agreement on an ITO, but their innovation had been greeted with public apathy, special interest opposition, and congressional backlash.

The focus on international agreement had led to a long gestation. As a result, the ITO missed the ground swell of support for international cooperation. The ITO was drafted in Washington (the Proposals), London, Lake Success, Geneva, and Havana between 1945 and 1948. During this long period of development, it became less relevant to a world perceived by many Americans as divided into two hostile economic camps. With the spread of communism and continued economic dislocation, U.S.-controlled, short-term initiatives seemed more important than the ITO, even to the ITO's most ardent advocates.

To a great extent, the ITO's problems stemmed from the actions of its architects. The ECEFP invited business groups to recommend investment provisions for the ITO and then ignored their suggestions, invited public comment but misjudged the sources of this comment as representative of the American public's perceptions, and stressed the importance of public communication but did not make such communication integral to their strategy. While they verbalized the need to work with Congress to achieve their goals, they devised much of their strategy without consulting Congress. They were surprised when members of the House and the Senate subsequently showed little interest and even open hostility toward the ITO and the GATT. They fiddled and delayed while the ITO's support dissipated.

These officials had a fallback position: under the GATT's aegis, trade liberalization became an international accomplishment, and further trade barrier reduction in 1948 would not require congressional review. Thus, it is not surprising that some administration officials began to find the GATT more attractive than the ITO.[64] By 1948, this approach betrayed the broader mechanism it had been developed to implement.

Many of the ITO's supporters still believed that the more comprehensive ITO best met the national interest. Moreover, their research indicated the public supported these plans.[65] But was such public support real or imagined? If it was real, why had it not translated into congressional support? The next two years revealed the answers to these questions.

7

Congressional Challenges and Public Apathy toward Trade, 1948–1949

No matter how much they desired to retreat from the world, Americans could not shirk the nation's international responsibilities.[1] The United States had a growing list of global obligations, including feeding Europe, preventing the spread of communism, and protecting the free world. Although the American people were gradually accepting these new responsibilities, they expected their government to resolve domestic problems first.

But the most powerful nation on earth seemed incapable of solving many of its own economic problems. Since the end of the war, the Truman administration had been bedeviled by labor upheaval, inflation, the need for jobs for veterans, and a lack of affordable housing.

Competing domestic and international priorities left the American people, Congress, and even Truman administration officials deeply divided. The 1948 debate over trade policies revealed the cleavage within the Truman administration and between Congress and the administration.

Many Republican members of the 80th Congress were determined to remake the Truman administration's trade policy and mechanisms. They questioned the strategy of trade liberalization and succeeded at redesigning the bureaucratic process for achieving tariff reduction. Supporters of trade liberalization found themselves on the defensive, struggling to preserve the right to negotiate trade agreements.

Ironically, it was in this environment that proponents of the ITO, both within the State Department and outside the government, finally organized to build a base of support for it. However, they found that the ITO's potential constituency was not particularly enthusiastic and too narrow to gain congressional approval. The public remained an untapped resource.

Trade: A Low Priority for Americans

In light of the nation's continued economic problems, it is not surprising that foreign policy, especially economic foreign policy, held little attraction for most Americans.[2] In March 1948, when some seven hundred Cincinnatians were asked which issues they took a keen interest in, 90 percent identified the cost of living and 68 percent identified U.S. relations with Russia, whereas only 27 percent named U.S. trade with other countries.[3]

Policymakers therefore found it difficult to make a strong case for trade liberalization. They tried to link the ITO to the more popular Marshall Plan but were relatively unsuccessful in showing how expanded trade would help U.S. and European economies. In a 1949 Survey Research Center poll, only a minority expressed "awareness of the economic advantages which come from cooperating with or helping other countries."[4] Yet Americans continued to be reluctant to support tariff reduction, even when they were informed how it would benefit European countries.[5] Moreover, ITO advocates did not effectively sell its ability to create U.S. jobs and spur economic growth. Some 55 percent of those polled by the National Opinion Research Center (NORC) in March 1949 believed the European Recovery Program (ERP) would help America's prosperity and security. Of this 55 percent, only 22 percent believed it could create U.S. jobs and stimulate domestic production and only 11 percent thought the plan would increase U.S. trade.[6]

Herein lay the problem for supporters of freer trade. Most Americans had little understanding of trade policies and mechanisms, had little or no interest in problems of foreign trade, and saw no direct benefits to themselves through expanded trade. Although they understood that economic dislocation abroad could affect the economic welfare of the United States, they did not associate the ITO with maintaining the health of the global economy or improving their standard of living. Polling data consistently reflected support for the objectives and process of trade liberalization, but further questioning revealed such support would diminish if the price were an individual's welfare. At the end of 1947, when asked if they favored the process of trade liberalization that allowed goods to come into the United States at lower tariff rates, some 67 percent of those polled said they were in favor, 11 percent were opposed, and 22 percent had no opinion.[7] In March 1948, NORC noted that of 1,289 adults polled, 22 percent thought they would be better off with higher tariffs, 38 percent favored lower tariffs, and 40 percent simply did not know. Moreover, attitudes toward future American business conditions did not have much relationship to an individual's attitude about trade liberalization.[8] Although most

Americans were now cognizant of U.S. interests overseas, they were not concerned with trade beyond U.S. borders.

Most Americans still did not understand what trade policies were supposed to achieve. In June 1949, although 73 percent of those polled recognized that the United States exported more than it imported, only 25 percent thought the United States should import more, 21 percent thought the United States was importing too much, and 28 percent felt the trade balance was about right.[9] Americans were no more knowledgeable about the General Agreement on Tariffs and Trade (GATT), which at least made the headlines. In December 1947, only 34 percent of 1,500 Americans polled by Gallup said they had heard of the GATT. In March 1948, only 32 percent of those polled by NORC said they had heard or read about the reciprocal trade agreements law. In April 1948, Gallup reported that 59 percent of those polled said they did not know what was meant by the term "reciprocal trade treaties."[10]

Ironically, in October 1948 some 59 percent of Americans polled said it was very important that all nations set up a special organization to increase world trade; 11 percent said it was not important, and 10 percent said they did not know. When asked whether the United States should join such an organization, 58 percent said yes, whereas 31 percent said no.[11] These polls, however, did not mean that it would be easy to translate general support for the goals of an international trade organization into political backing for a specific measure. Support for an ITO was "soft," probably reflecting what those polled thought they should say rather than what they really cared about. According to public opinion analysts, the polls revealing support for an international trade organization were an outgrowth of general enthusiasm for international cooperation rather than hard support for the ITO.[12]

Americans would have had to be educated—quickly and thoroughly —if they were to counterbalance the ITO's increasingly visible and vocal opposition. According to polling data, the most effective approach would be to show average citizens specifically how they could benefit from trade liberalization.[13] But the ITO's advocates ignored the people while working hard to gain the support of influential leaders in agriculture, labor, civic, and business groups. In this way, they hoped to build a counter constituency to match the well-organized special interests already in position to oppose the ITO.

The Marketing of the ITO

At the end of 1947, as the Havana Conference was under way, W.H. Baldwin, public relations man and longtime supporter of trade liberalization, urged William Clayton to rally the common interest early on in support of the ITO. Baldwin proposed forming a citizens' committee to coordinate the work of special interest supporters, to prepare material for the "molders of public opinion," and to do fieldwork around the country to educate the public. Baldwin suggested holding a community rally in favor of freer trade with the theme "Imports are silent partners in American pay envelopes." He said that such a theatrical approach would depict the Reciprocal Trade Agreements Act (RTAA) and the ITO in terms that voters could understand.[14] Although the idea of such a rally seems a bit farfetched, Baldwin was on the right track; the ITO needed a massive public relations program.

With the signing of the Final Charter, the articulation of the ITO became a Department of State responsibility. Clayton and senior State Department officials did not feel comfortable with Baldwin's approach. They were good at devising international economic policy but not at communicating with average Americans.[15] Certain that their objectives would serve the national interest, they believed the public did not understand the long-term benefits of increased trade. However, they took no responsibility for public ignorance or indifference toward the nation's economic interdependence.

These officials could see few advantages to trying to "market" the ITO to average citizens. Fearing Congress would tag any effort on behalf of the ITO as propagandizing, they made minimal efforts to educate the public. Nor did they urge the president to highlight the ITO. In an election year, the "bully-pulpit" was already overused to gain support for other urgent international issues.[16]

Many of these officials, however, knew the Committee for the Marshall Plan had helped "sell" the European Recovery Program (ERP) to the American people. Thus, they were receptive to working with outside support groups who could articulate the benefits of policies such as the ITO and increase the State Department's visibility and credibility. They were aware, however, of the dangers of overloading the public with issues in an election year. As before, State Department officials focused their efforts on gaining the support of concerned elites.

Department officials became increasingly sophisticated at assessing public opinion. They continued to sponsor polls, summarize editorials, and keep track of special interest statements on departmental policies including the ITO and the RTAA.[17] They used this information, however, to rebut elite opposition rather than to develop salient arguments that might turn average Americans into advocates.[18]

Monitoring and massaging elite opinion was a major focus of some State Department officials. They planned lunches with, gave speeches to, and participated in debates before representatives of the U.S. Chamber of Commerce, the Farm Bureau, the Congress of Industrial Organizations, the Council on Foreign Relations, and other special interest groups. Junior staff perused newspapers for editorials and drafted articles for numerous publications.[19] The department tried to coordinate government-wide support on the ITO, including support from the international institutions.[20] In preparation for the yet unscheduled hearings as well as for public debates and speeches, staff prepared issue papers and rebuttals to allegations about the ITO.[21]

But these government officials were better at developing policy than at managing or marketing it. The State Department was frequently reorganized, and staff work was redirected toward the newest, most compelling emergency.[22] Moreover, State Department officials did not know how to explain the complex ITO and show how it complemented the emergency foreign policy tools the administration had developed.

ITO supporters hoped to wrap the ITO with the banner of multilateralism to arouse public and congressional support. They tried to show the ITO's importance to the functioning of existing institutions such as the United Nations and the ERP. But to many Americans, internationalism had yet to prove itself. Peace had not returned, and multilateralism had resulted in two opposing approaches to global politics and economics. Moreover, as historian Richard Gardner noted, Europe's (especially Britain's) continued economic and financial problems seemed to show that codification of economic principles would not resolve trade and economic disputes between nations.[23] It is not surprising that outdated rationales based on little-understood concepts such as internationalism did not bring forth popular support.[24]

Moreover, ITO advocates did not link the ITO to current public concerns. For example, administration officials did not show how increased imports could reduce the need for taxes to fund foreign aid. Nor did they stress the ITO's benefits in concrete terms that citizens might easily understand, such as in new jobs created by increased trade or a greater choice of competitively priced goods at their local stores. Instead, they used vague and impersonal language to defend the ITO.

Prominent private citizens backed the government's efforts to build support for the ITO and the GATT. Their efforts were also directed toward business and labor groups rather than the general public. Although Clayton was no longer special adviser to the secretary of state, he helped create and sustain the Committee for the International Trade Organization to bolster departmental efforts. In contrast with its sister organization, which worked to build support for the Marshall Plan, the Committee for the ITO was relatively unsuccessful at organizing elite and grassroots support. To some extent, the committee floundered because of the difficulty of conveying this complex mechanism at that late date. To an even greater extent, the committee failed because business leaders did not support its work with their expertise and their dollars.

Clayton had a hard time finding a prominent business executive willing to chair the committee. After failing to engage well-respected business leader Philip Reed, chairman of General Electric, and his colleague W.R. Herod, president of International General Electric, Clayton was heartened to learn that William Batt, president of SKF Industries (makers of ballbearings), was willing to serve.[25]

Batt brought experience in business and government as well as a true commitment to the ITO. He had been vice chairman of the War Production Board and had served the U.S. government in other capacities overseas. But he had neither the influence of a Clayton or Reed with members of Congress nor the clout and associations in the business community that leadership of a major multinational corporation might bring. Nevertheless, Batt worked hard to build these contacts. As a result of his work with Clayton and the capable staff of the committee, more than one hundred prominent business leaders, academics, and civic and union leaders joined the committee to express publicly their support for the ITO.

Although Clayton and the committee sent out many letters, the response in the business community was mixed.[26] For example, the National Foreign Trade Committee, the most internationalist organization of business leaders, decided to oppose the charter. Its opposition was particularly disheartening to the ITO's architects because it had long supported increased trade. Later, the United States Associates of the International Chamber of Commerce, the U.S. Chamber of Commerce, and the National Association of Manufacturers expressed strong opposition.[27] Only the more liberal business organizations, such as the Committee for Economic Development (CED), and business-funded think tanks (the National Planning Association, the Twentieth Century Fund, the Brookings Institution, and the Carnegie Endowment) came out for the charter. The CED expressed its support with a reservation that Articles 11 and 12 (the charter's investment articles) not be approved. Business leaders were not enthusiastic about the ITO.[28]

Like their allies in the administration, Committee for the ITO staff did not try to turn average Americans into ITO advocates. To some extent, this can be attributed to the financial problems of the committee, which simply did not have the funds to finance a public relations program. Nor did the committee take advantage of its broad national membership to build grassroots support. Baldwin attributed this to the failure of business leaders to do their part to help the nation face its new responsibilities.[29]

Table 6. Committee for the International Trade Organization

Ashwell, Thomas W., publisher, Thomas Ashwell and Company, New York, N.Y.

Batcheller, Hiland G., president, Allegheny Ludlum Steel Corporation, Pittsburgh, Penn.

Benton, William, publisher, Encyclopedia Britannica, New York, N.Y.

Bimson, Walter, president, Valley National Bank, Phoenix, Ariz.

Bingham, Barry, *Courier-Journal,* Louisville, Ky.

Brown, Edward E., chairman of the board, First National Bank of Chicago, Chicago, Ill.

Brownlee, James F., chairman, Business Education Committee, Committee for Economic Development, New York, N.Y.

Bunker, Arthur H., Lehman Brothers, New York, N.Y.

Burt Clayton R., president, Potter and Johnston Company, Pawtucket, R.I.

Canfield, Cass, chairman of the board, Harper and Brothers, New York, N.Y.

Carey, James C., secretary-treasurer, Congress of Industrial Organizations, Washington, D.C.

Carson, James S., vice chairman of the board, Colonial Trust Company, New York, N.Y.

Cate, Garth, travel and trade director, Scripps-Howard Newspapers, New York, N.Y.

Clayton, William L., Anderson, Clayton, and Company, Houston, Tx.

Clement, Dr. Rufus E., president, Atlanta University, Atlanta, Ga.

Clothier, Dr. Robert C., president, Rutgers University, New Brunswick, N.J.

Collier, H.D., chairman of the board, Standard Oil Company of California, San Francisco, Calif.

Condliffe, Dr. J.B., Institute of Economics, University of California

Conway, Carle C., chairman of the board, Continental Can Company, New York, N.Y.

Cook, Everett R., Cook and Company, Memphis, Tenn.

Coward, H.A., vice president, Budd Company, Philadelphia, Penn.

D'Aquila, Frank P., sales manager, Iowa Manufacturing, Cedar Rapids, Iowa

Davis, Chester C., president, Federal Reserve Bank of St. Louis, St. Louis, Mo.

Davis, Tom J., attorney and counselor at law, Butte, Mt.

DeGolyer, Everett L., DeGolyer and MacNaughton, Dallas, Tx.

Dick, Jackson P., vice president, Georgia Power Company, Atlanta, Ga.

Dickey, John S., president, Dartmouth College, Hanover, N.H.

Dickinson, Mrs. LaFell, Keene, N.H.

Douglas, Donald W., president, Douglas Aircraft Company, Santa Monica, Calif.

Dunn, Gano, president, J.G. White Engineering Corporation, New York, N.Y.

Eichholz, Alvin, manager, World Trade Department, San Francisco Chamber of Commerce, San Francisco, Calif.

Fairbanks, Douglas Jr., "Westridge," Pacific Palisades, Calif.

Felder, William D., Jr., president, Texas Cotton Association, Dallas, Tx.

Fleming, Robert V., president, Riggs National Bank, Washington, D.C.

continued

Table 6. Committee for the International Trade Organization, continued

Folsom, Marion B., treasurer, Eastman Kodak Company, Rochester, N.Y.

Fox, Kirk, Ed., *Successful Farming*, Meredith Publishing Company, Des Moines, Iowa

Fox, Mattew, 445 Park Avenue, New York, N.Y.

Francis, Clarence, chairman, General Foods Corporation, New York, N.Y.

Franklin, John M., president, United States Lines, New York, N.Y.

Friele, Berent, International Basic Economy Corporation, New York, N.Y.

Friele, H.B., vice president, Nakat Packing Corporation, Seattle, Wash.

Galbraith, John K., lecturer, Department of Economics, Harvard University

Gifford, R.W., chairman of the board, Borg-Warner International Corporation, Detroit, Mich.

Hanes, John W., chairman, Executive Committee, United States Lines, New York, N.Y.

Hansen, O.C., president, World Trade Center, San Francisco, Calif.

Harrison, George M., grand president, Brotherhood of Rwy. and S.S. Clerks, Cincinnati, Ohio

Hecht, Rudolph S., chairman of the board, Mississippi Shipping Co., New Orleans, La.

Hegewisch, A.E., A.E. Hegewisch, New Orleans, La.

Heline, Oscar, president, Farmers Grain Dealers Association of Iowa, Marcus, Iowa

Heller, Robert, president, Robert Heller and Associates, Cleveland, Ohio

Hobby, Mrs. Oveta C., executive vice president, *Houston Post,* Houston, Tx.

Holliday, Wallace T., president, Standard Oil Company of Ohio, Cleveland, Ohio

Holmstrom, Andrew B., vice president, Norton Company, Worcester, Mass.

Horde, Dr., Frederick L., president, Purdue University, Lafayette, Ind.

Howard, G.K., vice president and general manager, International Division, Ford Motor Company, Dearborn, Mich.

Hoyt, Palmer, editor and publisher, *Denver Post,* Denver, Colo.

Hutchinson, R.A., president, Studebaker Export Corporation, South Bend, Ind.

Johnston, Eric A., president, Motion Picture Association of America, Washington, D.C.

Kanzler, Ernest, chairman, University C.I.T. Credit Corporation, Detroit, Mich.

Keenan, Joseph D., director, Labor's League for Political Education, Washington, D.C.

Kempner, H., Galveston, Tx.

Kendall, Henry P., president and treasurer, Kendall Company, Boston, Mass.

Keough, C.A., president, Ballthrall Trading Company, Philadelphia, Penn.

Kestenbaum, Meyer, president, Hart, Schaffner and Marx, Chicago, Ill.

Kline, Allan B., president, American Farm Bureau Federation, Chicago, Ill.

Knoizen, Arthur S., Joy Manufacturing Company, Pittsburgh, Penn.

Lazarus, Fred, Jr., president, Federated Department Stores, Cincinnati, Ohio

Lincoln, Murray, president, Coop. League of the U.S.A., Columbus, Ohio

Litchfield, P.W., chairman of the board, Goodyear Tire and Rubber Company, Akron, Ohio

continued

Table 6. Committee for the International Trade Organization, continued

Lukens, W.H., vice president—export, R.M. Hollingshead Company, Camden, N.J.
Lundborg, Louis B., vice president, Stanford University, Stanford, Calif.
MacNaughton, E.B., president, Reed College, Portland, Ore.
Marcus, Stanley, Neiman-Marcus, Dallas, Tx.
Marshall, M. Lee, chairman, Continental Baking Corporation, New York, N.Y.
McCormick, Charles P., chairman, McCormick and Company, Baltimore, Md.
McFadden, John H., Jr., Geo. H. McFadden and Brother, Memphis, Tenn.
McGowin, Earl M., vice president, W.T. Smith Lumber Company, Chapman, Ala.
Mead, George H., Mead Corporation, Dayton, Ohio
Monisgue, Gilbert H., counsellor at law, New York, N.Y.
Mooney, James D., chairman of the board, Willys-Overland Motors, Toledo, Ohio
Noble, Edward J., chairman of the board, American Broadcasting Company,
    New York, N.Y.
Northrop, Dr. Mildred B., professor of economics, Bryn Mawr College
Patterson, Hon. Robert P., Patterson, Belknap and Webb, New York, N.Y.
Patterson, W.A., president, United Air Lines, Chicago, Ill.
Patton, James G., president, National Farmers Union, Denver, Colo.
Pepper, G. Willing, vice president, Scott Paper Company, Chester, Penn.
Parker, Walter G., export manager, Marchant Calculating Machine Company,
    Oakland, Calif.
Peterson, Howard C., Fidelity-Philadelphia Trust Co., Philadelphia, Penn.
Pfeiffer, Curt G., senior councillor, National Council of American Importers,
    New York, N.Y.
Pickett, Clarence E., executive secretary, American Friends Service Co.,
    Philadelphia, Penn.
Potts, Frederic A., president, Philadelphia National Bank, Philadelphia, Penn.
Reed, Philip D., chairman of the board, General Electric Company, New York, N.Y.
Rosenthal, Morris S., president, Stein, Hall and Company, New York, N.Y.
Schacter, Harry W., president, Kaufman Straus Company, Louisville, Ky.
Scherman, Harry, president, Book-of-the-Month Club, New York, N.Y.
Schramm, James S., vice president, J.S. Schramm Company, Burlington, Iowa
Shotwell, Dr. James T., acting president, Carnegie Endowment for International
    Peace, New York, N.Y.
Sibley, John A., chairman, Trust Company of Georgia, Atlanta, Ga.
Sitterley, Eugene, publisher, *World's Business*, New York, N.Y.
Smith, Eugene B., Eugene B. Smith and Company, Dallas, Tx.
Smith, Marvin W., executive vice president, Baldwin Locomotive Works,
    Philadelphia, Penn.
Smith, Paul C., editor and general manager, *San Francisco Chronicle,* San
    Francisco, Cal.
Smith, Tom K., president, Boatmen's National Bank of St. Louis, St. Louis, Mo.
Sonne, H. Christian, president, Amsinck, Sonne and Company, New York, N.Y.
Speer, Talbot, president, Baltimore Sales Book Company, Baltimore, Md.

continued

Table 6. Committee for the International Trade Organization, continued

Staley, Eugene, economist, Palo Alto, Calif.
Storke, Arthur D., president, Climax Molybdenum Company, New York, N.Y.
Swope, Gerard, honorary president, General Electric Company, New York, N.Y.
Symington, C.J., chairman, Symington-Gould Corporation, New York, N.Y.
Taft, Charles P., Headley, Taft and Headley, Cincinnati, Ohio
Virden, John C., chairman, J.C. Virden Company, Cleveland, Ohio
Watzek, John W., Jr., Crossett, Watzek, Gates, Chicago, Ill.
Weil, Adolph S., Well Brothers, Montgomery, Ala.
Wetherill, Samuel P., president, Wetherill Engineering Company, Philadelphia, Penn.
Wheeler, W.H., Jr., president, Pitney-Bowes, Stamford, Conn.
Wilbur, Brayton, president, Wilbur-Ellis Company, San Francisco, Calif.
Wilkie, H.F., vice president, Joseph K. Seagram and Sons, Louisville, Ky.
Williams, Alfred H., president, Federal Reserve Bank of Philadelphia, Philadelphia, Penn.
Williams, Roger, chairman, Executive Committee, Newport News Shipbuilding and Dry Dock Company, New York, N.Y.
Winton, David J., chairman, Winton Lumber Company, Minneapolis, Minn.
Wynne, C.M., president, Overseas Industries, Chicago, Ill.

Source: Alphabet file, Truman Library

The marketing of the ITO in 1948-1949 failed to win it broad support or committed special interest support. Because 1948 was an election year, senior policymakers ignored the ITO. As the Charter languished, the arguments of ITO proponents began to reflect a growing recognition that maintaining presidential authority to negotiate trade agreements, rather than bringing the ITO to life, had to be the top trade policy priority.

The Battle over the Trade Agreements Extension of 1948

Trade policy, which had long been the scene of a tug-of-war between Congress and the executive branch, became a battleground in 1948. The 80th Congress was activist, responding to constant crises in Europe and Asia as well as at home. It was also a partisan Congress, and its members, especially Republican members, had more immediate priorities than the establishment of multilateral trade liberalization. Republican control of Congress affected the administration's willingness to keep the ITO as its cornerstone of foreign economic policy. With the 1948 renewal of the RTAA, Republicans for the first time could control the destiny of trade liberalization measures.[30]

The administration had already received many warnings from Congress and special interests about the fate of its foreign economic policy mechanisms. House Republicans and conservative Democrats were especially hostile to the mechanisms devised as part of the postwar planning process under Roosevelt and controlled by the State Department. Earlier hearings in 1947 on the ITO had made it clear that many members of Congress still did not understand the rationale for and the difference between the ITO and the GATT. Moreover, many on Capitol Hill saw both instruments as an abuse of executive authority under the RTAA. If they could not rein in the State Department at international negotiations, they would do their best to ensure that Congress maintained control over trade policy. Although the department recognized congressional dissatisfaction with its trade policy initiatives, its actions had not reassured opponents of trade liberalization. As in 1945, State Department officials were taken aback by the depth of hostility they encountered in Congress.[31]

As the Havana Conference began, congressional members of both parties criticized the department for its sloppy congressional relations. Representative Robert L. Doughton, senior Democrat on Ways and Means, said he was "distressed" that he had not been consulted. Representative Harold Knutson, Republican chairman of the Ways and Means Committee, expressed annoyance that no Republican from his committee had been named to the Delegation. In a March 1948 meeting with Winthrop Brown, Knutson criticized the department for its handling of both the GATT and ITO, complaining that the department had not kept Congress informed about the administration of the Act, had treated businessmen as "lepers" at Geneva, and had not invited any Republicans from Ways and Means to go to Havana. According to Brown, "He charged that the Department was simply trying to by-pass the Committee." Knutson added that he did not see why hearings were necessary, for the department had nothing to gain except "to admit publicly that the program was a failure."[32]

Supporters of trade liberalization both inside and outside the administration launched an all-out effort to sell the Trade Agreements Extension to influential special interests in the hope that they, in turn, would persuade Congress of its merits. This response, albeit last minute, illustrated the panic developing within the department and revealed the costs of the earlier failure to court and maintain alliances with these interests. From outside the government Clayton did what he could to help. He wrote letters to many business, labor, and farm leaders requesting their help in preserving the bill without crippling amendments. Along with other prominent Americans, he set up the Citizens' Committee for Reciprocal World Trade to mobilize public support. He even went "door to door" in the Senate to drum up congressional support. But Clayton was not optimistic: "I think the fate of the . . . Trade Agreements Program will be settled . . . by the High Command of the Republican party."[33]

In the hope of getting a better reception once the hearings began, the department tried to devise an approach to trade agreements that would meet congressional concerns while preserving the executive branch's full authority to negotiate these agreements. Joseph Coppock suggested making the act permanent, permitting unlimited cuts but providing for congressional veto of whole agreements (similar to the "fast-track" approach used today). Although experienced State Department officials such as Harry Hawkins and Willard Thorp favored this "constitutional approach," the suggestion was not approved.[34] The department proceeded with its request for a three-year extension.

Congress, however, had a different notion of how it should handle the renewal. Between May 3 and May 8, 1948, the Subcommittee on Tariffs and Foreign Trade of the House Committee on Ways and Means held hearings on H.R. 6566, which, as noted above, gave the Tariff Commission the responsibility for making recommendations on proper rates of duty and provided only for a one-year extension of the Act.[35] Although at first glance the proposed changes do not seem drastic, to many supporters of trade liberalization they seemed to have the potential to emasculate the act, reduce the State Department's authority to control the process, keep the administration on a short leash, and send notice to other nations that Congress was not in step with U.S. efforts to lead multilateral trade liberalization. The bill represented the second time the 80th Congress had taken responsibility for foreign economic policy away from the State Department; the precedent was the development of the Economic Cooperation Agency to implement the Marshall Plan.[36]

The chairman of the House Subcommittee on Tariffs and Foreign Trade, Bertrand W. Gearhart, announced that to expedite matters the hearings would be held in executive session; only experts on the Act could testify, and the hearings would be closed to the public. Gearhart, like Knutson, believed Congress was entitled to closed hearings because the State Department had devised and negotiated its policies behind closed doors. Moreover, he noted, public hearings on the act had already been held in April and May, 1947.

The House hearings were a series of attacks on State's policies and policymakers. In evidence of their lack of deference to the administration, the lead witness was not from the State Department or another executive branch agency. He was W. Wickliffe Rose, president of the American Tariff League and a well-known protectionist. It was not until the third day of hearings that administration officials were given the floor. Supporters of trade liberalization quickly responded, calling the hearings a "star chamber." The Citizens Committee for Reciprocal World Trade announced that it would invite all interested parties to appear at public hearings held simultaneously with the executive session in Washington.[37]

Both the Senate and the House hearings revealed that the State Department's strategy had engendered great mistrust. Repeating long-standing criticism, some opponents characterized American tariff policy as a pawn in the hands of diplomacy. The department, they said, had been allowed to abdicate its responsibility to American farmers, consumers, and manufacturers.[38] They used this argument to show how little the State Department cared about domestic economic conditions. Opponents also criticized the failure to involve interest groups and Congress in framing policy. Senators said the department kept its policy development and negotiating process closed, which justified greater congressional scrutiny.[39] To discredit the department's policymakers, their support for freer trade was associated with being "soft" on communism.[40] The RTAA was again linked to big business by Representative Gearhart, who stated that because big business had grown fat on protection in the past, it was now only fair to grant such protection to smaller business.[41]

The hearings revealed how poorly the rationale for the three instruments had been conveyed to Congress. House members accused the State Department of making the ITO a permanent trade agreements program. Some stated the United States would use the RTAA to commit itself to the ITO through the back door, and they feared the GATT was a little ITO. Finally, they implied the administration knew the ITO would never gain congressional approval, noting that although the ITO was ready, the administration was afraid to present it to the Congress.[42] At the Senate hearings, Clayton explained that the GATT was not a mini-ITO and that authority to negotiate the GATT was "implied" under the Reciprocal Trade Agreements Act. He tried to show deference to the Senate and noted that the GATT covered only commercial policy and not matters that might be considered treaties, but Eugene Millikin and many of his Senate colleagues were not convinced.[43]

Supporters of the RTAA did refine their arguments, attempting to demonstrate that trade liberalization met the realities of 1948 America. The RTAA was linked to the ERP, with proponents arguing that the United States could not ask other nations to reduce trade barriers under the ERP while Congress was repudiating the trade agreements. Supporters also argued that the United States must encourage free enterprise in the world at large to further free enterprise at home and around the world. Finally, they stressed that without U.S. leadership of global efforts to liberalize trade, the world might return to autarky. Again, opponents were able to respond that existing trade agreements had not prevented statism or the spread of communism.[44] They wondered how trade liberalization could make the world more stable.

Both opponents and supporters of the RTAA appealed to the interests of consumers. Opponents of the RTAA said consumers were ignored under the act, and an old populist argument for protection—that tariffs protect American consumers from foreign monopoly prices—also reappeared. The supporters of trade liberalization countered that all workers were as affected by high tariffs as consumers and that growing numbers of workers were dependent on exports.[45] This argument revealed how little State Department officials understood the public's view of tariff protection.

Although the Senate hearings were open, their tone was equally antagonistic to the Department of State and its program. Many of the arguments expressed in the House hearings were reiterated in the Senate. The RTAA's supporters in the U.S. Government were on the defensive; Senate opponents accused them of sins ranging from ineptitude to betrayal of the national interest. Senator Millikin did not play the good cop this year; instead, he took the lead in condemning the policy and the policymakers. He argued that the administration was unsure what it was going to do with the RTAA, suggesting that even the State Department viewed the RTAA as unimportant. Senator Albert W. Hawkes said the department had procrastinated on the renewal legislation and that the administration thus was not committed to its own program. Clayton was forced to defend the administration's steps to renew the act.[46]

The supporters of trade liberalization inside and outside the Government responded vigorously to these arguments. As before, they defined their strategy in terms of the national interest. Clayton said that "it is part of wisdom and statesmanship to arrive at a fair balance" of trade. He and others argued against giving the Tariff Commission greater authority, noting that the system had worked toward the national interest through an interagency process. "No concession is recommended unless it accords with the security interests . . . with the interests of agriculture . . . consumers, and more broadly, with the over-all foreign economic policy of the United States."[47] However, Clayton did not make his case by showing how these interests were reconciled.

Congress had a different concept of the national interest. It passed the Senate version of the Extension Act, which required the Tariff Commission to report to the president the lowest rate of duty that could be fixed on each dutiable item without causing or threatening serious injury to American producers. In addition to this "peril point" provision, the bill ended Tariff Commission participation in the negotiation of trade agreements and provided authority to negotiate trade agreements for only one

Table 7. Some Prominent Proponents and Opponents of 1948 Hearings on the Operation of the Trade Agreements Act

Some Proponents:	Some Opponents:
Agriculture: American Farm Bureau Federation, National Farmers Union, Dried Fruit Industry of California	*Agriculture:* National Grange, California Walnut Growers Association, National Cooperative Milk Producers Conference, Mushroom Growers Cooperative of Pennsylvania, American National Livestock Association, National Council of Farmer Cooperatives
Labor: International Ladies Garment Workers Union, Brotherhood of Railway Steamship Clerks, International Association of Machinists	
	Labor: American Wage Earners Protective Conference, Amalgamated Lace Operatives of America
Business: National Foreign Trade Council, Chamber of Commerce of the United States, United States Associates of the International Chamber of Commerce, National Council of American Importers, American Association of Port Authorities, H.J. Heinz Corporation, Spyros P. Skouras, president, Twentieth Century-Fox Film Corporation, New York, N.Y.	*Business:* American Tariff League, Rubber Manufacturers Association, Cotton Textile Institute, National Association of Wool Manufacturers, Vitrified China Association, National Renderers Association, Maine Sardine Packers Association, Candle Manufacturers Association, Synthetic Organic Chemical Association, American Glassware Association, National Association of Wool Manufacturers
Prominent Republicans: Charles P. Taft, Jacob Javits	
Prominent Advocates: Alger Hiss, Gerard Swope, chair of General Electric and chair of Citizens' Committee for Reciprocal World Trade	
Civic Groups: American Veterans Committee, Federal Council of Churches of Christ	

Source: House Committee on Ways and Means, *Testimony before the Subcommittee on Tariffs and Foreign Trade of the Committee on Ways and Means, on the Operation of the Trade Agreements Program,* 80th Cong., 2d sess., May 1948, iii–vi; and Senate Committee on Finance, *Hearings on H.R. 6566, An Act to Extend the Authority of the President under Section 350 of the Trade Agreements Act of 1930, as Amended and for Other Purposes,* 80th Cong., 2d sess., June 1948, iii–v.

year. As the bill revealed, Congress was determined to scrutinize membership in the proposed ITO as well as the relationship of the RTAA and the ERP. Both Houses wrote reports that state that the membership in the ITO must be reviewed in conjunction with renewal of the RTAA. The executive branch had been warned. President Harry S Truman signed legislation extending the Reciprocal Trade Agreements Act on June 26, stressing that the authority to negotiate trade agreements should not lapse.[48] But State Department officials now acknowledged that Congress had gained greater control over trade policy and that their strategy for the ITO must reflect that fact.

After their difficulties defending the RTAA, senior Truman administration officials decided not to waste their limited political capital on the ITO, and they postponed its presentation until the 81st Congress. They hoped that a Democratic victory would ensure a better future for their foreign economic policy objectives. Truman won the White House and Democrats regained greater control over the Congress.

By December 1948, ITO supporters had little to cheer them. Although Truman was vindicated by the election results, he had not received a mandate to proceed with trade liberalization. Moreover, his victory did not signal an energetic defense of the ITO. ITO proponents now had an organization to build support for the ITO, but it was neither well funded nor energetically supported. State Department officials were clearly pushing other priorities ahead of the ITO as it awaited formal presentation to Congress and a hearing date.

Clayton and Batt, the ITO's most visible and tireless proponents, were not optimistic. Clayton, believing he had failed to preserve the integrity of the Trade Agreements Program, became increasingly concerned about the fate of the ITO.[49] The next two years would show his concerns were well placed.

8

Dead on Arrival: The Fate of the ITO, 1948–1951

In October 1948, members of the National Association of Manufacturers, a lobbying group of large and small industrial companies, met to discuss the ITO. Executive Curtis Calder compared the ITO, a code for global trade, with the development of a penal code in a small town: One of its citizens said he wanted to be free to commit murder on Mondays, a second said that he wanted to commit larceny on Tuesdays, and a third said he wanted to commit arson on Wednesdays and Fridays. Calder concluded that no Americans would want to live in such a town with so many exceptions to the rules. But Wilbert Ward of the National City Bank (today's Citibank) criticized the analogy, noting that he didn't know any other world we could move to.[1]

Such a lack of enthusiasm for the ITO did not, however, mitigate the fact that twenty-three nations, including the United States, had already reduced their trade barriers.[2] In 1948, eleven other nations announced that they too desired to accede to the GATT. And the White House wanted that success to continue.

As the ITO remained on hold, senior Truman administration made a three-year renewal of the RTAA a priority. The hearings on the sixth renewal of the act showed the limits of their commitment to the ITO.

The hearings, which began in February 1949, were a milestone for supporters of multilateral trade liberalization. A fragile coalition of business, labor, education, and community leaders expressed support for trade liberalization as a means of maintaining the nation's economic health and as a tool for preventing the spread of communism overseas. But congressional countenance of trade liberalization as a policy objective did not translate into congressional or public approval of the specific mechanisms of the GATT or the ITO. Republican members also used the hearings to criticize the administration for not submitting the ITO charter to Congress at the same time the RTAA was under consideration.[3]

By the time President Truman submitted the final charter to Congress in April 1949, public attention was focused on the threat of strikes at home and the spread of communism overseas. Moreover, the final charter was long and complex. Few Americans could be enticed to read it; fewer still must have understood it. Most Americans did not believe they had much to gain or to lose from this innovation. Many influential business leaders, a key special interest constituency, did not support the ITO.

When the House finally held hearings on the ITO in 1950, perfectionists and protectionists forged an informal coalition to oppose the measure.[4] Because the ITO's supporters had not effectively made a case for it with the American people, the voices of its opponents drowned out its many advocates in business, civic associations, labor unions, and farm groups. The House hearings, however, did not kill this policy mechanism. The ITO was actually dead on arrival on Capitol Hill, where few Americans were interested in its revival.

Congressional Support, International Events, and the Fate of the ITO

Although the Democrats were in control again, the 81st Congress was not amenable to executive branch innovation. Nor were its members greatly supportive of multilateral initiatives, especially those held over from the Roosevelt administration.[5] The new Congress had its own interests and agenda, and trade policy was not high on its list. Red-baiting was, however, after Elizabeth Bentley and Whittaker Chambers charged that high administration officials had been members of Communist spy rings. Members of Congress recognized that the hearings on these allegations were likely to attract a great deal of attention and make or break some congressional careers. Among the accused Communist spies was Alger Hiss, who had worked in the Department of State on United Nations affairs. In his position as head of the Carnegie Endowment for International Peace, he had helped to gain outside support for the 1948 extension of the RTAA. His association with the ITO was minor, but in the heated environment of the early cold war, it was enough to damage both the ITO and its supporters.[6]

President Harry S Truman responded to these accusations with conviction, describing congressional concerns as misplaced, calling the accusations a "red herring," and urging Congress to deal with the very real problem of inflation. But his remarks did not dissuade the public, a majority of whom supported congressional investigations of "fellow travelers" in the executive branch. The accusations against Hiss fueled a growing perception that freer trade and multilateralism were policies deliberately designed by Communist sympathizers within the government to benefit the United States' cold war adversaries. Although the Soviets had in fact condemned the ITO, some special interest groups and members of Congress used the Hiss accusations to criticize the RTAA and later the ITO. After the Soviets exploded an atomic bomb in September 1949 and Hiss was found guilty of perjury on January 21, 1950, distrust of internationalist idealists grew. Red-baiting became a lens through which members of Congress, as well as average Americans, viewed policy innovations.[7] Many Americans now believed there was something drastically wrong with the foreign policies developed under Dean Acheson and other "New Deal liberals" and were leery of further New Deal international initiatives.

As foreign policy became more important, Congress was determined to obtain greater control over the growing number of programs and policies. The budget estimates for international affairs and finance in fiscal year 1948-49 came to about $7.2 billion, or some 18 percent of the entire national budget. The State Department, as well as over forty other departments and agencies, had acquired substantial new responsibilities in the nation's expanded international activities. Congress, which had never been fond of the State Department, was not prepared to open its pockets to fund many of the Department's initiatives. Congress used the power of the purse to ensure a modicum of State Department obeisance to congressional will and intent.[8]

Although the mood on Capitol Hill worried the Truman administration, they proceeded in an ad hoc manner. Inside the White House and the State Department, officials could not agree on the strategy for gaining congressional support of the Trade Agreements Act, the GATT, and the ITO.[9]

In May 1948, Undersecretary of State Robert A. Lovett urged the administration to postpone congressional consideration of the ITO, however, Lovett wanted to engage in battles over other priorities first. Not all of Truman's staff or the State Department shared Lovett's priorities.

Some administration officials had a different game plan, one more supportive of the ITO. On May 26, George M. Elsey, a White House aide, wrote to Special Counsel Clark M. Clifford, "The President doubtless has the legal right to retain the Charter . . . but I do not see that he has the moral right . . . . Can the President now say to the world . . . we aren't interested in the ITO?" David Bell, administrative assistant to the president, noted that if the charter were withheld, some opponents might presume the president "was hiding the results and not submitting them to the public." Despite the opposition of White House insiders Elsey, Bell, and Charles Murphy, also an administrative assistant to the president, the White House approved Lovett's recommendation.[10] But the debate over the ITO's fate continued.

At the end of 1948, officials did firm up several aspects of their strategy for the congressional hearings.[11] They decided that the State Department should handle the bulk of the hearings, on the assumption that other agencies might not "come through" for the ITO. This decision hurt the ITO. By keeping the work in State, they appeared to have alienated trade officials in other agencies such as Agriculture, Treasury, and Commerce and to have made it more difficult to present the ITO as a measure devised by all of these agencies in the national interest. Moreover, this strategy put additional burdens on the already overworked trade and public relations staff at the State Department. Officials also decided to leave the direct lobbying activities to their friends outside the government. As staff member Norman Burns noted, members of Congress should not be left with the impression that State had hired a high-class lobbyist "to work on them."[12]

State Department officials did not take advantage of the delay in presenting the ITO to Congress to build public support. They continued to take public support for granted. As Joseph Coppock wrote his superiors, "The informed and opinion-making public is aware of the ITO and generally in favor . . . . The energies of our limited group should not be spent at this time lecturing to public groups . . . . The situation may call for such a public effort at a later stage."[13] Presumably this later stage would come before congressional action.

Although the appointment of Dean Acheson as secretary of state in January 1949 raised the hopes of ITO proponents, their optimism was quickly dashed. Acheson had more pressing foreign policy priorities than this mechanism.[14] Like his boss, President Truman, Acheson knew when to cut his sails to fit the prevailing political wind. Both men couched the ITO in pretty words, but neither would use his political chits to gain its passage.

The first evidence of the administration's congressional strategy for the ITO and the GATT came in January 1949. In his state of the union address, President Truman requested that Congress approve the ITO Charter, and he recommended restoration of "the Reciprocal Trade Agreements Act to full effectiveness" with extension for three years. The second round of the GATT was scheduled to begin at Annecy, France, in April 1949; the administration needed renewed authority immediately. Trade policy officials redirected their attention to ensuring that the RTAA was extended: the Ways and Means Committee scheduled hearings on HR 1211, which was designed to correct the 1948 extension by getting rid of peril points, to return the tariff commission to the interagency process, and to provide for three years of trade liberalization authority.[15]

Some members of Congress made it clear that they believed that the RTAA and the GATT should be the administration's trade policy priorities. Senator Walter F. George, Chairman of the Finance Committee, warned Truman that the ITO and the RTAA must not be presented at the same time. He feared that Senator Millikin would stretch out the trade agreements hearings until the Presidential authority expired, preventing the administration from negotiating further trade agreements. Acheson warned his staff, "Please see that there is no slip-up." Taking this message seriously, the administration again decided to postpone congressional consideration of the ITO in an effort to push through renewed authority under the RTAA.[16] The ITO bride was becoming a bridesmaid to the GATT.

But the administration did firm up its congressional strategy for the ITO. On March 28, 1949, Acheson met with the president, Vice President Alben Barkley, Senator Scott W. Lucas, and Majority Leader John W. McCormack. The president decided that the ITO matter should go before Congress in two bills: one authorizing U.S. participation in the ITO, and the other providing for the necessary changes in U.S. legislation. The first of these bills would be sent to the Foreign Affairs and Foreign Relations Committees; the second, to the Ways and Means and Senate Finance Committees. Acheson delegated his assistant secretary for congressional relations, Ernest Gross, to handle the ITO bills, but made it clear that the Trade Agreements Program must come first. As a result, the ITO bills were not forwarded to Congress until later that year. On April 15, Will Clayton met with Senator George. Although the senator admitted he had once recommended postponing the ITO, he now said that "in view of the long delay . . . we should go ahead and present the charter to the Congress." Clayton then asked Senator George to serve as the leading advocate for the charter to counterbalance the knowledgeable opposition of Senator Millikin. But Senator George, unwilling to crawl out on that limb any further than the administration had, respectfully declined.[17]

Senator George's lack of enthusiasm for the ITO was shared by many members of Congress. None of Truman's allies on Capitol Hill wanted to lead the charge for the ITO Charter. They had already carried the ball for him on unpopular issues such as civil rights or Taft-Hartley legislation. The ITO's day on Capitol Hill would have to wait for the Trade Agreements Extension and other priorities.

The 1949 hearings on the Trade Agreements Extension Act took longer and were more difficult than administration officials expected. Although the House passed the bill on February 9, the Senate did not vote until September 15. Despite support on both sides of the aisle, the hearings were again contentious.[18] In contrast with past hearings, assistant secretaries and office directors, not senior officials, provided the main defense, a decision that hurt the RTAA as well as the ITO.

Assistant Secretary Willard Thorp, who was now in charge of the department's international economic policies (responsibilities that had been previously handled by Undersecretary Clayton), took a dispassionate approach to the trade hearings. He would not embellish his answers with his own convictions but answered only with dry facts that seemed to reflect a lack of enthusiasm for the trade policy mechanisms at issue.[19]

Congressional concerns echoed many of those expressed in the 1948 hearings. Some witnesses complained that low tariffs forced American workers to compete with slave or low-wage labor, that the State Department was secretive and bungling, and that it was determined to close American factories and lower the nation's standard of living. Opponents linked their criticism of the RTAA to the European Recovery Plan (ERP), stating that both programs were misguided. Some members noted that the GATT, building on the RTAA, was in fact a little ITO.[20] After administration witnesses argued that U.S. producers were, in fact, protected by the escape clause, opponents complained that the escape clause was worthless and that the administration's policies subsidized America's economic competitors.[21]

Republican members used the hearings to link the Democrats' policy innovations to Communist machinations and thus discredit the policies as well as the policymakers. Representatives Daniel A. Reed and Thomas A. Jenkins expressed concern about the Truman administration's failure to disclose the records of the Interdepartmental Committee on Trade Agreements, arguing that it was unconstitutional to withhold information from Congress on the rates of duty reductions to be recommended. After Truman decided that such records should not be disclosed, the two representatives used this decision to condemn the State Department and link it to Communist intrigue, accusing it of withholding information developed by and for the benefit of "fellow travelers," a term for Communists.[22] Echoing these thoughts, Senator George W. Malone argued that the department was "trying to undermine the basic economic structure of this country" and lower the U.S. standard of living, a process he described as "the third and final step of this very clever . . . program to . . . distribute the wealth of this Nation throughout the world."[23] Brown and other ITO advocates did not honor these allegations by refuting them.

At the Finance Committee's hearings, Senator Millikin took the lead in skewering the administration's proposals. He loved the arcane aspects of the law and used his experience on tariff policies to challenge the ad-

Table 8. Some Prominent Proponents and Opponents of 1949 Hearings on the Operation of the Trade Agreements Act

Some Proponents:	Some Opponents:
Agriculture: American Farm Bureau Federation, National Farmers Union, Dried Fruit Industry of California	*Agriculture:* National Board of Fur Farmers, National Grange, California Walnut Growers Association, National Cooperative Milk Producers Conference, Mushroom Growers Cooperative of Pennsylvania, American National Livestock Association
Labor: American Federation of Labor, Congress of Industrial Organizations, American Watch Assemblers	
Business: National Foreign Trade Council, W.R. Grace, National Council of American Importers, Chamber of Commerce of the United States, United States Associates of the International Chamber of Commerce, H.J. Heinz Corporation	*Labor:* Atlantic Fisherman's Union, American Wage Earner's Protective Conference
	Business: American Tariff League, Rubber Manufacturers Association, Cotton Textile Institute, National Association of Wool Manufacturers, Vitrified China Association, National Renderers Association, Maine Sardine Packers Association, Candle Manufacturers Association, Synthetic Organic Chemical Association, American Glassware Association, American Paper and Pulp Association
Prominent Republicans: Charles P. Taft, Senator Ralph Flanders	
Prominent Advocates: Senator Virgil Chapman, Gerard Swope, chair of General Electric and chair of Citizens Committee for Reciprocal World Trade	
Civic Groups: Peoples' Lobby, American Veterans Committee, Federal Council of Churches of Christ	*Prominent Opponents:* Senator Leverett Saltonstall

Source: House Committee on Ways and Means, *1949 Extension of the Reciprocal Trade Agreements Act Hearings on H.R. 1211, a Bill to Extend the Authority of the President under Section 350 of the Tariff Act of 1930, as Amended, and for Other Purposes,* 81st Cong., 1st sess., Jan. 24-Feb. 1, 1949, iii-vii; and Senate Finance Committee, *Extension of Reciprocal Trade Agreements Act: Hearings on H.R. 1211, an Act to Extend the Authority of the President under Section 350 of the Tariff Act of 1930, as Amended, and for Other Purposes,* 81st Cong., 1st sess., Feb. 17-23, 1949, iii-vii.

ministration. Winthrop Brown, and to a lesser extent Assistant Secretary Thorp, carried the department's main line of defense. They found the senator an effective quarterback, frequently scoring in his criticisms. Millikin spent days scrutinizing the RTAA, the GATT, and the ITO and questioning the need for three mechanisms to achieve trade liberalization. With Senators Robert A. Taft and Owen Brewster, he condemned the department's policies; they claimed that the one-year extension of the

RTAA in 1948 had been designed so that Congress could consider the RTAA, the GATT, and the ITO together. Millikin repeatedly asked why the ITO was withheld. The administration, he said, was using "a Judas goat to bring this country into the ITO without proper Congressional authority."[24]

State Department officials were not prepared to defend the administration's strategy for postponing the ITO. As a result, the Senate hearing became a referendum on the ITO as well as the GATT and the RTAA. Millikin was determined to show that the three mechanisms were connected morally and legally, but he mistakenly concluded the administration was fully committed to the ITO, noting that "the GATT is the tail to the ITO dog." Brown twice hinted that the department was willing to abandon the ITO, virtually conceding its demise. "The general agreement is so set up that it can stand on its own feet . . . . If the ITO does not come into being there will be consultation to see what should be done with the general agreement . . . . We would ask the Congress to make changes . . . to permit us to make this agreement definitely effective."[25] But this late-breaking conciliatory approach failed. Although the administration showed its willingness to toss the ITO to the congressional sharks, Millikin did not take the bait. Because Brown and other ITO advocates did not effectively explain why a more substantive ITO—as well as the GATT—was needed, this became the Senate's final hearing on the ITO.

Although supporters had a growing sense that the ITO was dead, the hearings were a watershed for multilateral trade liberalization. The policy was made acceptable to the American polity based on a belief that trade liberalization could help prevent the spread of communism overseas and keep the U.S. economy prosperous. Policymakers found they could accommodate protectionist special interests, maintain the support of freer traders, and achieve the broader goals of trade liberalization by making concessions to protectionist interests and members of Congress. But this tentative consensus did not lead to agreement on the policies and mechanisms to achieve multilateral trade liberalization.[26]

The consensus on multilateral trade liberalization was fragile also because it was built on an inherent contradiction. The consensus first took shape when representatives of protectionist special interests and members of Congress repeatedly stressed that they supported freer trade but that the situation of specific sectors merited protection. These sectors often justified their exemption from freer trade with a defense rationale, a popular argument in those years. When policymakers developed concessions to accommodate the sectors, many ITO supporters were concerned, although they recognized the need to compromise domestically to move ahead internationally. The development of the compromises ensured that multilateral trade liberalization would not be "pure," as sector-specific protection was patched onto the broader trade policies.[27]

Despite their success at achieving this consensus, State Department officials continued their charade of trying to get congressional approval for the ITO. After discussing the legislative schedule with key members of Congress, the president finally submitted the charter to Congress in April 1949, some thirteen months after its final negotiation.[28]

Truman used two principal arguments to justify congressional approval: the need to order international economic relations and the need to support international cooperation (and a stable world order) through the United Nations. But these arguments were not designed to convince the public or Congress that the ITO was a policy priority. Using blunt and repetitious rhetoric, the architect of the "Fair Deal" stressed the charter's innovative nature, twice describing it as "progressive" and as a step forward. Truman also linked the ITO to the ERP, noting that ERP "will be only partially realized unless we achieve a vigorous world trading system."[29] But his arguments were ill suited to the political realities of 1949. He did not explain how the ITO could achieve a vigorous world trading system when so many nations were short of dollars and had nothing to sell the United States and when other nations appeared so firmly opposed to freer markets in their home country. Moreover, his speechwriters did not root the ITO in long-standing U.S. economic and legal principles of equity, competition, and openness. It is not surprising that the charter appeared alien to many Americans, including members of Congress. At a time when many Americans believed international cooperation was a failed policy and perceived that the U.S. system was threatened by Communist regimes, Truman's arguments for the ITO were ineffective.

The president's presentation of the ITO charter to Congress contrasts with his presentation of the UN Charter. Clearly, the two instruments are very different and merited different introductions. But Truman personally delivered the UN Charter to the Senate, whereas the ITO received a speech some thirteen months after the final charter negotiation. Moreover, he made it clear that Congress must take the UN Charter as negotiated. "The choice before the Senate is now clear. The choice is not between this charter and something else. It is between this charter and no charter at all." Although the Congress faced a similar choice in the case of the ITO, Truman did not make a similar warning.[30]

Congressional delay followed the president's procrastination. On May 3, 1949, Judge John Kee, chairman of the House Foreign Affairs Committee, finally introduced House Joint Resolution 236, which provided for membership and participation in the ITO. But the minimum wage legislation, not the ITO, was the congressional priority in August.[31] The ITO bill had to wait.

The administration continued to make its foreign policy priorities clear to members of Congress. When Acheson testified in executive session on June 22, 1949, he left the Chairman of Senate Foreign Relations a memorandum on the administration's priorities. Although he stated that these priorities referred "to the timing of the consideration of the legislation and not to relative importance," it was clear what he meant. The ITO was not among the items for which the department urged "early consideration."[32]

William Batt went to Clayton urging him to gain top level support to set an immediate hearing date for the ITO. In June, Clayton called on Acheson, who reassured him that the administration would tell its allies on Capitol Hill that ITO hearings should start immediately.[33] But Acheson was giving a different message to the administration's friends on Capitol Hill.

State Department officials continued to work on gaining congressional and public approval of the ITO. In November, the department established a strategy board on the ITO, which recommended that the staff concentrate on "Congressional . . . cultivation" and on missionary work with civic, union, agricultural, and business groups. These officials worried about having a consistent governmentwide position on the ITO, fearing that Commerce Secretary Sawyer's "indifference showed evidence of permeating down to Commerce's technical people." Although they persevered on the ITO's behalf, growing numbers of officials acknowledged that the ITO was a lost cause.[34]

As the ITO awaited a hearing date, Assistant Secretary Thorp was given the responsibility of getting the ITO through Congress, but he was also directed not to work too hard on its behalf. At a November 23, 1949, meeting with Undersecretary of State James E. Webb and other senior officials, Thorp was told that the ITO's establishment must be "put in the proper perspective . . . . In dealing with the public and the Congress we must not give the impression that the Charter will answer the critical requirements." A senior congressional staff member warned State Department officials that the ITO was too "controversial" and "might well prejudice" the fate of other foreign policy measures. The ITO's opponents concluded that the administration was not deeply committed to the ITO, and they began to exploit the administration's delay and congressional inaction to oppose the ITO.[35]

As a result of the failure to push for hearings on the ITO, some of America's trading partners began to question the U.S. commitment to multilateral trade liberalization. State Department officials were forced to reassure other ITO nations that the ITO and the GATT remained central to the administration's foreign policies.[36] But many foreign diplomats were not convinced, because the United States seemed perfectly willing to abandon freer trade policies when it seemed politically expedient.[37] Their doubt about U.S. intentions had been growing since 1947, and this threatened the success of the next round of GATT negotiations.[38]

Some thirty nations, including eleven new contracting parties, sent delegates to Annecy, France, to begin the second round of GATT negotiations. Despite their considerable success in enlarging the international aegis of the GATT, American negotiators operated at a great disadvantage, because of their charade of support for the ITO and the GATT, as well as the delay in obtaining congressional approval of the sixth extension of the RTAA. When the British delegation wanted to bring into force the provisions of the Havana Charter governing international commodity agreements, the United States had to withhold approval. Delegates from other nations wanted "to use the machinery of the contracting parties" to prevent the world from being split into dollar and nondollar camps. The ITO was clearly designed to act on this sort of problem, but if U.S. officials encouraged recourse to the ITO, they would again be acting without congressional approval.[39] Moreover, although negotiations among the Contracting Parties (GATT members) were concluded in August, American negotiators could not sign the bilateral agreements under the GATT, for Congress had not given the executive branch the go-ahead for the Annecy negotiations. The United States had to mount "a strenuous diplomatic effort" to postpone the signing date to October 10, five days after Congress finally extended the RTAA. According to the delegation's capable leader, Woodbury Willoughby, these problems resulted "in a definite impression which could not entirely be dispelled, that the United States is withdrawing from the position of leadership" in developing the GATT and the ITO.[40] As foreign officials perceived the United States as less committed to the principles and mechanisms it had espoused since the war, they were less willing to bind their nations' economic future to such principles.[41]

Members of Congress and their staff showed that they had their own agenda. On November 29, Foreign Affairs Committee staff informed the State Department that the ITO would be the first new item of business on its agenda in 1950, but no date for these hearings was finalized.[42] Throughout 1950, the date for ITO hearings was repeatedly postponed, reflecting the lack of interest on the part of the executive and legislative branches.[43]

The Power of Delay

State Department officials, nevertheless, began to seek advice from members of Congress on how to handle these hearings. Because they sought that advice from traditional friends of freer trade rather than its opponents, they again missed an opportunity to disarm the opposition. Representative Jacob Javits stressed that the department must "make clear that the Charter wasn't going to hurt anybody in the United States; . . . that we should have good answers on the effect of the ITO on our agricultural policy[;] . . . that we make sure to satisfy any real or fancied special interests of members of the Committee before the hearings started." [44] Department officials listened to his advice and remained focused on special interests.

In their talks with business leaders, State officials discovered that several members of the business community preferred the GATT as the key mechanism for achieving trade liberalization. For example, Mr. Campbell of the United States Chamber of Commerce told Carl Corse that the Chamber would accept the ITO if it consisted only of chapter IV (the section on commercial policy.) Other business groups used the RTAA hearings as well as private meetings to suggest this policy alternative. However, State Department officials continued to argue that the GATT could not stand without the larger framework of the ITO.[45] They gave the business groups no indication that this was, in fact, their strategy, continuing the facade of support for the ITO.

These efforts did not advance the ITO on Main Street, Wall Street, or Capitol Hill. Winthrop Brown made one last stab at getting visible top-level support, calling George M. Elsey at the White House to complain that even Democrats were not coming through for the administration. "So many Democrats fail to come to meetings that a quorum is not present . . . . Furthermore, Judge Kee is now talking about taking up several 'non-controversial' . . . bills before turning to ITO. This means even less time would be available for ITO hearings . . . . To make matters worse, these dilatory tactics on the part of the House Committee have made many prospective witnesses restless." Elsey recommended that the president reemphasize his support for the ITO to the congressional leadership. On February 9, the president asked his secretary of state what the ITO's chances would be in Congress. When Acheson replied that its chances were doubtful, Truman said he thought "this even more reason for making the most vigorous efforts." But the president was unwilling to actively take part in its defense.[46]

Lacking full administration support, developments on the Hill continued to go against the ITO. When Senator Millikin threatened to transfer the ITO to the Senate Committee on Finance, Senator George, chair of the Committee on Foreign Relations, appeared unwilling to challenge this move. The press and public correctly interpreted this lack of interest as evidence of the administration's lack of commitment to the ITO.[47] Some of the ITO's allies began to criticize the administration's strategy in public.

The clerk of the House Ways and Means Committee wondered why the ITO had not gone first to this committee, with its thirteen members "ready to go down the line for you on . . . a logical extension of the Trade Agreements Act."[48]

A bad situation on Capitol Hill kept getting worse. On April 12, Elsey wrote to his boss that Judge John Kee, Chairman of the House Foreign Affairs Committee, finally had scheduled hearings on the ITO. "This action . . . raised the hopes of the ITO boys in State to a new high, only to have them disappointed by Senator Lucas' failure to include ITO on the "must" list for this session."[49] Acheson urged the president to speak with Senator Tom Connally about his views that the ITO should be enacted as soon as possible, and he warned that "Senators Ives, Millikin, and Lodge have been vocal in suggestions that the department should have consulted the Republicans in the Senate . . . . Republican opposition to the Charter bids fair to be both loud and voluminous." The Republican strategy was clear: they would insist that the ITO be reviewed by the Congress as a treaty, solely within the Senate's jurisdiction. Moreover, they proposed that Secretary Acheson delay action on the ITO as a goodwill gesture to bipartisan foreign policy. Senators Millikin, Brewster, and Homer Ferguson had already placed several comments to this effect in the *Congressional Record*.

On May 3, Acheson told the president that Judge Kee was a sick man who was already having a difficult time managing his own committee. Acheson advised Truman to commend Judge Kee "on his willingness to go ahead with the ITO hearings even in the face of strong Committee opposition" and to show his support by prodding the Democrats to attend the hearings. Truman restated his support for the ITO in Fargo, North Dakota, during his "report to the people" on May 13, and on May 22 he told Undersecretary Webb that the State Department should still press for the ITO.[50] He, however, remained unwilling to invest his administration's political capital on the new policy.

The ITO had not been helped by the two years of delay. Its comprehensive approach to trade policy now seemed naive and impractical. It became even harder for Clayton and Batt to get business support in their efforts to market the ITO. Clayton had to loan the Committee money to continue its efforts. By the end of 1949, the Committee for the ITO had to reduce its staff by 50 percent. With only two full-time staff members and no firm hearing date, the Committee found it difficult to map out an effective strategy for marketing the ITO.[51] As a result, the Committee was unable to counter the cumulative force of opposition arguments, public apathy, public suspicion of internationalism and big bureaucracies, and long-standing support for sector-specific protection.

The ITO's Final Hearing

Some two years after the final charter was signed, hearings finally began on April 19, 1950. The House hearings were well attended, but not by members of Congress. Witnesses often testified in front of crowds of representatives from special interest groups, with only two or three members of Congress present at a time. When Paul Hoffman, who headed European recovery efforts, came to testify, he waited for thirty-five minutes. Only one member of Congress showed up. Congressional supporters did what they could: Representatives Javits and James G. Fulton went out of their way to support both the ITO and the State Department, and the Democratic membership of the Committee on Ways and Means issued a statement in support of the ITO on April 28. But these actions were not enough to counter the well-framed arguments of the opposition, to compensate for the lack of administration interest, or to attract public interest in the ITO.[52] After several days of testimony, Chairman Kee decided to end his role in the charade. To speed up the hearings, he asked additional witnesses to file statements instead of appearing.

Two years of waiting for the hearing had given the State Department plenty of time to rehearse its arguments in support of the ITO and to rebut criticism. Despite such preparation, the rebuttals were relatively unsuccessful. ITO supporters attempted to make their case by arguing that opponents generally accepted the objectives of trade liberalization but rejected the specific measure. They criticized the opponents for proposing no alternative mode to achieve the objective of international trade expansion, but this argument did not make the very complicated ITO any more appealing.[53] ITO proponents did try to make positive arguments, noting how the ITO could have a constructive impact on world trade, that the ITO was rooted in U.S. principles of equality and openness, and that it would help retain trade in private hands. These arguments were too obscure. Only gradually could the ITO benefit the economy as a whole, whereas it could immediately hurt the farmer, worker, or business executive affected by foreign competition.[54] It is not surprising that only a few members of Congress were persuaded to go out on a limb in favor of the ITO. It held little appeal for them: it couldn't guarantee jobs or income to their districts.

In contrast, the arguments advanced by the ITO's opposition had greater political resonance because they were rooted in American economic tradition, in economic self-interest, and in current world events. Opponents stressed that the ITO was not in the U.S. interest, that it was inconsistent with U.S. practice, and that its many exceptions would render it ineffective. One of the most prominent arguments against the ITO was that it would surrender U.S. sovereignty to an international organization. At first glance, which is how many Americans saw the charter, it did appear that the United States was giving some of its authority to the ITO. ITO opponents pointed to Article 9, under which they said the ITO could direct the U.S. government to promote American economic development, and Article 11, which they said allowed the ITO to interfere with U.S. employment policy. For example, speaking on behalf of the American Bar Association, Albert Barnes warned, "The ITO is in effect an international constitution but it contains no bill of rights . . . and a firm commitment to rest control of our national resources and regulations of our international trade, with an international executive board in which the United States has 1 vote of 18." In questioning, Barnes admitted that he had similar concerns about the RTAA, but "these agreements do not control our domestic law." In short, to Barnes, the ITO not only ceded congressional authority to an international body but it also took away individual rights for review in the courts.[55] Although supporters argued that the ITO could not compel the United States to follow its decisions, these criticisms gained considerable support among business and labor leaders. Opponents also argued that the ITO would be a huge international bureaucracy engaged in international planning. Although proponents stated that the ITO's job would be to persuade government not to take various actions affecting trade, it was hard to convince opponents that by codifying exceptions the ITO was not condoning government intervention in trade.[56]

Opponents also used the ITO's commitments on full employment to show that the ITO was inconsistent with U.S. economic practice.[57] They argued that full employment was a code word for government intervention and state planning. In fact, the charter contained no commitment to assure employment but directed members to take action in a manner appropriate to each nation's economic culture. Although proponents attempted to reassure the concerned public that the federal government would have no greater responsibility than that already mandated in the Employment Act of 1946 (or in the United Nations Charter), opponents argued that the ITO required the federal government to intervene to maintain employment.[58] Some witnesses forcefully seized on the charter's provisions governing state trading to argue that the charter condoned and encouraged state trading, the antithesis of the U.S. free market system. At a time of anticommunist fervor and antipathy to the growth of government intervention in the economy, such arguments gained considerable support.[59]

Opponents also made a strong case that the charter was hypocritical and unrealistic. For example, the charter appeared to permit intergovernmental commodity agreements but to forbid restrictive business practices.

Why were international agreements to create an ordered world for coffee producers acceptable, whereas steel manufacturers could not form cartels to order their markets? ITO opponents also argued that the charter was riddled with exceptions. Although the exceptions were justified on the grounds that they were transitional measures to help ITO members recover from the economic impact of the war, opponents did not see them as transitional; they stressed that the charter condoned these exceptions and made them permanent.[60]

The House hearings were not followed by Senate hearings. Tom Connally, Chairman of the Senate Foreign Relations Committee, refused to establish a hearing date. He wrote Clayton that "five of our members are on the sub-committee handling the charges made by Senator McCarthy. . . . Even some of the Democrats feel . . . it would be unwise to undertake consideration."[61]

Ironically, the administration had not yet decided how to abandon the ITO without renouncing its underlying objectives. On May 26, 1950, White House aides Elsey and Charles Murphy met with Brown and Florence Kirlin of the State Department. They concluded it would be better to press the ITO to a vote in the House even at the risk of defeat on the floor. The president asked Judge Kee to report the ITO out of the Committee, but he never did.[62] On August 10, Judge Kee wrote to Truman about the hearings, noting, "Those favoring our adherence to the ITO predominated heavily . . . . Regrettably, it seems clear that pressure of other urgent business, and particularly legislation of an emergency nature, has made it impossible for the Congress to act upon the bill . . . before the contemplated date of . . . adjournment . . . . It would appear that our wisest course seems to be to reserve this important legislation for . . . next session, or later this year." The president wrote back on August 14, "I think we should keep on working at it."[63] But by this time even Clayton advised the department to drop the ITO.

In light of the attitudes of senior Truman administration officials toward the ITO, one must wonder why junior and mid-level officials such as Winthrop Brown, John Leddy, Joseph Coppock, Woodbury Willoughby, J. Robert Schaetzel, David Bell, and George Elsey, continued to work so hard on the ITO. First, they believed that a longer-term and more comprehensive approach to foreign economic policies was the only way to ensure a healthy U.S. and global economy. Moreover, many had begun their careers at State, had worked beside Harry Hawkins, Clair Wilcox, and William Clayton, and were devoted to the ideals that motivated the illustrious careers of these three men. Although these officials recognized that the world had changed (they would work just as hard on the GATT, the ERP, and other foreign economic policy mechanisms), they were understandably reluctant to give up on something that they believed in so strongly. Moreover, they did not drive America's foreign economic policy, and they had been directed to persevere. In the unstable political environment of the early cold war, policymakers with the best of intentions often stumbled.

The End of the ITO

At the end of 1950, State Department and White House officials finally decided how to end the pretense of full support for the ITO. On November 10, John Leddy drafted a memorandum for the president. "The ITO is no longer a practical possibility . . . . The need for a trade organization, however, is a matter of urgency. The international administration of the trade-agreements program will bog down unless we can set up a permanent international body . . . . We should drop the ITO and instead . . . seek from Congress, in connection with the renewal of the Trade Agreements Act, authority to participate in the establishment of an appropriate international organization under the General Agreement . . . . If Congress takes these actions, we will have managed to make effective . . . substantially all of the major parts of the ITO Charter . . . . There is . . . reason to believe that certain influential groups which have opposed the ITO . . . would support the addition of appropriate organizational provisions to the Trade Agreements Act if the ITO were withdrawn." On November 21, when Acheson presented this proposal to the cabinet, all members present concurred with the abandonment of the ITO.[64]

But trade policy officials were not ready to announce the demise of the ITO, recognizing that the status of the ITO could cause problems for the third round of GATT negotiations at Torquay. As a result, senior U.S. officials gave some of their allies misleading information on the status of the GATT and the ITO. During and after the House hearings, American diplomats tried to persuade other governments and international organizations that the United States would not abandon the ITO.[65] In August 1950, the State Department told Canadian trade officials that the administration would continue to push for the ITO but also asked the Canadians to call for the strengthening of international GATT machinery.[66] Meanwhile, the administration began to downplay the ITO in public statements.[67]

In December 1950, the rumors about the ITO were found to be true. A press release from Torquay stated, "The President has agreed that the proposed Charter for an International Trade Organization should not be re-submitted to the Congress."[68] In a message to the British, Winthrop Brown wrote, "the U.S. Government proposed . . . to build on the G.A.T.T.

Table 9. Some Prominent Proponents and Opponents of ITO

Some Proponents:	Some Opponents:
Agriculture: American Farm Bureau Federation	*Agriculture:* California Walnut Growers
Labor: Congress of Industrial Organizations, United Automobile Workers	*Labor:* American Wage Earners Protective Conference
Business: National Council of American Importers, American Cotton Shippers Association, Motion Picture Association, International and Comparative Law Section of the American Bar Association	*Business:* National Foreign Trade Committee, National Economic Council, American Tariff League, American Bar Association, National Association of Manufacturers, Illinois Manufacturers Association, Export Managers Club of Chicago, Rubber Manufacturers Association, Independent Petroleum Association of America
Civic and Religious: The Brookings Institution, League of Women Voters, Committee for Economic Development, National Planning Association, Lutheran Church, Baptists of the United States, American Unitarian Association	

Organizations supporting GATT, but not the ITO at the Hearings:
National Foreign Trade Council, Chamber of Commerce of the United States

Source: House Committee on Foreign Affairs, *United States in the International Trade Organization, Hearings on H.J. Res. 236, A Joint Resolution Providing for Membership and Participation by the United States in the International Trade Organization and Authorizing an Appropriation Therefor,* 81st Cong., 2d sess., Apr. 19-May 12, 1950.

and give it a rather more permanent organization which could function between the sessions." The British responded positively to this approach, recognizing that "there will be less resistance to the idea of American adherence to an already functioning body . . . than to the idea of the U.S. joining yet another abstruse international economic organization."[69]

The ITO was now officially dead, even though some U.S. government officials had not given up hope that it might yet again be revived and presented to Congress. Yet many of these officials found it difficult to admit that they had abandoned the ITO. Their compromise solution enabled them to kill the ITO without wielding the murder weapon.

In the next few years, Willard Thorp, Winthrop Brown, John Leddy, and others tried to strengthen the GATT's infrastructure. They believed the GATT needed a structure and international standing to ensure that rules governing trade were accepted and enforced. Both the Canadians and the Americans developed proposals, but they went nowhere in the early 1950s. As early as 1951, the British believed GATT was "already an adequate forum for the ventilation of divergencies on economic policy."[70] GATT remained an informal international organization, never formally approved by the governments of its contracting parties.

From 1948 to 1950, the Truman administration pretended to support the ITO without putting much energy behind their actions. This strategy, although a bit two-faced, reflected the strength of special interests and Congress. It was necessitated by the earlier failure of Truman and Roosevelt administration officials to develop a public constituency to counterbalance protectionist special interests. Nevertheless, it allowed the administration to achieve several objectives. First, mid-level officials could continue to fight for the ITO as Congress and special interests stomped it to death. The charade also permitted Truman administration officials to postpone the abandonment of the ITO until Congress had destroyed it. They did not have to repudiate a policy devised by their colleagues in the national interest. Finally, the strategy permitted the development of a fragile and enduring consensus in support of trade liberalization, albeit with safeguards for specific sectors. GATT became one of the most-often used tools in the U.S. policy tool box.

9

The Rise and Erosion of the Freer Trade Consensus and the Debate over NAFTA, 1949–1994

The American polity achieved a fragile consensus on trade policy in 1949. During the RTAA hearings, policymakers, representatives of special interests, and members of Congress concurred that America's leadership of global efforts to reduce trade barriers could help global prosperity and prevent the spread of communism. U.S. policymakers were not very concerned about GATT's small base of public support. Trade was not a burning issue for most Americans.[1]

By the mid-1950s, the GATT developed a special interest constituency consisting of exporters, some labor groups, internationalists, policymakers, journalists, and economists. These opinion leaders acted as a buffer between politicians and the public, criticizing protectionism and touting the benefits of freer trade.[2] Support of freer trade became a dogma among elites for the next three decades.[3]

The faith of these opinion leaders in the GATT seemed justified. Under its aegis, the world economy grew dramatically, but world trade grew even faster.[4] Important industries in the United States such as textiles, television, steel, and footwear did suffer from foreign competition, and workers lost jobs. However, most Americans benefited from this growth in world trade; as consumers they got a cheaper and more diverse supply of goods; as producers, most found new markets and growing employment; as taxpayers and voters, this economic growth came at little cost to the American economy as a whole or to American democracy.

GATT's purview grew dramatically in the years that followed. During the eight trade rounds, not only were tariffs reduced, but GATT's contracting parties agreed to rules reducing nontariff measures that restrict or distort trade. After the Tokyo Round of the GATT, the GATT also included a standards code (to discourage recourse to standards as a trade barrier—standards are regulations or legislation designed to protect citi-

zens' health and safety), a civil aircraft code, a procurement code, a subsidies code, an antidumping code, and rules on import licensing.[5]

Although GATT's purview now increasingly covered rules that had
once been solely domestic, GATT's structure remained ad hoc. As in 1947,
the GATT was essentially a set of accepted rules and a forum in which
countries could discuss and resolve trade problems as well as negotiate to
expand world trade. Aided by a small secretariat in Geneva, GATT's contracting parties made decisions by consensus. To ensure compliance with
the GATT, the GATT's secretariat relied on both formal and informal tools,
including consultation, pressure and diplomacy, periodic reviews, and
formal third-party adjudication by GATT legal panels.[6]

GATT's economic accomplishments did not, however, inspire congressional confidence. Congress consistently authorized a GATT disclaimer
in its extensions of the RTAA, stressing that congressional approval of the
act should not be construed as denoting approval or disapproval of the
GATT.[7] According to legal scholar Robert Hudec, "Congress was willing
to see GATT continue, but wished to preserve its own freedom of action."[8]
Congress had effectively drawn a "line in the sand" beyond which it
would not cede control over trade policy. And the American people did
not disagree with this assessment.

Public Opinion on Trade

Like the Congress, the American people never fully embraced freer trade
policies or the GATT. Americans accepted freer trade in theory, because
free markets were "the American way." But they often blamed trade policies for the nation's economic problems, especially when they saw that
their fellow Americans lost jobs.[9] As example, in 1993 *Newsweek* reported
that some 76 percent of its polling sample thought international trade was
"a good thing," yet some 77 percent thought imports bear some or a lot of
the blame for slow U.S. economic growth.[10] A 1993 Yankelovich poll asked
if past international trade agreements have caused U.S. jobs to be lost.
Some 76 percent said yes, while 15 percent said trade agreements have not
caused job loss.[11]

However, Americans were divided on the job impact of freer trade
policies. As voters left voting booths on election day 1992, 43 percent said
U.S. trade with other countries creates more jobs for the United States, 41
percent said it loses more jobs, and 5 percent said trade with other countries has no effect on jobs. But in March 1994, a Princeton Survey Research telephone poll of 2,001 adults found that 52 percent of those polled
believed that free trade agreements help the overall job situation, 32 per-

cent said they reduce jobs, and 15 percent said they didn't know.[12] Nonetheless, some Americans seemed to have concluded it was more important to preserve jobs than to benefit from trade. In a January 1992 *New York Times*/CBS poll of 1,281 Americans, 56 percent of those polled said it was more important to protect American industries and jobs by limiting imports than to allow free trade to buy good products at low prices.[13]

By the 1990s, the public had some awareness of the benefits of freer trade. Americans liked to choose between foreign and domestic goods and believed that having that choice has long-term positive effects for the economy as a whole. In a *USA Today* poll of 604 adults in February 1992, 85 percent said they made an effort to buy American whenever possible, but "only 40 percent of those polled agreed that the best thing for the U.S. economy . . . is to buy only U.S. goods." A 1993 *Newsweek* poll showed Americans "try to buy the best product" whether or not it is made in America. A 1994 Gallup Poll also revealed 82 percent weigh quality of a product, whereas only 34 percent always try to determine the source of products.[14]

Yet to many Americans, the benefits of cheaper goods did not outweigh their costs. Polling data revealed that Americans wondered if our nation's efforts on behalf of freer trade have benefited American workers and communities as much as their counterparts in other nations such as Japan, Germany, or Korea.[15] According to the Public Agenda Foundation, there was a widely held conviction that "something is wrong" with the U.S. economy, a "real fear that the country is skating on thin ice and that . . . we have lost something crucial to our success as a nation." Thus, it is not surprising that although Americans tout our "laissez-faire" economy, they also want policymakers to use trade restrictions to protect domestic industries and jobs.[16]

As in the post–World War II period, how one thought about trade reflected one's education and economic status. According to the Gallup Organization, there was a class and education gap between those Americans who saw trade as an opportunity and a job creator and those who saw trade as a threat. GATT was most likely to be opposed by those Americans living in families making under $20,000 a year and those without a college education. "It is favored most heavily by Democrats and people who consider themselves liberal," but "on balance Republicans and conservatives also favor GATT."[17]

However, polling data revealed that policymakers could not take middle-class support of the GATT for granted. As Daniel Yankelovich, America's premier public opinion analyst, noted in the 1990s, the globalization of the economy, corporate downsizing, and changes in technology were making many Americans feel insecure and scared. Although all of these factors were creating change, many Americans "blamed" U.S. trade policy.[18] Moreover, their fears were making them pessimistic. A September 1991 poll of 1003 Americans found some 60 percent of those polled believed the American standard of living was declining; this perception cut across income level and occupations. A 1995 poll of 1,249 adults found 67 percent thought the American dream had become harder to achieve in the past ten years.[19] According to the Times Mirror Center, "Middle income Americans express more pessimistic attitudes about future growth in this country than do those in the upper and lower income brackets." Perhaps more ominously, the children of the middle class were scared, too. The Times Mirror Center reported that "despite the overall improvement in the personal financial picture of Americans since 1992 . . . younger Americans . . . are least likely to be satisfied with the way things are going for them financially." Some 74 percent of those polled by Harris in 1995 believed the American dream will be harder to achieve in the next ten years.[20] Their fears about the future may make them more receptive to protectionist arguments. And in the 1980s and 1990s, Americans heard a lot about the need to protect their jobs, their communities, and their future.

New Challenges and Challengers to Freer Trade

As other nations became increasingly proficient at producing and distributing a wide range of goods and services, some workers, shareholders, and communities suffered. Profits tumbled in key industries such as steel and automobiles. Some products invented in the U.S.A. were no longer made in the U.S.A. America and Americans were addicted to imports. (See figure 1.)

Workers, executives, and shareholders of those companies hurt by foreign competition were doubly angry. They saw their government as ineffective; in their eyes, it unfairly continued to lower trade barriers while doing little to help workers, communities, or companies adjust. Groups such as the AFL-CIO worked on Capitol Hill to strengthen U.S. trade law to promote job and income security for U.S. workers.[21] Congress heard these concerns and made it easier for U.S. firms to gain protection against dumped or subsidized goods. High-tech industries such as semiconductors joined traditionally protectionist sectors such as steel in taking advantage of these changes.[22]

In this period, Congress became more receptive to new approaches to trade policy. Many of these new approaches were in accordance with GATT principles. But their growing appeal revealed that many members of Congress were concluding that a multilateral approach to trade was not always working in the interests of the American people.[23] For example,

Percent of real GDP

Source: Department of Commerce, from Economic Report of the President, 1994.

U.S. Trade as Share of Real Gross Domestic Product.

two influential policymakers, Congressman Richard Gephardt and Senator Daniel Patrick Moynihan, stressed that the United States should use its huge market as leverage to convince other nations to reduce their trade barriers. In their view, this would be the only way to achieve truly open markets.[24]

Some members began to call for a new approach to trade policy based on results, rather than rules. Advocates of a results-oriented trade policy believe U.S. producers do not often obtain the market shares they deserve because of covert forms of protection such as unrealistic health and safety standards or collusive business practices. Their prescription was not to abandon the GATT, but to redirect trade liberalization efforts toward achieving real market share results through bilateral negotiations with our major trading partners.[25] This results-oriented approach gained influence in the U.S. government, in academia, and in labor and business groups, such as the Council on Competitiveness and the Labor Industry Coalition for International Trade in the late 1980s.[26]

Congress also became receptive to new approaches to trade policy designed to restore American competitiveness. (Competitiveness is the ability to produce goods and services that meet the test of international markets while our citizens enjoy a rising standard of living.) As Laura

D'Andrea Tyson noted, "Free trade is not necessarily . . . the best policy. . . . U.S. policy should be guided by the principle of selective reciprocity and motivated by the goal of opening foreign markets." Tyson, along with other economists, called for a new trade policy "to deter or compensate for foreign practices that are not adequately regulated by existing multilateral rules."[27]

Questioning of America's trade policy was not limited to policymakers or confined to Washington. After two decades of trade deficits, a growing number of intellectuals, business leaders, academics, and religious and community leaders also began to debate the course of U.S. trade policy. They were motivated by the demise of the Soviet Union and the end of the cold war rationale for foreign policy. Very few opinion leaders argued for abandonment of the GATT, but their concerns revealed growing impatience with the effects of multilateral trade liberalization. Chief among their concerns was the impact of trade upon the American dream.[28]

Some economists noticed that two trends seemed to accompany America's integration in the world economy: America's standard of living stagnated about the same time that the United States experienced a rising income disparity between college-educated workers and those with little or no education. (See figure 2.) They wondered if America's trade policies had any relationship to these trends. To move the debate forward, two of America's premier think tanks, the Brookings Institution and the American Enterprise Institute, sponsored conferences. Even the Council of Economic Advisors focused on this issue in the *Economic Report of the President*.[29] Economists were as divided about the solutions as they were about the problem. While classical economists argued that these factors were best left to market forces, other economists such as Robert Reich and Laura D'Andrea Tyson argued that effective trade policies should link freer trade to policies that help workers, communities, and businesses adjust to foreign competition by upgrading worker skills.[30]

"Economic nationalists" and traditional isolationists such as columnist Patrick Buchanan had a different solution to the wage stagnation and economic insecurity of the late twentieth century. These traditional protectionists joined with neopopulists and religious fundamentalists seeking a return to traditional values and limited government. In the early 1990s they forged an anti–free trade and anti–big government alliance. They made no distinction between multilateral, regional, or bilateral approaches to trade liberalization. They simply wanted America to abandon freer trade policies.[31]

The visibility and political clout of this group was bolstered by the 1992 presidential campaign of billionaire (and independent) H. Ross Perot, who garnered some 19 percent of the vote. Not only did he criticize America's fiscal and budgetary policies, but he gained popular support for his opposition to the North American Free Trade Agreement (NAFTA). The NAFTA debate attracted a lot of public and media attention, as Americans debated whether NAFTA would lead to what Perot alleged, "a great sucking sound" of lost jobs and industries. Although some Americans did lose jobs, Perot's popularity had fizzled out by 1993. His organization, "United We Stand," however, had garnered a lot of public attention; it would continue to organize opposition to U.S. trade policies after the 1992 election. It would also put significant pressure on Republican members of Congress to take stands on the GATT and how it affected U.S. sovereignty.

Another source that would reinvigorate arguments for protectionism was a new social movement, the communitarian movement. Communitarians such as historian Christopher Lasch and sociologist Amitai Etzioni want a society based on values of social stability and justice, rather than one founded simply on market efficiency. They believe free trade threatens the social contract between American workers and American business, where workers are awarded with relatively high wages for labor peace and productivity.

Although not officially communitarians, growing numbers of opinion leaders began to make what sounded like communitarian arguments about trade. They included Michael Lind, senior editor at the *New Republic*; Edward Luttwak of the Center for Strategic Studies, a conservative/internationalist think tank; and Sir James Goldsmith, a British billionaire and member of the European parliament. Although the communitarian movement had little impact on policy, their views received media and congressional attention and helped make concerns about trade's impact on social stability a focus of the trade policy debate.[32]

But community activists (such as Public Citizen) as well as environmental groups (such as the Sierra Club) had a major impact on U.S. trade policy in the 1990s. In the late 1980s, during the Uruguay Round negotiations, Mark Ritchie of the Institute of Agriculture and Trade Policy (a Minnesota think tank) and Lori Wallach and Ralph Nader of Public Citizen awakened to the potential implications of multinational free trade policy for the achievement of their policy priorities. They had long viewed free trade policies as being in the corporate interest, but they came to believe that trade agreements could thwart the ability of the American people to determine health and safety standards at the state and local level. In 1991, 100 national organizations representing consumer, environmental, labor, family farm, religious and other civic groups banded together to promote "a citizens' agenda in U.S. trade policy." In 1993, the Citizens' Trade Campaign vowed "to implement a common strategy: to educate the public, media and elected officials . . . that citizens' interests are central to U.S. trade policy."[33]

·The Citizens Trade Campaign (composed principally of individuals with populist and leftward-leaning politics) would work with economic nationalists (composed principally of individuals with populist, conservative, and often rightward-leaning politics) and traditional protectionists (such as small businessmen and labor union officials) to oppose both NAFTA and GATT. They would return the trade policy debate to one about democracy as well as one about economics. But they also stimulated greater public interest in trade. As political analyst Kevin Phillips noted, this unusual coalition set out to prove that international economics was not beyond the bailiwick of the boobs on Main Street. Whereas the old protectionists expressed their frustrations by smashing Toyotas and Toshibas on Main Street and Capitol Hill, Public Citizen mounted a nationwide campaign to educate the public about how freer trade policies may affect the achievement of other policy goals.[34] This focus on winning the hearts and minds of the public gained U.S. trade policy public as well as media attention.

In 1993, trade became the talk of the town, as Americans debated whether to create the NAFTA.[35] Bilateral free trade agreements such as NAFTA are in accordance with GATT principles. The United States had established free trade agreements with Israel and Canada in the 1980s. But this would be the first time that the United States had contemplated a truly open trade agreement with a low-wage nation, with relatively weak labor, health, and environmental laws.[36] The NAFTA would deflect the attention of trade negotiators and Congress from the Uruguay Round. But NAFTA would help make trade policy more democratic, by educating and involving more Americans in trade.

The NAFTA Debate

NAFTA raised the visibility of trade because it made the debate over trade easy to understand. Although the NAFTA raised questions about environmental protection, immigration, drug interdiction, and democracy, the bulk of the NAFTA debate focused on one question—would NAFTA create or destroy jobs? A surprisingly large number of Americans found that interesting. In November 1993, 68 percent of those polled by Gallup said they followed NAFTA news closely. This compared favorably with the 77 percent who followed the O.J. Simpson case—the trial of a famous football star on murder charges.[37]

The NAFTA debate was American politics at its best, creating some unusual coalitions in support and in opposition. For example, the NAFTA was endorsed by all of America's living presidents, the U.S. Chamber of Commerce, the traditionally protectionist American Textile Manufacturers Institute, and the National Wildlife Federation. The Humane Society, Americans for Democratic Action, the National Consumers League, the National Family Farm Coalition, the United Auto Workers, the United Church of Christ, and the United Methodist Church joined to oppose the NAFTA. Opponents had a variety of concerns: many environmentalists feared that NAFTA would lead to greater environmental degradation, labor unions argued that factories would move jobs to Mexico, and progressives argued that the NAFTA was undemocratic and favored "big business."

However, President Clinton's chief trade negotiator, Ambassador Mickey Kantor, diffused some of this opposition. As the U.S. Trade Representative Kantor negotiated side agreements on labor and the environment.[38] Ultimately, NAFTA was endorsed by six environmental groups, including the Environmental Defense Fund, National Wildlife Federation, and the National Resources Defense Council, in the belief that border environmental conditions could be improved and that NAFTA's provisions would not undermine environmental protection.[39]

Although the Clinton administration had won support from some environmentalists, NAFTA would prove to be a tough sell. Proponents launched a major public relations initiative. At the White House, Clinton recruited Chicago politician and lawyer William Daley and former Republican congressman and Brookings Institution scholar William Frenzel to build bipartisan congressional support. To show how important the Clinton administration viewed NAFTA, this last-minute effort was run out of the White House "war room." The administration organized a "Product Day" at the White House, highlighting the big and small businesses that sell goods and services to Mexico. Proponents inside and outside government organized elite support to illustrate that business, foreign affairs, and community leaders were united in support of NAFTA. And they orchestrated public opinion by characterizing all NAFTA opponents as isolationists, fearful of change, and defeatist.

The turning point of the debate came when the administration was able to make Ross Perot the symbol of NAFTA opposition. On November 9, 1993, millions of Americans tuned into CNN (the Cable News Network) to watch Vice President Al Gore Jr. debate businessman H. Ross Perot on NAFTA. Gore not only calmly defended NAFTA, he seemed to link Perot, a man who made his fortune creating a high-tech industry (data processing), with old ideas and traditional fears about economic change.[40] Gore linked support of free trade to the future. Soon after, Congress narrowly passed NAFTA.

Gattzilla, representing GATT opponents' feeling that GATT was crushing democracy. Cartoon by Alex Garcia. Courtesy of Public Citizen

NAFTA's Effect on the GATT/WTO Debate

In this environment, the Clinton administration would seek support for congressional approval of the Uruguay Round, creating a new organization to govern trade, the World Trade Organization. But the NAFTA victory came at a real price for the GATT/WTO. Proponents of the GATT seemed to believe that it would arouse less opposition than the NAFTA, because the opposition (and its benefits) were more diffused. The White House also seemed to presume that bipartisanship and business support would sweep the GATT to victory. But the business community was slow to organize on behalf of the GATT/WTO. Until the last minute, business interests seemed more enthused by NAFTA. Moreover, the business community was divided about the Uruguay Round; many business leaders were waiting to see the specifics of the congressional implementing legislation.

Popular support for the Uruguay Round and the creation of the WTO was also not ensured among the American people. The NAFTA debate had conveyed a message that free trade agreements served the interest of big business and not necessarily that of the man and woman on the street. Moreover, the NAFTA debate had taught a very diverse opposition of environmentalists, isolationists, economic nationalists, and social activists how to work together to educate the public at the national and grassroots levels. Finally, the debate taught these opponents how to talk about trade in ways that the public could relate to and in forums to which the general public would listen. This experience, however, did not pay off in an increased ability to motivate the public. Although growing numbers of Americans had been awakened to the implications of free trade policy, they seemed less engaged by the GATT/WTO debate than by NAFTA.

The NAFTA debate did forge a lasting bond among a diverse group of Americans galvanized in opposition to trade. They created an Internet bulletin board with updates on the Uruguay Round on Capitol Hill and used faxes, computers, modems, and talk shows to unite widely dispersed Americans. Bruce Warnick, a volunteer for United We Stand, sent faxes around the United States, directing citizens to call their legislators in opposition first to NAFTA, then to GATT. Warnick was credited with convincing many Republican leaders to question the WTO.[41]

The NAFTA debate also marked the emergence of a new means of influencing trade policy—the radio talk show—and a new tool for understanding the trade policy-making process—C-Span. Radio talk shows provided a means for the public to debate trade policy and to ask questions of influential opinion leaders. C-Span covered the hearings and congressional debate. During the Uruguay Round's months on Capitol Hill, this cable news channel would reveal the progress of the implementing legislation deal-making process.[42] For growing numbers of Americans, these venues became a major source of insight into the costs and benefits of America's trade policies.

Although print and television newscasters also covered trade policy, they were less attentive to the implications of the Uruguay Round for the American people and the polity. They covered the implementing legislation like a campaign or a horserace and they tended to emphasize the negative. Headlines described trade policy—not as a win-win exchange among nations and peoples, but as a competition or a "zero-sum game." Television and radio news referred to America's trade "wars" with Japan and China and described the European community as "fortress Europe." *The Wall Street Journal* and *Business Week* were notable exceptions.[43]

Thus, it was not the debate over multilateral trade liberalization, but rather the NAFTA, a regional free trade agreement, that awakened the American people to trade. And their awakening was accompanied by growing dissension among America's opinion leaders as to the benefits of multilateral trade liberalization. It was unclear how Americans would respond to the supposedly less controversial but economically more important Uruguay Round.

10
Present at the Creation of the WTO, 1986–1994

In a 1993 speech early in his presidency, Bill Clinton acknowledged his own ambivalence about American leadership of global efforts to liberalize trade through the GATT. "For all the . . . opportunity in this global economy, an American cannot approach it without mixed feelings." The president admitted that freer trade policies had led to job loss and lowered wages for some Americans, but then he argued, "Far more is at stake. For this new fabric of commerce will also shape global prosperity or the lack of it, and with it the prospects of people around the world for democracy, freedom and peace." Clinton warned his fellow citizens that if they want a better future for their children, Americans must continue to reach outward.[1]

The president was not alone in his ambivalence about the costs and benefits of free trade. On Capitol Hill, members of Congress developed a multitude of new approaches to trade policy. None of these approaches repudiated U.S. leadership of the GATT, but they signaled a growing disenchantment with the results of multilateralism. And this questioning was not confined to Washington. Although many Americans recognized that they benefited from imported cars, clothes, wine, and televisions, they were not sure that American leadership of the GATT would ensure a sunny future for their children.[2]

In 1994 the Clinton administration sought approval for the eighth round of trade barrier reductions under the GATT. This round established a new World Trade Organization (WTO) to administer the agreement.[3] This chapter focuses on this debate. The WTO is not the ITO reborn; each is a product of its own economic and political times.[4] Most Americans, including many members of Congress, had never heard of the ITO. Yet the failure of the ITO haunted the deliberations over the GATT/WTO. As in the postwar era, proponents saw in this innovation a way to keep the U.S.

economy growing. Opponents saw a threat to American democracy and expressed fears that the American dream might be fading for their children.[5]

Neither the president nor Congress moved rapidly on GATT in 1993-94. The president's top priority was health care reform. GATT opponents constructed a variety of roadblocks, and Democrats and Republicans on Capital Hill found many reasons to stall development of the implementing legislation.[6] Nor was the public screaming for congressional action. Most Americans had little understanding of the GATT and were increasingly frustrated with international organizations (the United Nations was faulted for its failure to prevent violence in Somalia and Bosnia). And policy-makers did little to tell them why the GATT needed to be transformed into a new international organization, the World Trade Organization, when the GATT had worked so well for almost fifty years.

Congress and the World Trade Organization

Policymakers and opinion leaders were the force behind the creation of the WTO. In the United States and overseas, policymakers recognized that GATT was hampered by the lack of a formal institutional structure and rules tying together all of the GATT and its ancillary codes (such as the subsidies codes). Since membership in the codes was optional, GATT contracting parties did not adhere to all the side codes. In addition, GATT's contracting parties continued to develop creative ways to avoid or misinterpret GATT rules. International business executives, academics, members of Congress, and trade policy officials among others, concluded that GATT's lack of a formal structure was a "birth defect" that needed to be fixed.[7] But the public was unaware of the need for surgery.

Reagan, Bush, and Clinton administration trade policymakers recognized that GATT needed a stronger institutional standing, but they were not enthusiastic about creating a new international organization to govern world trade. Nonetheless, they accepted creation of a firmer foundation for GATT as an important Uruguay Round objective. But the round dragged on for more than seven years. In an effort to move the negotiations forward, in December 1991, the director general of the GATT, Arthur Dunkel, proposed and published a comprehensive text of the draft agreement, which was leaked to Public Citizen, a consumer activist group (home to the Citizens' Trade Campaign). This action forced trade negotiators to identify their positions on the draft text.[8] It also allowed proponents and opponents of the GATT to see firsthand where the negotiations were going and to comment on them. Much of the ensuing debate focused on a tentative draft of a new charter for a multilateral trade organization and its perceived effect on U.S. sovereignty.

Despite the very real differences among nations as to the responsibilities of this proposed organization, on December 15, 1993, 117 nations finally reached agreement on the Uruguay Round and the new structure for the GATT, to be called the WTO. The WTO Charter provided legal authority for a secretariat, a director general, and a staff. It also included a strengthened and unified dispute settlement mechanism.[9]

As with the GATT, the proposed WTO could not force changes in U.S. law. If a WTO panel found the United States in violation of the trade rules established under the WTO, the United States had several options: it could change its laws or regulations; it could offer compensation through lowered trade barriers in other areas; or the United States could accept equivalent foreign retaliation through increased barriers to U.S. exports.[10] These same options existed under the GATT, but they were not well understood by members of Congress or the general public.

Clinton administration officials argued that the new WTO was simply an evolution of the GATT, which would "encompass the current GATT structure and extend it to new disciplines that have not been adequately covered in the past. . . . The organization would not be different in character from that of the existing GATT secretariat."[11] Eminent legal scholar John H. Jackson took a slightly different tack. He noted that because the WTO addresses how decisions should be made, "there are more legal grounds to challenge WTO decisions," and "thus the protection of national sovereignty built into the WTO . . . [is] substantially enhanced over the GATT." Given America's great weight in the trading system, it is unlikely that the WTO could force the United States to substantially change its behavior or laws. However, he concluded that "the WTO has no more real power than that which existed for the GATT."[12]

But many prominent groups and individuals did not see the WTO as a simple evolution of the GATT. They joined together to question turning the informal GATT into a formal WTO. To these Americans of the right and left, the Uruguay Round would not only create a new international entity, but it would be undemocratic and unresponsive to public concerns. According to former California governor Edmund G. "Jerry" Brown, "Instead of democratic decisions made at the state and local level, under GATT . . . we would all be subjected to a supergovernment of unelected trade bureaucrats."[13] Some opponents wondered if consumer or environmental concerns could even be heard at the international level. As Mark Ritchie and Karen Lehman of the Institute for Agriculture and Trade Policy noted, the WTO may "make it extremely difficult for citizens to continue to use the democratic process to push for further progress."[14]

Even supporters of the strengthening of the GATT infrastructure questioned the WTO's effects on sovereignty. Clyde Prestowitz, former trade negotiator and president of the Economic Strategy Institute, noted that "the environmentalists . . . are correct when they express their concern for the potential reversal of U.S. regulations via findings of the WTO."[15]

Throughout 1994, Americans expressed concern about the GATT/WTO. In a unusual press conference, Ralph Nader, liberal icon and founder of the consumer movement, joined forces with Patrick Buchanan, 1992 presidential candidate, news columnist, and conservative icon, to denounce the WTO's perceived impact on U.S. sovereignty.[16] Some industry representatives were opposed to the enhanced dispute settlement mechanism, which established a more formal legalistic process by which disputes would be reviewed and settled. Many of these opponents, however, were mollified by changes to the implementing legislation.[17] Democratic Representative Jill Long and Republican Senators Larry Pressler, Jesse Helms, and Larry Craig, among others, expressed concern that this new WTO would be undemocratic, make decisions in a closed manner, and be staffed by unresponsive faceless bureaucrats. In May, Senators Helms and Pressler raised questions as to why the Uruguay Round was not being submitted to the Congress as a treaty, given that it created a new international organization. Fifty-five members of the Congress (both Democrats and Republicans) urged President Clinton to delay the vote on the Uruguay Round until July 1995.[18]

Deadlines and Money Politics

But delay could jeopardize congressional passage of the Uruguay Round. The Congress had given the administration "fast-track authority," which required that once the president formally submitted implementing legislation to the Congress, both houses had to vote up or down on the bill without changes within ninety days. This did not mean there would be no debate or changes to the implementing legislation in the months prior to its submission. Nonetheless, the fast-track time clock would prove to be a major problem for the GATT/WTO; its requirements would further an impression that the GATT/WTO and U.S. trade policy were undemocratic.

The Uruguay Round's travels through the Congress were also hampered by the issue of funding the revenue shortfall resulting from the Uruguay Round's substantial tariff reductions. The Budget Enforcement Act of 1990 established "pay-as-you-go mechanisms to ensure that any new entitlement or receipt legislation will not increase the deficit." New legislation which decreases federal receipts (such as tariff reductions under the Uruguay Round) "triggers automatic spending reductions unless the costs of the legislation are offset." (The Congressional Budget Office estimated the five-year revenue loss from the Uruguay Round at some $12 billion.) House Republican Whip Newt Gingrich demanded that the administration change the budget rules used to assess the cost of trade agreements "or make a commitment not to raise taxes to offset the revenue cost of the Uruguay Round."[19]

The funding requirements were further complicated by Senate budgetary requirements. Senate rules required fiscal offsets for ten years, which the Senate Budget Committee estimated at a whopping $43 billion. (But this amount went unquestioned because the administration refused to offer funding proposals for the ten-year amount and the Congressional Budget Office refused to offer ten-year cost estimates for the GATT or any other legislation.) To get around the ten-year rule, the administration decided to ask for a waiver of the Senate's budget rules. Thus, Senators would not only have to vote on the GATT/WTO implementing legislation, but sixty senators would have to approve an exemption to the Senate's budget rules.[20]

GATT funding created a great problem for the administration. Policymakers wanted to argue that the Uruguay Round would be a net tax cut for American consumers and producers. But the administration did not want to tackle trying to change the budget rules; they feared it would open the door to other tax cuts and thus increase America's already large budget deficit. Administration officials also recognized that any changes that they proposed, whether revenue enhancements or budget reductions, would arouse opposition, and that opposition would hurt the GATT/WTO on Capitol Hill. Finally, the administration would have to use up some of its limited political capital on the funding question, leaving less for the GATT/WTO.[21]

The funding problem helped make the GATT/WTO debate more partisan, but it also brought to the fore concerns about democracy and U.S. trade policy. The administration worked for months to find ways to balance the tariff cuts with revenue increases and spending cuts.[22] Draft legislation slowly worked its way through the Senate Finance and House Ways and Means Committees.[23] As it traveled through the Congress, prominent Republicans and Democrats used the debate to project their own views of trade policy (for example, Senator Ernest F. Hollings) or to advance their political careers (Senator Robert Dole and Congressman Newt Gingrich). They showed a willingness to play politics with the fate of the Uruguay Round. And they often used the sovereignty issue as a tool to challenge presidential leadership on trade.

Focusing on Opinion Leaders

Like the policymakers who preceded them, the Clinton administration did not focus on winning the hearts and minds of average Americans.[24] Although key trade policy officials appeared on talk shows to parry with the pundits, they rarely met with members of the general public to hear their concerns about the Uruguay Round. Proponents focused on opinion leaders in Congress, in the media, in business, and in the community.

The administration initially relied on old arguments about jobs and economic growth to defend the WTO. In speeches, letters, and official documents, the administration stressed that the GATT agreement would create jobs for "hundreds of thousands of Americans" and set up a more effective "foundation for prosperity." The Department of Commerce prepared estimates of the GATT's impact on jobs and economic growth for each state and for each major sector of the economy.[25] Proponents also argued that the GATT would bring future prosperity, noting that the emerging markets of Poland, China, Chile, Brazil, . . . were the markets of the future. Their demand for U.S. goods would raise the U.S. standard of living by providing high-paying jobs.[26] But this indirect argument did not seem to reassure many Americans.

Proponents outside the government also focused on building the support of elites. They formed a coalition, the Alliance for GATT NOW, to act as a clearinghouse for information on the Uruguay Round, to lobby members of Congress and editorial boards, and to organize general support for the Round. The alliance eventually had a membership of more than 200,000 small and large businesses. It also included business and agricultural associations. However, because no community or labor groups joined the Alliance, the GATT/WTO (like the NAFTA before) was vulnerable to arguments that it was designed to benefit big business rather than average Americans.

Although some business leaders were very concerned about public opinion, the Alliance did not focus on gaining grassroots support for the GATT/WTO. For example, the Alliance commissioned a poll of public opinion on the GATT, which indicated that the more information people received about GATT, the more likely they were to support it. But the Alliance used the poll to convince lawmakers of public support, rather than as a tool to find areas of public concern or misunderstanding and address them.[27]

GATT/WTO proponents' focus on Congress was understandable. Because the Uruguay Round was so broad and so controversial, there were many hearings on various aspects of the Round during the 103d Congress.[28] But the implications of changing the GATT to the WTO was never

To show that GATT was a "home run for America," the Alliance for GATT NOW issued collector cards. GATT All-Stars included Presidents Reagan, Bush, and Clinton. The set included cards that analyzed GATT's effect on the fifty state economies. Courtesy of the Alliance for GATT NOW

far from the debate. The Senate Commerce, Senate Foreign Relations, and House Ways and Means Committees held specific hearings on the WTO and how this new institution might affect U.S. law.[29]

To bolster support for the WTO, the administration relied on a bipartisan coalition of leaders, including Republican Senator Bob Packwood, Representative Bill Archer, and Representative Jim Kolbe. In testimony to the House Ways and Means Committee, U.S. Trade Representative Ambassador Mickey Kantor noted that "everyone from Consumers Union, from . . . Jack Kemp to Judge Bork . . . have said that U.S. sovereignty is not affected, in fact may even be enhanced."[30] The administration distributed a letter to every member of Congress discussing its dispute settlement mechanisms, how decisions would be made in the WTO, and how these decisions affect U.S. law. The letter stressed that legal scholar John H. Jackson, Nixon administration official Peter Suchman, and Heritage

Foundation (a conservative think tank) economist Joe Cobb all support the WTO and believe it will not negatively affect U.S. sovereignty. The letter also included an analysis by conservative law professor Robert Bork. Cobb was vilified for his support of economic internationalism in many right-wing papers. But he went on the counterattack, linking anti–WTO sentiment to support for big government. He issued a memorandum to every Senate and House Republican staff member, noting that the only real threat to U.S. sovereignty is traditional protectionism, "the concerted effort by special interests . . . to focus all power over the American economic system in the hands of Congress and the bureaucrats in Washington."[31]

The Cobb and Bork analyses helped give "cover" to Republicans and conservatives concerned about sovereignty. But they were still vulnerable to the concerns about sovereignty presented by Harvard legal scholar Lawrence Tribe, Reagan administration lawyer Bruce Fein, a letter signed by forty state attorneys general, and the arguments of the Senate's reigning constitutional scholar, Robert Byrd.[32] Throughout 1994, Congress remained concerned that the WTO would weaken U.S. law.[33]

Not surprisingly, the history of the ITO haunted the GATT/WTO debate, as the sovereignty issue gained increasing attention. Proponents frequently defended the WTO by saying it was not the ITO. Both the *Wall Street Journal* and *Time* wrote articles about how the WTO congressional debate mirrored congressional debate about the ITO. And Senator Daniel Patrick Moynihan, chairman of the Senate Finance Committee, kept reminding his colleagues of the ITO's fate on Capitol Hill.[34]

Many of the arguments against the WTO echoed those against the ITO. For example, as with the ITO, opponents would preface their opposition by saying, "I am a free trader, but . . ." They delivered a message that the WTO wasn't worth the price in U.S. sovereignty or in the thwarted achievement of other policy goals.[35] As in the postwar period, the legal community was divided. In 1994, law professors Lawrence Tribe, Anne-Marie Slaughter, Richard Parker, and William Lovett questioned the WTO's potential impact on democratic self-government. But speaking for the American Bar Association, attorney Claire Reade said that the ABA viewed the WTO as not detracting from U.S. domestic legal powers, and she announced that the ABA supported the WTO.[36]

As in the postwar period, some opponents argued that American workers could not compete against these low-wage foreign competitors; in 1994 they warned that the GATT/WTO would decimate U.S. jobs. But the GATT/WTO's proponents argued just the opposite—echoing the ITO's architects, they presumed it would create jobs, especially high-wage jobs.[37] And opponents again used the job-loss issue to bash U.S. policymakers. Tulane economist and law professor William Lovett condemned U.S. economic leadership, noting that jobs had been lost because the United States failed to use its bargaining leverage effectively under the GATT. Sounding like Representative Jacob Javits, who so eloquently defended the ITO, Senate Majority Leader George J. Mitchell of Maine countered that "we should not measure this trade agreement against a perfect and unrealizable ideal. . . . We don't trade with countries made in heaven."[38]

During the ITO debate, policymakers had insisted on a comprehensive approach to trade policy to link foreign and domestic policy goals. During the GATT/WTO debate, however, new interest groups (principally environmental, citizens, and labor groups) were the ones calling for a more comprehensive approach to trade policy. They recognized that trade policy could thwart the achievement of equally important domestic policy objectives such as protecting the environment or encouraging the survival of small family farms. To a certain degree they succeeded; even some business leaders argued that domestic and trade policy goals needed to be better reconciled and that was an appropriate function for a WTO.[39]

But to many Republicans and business leaders, such linkages were anathema.[40] Congressman Newt Gingrich pressed Ambassador Kantor about whether he would use the WTO "to expand labor and environmental standards," thereby transforming the GATT into more than a trade agreement. Kantor responded by saying that "addressing the intersection of labor standards and . . . environment and trade will only help enhance a world trading system."[41] Ironically, many of the same "purists" in business and in the Congress would find themselves defending a GATT/WTO that included a Committee on Trade and the Environment and congressional implementing legislation that would direct the president to seek a working party on labor standards within the WTO.[42]

This was not the only blurring of positions. On one hand, administration officials argued that the U.S. must approve the Round to maintain U.S. leadership and status. But their push for the WTO was an implicit acknowledgment that, given America's declining economic clout, the United States needed a strong international organization to change the behavior of its trading partners. In effect, this view acknowledged that the United States could no longer use the pressure of access to America's enormous market to bludgeon its trading partners into behaving correctly. Ambassador Jules Katz, who had been a key negotiator, noted the irony in the sovereignty arguments against the WTO. He stressed that because the WTO's infrastructure is "bare-boned," the WTO will not be strong enough to provide the "effectiveness of the kind that sometimes we seek." Claude Barfield of the American Enterprise Institute noted that the WTO

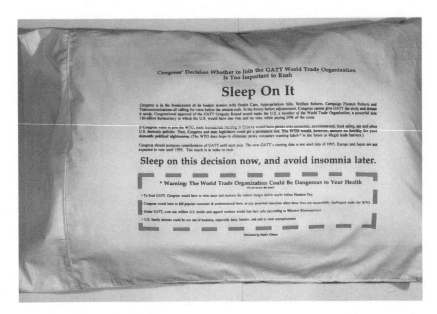

Days before the vote on GATT, Public Citizen went door to door in Congress with pillowcases suggesting that Congress "sleep on it." Courtesy of Public Citizen

would probably not improve on the GATT's ability to get countries to abide by the rules.[43]

GATT/WTO opponents also offered confusing and sometimes exaggerated arguments. Democratic Senator Ernest Hollings argued against the GATT/WTO because he believed free trade had only hurt the United States and the American people. He noted that nations such as Japan had been especially skillful at exploiting the GATT to expand their share of the U.S. market. He then argued that the United States should behave more like Japan, a nation that had grown rich because of its focus on trade.[44] Charles McMillion, an economist and head of MBG Information Services, said about GATT claims, "not since the Vietnam War has our government and media lied to us so outrageously." In a telephone discussion, Dr. McMillion clarified that the administration never mentioned how imports affected jobs in America; they only focused on how exports "create" jobs. Therein lay the "lie."[45]

The debate over GATT/WTO raised important real questions about whether or not American law and institutions *should* adapt to the global economy. To some opponents, the WTO would not only affect the ability of individuals to influence government; it would also upset federal-state relations. One of the most interesting arguments used by WTO opponents

Concerned about the ticking legislative clock, the Alliance distributed this pamphlet to Congress. Alliance for GATT NOW

was that of states' rights—the rights of states to preserve their standards for health and safety. On June 27, 1994, twenty-two state attorneys general wrote President Clinton asking the administration to "explain how states will be able to defend their laws from foreign challenges before World Trade Organization panels." They also asked if implementing legislation can guarantee that the federal government will accept trade sanctions rather than pressure states to change state laws that are successfully challenged in the WTO."[46] Sierra Club attorney Patti Goldman noted, "The current structure gives the federal government the power through preemption, withholding federal funds, and litigation to compel changes in state laws that conflict" with trade agreements. Although the administration will consult with state governments on state standards, the federal government has the power to "trump" state law. In advertisements opposing the WTO, the Sierra Club argued that foreign nations will use the GATT/WTO to challenge these laws, noting "every state is affected."[47]

Senator Bob Dole, the Republican leader, heard the concerns about sovereignty. On August 28, Senator Dole wrote an editorial in the *Wichita Eagle* suggesting that members of Congress should take their time in assessing the GATT/WTO. Although Dole stated he was "not trying to hustle opposition to the GATT," he argued that the administration was ignoring legitimate concerns about how the GATT/WTO would affect American laws and practice. Dole said he was receiving about two thousand phone calls each day on GATT. GATT/WTO proponents were alarmed by Dole's actions, for he had long supported both internationalism and free trade. Tom Mann, director of Governmental Studies at the Brookings Institution gave two interpretations of the senator's actions: he could be interested in embarrassing the president, or he could be unravelling the GATT by stalling. To satisfy Senator Dole's concerns, the Clinton administration agreed to support legislation that would establish a panel of judges to review the WTO panel decisions that the United States loses. If the judges decided that three WTO panels have exceeded their authority in finding against the United States, it would trigger a process under which the U.S. could pull out of the WTO. (However, this "three strikes and we're out" provision did not appease some Americans concerned about sovereignty, because the standard of review would be very difficult to meet.) The U.S. trade representative also agreed to submit an annual report on the WTO and the openness of the decisionmaking process. With these changes, Senator Dole promised to support the GATT/WTO.[48]

Dole was not the only "supporter" of the GATT to question the WTO's impact upon U.S. sovereignty. In an April television interview, Representative Newt Gingrich linked the proposed World Trade Organization to "this mess in Bosnia and the United Nations' incompetence." He asked if Americans "really want to create the United Nations of world trade?" Nor was such questioning limited to Republican members of Congress. In Senate testimony, James Fallows, Washington editor of the *Atlantic Monthly,* noted that he supported the GATT/WTO, but he warned that it couldn't meet U.S. expectations and harmonize the world's varied economic interests.[49] These concerns were understandable. But ambivalence about the WTO, especially among Republicans, served to legitimize fears about its potential impact on U.S. sovereignty.

The Committee on Government Affairs reported the bill "without recommendation," noting that the authority of the World Trade Organization does not supersede the sovereign powers of state governments or the federal government. However, the committee issued a warning about the WTO's potential impact on U.S. sovereignty. "This Committee takes very seriously the issue of Federalism."[50] They promised to hold executive branch officials accountable to ensure that U.S. sovereignty is protected and that the WTO become more democratic.

On September 27, final drafts of the implementing legislation were introduced in both Houses and referred to the relevant committees of jurisdiction. The ninety-day time clock had begun, and it included the mid-

Ambassador Michael Kantor and Vice President Albert C. Gore Jr. at a press conference on Capitol Hill hosted by the Alliance for GATT NOW and arranged by the Fratelli Group. Photos by John Harrington. Courtesy of the Fratelli Group

term election in November. But a Democratic senator, Ernest Hollings, stopped the clock, holding the implementing legislation in his committee, the Senate Commerce Committee, for forty-five days. The vote was delayed until after the congressional election. The House was scheduled to return on November 29, 1994, for the sole purpose of considering the Uruguay Round agreement. The Senate was now scheduled to reconvene on November 30 and to vote on the agreement on December 1. Supporters worried that a lame-duck session might not have the political will to approve U.S. participation in this new international organization.

This concern helped invigorate the GATT/WTO's proponents. Business groups tried to keep the GATT/WTO from becoming an election-year issue, and they stepped up their lobbying with a multimillion dollar media campaign. Some fifty newspapers endorsed the GATT/WTO, including all of the nationwide papers (*USA Today, Wall Street Journal, Journal of Commerce, Washington Post,* and *New York Times*). The Alliance for GATT NOW sent out press releases noting that former trade officials, forty governors, former presidents, and 450 leading economists endorsed the Uruguay Round. They issued fact sheets on the budget waiver, the costs of delay, and myths and realities regarding the sovereignty issue.[51] Moreover, they spent money defending the GATT/WTO with a nationwide series of television advertisements (two of which linked GATT to baseball) and a targeted series of print advertisements in key newspapers.

GATT A HOME RUN FOR AMERICA

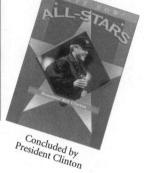

Started by
President Reagan

Negotiated by
President Bush

Concluded by
President Clinton

The General Agreement on Tariffs and Trade Will:

- Add between $100 and $200 billion to the U.S. economy once it is fully implemented.

- Create over 1 million jobs—jobs that pay more than the average U.S. job.

- Allow U.S. companies to export more goods, services, and agricultural products.

- Cut tariffs on U.S. goods exported to foreign countries. Foreign countries have more trade restrictions on U.S. exports than we have on their imports.

- Protect U.S. "intellectual property" such as patents, trademarks, and copyrights from foreign piracy, helping leading U.S. industries such as entertainment, pharmaceutical, high technology, and computer software.

- Make sure that all 120 nations that sign the GATT play by the same rules we do.

Paid for by the Alliance for GATT NOW.

Alliance for GATT NOW

Alliance for GATT NOW

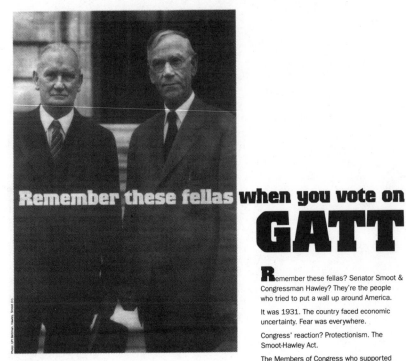

Remember these fellas when you vote on

GATT

Remember these fellas? Senator Smoot & Congressman Hawley? They're the people who tried to put a wall up around America.

It was 1931. The country faced economic uncertainty. Fear was everywhere.

Congress' reaction? Protectionism. The Smoot-Hawley Act.

The Members of Congress who supported that bill attached their names to one of the most infamous – and destructive – pieces of legislation ever passed by the United States Congress.

Now, it's 1994. The country faces economic uncertainty.

What will Congress do?

Vote America's Future.
Vote GATT.

With GATT, Congress has an historic opportunity to open foreign markets to American products and services and reject protectionism. A vote for GATT will add billions to the U.S. economy and create new high-paying American jobs.

GATT gives us the largest global tax cut in history, stops foreign countries from cheating on trade and makes over 120 nations play by the same rules we do.

So, when you vote on GATT, keep these two fellas in mind.

And remember: History has not been kind to those in Congress who embrace protectionism.

Representative Willis Hawley on left, Senator Reed Smoot on right. Alliance for GATT NOW

WHILE THE MEDIA SLEPT,

THE GATTISTAS TIGHTENED THEIR GRIP ON AMERICA.

The major media coverage this year of the Uruguay Round of the General Agreement on Tariffs and Trade (GATT) establishing the World Trade Organization (WTO) is classic official policy journalism. Government and other pro-GATT statements and reports were extensively covered; critical statements, testimony, reports and events were mostly ignored. Here are some samples of what major media editors and reporters rejected as non-newsworthy:

1. Fifty-one leaders of news organizations and media groups sent a letter to President Clinton on September 14, 1994 denouncing the secrecy and inaccessibility of the WTO's deliberations as "an affront to the democratic traditions of this nation." Not newsworthy -- no coverage

2. More than 30 State Attorneys General and other state officials protested incursions on state sovereignty by the WTO's secret tribunals in a letter to Clinton July 6, 1994. Not newsworthy -- no coverage

3. Native American tribes issued a statement on November 13, 1994 criticizing the Clinton Administration for not consulting them about GATT/WTO agreement and declaring that tribal sovereignty is not subject to WTO jurisdiction. Not newsworthy -- no coverage

4. Six Committees of Congress held hearings earlier this year which included critics from a wide range of constituencies. Not newsworthy -- no coverage

5. A dozen news conferences presenting new information were held by labor, consumer, environmental, farm, church and animal rights groups. All not newsworthy -- no coverage. News conferences aside, the positions of these groups were later reduced to one sentence objections.

6. House and Senate critics staked out positions on the budget waiver and the timing of the vote. Budget Director Alice Rivlin sent a letter to Senators declaring "...we do not believe it is necessary to sacrifice budget discipline to pass GATT in the Congress. In fact, we fear that if Congress were to reverse the progress that has been made on budget discipline over the past few years, we could lose more than we would gain from the GATT accords." Not newsworthy -- no coverage

7. Over 130 Americans urged deferral of the GATT/WTO vote until next year in an August 8, 1994 letter to Clinton, including such opposites as Gloria Steinem and Phyllis Schlafly, and Pat Buchanan and James MacGregor Burns. Not newsworthy -- no coverage

8. A major controversy, initiated by Senator Robert Byrd, over whether the GATT/WTO should be considered a treaty (requiring 2/3 ratification by the Senate) or a trade agreement (requiring a majority vote in both Houses) was presented before the Senate Commerce Committee on October 18, 1994 by leading constitutional law specialists. Not newsworthy -- no coverage

9. A report by Georgetown University Law Professor Robert Stumberg listed many California laws at risk to challenge under the proposed GATT/WTO. Not newsworthy -- no coverage

10. Reports this spring by Japan, the European Community and Canada asserted the probable illegality under GATT/WTO of numerous federal and state consumer, environmental, workplace, tax laws and other authorities such as Super 301 affecting American living standards. Not newsworthy -- no coverage

11. Analyses demonstrating the fanciful figures on alleged financing of the Pact, on the GNP benefits and job gains from the WTO agreement were publicly released. Not newsworthy -- no coverage

12. The detailed structure of the WTO, with only 120 nation members, has a one nation-one vote policy, no veto rights, secret tribunals and standards harmonization mandates. Not newsworthy -- no coverage. Major media preferred to repeat the White House's disinformation on this topic.

13. Authentically, dramatic Senate hearings were held on September 12, 1994 on brutalized child labor in foreign countries producing goods for the U.S. market and how a proposed U.S. ban on such products by 14 Senators would be GATT/WTO illegal, later verified by the Congressional Research Service. Not newsworthy -- no coverage

14. Although the media cover themselves, they failed to cover this deplorable year-long official policy journalism. They missed story after important story. Even the irony of these major newspapers editorializing in favor of GATT/WTO, while their own reporters would be prohibited from covering WTO proceedings, went unnoticed.

The opponents of the GATT/WTO received little coverage even though they pushed Congress to postpone the GATT vote from April to June to August to September and now to a lame duck session where some 90 job-seeking lame ducks are returning to vote on this momentous matter.

The only two polls conducted by reputable polling firms have registered major skepticism and large majorities against various dimensions of this legislative package behind the GATT/WTO.

It is true, as reporter David Sanger of the New York Times has written (11/20/94): "Over the past year the Administration tried desperately to keep anyone from noticing GATT." But apart from some professional reporting by one wire service, some radio shows and an occasional regional paper feature:

WHY DID THE MEDIA LET THE CLINTON ADMINISTRATION MANAGE THEIR NEWS AND DEFINE THE NON-NEWS FOR THEM?

Congressional Accountability Project, Public Citizen

Senators Campbell, Grassley, Warner, Kohl and D'Amato:

Remember when you opposed *"any effort"* to waive the budget for GATT?

United States Senate

WASHINGTON, DC 20510

July 15, 1994

President William J. Clinton
The White House
1600 Pennsylvania Avenue, N.W.
Washington, D.C. 20500

Dear President Clinton:

We write to ask that you join us in opposing any effort to waive provisions of the Budget Enforcement Act for the General Agreement on Tariffs and Trade (GATT) implementing legislation and avoid the requirement that such legislation be fully funded.

Some of us support GATT, others of us oppose the agreement, and still others of us have yet to make a decision, but we are united in our concern about the precedent waiving the provisions of the Budget Enforcement Act could set, undermining our ability to make further progress in lowering the deficit now and in the future.

We are confronted on a regular basis with having to make tough decisions on worthy programs because of our budget rules, and rightly so. **The federal budget deficit must be brought down.**

That GATT is significant is clear, but **the importance of an issue should not determine whether or not it should conform with the budget rules we have set for ourselves.** Indeed, the true test of our resolve to bring the deficit under control is our willingness to apply the budget rules to the important issues.

We recognize your commitment to passing GATT implementing legislation. Your support for making that legislation comply with the budget rules will be all the more meaningful because of that commitment, and **we hope you will join us in this effort to oppose any effort to dodge this responsibility.**

Sincerely,

(Emphasis added)

The Voters Do.

Will you __break__ your word and __bust__ the budget?

Don't Waver on the Waiver.
Don't Bust the Budget for GATT!

Citizens Trade Campaign 1025 Vermont Avenue, NW, Suite 300, Washington, DC 20005. (202) 879-4297

Citizens Trade Campaign, Public Citizen

Meanwhile, WTO opponents, like ITO opponents, forged a broad coalition well versed in influencing Washington. WTO opponents included neopopulists, the NAACP, United We Stand, small farmers, the AFL-CIO, small business, isolationists, business leaders, human rights activists, libertarians, environmentalists, and community activists. In contrast with the NAFTA, the environmentalists did not break ranks—they remained united in opposition to the GATT/WTO.[52]

The glue holding this diverse coalition together was the sovereignty issue. The opposition lobbied and made the rounds of talk shows and community centers. While Public Citizen condemned GATTZILLA, United We Stand protested "the general agreement on tyranny and treason." An articulate lawyer from Public Citizen, Lori Wallach, and devoted "economic nationalist" Bruce Warnick, worked hard to ensure that concerns about sovereignty got a lot of attention on Capitol Hill.[53]

On September 14, some fifty members of the Fourth Estate wrote President Clinton a letter arguing that the WTO proposal was "an affront to the democratic traditions of this nation." Writing "as advocates for openness in government," they argued not against the WTO per se but against its decisionmaking procedures. Among more than fifty signatories were the president of the Society of Professional Journalists and the editors of the *Cincinnati Enquirer,* the *Detroit News,* the *Detroit Free Press, USA Today,* and the *Miami Herald.* Many of their papers had endorsed the GATT/WTO, but the writers believed it did not "conform with democratic practices and principles."[54] Their arguments about the undemocratic nature of GATT were bolstered when it became public knowledge that the *Washington Post,* one of America's most influential papers, had strongly editorialized for the GATT at the same time a *Post* subsidiary was positioned to benefit from financing rules arranged in the GATT implementing legislation.[55] As trade analyst I.M. Destler noted, this only reinforced the idea "pressed by Nader, Perot and their allies—that the GATT legislation was the very sort of secret, inside deal and back scratching among narrow interests in Washington." Opponents of the GATT/WTO told the public "The corporate pressure to pass GATT is immense."[56]

Public Citizen tried to alert the public that congressional approval of GATT was undemocratic. They noted most members of Congress hadn't read the implementing legislation and had no idea about the powers of the WTO. To get public attention, Ralph Nader, the founder of Public Citizen, challenged every lawmaker to take a quiz on the GATT. Only one senator, Hank Brown of Colorado, took him up on the quiz. Afterward, the senator noted that he was persuaded to vote against the GATT. Although a few journalists covered the quiz, it actually attracted little attention. Like the editors' letter and the *Washington Post* "deal," the quiz did not create the public concern that Public Citizen had hoped.[57] To derail the GATT/WTO, opponents of the GATT next looked to the 1994 congressional election.

At first, the GATT/WTO looked iffy. The Republicans won a majority in both Houses, and the media interpreted their victory as a repudiation of President Clinton's leadership. Despite the fifty-year record of trade bipartisanship, some Republicans seemed willing to deny Clinton a victory to show their power. Moreover, the administration could not necessarily count on the Democrats. On one hand, retiring and defeated members could vote however they wanted, without voter punishment. On the other hand, their vote could be discredited as not legitimately reflecting their constituents. GATT opponents argued that a vote on GATT could be illegitimate, because many of the voting lawmakers were defeated or retired. On November 10, Senators Jesse Helms, Strom Thurmond, and Larry Craig wrote to Senator Dole, urging that Congress delay consideration "in light of our Party's victory on November 8."[58]

But supporters began a deluge of positive public relations for the GATT/WTO. Administration officials went on the stump for the GATT, trying to create the impression that a GATT/WTO win was inevitable. At a speech at Georgetown University, President Clinton described the GATT vote as a test of "what kind of country we are and what kind of people we're going to be." After he got Dole's support, Clinton expressed confidence that the GATT would pass the Congress. However, the chair of the Senate Finance Committee, Daniel Patrick Moynihan, was not sanguine. He warned on *This Week with David Brinkley* that "the most important vote of the decade" does not have enough votes.[59]

The president's optimism stemmed from his belief that Republicans held the key to the GATT victory. Despite the opposition of prominent Republicans such as Ross Perot and Pat Buchanan, the Republican party leadership kept members in line. Proponents did not focus on the concerns of left-leaning Democrats, who feared the GATT/WTO's impact on their constituents. There were few arguments made that would appeal to these Democrats, concerned about the GATT's effect on the poor, on labor, and on the environment.[60]

Despite the forceful arguments of labor, environmentalists, isolationists, and other groups, the Congress overwhelmingly voted in favor of the GATT/WTO. Seventy-six percent of both houses voted in favor of the WTO.[61]

The Public and the WTO/GATT Debate

Given the debate on sovereignty, on state-federal relations, and the relationship between trade policy and other policy goals, public opinion

Table 10. Some Prominent Proponents and Opponents of WTO

Some Proponents:	Some Opponents:
Agriculture: National Association of Wheat Growers, American Farm Bureau	*Agriculture:* National Farmers Union, American Corn Growers, National Soybean Association
Labor: None	*Labor:* AFL-CIO, International Brotherhood of Teamsters, Amalgamated Clothing and Textile Workers Union, International Ladies Garment Workers Union
Business: Alliance for GATT NOW, Coalition of Service Industries, Securities Industry Association, Motor and Equipment Manufacturers Association, American Furniture Manufacturers Association, National Association of Manufacturers	*Business:* American Iron and Steel Institute, Manufacturing Policy Project, Pantagonia Company
Prominent Americans: Congressman Jim Kolbe, former congressman Bill Frenzel, legal scholar and former judge Robert Bork, legal scholar John H. Jackson, former trade negotiator Jules Katz, investment banker Felix G. Rohaytn	*Prominent Individuals:* consumer advocate Ralph Nader, legal scholar Bruce Fein, business leader Ross Perot, Phyllis Schlafly, Jesse Jackson, former governor Jerry Brown
Citizens Groups: Consumers Union	*Citizen's Groups:* Sierra Club, Defenders of Wildlife, Public Citizen, National Wildlife Federation, Food for Peace, United We Stand America, Friends of the Earth, National Consumers League, NAACP

Sources: Senate Finance Committee, *Results of the Uruguay Round Trade Negotiations Hearings,* 103rd Cong., 2d sess., Feb. 8-Mar. 23, 1994; House Committee on Ways and Means, *The World Trade Organization Hearing,* 103d Cong., 2d sess., June 10, 1994; and Senate Committee on Commerce, *GATT Implementing Legislation Hearings.*

should have been the great tug-of-war. But that is not what happened. The public remained an untapped potential source of support.[62]

Polls revealed three major insights about public opinion: the public was apathetic, most Americans still knew very little about the GATT, and the more Americans heard about the GATT/WTO, the more likely they were to support it. This may explain why concerns about sovereignty did not derail the GATT/WTO.[63] For example, a July telephone survey of 3,800 Americans found 62 percent favored free trade agreements such as NAFTA and GATT; only 28 percent opposed them. On December 1, 1994, the day of the Senate vote, of some 1,511 adults polled by Princeton Survey Research Associates only 44 percent followed the GATT debate, but

64 percent of those 44 percent who followed the debate closely said they supported the GATT agreement, whereas 28 percent opposed.[64] An NBC/ *Wall Street Journal* poll in December 1994 found that 42 percent thought the GATT would be a good thing, 17 percent considered it a bad thing, and 39 percent said they didn't know enough about GATT to say.[65]

Grassroots organizations, however, did not ignore the public. Greenpeace and Public Citizen went door to door to oppose the GATT. Using new technologies, United We Stand linked a wide range of opponents to policymakers. Yet they failed to motivate the public to rise up and oppose the WTO.

The Achievement of the WTO

In light of growing questioning about the benefits of freer trade, new protectionist activism, and a generally apathetic public, how can we explain the achievement of the GATT/WTO? Ever so gradually, consciously and unconsciously, the American people are adapting to global economic interdependence. We sense it in the wages we get at work and in our inability to keep drugs, pollution, and disease from our shores. The approval of the WTO was a tacit recognition by Congress that we Americans live in the global village—there is no other village we can move to. But it was also an implicit recognition of our declining economic clout. The United States needs the WTO.

Conclusion:
Democracy and Economic
Interdependence

The March 30, 1995, letter from Senators Bob Packwood and Daniel Patrick Moynihan to the president of the United States was brief and to the point. "We are writing to propose that the WTO establish its headquarters not in Geneva (where it will be viewed as simply a continuation of the GATT) but . . . here in Washington, D.C. Locating the WTO's permanent headquarters in Washington would do much to . . . help build the support of the American public for its work." In this way, the United States could address the concerns about sovereignty that were at the "heart of last year's debate" by making the new international organization "easily accessible to our citizens."[1]

As the twentieth century comes to a close, no American can escape the global economy. Every hour of every day we see, smell, hear, taste, touch, read, or use goods and services traded between the United States and other nations. How we as citizens, taxpayers, producers, consumers, and shareholders manage America's trade policies affect the kind of jobs that we hold, the cost and diversity of the things we buy, the health of our economy and our environment, and even economic opportunities for our children. Trade policies stand at the heart of the American dream.

There are lessons in the ITO and the WTO for policymakers and the public. Both of these proposals raised important questions about the relationship between the global economy, American institutions, and American values. Like the ITO, the WTO brought to the fore concerns about sovereignty, the ability of American workers to compete with low-wage workers, and America's ability to compete with different forms of capitalism. As the two senators recognized, the ability of the GATT/WTO to open markets, settle trade disputes, enforce trade rules, and help produce rising standards of living for more of the world's people will depend on the commitment of its members. The continuing support of the American people for the WTO will depend on a greater degree of public understanding of how global economic interdependence affects our economy and our democracy.[2]

The Public, Policymakers, and the ITO

The debate over the ITO was a lost opportunity to involve the American people in developing instruments to shape the global economy. In contrast with the architects of the European Recovery Plan and the United Nations, the ITO's architects barely explained why radical changes to the nation's trade policies were necessary. Because they did not root their arguments for the ITO in American economic and political tradition, they were unable to counter protectionist sentiment. Moreover, because they did not find a way to link multilateral trade liberalization to the economic circumstances of the voting public, their arguments for the ITO and the GATT had little political resonance.

The early development of the ITO and the GATT was insular and secretive. State Department officials did not begin consultations with concerned interest groups until 1946 or hold public hearings on the plans until 1947. While they verbalized the need to work with the Congress to achieve their goals, they devised much of their strategy without consulting Congress.

Neither Roosevelt nor Truman administration officials developed effective arguments to awaken the American public to the potential benefits of the ITO and the GATT. The ITO's architects frequently changed their rationale for the ITO during its short life. They began by justifying the ITO on the belief that international economic cooperation could help prevent war. But during the peak of public support for internationalism in 1945-46, the ITO had not even been pushed through its first international negotiation.

After 1946, policymakers found it very difficult to explain to the public why the United States needed to create an international institution to codify world trade. Most Americans did not perceive trade liberalization as crucial to developing an orderly and prosperous U.S. economy or global peace. U.S. government officials argued that a multilateral system of freer world trade would complement the economic and military efforts of the noncommunist nations in promoting a common cause against the threat of the Soviet Union. Taking in more imports, they told Americans, could both spur European recovery and lessen the appeal of communist regimes. But the connection between increased trade, imports, and communism seemed obscure to many Americans. How could increased trade prevent the spread of communism? Policymakers explained this connection inadequately, so the public did not develop any marked enthusiasm for this reconfiguration of the national interest.

American fear of communism dealt a mortal blow to the ITO. After 1948, many Americans saw in the final charter of the ITO the unacceptable extension of parameters for government intervention in the economy. They feared this meant the decline of America's liberal democratic tradition; they saw various forms of government intervention from the TVA in the United States to total state control of production in the Soviet Union as the same thing: "planning." They believed the ITO legitimized government control at the international level and warned that the U.S. system of free enterprise could be stifled by global economic regulation.

Moreover, because it included nations with very different economic systems, the ITO seemed to condone trade between free-market economies and statist economies, the very type of system the United States opposed. In this environment, the ITO appeared hypocritical as well as ineffective. Once the centerpiece of foreign economic policy, the ITO had now become a subsidiary weapon to stop the spread of communism. When its purpose was redefined to beat back communism, the complex ITO lost its moorings and its credibility.

Proponents of freer trade rarely used domestic economic conditions to justify the ITO or the GATT to the American people through the crucial years of proposal development (1943-45), negotiation (1945-47), and public scrutiny (1948-51). Postwar America, however, was a potentially ripe market for increased imports. Several concepts might have resonated with the man and the woman on the street. As the State Department's own polls showed, in 1945-50, people were more conscious of the threat of foreign products to their jobs than of the opportunity for cheaper imports and increased exports. Thus, a carefully crafted emphasis on how trade creates more jobs than it destroys might have helped to build public support. Between 1945 and 1947, however, these officials missed an opportunity to link voter self-interest to freer trade policies. By showing how imports could alleviate goods shortages and hold down the cost of living—two economic issues that deeply concerned most voters—they might have built public understanding and support.

The public wanted policymakers to give them more information about the world economy. Although 70 percent of 1,289 Americans polled by the National Opinion Research Center (NORC) in March 1948 thought the United States should take an active role in the world, 63 percent believed officials of the U.S. government were "not telling the people all they should about our foreign policy."[3] In 1949, when NORC asked Americans which policies they would like to know more about, some 14 percent, the largest percentage, felt the government should tell the people more about its economic relations abroad.[4]

Ambivalence and Indecision Among Executive Branch Policymakers

The failure to create public understanding of this final international institution was, to a great extent, a failure of leadership. Neither Roosevelt nor Truman devoted much effort to creating public understanding of America's interdependence in the world economy. Moreover, the ITO never benefited from consistent support at the highest levels of government. Trade policy was not a key concern for Roosevelt. By 1945, even Cordell Hull seemed unwilling to explain why trade and employment policies needed to be linked in a new international organization. Although Truman seemed interested in the ITO, he was not willing to expend political capital on its behalf. Verbiage about the importance of increased trade could not disguise the fact that these senior officials, like most Americans, did not see the ITO or the GATT as crucial policy tools. Given the press of events, this is understandable.

However, officials at the working level also bear much of the blame for the abandonment of the ITO. The ITO's architects were so sure that the ITO met the national interest that they did not involve the members of the concerned public or Congress in its development until 1947. After these officials responded to the concerns of business interests about the ITO's investment clauses, they ended up with an ITO that left many supporters of trade liberalization disappointed and many business leaders alienated. Although they organized hearings around the nation to encourage grass-roots comment on the ITO, they set up no permanent channel for members of the public to speak with State Department officials about trade policies.

After 1947, the Republican-controlled Congress and protectionists used the RTAA hearings to challenge the administration's plans. Protectionist members of Congress were able to take advantage of the fact that several Republicans and Democrats were alienated by the State Department's manner of presenting the ITO. The Truman administration delayed telling Congress for two years whether the ITO would be presented as a joint resolution or a treaty. As the congressional calendar became crowded with emergency legislation, the administration discovered it had used up some of its limited goodwill on the emergency loan to Britain in 1946 and much of the rest on the ERP. Without a significant constituency, the ITO had to wait and would still be waiting as the political and economic environment changed dramatically.

A Policy Alternative

The development of the GATT made the case for the ITO even weaker. Many members of Congress and the concerned public did not understand the rationale for passing both measures. The congressional and public hearings on the ITO in 1947 revealed considerable support for the GATT's more limited approach to trade liberalization, but the ITO's architects ignored these signals. At the same time, some ITO opponents tried to discredit the ITO by linking its supporters to communism. In the face of these developments, the ITO's day on Capitol Hill was again postponed. The policy's supporters debated whether the RTAA, the ITO, the GATT, or all three should be given top priority. Their indecision lessened their credibility, and over time this undercut the likelihood of congressional approval of the ITO.

But in 1950 the administration's vacillation came to a halt. Why was the administration suddenly willing to abandon the ITO? Truman had to defend two of his administration's own foreign policy inventions, the Marshall Plan and the Point IV Program (a foreign assistance program). The administration had not developed the ITO, and many of its prominent foreign economic policy officials thought that it was no longer the right mechanism for the times. Confronted with one crisis after another, these officials turned to short-term tools that were more flexible than the ITO. In addition, because opponents had successfully linked it to communism, the ITO was tainted. The ITO had never been popular, and the administration did not want to risk its political capital on this policy mechanism when it had the alternative of the GATT. Finally, administration officials understood that they would need the support of influential elites in business, labor, farm, and civic groups to achieve their larger foreign policy goals. Several of the most prominent business associations supported abandoning the ITO for the GATT. As a result, by 1949, growing numbers of State Department officials believed they could appease ITO supporters by enhancing the GATT.[5]

The Achievement of the WTO

Like Harry Truman, Bill Clinton did not make the GATT/WTO his top priority. In his view, he had been elected to focus on domestic policies, such as healthcare and welfare reform. However, he soon found himself defending major trade policy innovations—the NAFTA and then the GATT/WTO.

In getting approval of the Uruguay Round and the new WTO, the Clinton administration and WTO proponents had to prevail in a Congress divided not just along party lines or by attitudes toward free trade, but also divided by attitudes about financing government. The debate was colored by very real concerns that the U.S. could lose control of its health, environmental, workplace, and safety standards. The NAFTA had strained the president's relations with his party's traditional constituents such as labor, Progressives, and environmentalists. Opponents linked NAFTA to the interests of big business and not to the interests of average Americans. The Clinton administration responded by arguing that highwage, high skills jobs created by demand from emerging markets would keep the American dream alive.

The WTO, like the ITO, was complex and legalistic. Few Americans read the 655 pages of implementing legislation, which were accompanied over a thousand more pages of agreements, a statement of administrative action, and supporting statements. The magnitude of the legislation—its complexity and the need to juggle funding—furthered an impression that the WTO and U.S. trade policy were undemocratic. This was exacerbated by the time constraints inherent in the fast-track legislation. Thus, it was hard to counter perceptions that the whole Uruguay Round arrangement was being shoved down the American people's collective throat.

Although Congress had urged policymakers to strengthen the GATT, the Reagan, Bush, and Clinton administrations had not fully explained the rationale for such a new international organization. And their arguments were confusing. Proponents argued that the WTO was simply an evolution and enhancement of the GATT. But that argument diluted one of the rationales for creating the WTO: that it would improve on the GATT by remaking it. Was it toothless, or was it the future policeman of world trade?[6]

Like ITO proponents, GATT/WTO proponents focused their efforts on opinion leaders. But opinion leaders who supposedly supported freer trade were equally divided about the relationship of the GATT/WTO to the United States. Both Senator Robert Dole and Congressman Newt Gingrich expressed worries about the WTO, adding legitimacy to the notion that the WTO subverted sovereignty. And they seemed perfectly willing to join opponents of multilateral free trade in delaying the vote. What was the public to think when their leaders were so divided?[7]

As the Clinton administration made its case to opinion leaders, opponents took to the streets, the Internet, and the airwaves to question the WTO/GATT. They found a diverse audience: among progressives concerned about social injustice, among economic nationalists, among environmentalists, and among growing numbers of Americans who believed that the U.S. was not "winning in world markets" and who feared their children would pay a price.[8]

Issues of access, full disclosure, and federal-state relations soon came to the fore in the WTO debate. Clinton administration officials were less effective at responding to very real concerns about democracy, which were raised by the negotiating process (where secrecy is required), the fast-track process (where Congress can only vote up or down on the entire implementing legislation in the ninety-day period); the deals struck to make up for the funding of the GATT/WTO; and the relationship of the WTO to American institutions and policy priorities. Yet most Americans did not understand or share these concerns about democracy. They were not engaged by the debate.

The GATT/WTO, in contrast with the ITO/GATT, benefited both from top administration and special interest support. Although business was divided on the GATT/WTO, many of America's largest companies (the Fortune 500) and their suppliers were on board and willing to use their political and economic clout to make their case with the Congress and opinion leaders. The GATT/WTO also garnered the support of America's most prominent consumers group, Consumers Union. In a series of eloquent speeches, the president linked support for freer trade to the American dream, to the hopes and fears of Americans. He seemed to have convinced crucial members of Congress who were willing to link good jobs to future markets. As Senator Barbara Mikulski noted, "I am a blue-collar Senator. . . . In the last decade, working people have faced the loss of jobs, lower wages and a reduced standard of living. . . . But voting against GATT will not save those jobs. . . . I am voting for GATT to generate more exports, to create more jobs."[9]

Although the Uruguay Round received a resounding vote of support in both Houses of Congress, ultimately, the Congress did not resolve the fundamental issue that had also bedeviled the ITO: what is the relationship of trade policies to the achievement of other policy goals, and how should the world trade organization address these "national" issues? Should the WTO and future trade agreements be limited strictly to trade policy, or is it also necessary to develop codes to cover the environment, health and safety standards, and workers' rights? These questions will continue to bedevil trade negotiations and the working of the WTO.

Democratizing Trade Policy in the U.S. and at the WTO

U.S. membership in the WTO will be a test of our democracy's ability to adapt to a world where transactions, corporations, and technology are global but where our institutions, political allegiance, and culture remain national.[10] Harlan Cleveland, a former Marshall Plan official, noted, the global free market will require "a global public sector to keep it more or less free by keeping it reasonably fair" and by balancing "liberty and equality" and "efficiency and fairness."[11] These are the values that we Americans cherish and want to encourage overseas. Ironically, these concerns have barely been addressed by WTO opponents, who have presented no real alternatives to the WTO.

Historians must always be careful when they use history to prescribe current policy options.[12] I therefore make some cautious recommendations. First we must create a level of public understanding of trade policy commensurate with the importance of trade to the American economy. This requires that we find ways to make trade policy interesting to the American people. Trade policy should be a topic discussed in civics classes in America's high schools and on shop floors. Policymakers should hold televised town-hall meetings to discuss how trade policy affects us in our many roles: as taxpayers, citizens, producers, consumers, friends of the earth, and shareholders. The president should play a more prominent role in educating Americans to the reality of global economic interdependence.

Because many Americans see trade policy as an issue about jobs, proponents must acknowledge that U.S. trade policy has resulted in some job loss. But policymakers should also let the record of freer trade policies speak in a comparison of jobs lost and gained, in benefits and costs to the unskilled as well as to skilled workers, in benefits and costs to American health and environmental standards, and in its effect upon the American democracy. Policymakers must be truthful about the distributional consequences of freer trade and the need to develop effective mechanisms to help those workers, localities, and industries that bear the costs of trade liberalization.[13] This will allow the public to get a better understanding of how trade policy affects the achievement of other policy goals.

Second, we must continue to broaden the trade policymaking process in the United States. Under Ambassador Mickey Kantor, the Office of the U.S. Trade Representative created a channel to discuss trade issues at the state, local, and federal levels, and he appointed key state and local officials to the government's main trade policy advisory committees.[14] The Clinton administration also established a Trade and Environment Policy Advisory Committee to assist the president with issues involving trade and the environment.[15] Finally, despite the opposition of business leaders and Commerce Department officials, the Trade Representative has also opened up some of the advisory committee meetings to public observers. Because the trade policymaking process often requires secrecy, Americans are struggling to find a new balance between sunshine and efficacy.[16]

But policymakers should heed concerns about the effects of global economic interdependence on U.S. democracy. The fears about sovereignty are fears about the survival of American policy objectives and institutions. Americans are learning that many of our policy problems are global in reach and thus, to fully address these problems, we must devise global responses.[17]

Although the United States was the main force behind international institutions such as the World Bank and the GATT, these institutions do not function according to U.S. standards of equity, openness, and democratic decision making.[18] Although the American variant of openness may not become the GATT model, U.S. policymakers must continue to make GATT/WTO more open to public scrutiny and involvement.[19] Pressure for greater openness is also coming from the public: a growing body of Americans of the Right and the Left are working to make the WTO (and other multilateral institutions) more accountable and democratic.[20]

Third, we must be more honest about the implications of a successful and more democratic WTO. The World Trade Organization holds the potential to regulate international business across borders. If policy-makers around the world succeed at making the WTO more accountable and responsive, this may undermine the legitimacy of the nation-state as "the sole conveyor of its citizens' interests."[21] To tame global problems, the WTO may then become a true superstate, as some of its opponents have alleged. A strong and successful WTO may force Americans to rethink how we are governed.

In testimony to the Senate Foreign Relations Committee, Ralph Nader noted, "When historians look back on this period . . . either they will focus on it as a moment in which the Congress resisted the anti-democratic WTO or they will view it as the moment in which Congress ceded authority to safeguard the interests of this country and its inhabitants to this new autocratic international body."[22]

Nader has underestimated the flexibility of the American democracy. As President Truman recognized, public policy is derived from the people. The opportunity to reconcile American democracy and global economic interdependence still exists. As the public becomes more cognizant of the costs and benefits of global interdependence, they will remake trade policy to promote democratic ideals or they will find new tools to order the chaotic world economy.[23]

Notes

Introduction

1. Richard P. Stebbins and the Research Staff, *The United States in World Affairs, 1949* (New York: Harper and Brothers, 1950), 28.

2. On September 9, 1994, pollsters Hart and Teeter surveyed Americans about GATT. Although some 24 percent favored approval of the GATT, some 61 percent said they didn't know enough about GATT to say what they thought. N.a., "Opinion Outlook: Views on the Economy, Thinking about Trade," *National Journal,* Oct. 22, 1994, 2482. On November 28-29, 1994, Gallup surveyed 1,016 adults. Although some 23 percent favored GATT, 63 percent of those surveyed said they didn't know enough about GATT to say. Lydia Saad, "GATT Still a Mystery to Most Americans," Gallup Poll News Service, Dec. 1, 1994.

3. Mickey Kantor believes the debate over extending the North American Free Trade Agreement to Mexico awakened public interest in trade and stimulated new interest group opposition (e.g. that of the environmentalists). Interview with Ambassador Michael Kantor, U.S. Trade Representative, Jan. 16, 1995.

4. William Jefferson Clinton, "Remarks by the President at Signing of General Agreement on Tariffs and Trade," Dec. 8, 1994. For debate on trade, see Jack Anderson and Michael Binstein, "Kantor's Advice," *Washington Post,* Jan. 29, 1995; George Raymond Tyndall, "Trade Accords Have Sown Violent Seeds," Letter to the Editor, *New York Times,* Jan. 1, 1995; Richard Sennett, "Back to Class Warfare," *New York Times,* Dec. 27, 1994; and Owen Ullman, "A Presidential Train Wreck," *International Economy* (Nov./Dec. 1994): 6-9, 58.

5. One hundred twenty-three nations were affiliated with the GATT. GATT had no members but rather contracting parties. The GATT provided these nations with both a code of rules and a forum in which countries could discuss and overcome their trade problems and expand world trade. William Jefferson Clinton, "Memorandum for the United States Trade Representative: Trade Agreements Resulting From the Uruguay Round of Multilateral Trade Negotiations," Dec. 15, 1993, 3, 26, 27; GATT Secretariat, "Final Act Embodying the Results of the Uruguay Round of Multilateral Trade Negotiations," Dec. 15, 1993, Annex IV, 91; and U.S. Trade Representative, *A Preface to Trade* (Washington, D.C.: GPO, 1982), 5.

6. John H. Jackson, "The World Trade Organization, Dispute Settlement, and Codes of Conduct," in *The New GATT: Implications for the United States,* ed. Susan M. Collins and Barry P. Bosworth (Washington, D.C.: Brookings Institution, 1994), 63-75.

7. Economic conditions during the Great Depression had a major influence upon many of the ITO and GATT's architects. These men and women had different backgrounds, education, and political views; they were not all "ivy leaguers," all economists, all lawyers, or all Democrats; however, they shared a belief that global trade liberalization could create jobs for Americans. For example, Dean Acheson was a corporate lawyer. Will Clayton, who headed efforts on the ITO between 1945 and 1948, was a self-made man who had established a large trading company. At the office director level, Clair Wilcox was an academic economist, and Winthrop Brown, Harry Hawkins, and Paul Nitze were all State Department officials. Junior staffers who worked on the ITO include John Leddy, who joined the State Department from George-town University, Raymond Vernon, who joined from City College, and J. Robert Schaetzel, who came from the Bureau of the Budget. All except Clayton were college educated, with a strong background in economics.

8. Among the special interests who saw long-term economic gain from the ITO were internationalist executives at companies such as General Electric and Pillsbury; business associations such as the Committee for Economic Development; and labor unions such as the CIO. However, these groups also supported the ITO because they believed in international cooperation and in America's responsibility to aid European reconstruction. Their members were not simply motivated by the potential of profits from foreign markets. Thus, unlike some historians, I do not see this period as one in which internationalist big business triumphed. Robert M. Dallek, *Franklin D. Roosevelt and American Foreign Policy, 1932-1945* (New York: Oxford Univ. Press, 1979); Lloyd C. Gardner, "The New Deal, New Frontiers, and the Cold War: A Reexamination of American Expansion, 1933-1945," in *Corporations and the Cold War,* ed. David Horowitz (New York: Monthly Review Press, 1969); Thomas J. McCormick, *America's Half-Century* (Baltimore: Johns Hopkins Univ. Press, 1989); and Thomas Ferguson, "From Normalcy to the New Deal: Industrial Structure, Party Competition, and American Public Policy in the Great Depression," *International Organization* 38 (winter 1984): 93.

9. The best analyses of the ITO are William Diebold Jr., "The End of the ITO, *Essays in International Finance* 16 (Oct. 1952); Clair Wilcox, *A Charter for World Trade* (New York: Macmillan, 1949); and Richard N. Gardner, *Sterling Dollar Diplomacy in Current Perspective* (New York: Columbia Univ. Press, 1980).

10. Diebold, "The End of the ITO," 1, 5, 6.

11. It was only in the late 1940s that the public came to accept the costs of pro-viding open markets and foreign aid in order to prevent the spread of communism. Susan Aaronson, "The Irony of Persistence on Solving World Trade Woes," *International Economy* 4 (Aug./Sept. 1990): 30-31.

12. Much of the discussion about the ITO centered on Articles 3 (1) and 21 (4b) of the Final Charter, which linked full employment and trade. As the "cold war" be-gan to heat up in these years, opponents framed the debate as a choice between economic freedom or socialism. Philip Cortney, *The Economic Munich* (New York: Philosophical Library, 1949), ix, 17.

13. Diebold, "The End of the ITO," 1, 5, 6.

14. Paul G. Hoffman, *Peace Can Be Won* (Garden City, N.Y.: Doubleday, 1951), 87.

15. There is no consensus on the demise of the ITO. The few analysts who have examined it mainly attribute its demise to the lack of business support or to bureau-cratic politics (Congressional/Executive branch disputes on trade policy). Otis L. Graham Jr., however, briefly discusses the ITO in his history of industrial policy. He believes the ITO "was plainly meant to be an instrumentality capable of analyzing industrial policies internationally." It was thus perceived as a superstate. (*Losing Time:*

The Industrial Policy Debate, Cambridge, Mass.: Harvard Univ. Press, 1992), 299. Two historians briefly discuss the ITO in their books: Robert A. Pollard, *Economic Security and the Origins of the Cold War, 1945-1950* (New York: Columbia Univ. Press, 1985); and Randall Bennett Woods, *A Changing of the Guard: AngloAmerican Relations, 1941-1946* (Chapel Hill: Univ. of North Carolina Press, 1990), 188, 218.

Even the architects of a multilateral approach to trade policy disagree on why the ITO was abandoned. While in the Commercial Policy Division at the Department of State, William Diebold Jr. helped develop a multilateral approach to trade. He later pushed for increased support of multilateralism through his influential writing and his service at the Council on Foreign Relations. In his wonderful essay "The End of the ITO" (14, 24), he blames the rigidity of American businessmen, especially perfectionists, for its defeat. Raymond Vernon worked for the State Department on trade and investment policies before he launched his distinguished career in private industry and at Harvard University. He blames the ITO's demise on protectionism and inept government marketing. Vernon, "America's Foreign Trade Policy and the GATT," *Essays in International Finance* 21 (Oct. 1954): 6. Dean Acheson, who served Truman as secretary of state, believed that the ITO failed because of Republican opposition. Dean Acheson, *Present at the Creation* (New York: Norton, 1969), 133.

16. Robert E. Hudec, *The GATT Legal System and World Trade Diplomacy* (New York: Praeger, 1975), 63, 355, 356 n 17; and Kenneth W. Dam, *The GATT: Law and International Economic Organization* (Chicago: Univ. of Chicago Press, 1970), 337-38.

17. I.M. Destler, *American Trade Politics: System Under Stress,* 2d ed. (Washington, D.C.: Institute for International Economics with the Twentieth Century Fund, 1992), 44-63; and Jeffrey J. Schott, *The Uruguay Round: An Assessment* (Washington, D.C.: Institute for International Economics, 1994), 4-39.

18. Telephone interview with Catherine Fields, Office of the General Counsel, United States Trade Representative, May 1, 1994; and Omnibus Trade and Competitiveness Act of 1988, P.L. No. 100-418. The first trade negotiating objective for the United States in the 1988 act was "to provide for more effective and expeditious dispute settlement mechanisms and procedures." Also see Clinton, "Memorandum for the United States Trade Representative, "Trade Agreements Resulting from the Uruguay Round," Dec. 15, 1994, 26.

19. Michele Galen and Mark N. Vamos, "Portrait of an Anxious Public," *Business Week,* Mar. 13, 1995. In this Harris/*Business Week* poll of 1,249 adults conducted Feb. 16-19, 1995, 85 percent blamed global competition for the stagnation in incomes for working Americans; 90 percent blamed the decline of the manufacturing economy.

20. Susan C. Schwab, *Trade-offs: Negotiating the Omnibus Trade and Competitiveness Act* (Boston: Harvard Business School Press, 1994), 27-47.

21. The most revealing survey of public opinion on trade policy in this period is the National Opinion Research Center (NORC), "The Public Looks at Trade and Tariff Problems," University of Chicago, 1947. For an overview of American attitudes toward the ITO in 1948-49, see Gabriel A. Almond, *The American People and Foreign Policy* (New York: Harcourt, Brace, 1950), 169, 176, 180, 182.

22. For example, a 1946 State Department poll revealed that although 75 percent of those polled understood that the United States must buy foreign goods in order to sell goods abroad, only about one-third of those polled thought they would be better off. For an overview of American attitudes in 1946 toward trade liberalization, see S. Shepard Jones to Mr. Brown, Nov. 7, 1946, box 98, in Record Group 59, Lot File 57D-284. These are the International Trade Files at the National Archives (hereafter LF 57D-284). I am grateful to Kathy NiCastro for her help with these records.

23. John Morton Blum, *V Was for Victory: Politics and American Culture during*

World War II (New York: Harcourt, Brace, Jovanovich, 1976); William H. Chafe, *The Unfinished Journey: America since World War II* (New York: Oxford Univ. Press, 1986), 10-11; Eric F. Goldman, *The Crucial Decade—And After: America, 1945-1960* (New York: Vintage Books, 1956), 12-28.

24. Pollsters say that polls reveal ambivalent data when policy is confusing and involves conflicting goals, clashing values, or other complexities. Michael R. Kaygay, "Why Even Well-Designed Polls Can Disagree," in *Media Polls in American Politics,* ed. Thomas E. Mann and Gary R. Orren (Washington, D.C.: Brookings Institution, 1992), 114-15.

25. Although imports grew significantly in the years 1939 through 1950, they did not grow as fast as real gross national product. Nevertheless, even though the United States was less dependent on foreign markets than many other nations, international trade had become increasingly important to the health of individual sectors such as those involving crude material exports and crude foodstuff imports.

26. Destler, *American Trade Politics,* 62.

27. Andrew Kohut and Robert C. Toth, "Trade and the Public," Times Mirror Center for the People and the Press," Dec. 13, 1994, 1-3; Robert C. Toth, "America's Place in the World," Times Mirror Center for the People and the Press, Nov. 1993, 21; and Robert L. Paarlberg, *Leadership Abroad Begins at Home: U.S. Foreign Policy after the Cold War* (Washington, D.C.: Brookings Institution, 1994), 100.

28. Robert S. Greenberger, "Cold Shoulder: As Global Crises Mount, More Americans Want America to Stay Home," *The Wall Street Journal,* Oct. 28, 1993, A1.

29. Globalization increased most rapidly from the sixties and seventies through the 1980s, whereas wage inequality increased dramatically in the 1980s. See Paul Krugman and Robert Z. Lawrence, "Trade, Jobs, and Wages," NBER Working Paper no. 4478, Sept. 1993; and Robert Z. Lawrence and Matthew J. Slaughter, "International Trade and American Wages in the 1980s: Giant Sucking Sound or Small Hiccup?" *Brookings Papers on Economic Activity, Microeconomics* 2 (1993):161-23. Also see Paul Krugman, *Peddling Prosperity: Economic Sense and Nonsense in the Age of Diminished Expectations* (New York: Norton, 1994), 146-50; and Council of Economic Advisors, *Economic Report of the President,* Feb. 1994, 212-14.

30. Gary Clyde Hufbauer, ed., *The Free Trade Debate: Reports of the Twentieth Century Fund Task Force on the Future of American Trade Policy* (New York: Priority Press, 1989), 3-53.

31. Among those positing new approaches to trade policy were Laura D'Andrea Tyson (chair of the Council of Economic Advisers and the National Economic Council under President Clinton) and Lester Thurow (dean of the MIT School of Business). See Paul Krugman, *Strategic Trade Policy and the New International Economics* (Cambridge: MIT Press, 1994); Tyson, *Who's Bashing Whom? Trade Conflict in High Technology Industries* (Washington, D.C.: Institute for International Economics, 1992); and Lester Thurow, *Head to Head: The Coming Economic Battle among Japan, Europe, and America* (New York: Morrow, 1992).

32. Hufbauer, ed., *Free Trade Debate,* 3-53; Destler, *American Trade Politics,* 41-64, 153-56.

33. Christopher Lasch, *The Revolt of the Elites and the Betrayal of Democracy* (New York: Norton, 1994); Michael Lind, "Spheres of Affluence," *American Prospect* 16 (winter 1994): 91-99; Barry Bluestone, "The Inequality Express," *American Prospect* (winter 1995), 81-93; discussion with Ambassador Rufus Xerxa, Deputy U.S. Trade Representative, Jan. 5, 1995; Edward N. Luttwak, "Will Success Spoil America?" *Washington Post,* Nov. 27, 1994, C1; Richard Harwood, "When News Drowns Out Truth," *Washington Post,* Dec. 17, 1994, A27; and Citizens' Trade Campaign, "Our

Jobs, Our Environment, Our Future: An Introduction to the Citizens Trade Campaign" (Washington, D.C.: Citizens' Trade Campaign, 1993).

34. Dan Balz, "Buchanan Says He'll Form Panel on Presidential Race," *Washington Post,* Feb. 16, 1995, A9; Jim Hoagland, ""A Turn Inward," *Washington Post,* Jan. 10, 1995, A17; "House Republicans Warn Freshmen May Oppose New Trade Initiatives," *Inside U.S. Trade,* Feb. 10, 1995, 1, 19; Peter Behr, "GATT Is Legislative Landmark, but Trade Remains a Divisive Issue," *Washington Post,* Dec. 2, 1994, A26; David E. Sanger, "Senate Approves Pact to Ease Trade Curbs: A Victory for Clinton," *New York Times,* Dec. 2, 1994, A1; and telephone interviews, Jim Jontz, Citizens' Trade Campaign, Feb. 21, 1995, and Kevin L. Kearns, president, U.S. Business and Industrial Council, Feb. 22, 1995.

35. Richard Harwood, "When 'News' Drowns Out Truth," *Washington Post,* Dec. 17, 1994, A27; and "GATT Opponents to Target Clinton-Dole WTO Review Body in New Congress," *Inside U.S. Trade,* Dec. 16, 1994, 21. On disillusionment with internationalism, see Paarlberg, *Leadership,* 48-53.

36. Political scientist Daniel Verdier and economist Russell D. Roberts are important exceptions. Verdier argues that voters do play an important role in trade policy: *Democracy and International Trade: Britain, France, and the United States, 1860-1990* (Princeton: Princeton Univ. Press, 1994), xvii. Roberts has helped to build greater understanding of trade policy with *The Choice: A Fable of Free Trade and Protectionism* (Englewood Cliffs, N.J.: Prentice-Hall, 1994).

37. Mancur Olson Jr., *The Logic of Collective Action: Public Goods and the Theory of Groups* (Cambridge: Harvard Univ. Press, 1965).

38. E.E. Schattschneider, *Politics, Pressure, and the Tariff* (New York: Prentice Hall, 1935), 225n.

39. Thomas W. Zeiler, *American Trade and Power in the 1960s* (New York: Columbia Univ. Press, 1992), 9, 13-17.

40. Robert W. Barrie, *Congress and the Executive: The Making of the United States Foreign Trade Policy, 1789-1968* (New York: Garland, 1987); and Robert A. Pastor, *Congress and the Politics of U.S. Foreign Economic Policy, 1929-1976* (Berkeley: Univ. of California Press, 1980). Historians often use the corporatist model to assess the interaction between government officials and special interests. It is also called corporate liberalism, institutionalism, and associationalism. See Ellis W. Hawley, "The Discovery and Study of a 'Corporate Liberalism'," *Business History Review* 52 (autumn 1978): 317; Michael J. Hogan, "Corporatism, a Positive Appraisal," *Diplomatic History* 10 (fall 1986): 363-72; and Thomas J. McCormick, "Drift or Mastery? A Corporatist Synthesis for American Diplomatic History," *Reviews in American History* 10 (Dec. 1982): 318-30.

41. John S. Odell, "Understanding International Trade Policies: An Emerging Synthesis," *World Politics* 43 (Oct. 1990): 139-40, 141, 152-55.

42. Some historians have begun to show that the opinions of the unorganized public has affected trade policies. James Bellamy Beddow, "Economic Nationalism or Internationalism: Upper Midwestern Response to New Deal Tariff Policy," Ph.D. diss., University of Oklahoma, 1969. In this regard, historian Beth McKillan criticizes the corporatist model of interest group/government official interaction for ignoring public opinion. See McKillen, "The Corporatist Model, World War I, and the Public Debate over the League of Nations," *Diplomatic History* 15 (spring 1991): 171-72. Political economist G. John Ikenberry also argues that because public opinion constrains policymakers, researchers should study the general public and not just the behavior of elites. Ikenberry, "Conclusion: An Institutional Approach to American Foreign Economic Policy," in *The State and American Foreign Economic Policy,* ed. G. John Ikenberry, David A. Lake, and Michael Mastanduno (Ithaca: Cornell Univ. Press, 1988), 222.

43. Historians have long struggled with the problem of portraying public opinion. They have debated how to differentiate elite and "anonymous" (mass) opinion; how to find reliable sources for public opinion; how public opinion influences policy making and policymakers; and when public opinion affects policy-makers. Murray Edelman, *Political Language: Words That Succeed and Policies That Fail* (New York: Academic Press, 1977), 49-55.

44. See Robert D. Putnam, "Bowling Alone: America's Declining Social Capital," *Journal of Democracy* 6 (Jan. 1995); 72. He notes that reported union membership declined by some 40 percent from 1975 to 1991. Rather than joining unions or clubs, Americans are joining grassroots organizations such as the Sierra Club or the American Association of Retired People, where they are loosely linked by mailing lists, dollars, and ideology.

45. Interview with Ambassador Mickey Kantor, Jan. 13, 1995; telephone interview with Anne Luzzatto, Assistant U.S. Trade Representative, Jan. 11, 1995; and interview with Ambassador Rufus Xerxa, Deputy U.S. Trade Representative, Jan. 5, 1995. Also see Ullman, "A Presidential Trade Wreck," 58.

46. Richard Morin, "Public Growing Wary of GOP Cuts," *Washington Post,* Mar. 21, 1995, A1; and Thomas E. Mann and Gary R. Orren, eds., *Media Polls in American Politics* (Washington, D.C.: Brookings Institution, 1992), 15-17.

47. See Michael R. Kaygay with Janet Elder, "Numbers Are No Problem for Pollsters, Words Are," *New York Times,* Aug. 9, 1992, Week in Review, 5.

1. The Roots of Multilateral Trade Policy

1. Cordell Hull, *The Memoirs of Cordell Hull* (New York: Macmillan, 1948), 1: 80-85. Parts of this chapter were published in Susan Aaronson, "How Cordell Hull and the Postwar Planners Designed a New Trade Policy," *Business and Economic History,* 2d ser., 20 (1991): 171.

2. Hull, *Memoirs,* 133.

3. Address by Francis B. Sayre, "Liberal Trade Policies: The Basis for Peace," May 14, 1937, in U.S. Department of State, *Commercial Policy Series,* nos. 37-55, (Washington, 1937), 1019; Hull, *Memoirs,* 357; and Stefanie Ann Lenway, *The Politics of U.S. International Trade* (Marshfield, Mass.: Pittman, 1985), 67.

4. Destler, *American Trade Policies,* 15-16.

5. William B. Kelly Jr., "Antecedents of Present Commercial Policy, 1922-1934," in *Studies in United States Commercial Policy,* ed. Kelly (Chapel Hill: Univ. of North Carolina Press, 1963), 10-11; and Charles P. Kindleberger, "U.S. Foreign Economic Policy, 1776-1976," *Foreign Affairs* 55 (Jan. 1977): 396, 399.

6. Three good overviews of U.S. trade policy are Kelly, "Antecedents," 10-11; Thomas K. McCraw, "Mercantilism and the Market: Antecedents of American Industrial Policy," in *The Politics of Industrial Policy,* ed. Claude E. Barfield and William A. Schambra (Washington, D.C.: American Enterprise Institute, 1986), 33-39; and Kindleberger, "U.S. Foreign Economic Policy," 396, 399.

7. John M. Dobson, *Two Centuries of Tariffs: The Background and Emergence of the U.S. International Trade Commission* (Washington, D.C.: GPO, 1976), 6-7; and Destler, *American Trade Politics,* 14.

8. James A. Field Jr., "All Economists, All Diplomats," in *Economics and World Power,* ed. William H. Becker and Samuel F. Wells Jr. (New York: Columbia Univ. Press, 1984), 7.

9. Kelly, "Antecedents," 25.

10. Pastor, *Congress and the Politics,* 73-74; and Dobson, *Two Centuries,* 8. The classic study on tariffs is by the first chairman of the Tariff Commission, Frank W. Taussig, *The Tariff History of the United States* (New York: Putnam, 1931).

11. The U.S. government occasionally acted to open foreign markets in support of special trade interests, but such actions were "exceptional and cautious." Kinley J. Brauer, "The Diplomacy of American Expansionism," in Becker and Wells, eds., *Economics and World Power,* 113-14.

12. Raymond A. Bauer, Ithiel de Sola Pool, and Lewis Anthony Dexter, *American Business and Public Policy* (New York: Atherton Press, 1963), 12-13; and Kelly, "Antecedents," 3. The "American government apparatus was not developed in ways that allowed policymakers to pursue state interests." John G. Ikenberry, "Conclusion: An Institutional Approach to American Foreign Economic Policy," in Ikenberry, Lake, and Mastanduno, eds., *The State,* 232.

13. Alfred D. Chandler Jr., *Scale and Scope: The Dynamics of Industrial Capitalism* (Cambridge: Harvard Univ. Press, 1990). A manufacturer able to sell larger volumes of output could realize significant economies of scale by building a state-of-the-art, labor-saving plant. Producers could also realize economies of scope by manufacturing a number of products in a single facility, using similar materials and processes.

14. Until World War I, the United States was a debtor nation. During most of this period, tariff policies did not quash increasingly vibrant trade. From 1874 until the turn of the century, the United States was able to pay this debt by a surplus of exports over imports. But by the 1914, the United States had become a net creditor. The changed position "from a debtor to a creditor suggested lower tariffs." Kelly, "Antecedents," 4; and U.S. Department of Commerce, *Historical Statistics of the United States: Colonial Times to 1970* (Washington, D.C.: GPO, 1971), 865-69.

15. Bauer, de Sola Pool, and Dexter, *American Business,* 20-21.

16. Some business leaders organized trade associations to seek government assistance in advancing international sales and some government officials sought to forge institutional links to the business community to spur foreign trade. Consular appointments were taken out of the patronage system, and the consular service became more effective at representing American interests abroad. William H. Becker, "America Adjusts to World Power," in Becker and Wells, eds., *Economics and World Power,* 175-81; Richard Hume Werking, "Bureaucrats, Businessmen, and Foreign Trade: The Origins of the U.S. Chamber of Commerce," *Business History Review* 52 (autumn 1978): 322-23; Mira Wilkins, *The Emergence of Multinational Enterprise: American Business Abroad from the Colonial Era to 1914* (Cambridge: Harvard Univ. Press, 1970), 120-25; and Mira Wilkins, *The Maturing of Multinational Enterprise: American Business Abroad from 1914 to 1970* (Cambridge: Harvard Univ. Press, 1974).

17. Pastor, *Congress,* 75-76; and Robert Wiebe, *Businessmen and Reform: A Study of the Progressive Movement* (Cambridge: Harvard Univ. Press, 1962), 128-29, 149, 222-24.

18. Wiebe, *Businessmen and Reform,* 207-8, 212-14; David Lake, "The State and American Trade Strategy in the Pre-Hegemonic Era," in Ikenberry, Lake, and Mastanduno, eds., *The State,* 50; and Pastor, *Congress,* 76.

19. Destler, *American Trade Politics,* 15-16; and Schattschneider, *Politics, Pressure, and the Tariff,* 85.

20. Quotation from Kelly, "Antecedents," 7-10; see also Bauer, de Sola Pool, and Dexter, *American Business,* 17; and Pastor, *Congress,* 77.

21. Melvyn P. Leffler, "Expansionist Impulses and Domestic Constraints," in Becker and Wells, eds., *Economics and World Power,* 227-28, 231.

22. Kelly, "Antecedents," 11-12, 27; and Francis Sutton, Seymour E. Harris, Carl

Kaysen, and James Tobin, *The American Business Creed* (Cambridge: Harvard Univ. Press, 1956), 210.

23. Policymakers said Smoot-Hawley would increase American jobs and the livelihood of American producers. For a good understanding of the power of protectionist ideology, nothing compares with Schattschneider, *Politics, Pressure, and the Tariff,* 83, 89, 145, 146, 162-63. Also see Raymond Mikesell, *United States Economic Policy and International Relations* (New York: McGraw-Hill, 1952), 17-18, 60-77.

24. Mikesell, *U.S. Economic Policy,* 62-63; Dobson, *Two Centuries,* 73-74; David A. Lake, *Power, Protection, and Free Trade* (Ithaca: Cornell Univ. Press, 1988), 7, 191; and Pastor, *Congress,* 77-78. However, Ohio University historian and former International Trade Commission chair Alfred Eckes Jr. has published a study that challenges the thesis that Smoot-Hawley was America's most protectionist tariff; *Opening America's Market: U.S. Foreign Trade Policy Since 1776* (Chapel Hill: Univ. of North Carolina Press, 1995), 100-139.

25. Goldstein, "Ideas, Institutions, and American Trade Policy," 182-83, 187, and Haggard, "Institutional Foundations of Hegemony," 90-94, 117-19, both in Ikenberry, Lake, and Mastanduno, eds., *The State;* Lake, *Power, Protection, and Free Trade,* 203; and Pastor, *Congress,* 81.

26. The Great Depression persisted throughout the 1930s. In 1933, approximately 25 percent of civilian laborers had lost their jobs; in 1938, 19.1 percent were unemployed; and in 1941, 9.9 percent were unemployed. Louis Galambos and Joseph Pratt, *The Rise of the Corporate Commonwealth* (New York: Basic Books, 1988), 101. The average U.S. unemployment rate was the highest among the industrialized nations in the decade. Michael A. Bernstein, *The Great Depression: Delayed Recovery and Economic Change in America, 1929-1939,* (Cambridge: Cambridge Univ. Press, 1987), 3. For information on how unemployment affected people's attitudes about government, see Dexter Perkins, *The New Age of Franklin Roosevelt, 1932-1945* (Chicago: Univ. of Chicago Press, 1957), 1-3, 12, 13; and Goldman, *Crucial Decade,* 5-6.

27. Laissez-faire, neoclassical theory said that free markets should set prices, rent (on money, people, and products), and working conditions. The theory posits that free markets would self-correct in times of depression or inflation. But in his pathbreaking book, *The General Theory of Employment, Interest, and Money* (New York: Harcourt, Brace, 1936), John Maynard Keynes challenged the notion that the business cycle was fully self-correcting. He showed that when too many people are unemployed, individuals and businessmen have little money to spend or invest and business has little incentive to invest. The economy could achieve equilibrium at a very low level of employment. Government could disrupt this equilibrium and push the economy to a higher level of employment, using fiscal or monetary policies. But by calling for government action, Keynes's ideas threatened laissez-faire ideology and the traditional notion of government's proper role. Never before had government been asked to do so much to solve economic problems. See Robert M. Collins, *The Business Response to Keynes, 1920-1964* (New York: Columbia Univ. Press, 1981), 1-3, 212; especially the Roosevelt quotation on p. 2.

28. In this book, I will use *free trade* and *freer trade* as synonymous terms. However, there is no truly free trade in the world economy. Nations intervene in various degrees. I gained a better understanding of how the planners tried to reconcile trade and employment in an interview with William Diebold, July 12, 1990. Also see Alvin H. Hansen, Harvard economist and former Federal Reserve official, *America's Role in the World Economy* (New York: Norton, 1945), 91-93. On reconciling these two economic policy goals, see Conference memo, "Post War International Economic Policies and Their Relation to Domestic Policies," Aug. 24, 1942, 1, box 14; and Harry

Hawkins to Acheson, Welles, and Hull, Aug. 4, 1941, box 5, both in Assistant Secretary Dean Acheson Records at NA, hereafter Acheson Records.

29. Freer trade policies call for the reduction or abandonment of government-erected impediments to trade, such as tariffs or quotas. On one hand, cheaper imports enable consumers to buy more foreign and domestic goods, creating more jobs. But cheaper imports can put manufacturers out of business and price well-compensated workers out of jobs.

30. Henry J. Tasca, *The Reciprocal Trade Policy of the United States: A Study in Trade Philosophy* (Philadelphia: Univ. of Pennsylvania Press, 1938), 17-25.

31. Congress passed conflicting legislation, including the National Industrial Recovery Act and the Agricultural Adjustment Act, which authorized the imposition of tariffs and quantitative restrictions on imports if they interfered with domestic programs designed to raise prices of agricultural and industrial products. Some analysts believe that Roosevelt's refusal to work for international economic cooperation divided the world economy into trading blocs (the Gold Bloc: France, Belgium, the Netherlands, and Switzerland) and the Sterling area (the British Commonwealth). Hull concluded the conference failed for two reasons: the lack of public opinion supporting trade liberalization, and the "engrossment of many nations with emergency treatment of panic conditions." Hull, *Memoirs,* 248-69; Kindleberger, "U.S. Foreign Economic Policy," 404; and Kelly, "Antecedents," 63-66.

32. Verdier, *Democracy and International Trade,* 195.

33. Dobson, *Two Centuries,* 74-75; Tasca, *Reciprocal Trade Policy,* 29; and John Day Larkin, *Trade Agreements: A Study in Democratic Methods* (New York: Columbia Univ. Press, 1940), 121

34. Hull, *Memoirs,* 352-77; and Tasca, *Reciprocal Trade Policy,* 31-33.

35. To answer the concerns of opponents that the act was an unconstitutional delegation of power, State Department lawyers poured over the history of executive agreements. The department issued memoranda arguing that the president can negotiate trade agreements as executive agreements. N.a., n.d, "Memorandum on Constitutionality of Trade Agreements Act" and "A Tentative List of Topics on Which Memoranda Might Be Prepared in Connection with Renewal of the Trade Agreements Act," 1937, both in box 46, RG 57D-284, NA.

36. Tasca, *Reciprocal Trade Policy,* 33-38. Members also objected to other aspects of the bill.

37. Haggard, "Foundations of Hegemony," 112-13; Larkin, *Trade Agreements,* 11-12.

38. Tasca, *Reciprocal Trade Policy,* 66-67; and Larkin, *Trade Agreements,* 65-67. Section IV of the act provided that reasonable public notice of the intention to negotiate an agreement should be given so that any interested party can present its views.

39. Larkin, *Trade Agreements,* 6-48.

40. John M. Letiche, *Reciprocal Trade Agreements in the World Economy* (New York: King's Crown Press, 1948), 18-19; and Verdier, *Democracy and International Trade,* 196-97.

41. Tasca, *Reciprocal Trade Policy,* 290.

42. Robert Hathaway, "Economic Diplomacy," in Becker and Wells, eds., *Economics and World Power,* 287-96; Lake, *Power, Protection, and Free Trade,* 205-6; Pastor, *Congress,* 87; and Harry C. Hawkins and Janet L. Norwood, "The Legislative Basis of U.S. Commercial Policy," in Kelly, ed., *Studies in U.S. Commercial Policy,* 73, 75.

43. U.S. Department of State, *The Reciprocal Trade Agreements Program of the United States* (Washington, D.C.: GPO, 1938), 3-4; Haggard, "Foundations of Hegemony," 93-94; Kelly, "Antecedents," 49-63; Goldstein, "Ideas," 182-83, 187; and Hawkins and Norwood, "Legislative Basis," 100.

44. Haggard, "Foundations of Hegemony," 112-13; and Verdier, *Democracy and International Trade*, 195-96.

45. Kelly, "Antecedents," 73-75; and Haggard, "Foundations of Hegemony," 93-94.

46. Historians, political scientists, and economists have plowed through the fertile fields of this pathbreaking legislation. Most analysts have not focused on two revolutionary concepts implicit in the legislation: a coupling of freer trade and U.S. jobs and a linkage of the U.S. economy to the world economy. Lenway, *Politics of U.S. International Trade*, 67 (a political science view); Mikesell, *U.S. Economic Policy*, 61-67 (an economist's and insider's view); and Lloyd Gardner, *Economic Aspects of New Deal Diplomacy* (Madison: Univ. of Wisconsin Press, 1964), 39-43 (a historian's view).

47. Franklin D. Roosevelt, "Message from the President of the United States Transmitting a Request to Authorize the Executive to Enter into Executive Commercial Agreements with Foreign Nations," in Tasca, *Reciprocal Trade Policy*, 299-301. The preamble of the act emphasized that increased trade would restore the American standard of living. See also Hull, *Memoirs*, 357; and Pastor, *Congress*, 80.

48. Hadley Cantril, *Public Opinion, 1935-1946* (Princeton: Princeton Univ. Press, 1951), 122, polls #4, 6, 7.

49. Ibid., 124, poll #19.

50. Ibid., 124, #22.

51. Tasca, *Reciprocal Trade Policy*, 293.

52. Telegram, Undersecretary of State Welles to the Secretary of State, Mar. 14, 1940, in Department of State, *Foreign Relations of the United States 1940* (hereafter *FRUS*) (Washington, D.C.: GPO, 1959), 16.

2. Linking Jobs to Trade Policy, 1939-1942

1. Letiche, *Reciprocal Trade Agreements*, 27, 60; and Galambos and Pratt, *The Rise of the Corporate Commonwealth*, 101, table 5.1. Some of the increased exports stemmed from greater demand for U.S. manufacturers and war material such as aircraft, machinery, lubricants, and chemicals.

2. Harley Notter to Mr. Duggan, Aug. 3, 1939, box 108, in Records of Harley Notter, Record Group 59, at NA (hereafter Notter Records). Also Harley Notter, *Postwar Foreign Policy Preparation* (Washington, D.C.: Department of State, 1949), 15.

3. See, for example, the records of the Postwar Planning Committee of the National Association of Manufacturers, boxes 288 and 289, accession 1411, in the Hagley Museum and Library, hereafter HML; and Notter, *Postwar*, 19.

4. Leo Pasvolsky was special assistant to the U.S. secretary of state, 1936-1938. He left the department for the Brookings Institution, then returned in 1939. Notter, *Postwar*, 24.

5. Hull, *Memoirs*, 1625-28. I am defining the postwar planners as those individuals actively involved in U.S. government efforts to plan the peace. They included civil servants and political appointees and were principally inside government, although some academics, consultants, business leaders, and labor officials also served this process from outside the government. The bulk of postwar planning was developed under the aegis of the Department of State; however, other agencies took the lead in certain areas. For example, the Treasury Department, under the direction of Harry Dexter White, planned postwar monetary policies and institutions. The Agriculture Department did much of the planning for the 1943 United Nations Conference on Food and Agriculture. Notter, *Postwar*, 107, 145.

6. For information as to how this perspective evolved, see Hull, *Memoirs*, 133; E.F. Penrose, *Economic Planning for the Peace* (Princeton: Princeton Univ. Press, 1953),

15; and Hansen, *America's Role in the World Economy,* 91-93. Also see two speeches by Cordell Hull, "The Outlook for the Trade Agreements Program," *Commercial Policy Series* 54 (Washington, D.C.: Department of State, 1938): 9-10; and Cordell Hull, "Foreign Trade, Farm Prosperity, and Peace," *Commercial Policy Series* 44 (Washington, D.C.: Department of State, 1938): 4-6, 13-15.

7. By the end of 1941, the staff had grown to eleven. Notter, *Postwar,* 38-39, 53.

8. Hawkins was chief of the Division of Trade Agreements. On Hawkins' relationship with Hull, see Oral History interview with John M. Leddy, June 15, 1973, 6-12, HSTL; and Oral History interview with Winthrop A. Brown, May 25, 1973, 4, HSTL. Twenty-two trade agreements were negotiated in 1934-49; only six in 1940-45. See draft chapter, "Division of Commercial Policy," 78, 96-98, 191, Notter Records.

9. Notter to Pasvolsky, Sept. 5, 1941, "The Transformation of the Division of Special Research from an Emergency to a Permanent Status," 1, box 11; "Division of Commercial Policy," 1-2, 151, box 32; and "Post-War Economic Problems," box 32, all in Notter Records. As an example of Hawkins's attempt to work with Pasvolsky's division, see memorandum, Harry Hawkins to W. Rostow, Sept. 9, 1942, box 5, Acheson Records.

10. The committee tried to organize a conference of neutrals on economic issues, but it came to naught. By May 1940, Germany had conquered Denmark, the Netherlands, Luxembourg, Belgium, and France, and the conference was abandoned. Hull, *Memoirs,* 1626-28; and Department of State, *FRUS 1940,* 1:1-122.

11. Notter, *Postwar,* 29-31; "Interdepartmental Group to Consider Post-War International Economic Problems and Policies," May 1940-Feb. 1942; and "Interdepartmental Group to Consider Post-War International Economic Problems and Policies," Dec. 18, 1940, both in box 11, Notter Records.

12. Hawkins to Acheson, Welles, and Hull, Aug. 4, 1941, 17, box 5, Acheson Records. On the linkage of bilateral negotiations with Britain to future multilateral agreements, see Wadleigh to Notter, "Basic Problems and Policies of Post-War International Economic Relations," 9, 1941, Notter Records; and Pasvolsky to Hull, "Possibilities of Conflict of British and American Official Views on Post-War Economic Policy," 5, box 2, in Records of Leo Pasvolsky, RG 59, NA, hereafter Pasvolsky Records. Pasvolsky notes, "Each of our countries is so important that if policies fail in adoption in one they will be doomed in the other and everywhere."

13. It was not easy to build a U.S. constituency in favor of lend-lease. Arthur H. Vandenberg Jr., *The Private Papers of Senator Vandenberg* (Boston: Houghton Mifflin, 1952), 9-13; and Hull, *Memoirs,* 922-25.

14. Lend-lease was President Roosevelt's idea. Alan Nevins, *The New Deal and World Affairs* (New Haven: Yale Univ. Press, 1950), 37-38, 43, 223-24; and Hull, *Memoirs,* 872-74, 925.

15. The lend-lease agreement committed the signatories "to promote mutually advantageous economic relations" and the betterment of worldwide economic relations. It provided for agreed action "directed to the expansion by appropriate international and domestic measures of production, employment and the exchange and consumption of goods." George M. Fennemore, "The Role of the Department of State in Connection with the Lend-Lease Program," 9, 1943, 79, box 14, Notter Records.

16. "Draft Study on Background of ITO," June 29, 1948, 3, box 3, LF 57D-284. The United States would provide the goods with terms of payment to be settled later. N.a., "Lend-lease," Aug. 2, 1946, box 13, Notter Records.

17. Consequently, the postwar planners would now have to balance the aspirations of our lend-lease partners with those of our own. It was very difficult for the postwar planners to balance domestic and foreign objectives for the peace. See speech

by Sumner Welles, undersecretary of state, Apr. 12, 1943, in Commercial Policy General File II, 280, 285 in box 23, RG 353, lot file 122, NA. Some nations grew to resent how lend-lease linked America's peacetime objectives with her wartime clout. This will be illustrated later, as we review the lend-lease negotiations with the British.

18. "The Division of Commercial Policy," 7, box 32, Notter Records.

19. William H. Diebold Jr., interview with author, July 12, 1990. Mr. Diebold served part-time with the Division of Special Research and the Council during this period. Also see Francis P. Miller, administrative secretary, Council on Foreign Relations, to Leo Pasvolsky, Dec. 11, 1941, file 4; and Walter H. Mallory, executive director, Council on Foreign Relations, to Pasvolsky, file 8, both in box 2, Pasvolsky Records.

20. For evidence of the Council's general support of policies to free trade, see Robert D. Schulzinger, *The Wise Men of Foreign Affairs* (New York: Columbia Univ. Press, 1984), 36, 47, 69, 85-86.

21. Notter, *Postwar,* 56-58; and Gardner, *Sterling-Dollar Diplomacy,* 4, 15.

22. Henry Wallace, *America Must Choose: The Advantages and Disadvantages of Nationalism, of World Trade, and of a Planned Middle Course* (New York: Foreign Policy Association and World Peace Foundation, 1934). See Acheson to Hawkins, July 31, 1941, file 1; and Charles Yost to Dean Acheson, "Prospective Functions of the Board of Economic Warfare," Dec. 22, 1941, 1, 2, 11, 12 both in box 1, Acheson Records. For a good understanding of Henry Wallace's hopes for future international economic policies, see Norman D. Markowitz, *The Rise and Fall of the People's Century* (New York: Free Press, 1973), 66.

23. Hull, *Memoirs,* 1631; and memorandum by Charles Yost, "Possible Steps in the Conduct of Liaison," June 4, 1942, box 11, Notter Records.

24. Acheson to Milo Perkins, May 19, 1942, box 12; and memorandum by Mary Jane Carder, Apr. 15, 1942, box 1, both in Acheson Records. State was seen as a model of interagency relations, "The Division of Commercial Policy," 195, box 32, Notter Records.

25. The postwar planners had initially controlled the information the public received about their plans. But Hull had to go public to gain support for their efforts. "Notter's Recollections"; and Division of Special Research, Staff memo 26, Feb. 22, 1942, both in box 11, Notter Records.

26. Notter, *Postwar,* 42-43.

27. See Leland M. Goodrich, ed., *Documents on American Foreign Relations* (Boston: World Peace Foundation, 1942): 4:1-4, 13-15 (hereafter cited as *Documents*); and Hull, *Memoirs,* 1630-32. These speeches paid off in developing some congressional support for the planning process. Notter, *Postwar,* 45-57.

28. Mikesell, *U.S. Economic Policy,* 119; and William Diebold Jr., *New Directions in Our Trade Policy* (New York: Council on Foreign Relations, 1941), 144. According to E.F. Penrose, economic advisor to America's ambassador to Great Britain, "there was fuller appreciation of the dependence of trade policy on internal employment policy," a key concern throughout Europe. Penrose, *Economic Planning for the Peace,* 15. For a private sector view see *Proceedings of the 239th Meeting of the National Industrial Conference Board,* Jan. 22, 1942, 28-30, accession 1057, HML. Many Europeans feared that the United States might experience another depression and cut off trade. N.a., *Major Problems of United States Foreign Policy 1947: A Study Guide* (Washington, D.C.: Brookings Institution, 1947), 25-26.

29. See "Public Attitudes on Commercial Policy in the United States and Great Britain: A Summary," Nov. 14, 1944, 1-2 in file 11, Special Committee on the Relaxation of Trade Barriers, box 104, LF 57D-284; and "American Public Attitudes on World Trade Issues," Nov. 46, 7, Papers Used at Press Conference file, box 98, LF 57D-284.

Also see Mikesell, *U.S. Economic Policy,* 121-23; and Percy W. Bidwell, *A Commercial Policy for the United Nations* (New York: Committee on International Economic Policy in Cooperation with the Carnegie Endowment for International Peace, 1945), 8-9, 34-35.

30. House Committee on Ways and Means, *Report to Accompany H.J. Res. 407: Extending the Authority of the President under Section 350 of the Tariff Act of 1930, as Amended,* 76th Cong., 3d sess., Feb. 14, 1940, H.R. 1594, 1-3.

31. Ibid., 3; and Minority Views, *Part 2,* 76th Cong., 3d sess., Feb. 16, 1940, 4, 5, 10, 14.

32. Joe R. Wilkinson, *Politics and Trade Policy* (Washington, D.C.: Public Affairs Press, 1960), 20-22.

33. Minutes, International Relations Subcommittee, Committee on Postwar Problems, National Association of Manufacturers, Mar. 20, 1942, series V, box 6, accession 1411, HML. Also see Carter Goodrich, chairman, International Labor Office, to Sumner Welles, Mar. 16, 1942, box 2; Joseph Jones to Pasvolsky, Nov. 20, 1942, box 3; and J.O. Downey of General Motors to Pasvolsky, June 5, 1942, box 3, all in Pasvolsky Records.

34. No author, but I believe this was Joseph Jones, to Pasvolsky, Sept. 24, 1942; and Charles Yost to Pasvolsky, Apr. 14, 1942, both in box 3, Pasvolsky Records.

35. "Draft Study on Background of ITO," June 29, 1948, 4, Background/ITO file, box 3, LF 57D-284; and Notter, *Postwar,* 49.

36. Memorandum by Lewis, in Sumner Welles's memoranda of conversation, "History of Negotiations with Responsibilities to Point Four of the Atlantic Charter," box 13, Notter Records.

37. For a good analysis of the perceptions on the U.S. side and on the British side, see Harley Notter, "Comment on the Atlantic Joint Declaration of President Roosevelt and Prime Minister Churchill, Aug. 14, 1941," Atlantic Charter file, box 13, Notter Records; and Pasvolsky to Hull, "Possibilities of Conflict of British and American Official Views," Dec. 12, 1941, box 2, Pasvolsky Records. Preferences were a force for solidarity within the Commonwealth. Many British people felt it inappropriate that the United States, a country that was not in the war, was suggesting that Britain abandon its preferences, which benefited the nations that fought side by side with the British, such as Australia and Canada. See Penrose, *Economic Planning for the Peace,* 19-20. At the same time, many Americans felt they had long been abused by the British on trade (from the colonial era to the present) and preferences continued this abuse. See Gardner, *Sterling-Dollar Diplomacy,* 18-19.

38. "Draft Study on Background of ITO," June 29, 1948, 4, Background/ITO file, box 3, LF 57D-284.

39. The Atlantic Charter called upon nations to endeavor, "with due respect for their existing obligations, to further the enjoyment by all States, great or small of access, on equal terms, to the trade and to the raw materials of the world." The signatories declared that "they desire to bring about the fullest collaboration between all nations in the economic field with the object of securing for all, improved labor standards, economic advancement, and social security." "President Roosevelt's Message to Congress," Aug. 21, 1941, in Goodrich, *Documents,* 4:10-12.

40. Harley Notter, "Comment on the Atlantic Joint Declaration," Sept. 11, 1941, 14-25, box 13, Notter Records. As examples of the questions raised, what did the pledge "access on equal terms" mean (pp. 15-18)? Did the Charter's Point Four call for international planning (pp. 19-21)? How permanent would Anglo-American cooperation be?

41. Notter, *Postwar,* 62; and Goodrich, *Documents,* 4:203.

42. The first quotation is from the "four freedoms" speech; the second quota-

tion is from Point Five, the Atlantic Charter, in Notter, *Postwar,* 42-43, 50. Also see memorandum by Wadleigh, "Basic Problems and Policies of Post-War International Economic Relations," 9, 1941, 1, 12, 13, 53, box 13, Notter Records.

43. Hawkins's division gained overall responsibility for commercial policy in 1941. "Draft Study on Background of ITO," June 29, 1948, 3, 5-7, Background/ITO file, box 3, LF 57D-284; and "Division of Commercial Policy," Notter Records. Paslovsky's Division of Special Research also worked on these issues, and its staff was expanded too. William Diebold Jr., interview with author, July 12, 1990; and Notter, *Postwar,* 79-80, 154-55.

44. The Trade-Agreement Program (under the RTAA) could foster multilateral trade liberalization because the trade agreements program extended benefits to all nations that traded with RTAA signatories. Hull, "Foreign Trade, Farm Prosperity, and Peace," 12, 14-16 and Hull, "The Outlook for the Trade-Agreements Program," 9-10. Also see Hull to Howard Coonley, president of the National Association of Manufacturers, Oct. 18, 1939, tariff file 2, box 855.3 in accession 1411, HML; and memorandum to Mr. Pasvolsky, Dec. 11, 1941, 1, 4, 5, box 32, Notter Records.

45. Dean Acheson, memorandum of conversation, July 28, 1941, *FRUS 1941,* (Washington, D.C.: GPO, 1959), 3:11-13. There were many in the Labour party who felt strongly that domestic and international markets could not be left solely to the invisible hand of market forces. These individuals believed that the visible hand of government should be used to maintain full employment. Hawkins to Acheson, Welles, and Hull, Aug. 4, 1941, 17, box 5, Acheson Records.

46. See "Public Attitudes on Foreign Policy, Special Report," Nov. 14, 1944, 3 in file 11, Special Committee on the Relaxation of Trade Barriers, box 104, LF 57D-284.

47. Lord Keynes to Acheson, July 29, 1941, file 4, box 2, Pasvolsky Records.

48. See notes that follow and memoirs of varied participants in the discussions with Keynes. As example, E.F. Penrose decided "in discussions with Mr. Keynes it would be wise to accept unreservedly the view that . . . free trade would be lost unless a high level of employment were maintained." Penrose believed that Hawkins and Hull had to prove that they were progressive in outlook "and under no illusion that freer trade alone was a panacea for all economic ills." Penrose, *Economic Planning for the Peace,* 15-16, 18. Keynes wrote to Acheson, "Forgive my vehemence. This is my subject. I know, or partly know, what I want. I know, and clearly know, what I fear." Keynes to Acheson, July 29, 1941, box 5, Acheson Records. Acheson described Keynes as one of the most brilliant men, though "to some he appeared arrogant." Keynes was "genuinely doubtful about our ability to see clearly into the postwar world." He was distrustful of American intentions. Acheson, *Present at the Creation,* 22, 29, 31.

49. Keynes was not easy to read, as several of his most prominent followers noted. But soon growing numbers of economists, students, and government officials read his influential book, *The General Theory of Employment, Interest, and Money.* During the Depression, many individuals influenced by Keynes moved into U.S. government agencies. As John Kenneth Galbraith noted, "Keynes was deeply dependent on his prophets" to spread his word. John Kenneth Galbraith, *Economics, Peace, and Laughter* (Boston: Houghton Mifflin, 1971), 49; Alan Sweezy, "The Keynesians and Government Policy, 1933-1939," *American Economic Review* 62 (May 1972): 116, 122; and Walter S. Salant, "The Spread of Keynesian Doctrines and Practices in the U.S.," in Omar F. Hamouda and John N. Smithin, eds., *Keynes and Public Policy after Fifty Years* (New York: New York Univ. Press, 1990), 1:65-76.

50. Alvin H. Hansen, *A Guide to Keynes* (New York: McGraw-Hill, 1953), 226-27; and David Calleo, "Keynes and Pax Americana," in *The End of the Keynesian Era,* ed. Robert Sidelsky (New York: Holmes and Meier, 1977), 96.

51. Examples of the focus on Keynes's views include Harry Hawkins to Acheson, Welles, and Hull, Aug. 4, 1941, quotations on pp. 1, 3; Keynes to Acheson, June 4, 1941, both in box 5, Acheson Records; and Hawkins to Pasvolsky and Acheson, Apr. 21, 1942, box 2, Pasvolsky Records. Keynes served the British government as director of the British Supply Council in North America in 1941-42.

52. Keynes's views on trade policy contrasted with those in the Department of State, where freer trade was seen as integral to global economic growth. He was, after all, most concerned with Britain's increasingly precarious economic position and her employment problem. Keynes is quoted in Hansen, *Guide to Keynes,* 215.

53. The "new and better" quotation is from Lord Keynes to Acheson, July 29, 1941, box 5, Acheson Records. Also see memorandum to Acheson, Welles, and Hull, Aug. 4, 1941, 8-9, box 5, Acheson Records; and Hawkins to Acheson, Aug. 1, 1941, file 4, box 2, Pasvolsky Records.

54. Protectionism and bilateralism had been discredited among the State Department staff after Hull won his battle with George Peek, President Roosevelt's trade adviser, in 1934. See Dallek, *Roosevelt,* 84-93. For evidence of the influence of freer trade views on the staff of the State Department see Oral History interview with Raymond Vernon, July 19, 1973, 41-45, HSTL; Oral History interview with Winthrop G. Brown, May 25, 1973, 4-5, HSTL; and Oral History interview with John M. Leddy, June 15, 1973, 8-12, HSTL.

55. Hawkins to Acheson, Aug. 1, 1941, in file 4, box 2, Pasvolsky Records.

56. In July 1941, Keynes came to Washington to explain British views and explore American views on economic policy. He was handed a draft of Article VII containing a strict commitment to nondiscrimination (and no commensurate American actions). His objections led to a new draft. This draft, prepared toward the end of 1941, called for "agreed action directed to the expansion, by appropriate international and domestic measures of production, employment and the exchange and consumption of goods." This was the first mutual acknowledgment that the "maintenance and expansion of trade and production were complementary aims." This new draft also stated that the elimination of discrimination was to occur with the reduction of tariffs and other trade barriers. See Department of State, *FRUS 1941,* 3:11-15; and Acheson, *Present at the Creation,* 29-33.

57. The Americans recognized that to get British support they would have to reduce tariffs dramatically. Hawkins to Acheson, Aug. 1, 1941, *FRUS 1941,* 3:21.

58. They were concerned about "approving any arrangement which seemed to make the dismantling of Commonwealth economic arrangements the 'price' of Lend-Lease aid." See Dean Acheson, memoranda of conversation, Oct. 3, 1941; and Sumner Welles, memoranda of conversation, Oct. 19, 1941, *FRUS 1941,* 3:38-40.

59. *FRUS 1941,* 3:49-50. British officials were "dismayed by a proposal to make their chief import dearer." Penrose, *Economic Planning for the Peace,* 66-67. A draft convention was drawn up for submission to an international wheat conference to be held at a propitious time. The original approach to the wheat agreement was abandoned.

60. For the final communique of the International Wheat Meeting, Washington, Aug. 4, 1941, see Goodrich, *Documents,* 4:713-18.

61. *FRUS 1941,* 3:36-53. A summary of the U.S. government position is on pp. 47-49. For a text of the final draft of Article VII, see Goodrich, *Documents,* 4:235-37.

62. The marketing of the program in each nation furthered the potential for misunderstandings in the future. President Roosevelt told the Congress that the United States was receiving a benefit—it would "promote mutually advantageous economic relations between them." "99 Day Report of the President on the Lend-Lease Act,"

June 11, 1942, Goodrich, *Documents,* 4:233-34. Churchill and other prominent officials told the British people that Article VII did not really provide for the elimination of Imperial Preferences. Gardner, *Sterling-Dollar Diplomacy,* 64-65.

63. Quotations from "Post-War International Economic Policies in Their Relation to Domestic Policies," Aug. 24, 1942, 1, box 14, Acheson Records; and memorandum by Wadleigh, "Basic Problems and Policies of Post-War International Economic Relations," Sept. 1941, 1, 12, 13, 53, box 13, Notter Records.

64. Confidential memorandum to Ambassador Winant, Aug. 22, 1942, box 14, Acheson Records.

65. Wilcox, *Charter,* 63; and Mikesell, *U.S. Economic Policy,* 61-67.

66. An example of a horizontal reduction would be to *uniformly* (across the board) cut tariffs by a certain percentage—say, 50 percent of 1930 tariff levels. George M. Fennemore, "The Role of the Department of State . . . ," Sept. 1943, 85-87, box 14, Notter Records. As early as 1942, some members of Congress expressed concern about executive authority to act on economic postwar planning under Article VII. Representative Charles Dewey to Pasvolsky, box 3, Pasvolsky Records; Rostow to Acheson, Dec. 28, 1942; and Hawkins to Rostow, Jan. 21, 1943, both in box 3, Acheson Records.

67. Memorandum by Cordell Hull, "Post-War Planning," Aug. 24, 1942, 2, box 5, Acheson Records.

68. The Advisory Committee included ten government outsiders as well as five senators and three representatives. Nongovernmental members included Isaiah Bowman, president of Johns Hopkins University; Hamilton Fish Armstrong, editor of *Foreign Affairs;* and Anne O'Hare McCormick, foreign affairs editor of the *New York Times.* Members from the American Federation of Labor and the Congress of Industrial Organizations were also invited to participate. Notter, *Postwar,* 58-59, 63-65, 72, 92-93.

69. In addition to five senior officials from the Department of State (Dean Acheson, Leo Pasvolsky, Herbert Feis, Adolph A. Berle Jr., and Harry Hawkins), members included Harry Dexter White, assistant to the secretary of the Treasury; Paul Appleby, undersecretary of agriculture; and Louis H. Bean, a senior official of the Board of Economic Warfare. Benjamin Cohen represented the president. Outside members were also selected for their expertise on trade policy. In July 1942, Norman H. Davis, president of the Council on Foreign Relations; Brooks Emeny, director of the Council of Foreign Affairs of Cleveland, Ohio; and Robert J. Watt, international representative of the American Federation of Labor, joined the committee. Prominent economists Percy Bidwell and Jacob Viner, senior labor union officials, and the president of the United States Chamber of Commerce, Eric A. Johnston, also participated in the committee's work. The Subcommittee on Economic Reconstruction (headed by Assistant Secretary Berle) was formed to address problems of relief and reconstruction. Notter, *Postwar,* 73, 76-77, 136.

70. Eleanor E. Dennison, "The Development of the Charter for an International Trade Organization: A Case Study of Interdepartmental Relationships," Aug. 13, 1948, 3, miscellaneous correspondence file, box 3, LF 57D-284.

71. In the period from February 20 to July 1942, the Acheson subcommittee had the following members: Acheson, Berle, Feis, Hawkins, and Pasvolsky of State; a representative of Treasury (later Harry Dexter White); and Mr. Appleby; Mr. Bean; and Mr. Cohen of other agencies/departments. In the period from July 1942 to March 1943, the members of the Acheson subcommittee included nongovernmental members Davis, Emeny, and Watt, none of whom represented congressional or protectionist interests. Acheson, Pasvolsky, and Hawkins remained as State representatives, and Appleby and Cohen remained from other agencies. It is important to note that several congressmen

served the Postwar Advisory Committee and other subcommittees, but none served on this subcommittee during this period. Notter, *Postwar,* 73-81, 136-37. In 1943, American business representatives called on government to include them in the postwar planning. See Press Release, "NAM Urges Government Use Businessmen to Assist fn Solving Postwar Problems," June 4, 1943, 1, accession 1411, box 288, HML.

72. He replaced the economic subcommittees with a fourth group, the Committee on Post-War Foreign Economic Policy, on Apr. 9, 1943. Memorandum to Acheson, "Organization of Economic Work," Jan. 11, 1943, box 1, Acheson Records. Ambassador Myron C. Taylor was designated to direct the Committee in the absence of Secretary Hull; thus, it became known as the Taylor Committee. This committee included several individuals outside the government including Isaiah Bowman of Johns Hopkins; Eric A. Johnston of the Chamber of Commerce; and Philip Murray of the CIO. Yet even this group would be transitional; it met several times in the summer, but was not reconvened as a whole after July 1943. Notter, *Postwar,* 73, 138-40.

73. In the fourth and last meeting of the full Advisory Committee on May 2, 1942, Hull expressed concern that interest groups would fight innovative plans for the peace. Notter, *Postwar,* 92; and Hull, *Memoirs,* 1178-79.

74. Memorandum to Leo Pasvolsky, Aug. 24, 1942, 1, file 2, box 3, Pasvolsky Records.

75. "Economic safety for the America of the future is threatened unless a greater economic stability comes to the rest of the world." "President Roosevelt's Message to the 78th Congress on the State of the Nation," Delivered before a Joint Session of Congress, Jan. 7, 1943, in *War and Peace Aims of the United Nations,* ed. Louise W. Holborn (Boston: World Peace Foundation, 1948), 103. Thus, the postwar planners sought economic security for the American economy through trade liberalization. But to achieve this state of security, the postwar planners promoted an international innovation. Galambos, "Technology, Political Economy, and Professionalization," *Business History Review* 57 (winter 1983): 485.

76. Many Americans saw a full employment policy as close to socialism. Acheson, *Present at the Creation,* 32. To Penrose, this linkage of laissez-faire to Keynesian economics showed that British and American economists "accepted the view that the maintenance and expansion of trade and production were complementary aims." Penrose, *Economic Planning for the Peace,* 12, 29. According to John Leddy, "There were many economists and others who thought that an excessive concern with full employment would lead to rigid controls and socialist planning." Oral History interview with John Leddy, June 15, 1973, 64-74, HSTL.

77. Memorandum to Acheson, Oct. 28, 1942; and Rostow to Acheson, Dec. 28, 1942, both in box 3, Acheson Records.

78. Memorandum by Cordell Hull, "Post-War Planning," Aug. 24, 1942, 2, box 5, Acheson Records. I take this language from "American Public Attitudes on World Trade Issues," Nov. 7, 1946, 3, Box 98, LF 57D-284.

3. Gaining Congressional Approval for Multilateral Trade Liberalization, 1943-1945

1. The Republican Post-War Advisory Council adopted resolutions on postwar domestic and foreign policy at Mackinac, Michigan, in September 1943.

2. Lionel Robbins and James Meade were economists who served the British government during the World War II. They later became noted academic economists. Each man kept a diary of his negotiations with the Americans in the years 1943-45. In his diary, Robbins noted the Lippman quote. Susan Howson and Donald Moggridge,

eds., *The Wartime Diaries of Lionel Robbins and James Meade, 1943-1945* (New York: St. Martin's Press, 1991).

3. Cordell Hull, radio address, "Our Foreign Policy in the Framework of Our National Interests," Aug. 12, 1943, in Notter, *Postwar,* 165.

4. "Preliminary Report of the Special Committee on the Relaxation of Trade Barriers," draft, Nov. 1, 1943, 2, 7, 15, 19, 20, box 51; and "United States Post-War Commercial Policy," Nov. 18, 1944, 7, box 13, both in Notter Records.

5. Notter, *Postwar,* 140, 179-82, 358, 537-40. This committee began as a sub-committee of the short-lived Taylor Committee, and later was made part of an inter-agency committee called the Executive Committee on Economic Foreign Policy. It had no nongovernmental or congressional members. Its members included government officials from the State, Agriculture, and Commerce Departments as well as from the Tariff Commission and two wartime agencies.

6. "Preliminary Report of the Special Committee on the Relaxation of Trade Barriers," draft, Nov. 1, 1943, 15, 17, 19, 21, box 51, Notter Records. Also see "Progress Report: Special Committee on the Relaxation of Trade Barriers," Dec. 8, 1943, 9, LF 57D-284; and Notter, *Postwar,* 182 n 9 and 358.

7. "Preliminary Report of the Special Committee on the Relaxation of Trade Barriers," draft, Nov. 1, 1943, quotations on pp. 20-22, box 51, Notter Records.

8. "Progress Report," Dec. 8, 1943, 16-17, box 20, LF 57D-284.

9. "Progress Report," Dec. 8, 1943, 16-21, box 20, LF 57D-284.

10. James T. Patterson, *Congressional Conservatism and the New Deal* (Lexington: Univ. of Kentucky, 1967), 334-37; Mary Hedge Hinchey, "The Frustration of the New Deal Revival, 1944-1946" (Ph.D. diss., University of Missouri, 1965), 6; and Richard N. Chapman, *Contours of Public Policy, 1939-1945* (New York: Garland, 1981), 268-69.

11. House Committee on Ways and Means, *Hearings on H.J. Res. 111, Extension of Reciprocal Trade Agreements Act,* 78th Cong., 1st sess., Apr. 12-23, 1943.

12. *Hearings on H.J. Res. 111,* 111, 182, 498, 622, 648.

13. For example, the National Association of Manufacturers worried whether the free enterprise system could survive the war. When the war ended, government should not try to "run enterprise." *NAM News,* Jan. 15, 1944, 1, 4, file "Postwar News Section 3," box 288, acc. 1411, HML. For some of the concerns of Congress, see "Congress Will Draw Its Own Postwar Plan," 1, in same newsletter. Also see Richard E. Darilek, *A Loyal Opposition in Time of War* (Westport, Conn.: Greenwood Press, 1976), 104; and Roland N. Young, *Congressional Politics in the Second World War* (New York: Columbia Univ. Press, 1956), 180-83. For linkage with the New Deal, see "An Alternative Post-War Program," Jan. 25, 1943, box 4, Pasvolsky Records.

14. House Committee on Ways and Means, *Hearings on H.J. Res. 111,* 168-69, 205-6, 230, 314, 417, 624, 694.

15. Ibid., quotations on undemocratic process, totalitarian analysis, 223, 407, 411, 417, 654, 933, 988; and quotations on Congress delegating its power, 209, 394, 400, 665, 691, 1084, 1089.

16. Ibid., 472-73, 496, 597, 607, 769, 806, 933, 985, 1000.

17. Ibid., 472, 586, 696, 699, 722, 835, 865, 1080.

18. John Patterson, "Republican Attitude on International Cooperation Reflected in Congressional Debate on the Trade Agreements Program," June 12, 1943, 6-7; and Acheson to Pasvolsky, Sept. 9, 1943, both in box 4, Pasvolsky Records.

19. U.S. Tariff Commission, *Operation of the Trade Agreements Program, June 1934 to April 1948* (Washington, D.C.: GPO, 1948), 15.

20. Darilek, *Loyal Opposition,* 66-68; and Hinchey, "The Frustration," 10.

21. This was the shared observation of Lionel Robbins and James Meade, who became close with many of the U.S. trade policy planners in this period. Howson and Moggridge, eds., *Wartime Diaries,* 21-22, 25, 121-22.

22. The Board of Trade was in charge of domestic and foreign commerce in Great Britain. Gardner, *Sterling-Dollar Diplomacy,* 103; Penrose, *Economic Planning for the Peace,* 94-95; and Howson and Moggridge, eds, *Wartime Diaries,* 110-11.

23. Woodbury Willoughby to William Fowler, Aug. 23, 1943; and Attachments, "Commercial Policy: Introductory Note," and "Commercial Policy: Illustrative Outline of Proposals," Aug. 17, 1943, all in box 19, LF 57D-284. The negotiators broke up into several committees to discuss specifics. "Informal Economic Discussions, Committee on Measures for Stimulating Commerce," Oct. 11, 1943, box 19, LF 57D-284. For a British perspective see Howson and Moggridge, eds., *Wartime Diaries,* 104-49. Also see Notter, *Postwar,* app. 30, 562-64. Both British and American delegations included all of the relevant government agencies. Fuqua, Leddy, and Stinebower were economists in the Department of State. Leddy drafted much of the GATT.

24. "Commercial Policy Introductory Note," 1, 4, 5, box 19, LF 57D-284.

25. Draft Minutes of Committee on Measures for Stimulating Commerce, Oct. 11, 1943, 2-5, box 194, LF 57D-284; "Cartel Subcommittee Minutes," Oct. 20, 1943, 5-7, box 19, LF 57D-284; and "Commercial Policy Introductory Note," 5, box 19, LF 57D-284.

26. "Informal Exploratory Conversations between Officials of the United States and Canada Regarding the Formulation of an Agenda for Discussions Looking toward the Implementation of the Principles Enunciated in the Exchange of Notes between the United States and Canada on November 30, 1942," Feb. 14, 1944, 1-3, box 20, LF 57D-284; and "United States Post-War Commercial Policy, Multilateral versus Multilateral-Bilateral Action Background Statement," Nov. 1944, 15, box 7, LF 57D-284.

27. Penrose, *Economic Planning for the Peace,* 92-94; and memorandum to the Executive Committee on Economic Foreign Policy from the Committee on Trade Barriers, ECEFP D62/44, Oct. 4, 1944, box 18, LF 57D-284.

28. "Progress Report," Dec. 8, 1943, 3, box 20, LF 57D-284.

29. Howson and Moggridge, eds., *Wartime Diaries,* 18.

30. Ibid., 15 Oct. 1943, 139 and 13 September, 1943, 101.

31. Memorandum for the Secretary, Oct. 6, 1943, box 41, LF 57D-284; "Bases of Our Program for International Economic Cooperation," submitted Oct. 22, 1943, box 20, LF 57D-284; and Notter, *Postwar,* 198-99, 562-64.

32. "Post-War Commercial Policy of the United States," PWC-52, Mar. 6, 1944, 3-5; "Summary of Statement on Post-War Commercial Policy of the United States," PWC-57, Mar. 6, 1944, box 20, LF 57D-284; and cover memorandum by Woodbury Willoughby, Mar. 7, 1944, box 20, LF 57D-284. Invitations to undertake similar discussions were extended to the Soviet and Chinese governments. "Progress Report on Post-War Programs," n.d., 3, box 145, LF 57D-284.

33. Notter, *Postwar,* 199.

34. Woodbury Willoughby, "Views of the Undersecretary of Commerce on the Implementation of Article VII," Feb.-June 1944, box 20, LF 57D-284.

35. "Procedure for Trade and Employment Conference," May 21, 1945, box 88, LF 57D-284.

36. Darilek, *Loyal Opposition,* 182; Robert A. Divine, *Foreign Policy and U.S. Presidential Elections, 1940-1948* (New York: New Viewpoints, 1974); and Charles John Graham, "Republican Foreign Policy, 1939-1952," (Ph.D. diss., Univ. of Illinois, 1955), 87-92, 117-19. Darilek believes this consensus was less a result of Republican conversion to internationalism and more a strategic response to a hazardous situation.

37. Ruth Russell, *A History of the United Nations Charter: The Role of the United States, 1940-1945* (Washington, D.C.: Brookings Institution, 1958), 125.

38. Ibid., 125, 225, 275, 594-95. These officials held some 115 meetings with representatives of religious, education, business, labor, and veterans groups from October 16, 1944, to December 20, 1944.

39. The period of preparation for U.S. proposals on an international security organization covered December 9, 1943 to July 8, 1944. Notter, *Postwar,* 215, 246-69, quotations on p. 269; and "Informal Political Agenda Group," IO Minutes, International Organization Discussions, Apr. 10, 1944, box 53, RG 353, Lot File 122, Inter- and Intra Departmental Committees of the Department of State, hereafter RG 353, LF 122. Also see Russell, *History of U.N. Charter,* 935; Hull, *Memoirs,* 1656-1713; and Robert C. Hilderbrand, *Dumbarton Oaks: The Origins of the United Nations and the Search for Postwar Security* (Chapel Hill: Univ. of North Carolina, 1990), 27-29, 56-58, 150-51.

40. Russell, *History of U.N. Charter,* 935-47.

41. Armand Van Dormael, *Bretton Woods: Birth of a Monetary System* (New York: Holmes and Meier, 1978), 219.

42. Ibid., *Bretton Woods,* 169-85, 240-65; and Alfred Eckes Jr., *A Search for Solvency: Bretton Woods and the International Monetary System 1941-1971* (Austin: Univ. of Texas Press, 1975), 169-210, Taft quote is on p. 196.

43. Emilio G. Collado to Secretary Hull, Mar. 30, 1944, box 2, Pasvolsky Records. For Acheson quotation see Acheson, *Present at the Creation,* 108. It is important to note that many bankers and business leaders were opposed to the BWI.

44. "Implementation of Post-War Commercial Policy Objectives," Feb. 15, 1945, box 13, Notter Records; and memorandum, June 30, 1945, box 88, LF 57D-284.

45. Proposal B suggested negotiating bilateral agreements that would incorporate selective tariff reductions. Although this proposal could be effected under the TAP, it would not provide an adequate incentive for nontariff barrier reduction because the amount of concessions would be unclear. Proposal C was a commitment to negotiate bilateral agreements covering trade barriers of all kinds. Like B, this proposal could be effected under the TAP, but it too would not be an adequate incentive for nontariff barrier reduction, because the extent of trade barrier reduction ultimately achieved might be problematical. In addition, the British believed these approaches should only be used as a last resort since they had such serious disadvantages. Proposal D called for horizontal tariff reduction plus a commitment to negotiate bilateral tariff agreements. This proposal would utilize the TAP, provide negotiating nations with a clearer commitment on U.S. tariff cuts, and therefore better induce them to reduce nontariff barriers. But would Congress approve this change to the TAP allowing horizontal tariff reduction? Memorandum by John Leddy, n.d., 13-21, box 19, LF 57D-284. The Canadians much preferred Proposal A but were willing to consider C. "Informal Exploratory Conversations," Feb. 14, 1944, 3-4, box 20, LF 57D-284.

46. Memorandum by John Leddy, n.d., 3-12, box 19, LF 57D-284; and "Multilateral vs. Multilateral-Bilateral Action Background Statement," Nov. 1944, box 7, LF 57D-284.

47. Memorandum by John Leddy, n.d., 24-33, quotations on pp. 27, 33, box 19, LF 57D-284. For confirmation that most of the trade policy planners preferred this approach, see Clayton to Fowler, Dec. 31, 1944; and Fowler to Leddy, Dec. 29, 1944, both in box 60, LF 57D-284.

48. William A. Fowler, "Legislative Program on Trade Barriers," Feb. 8, 1945, box 47, RG 353, LF 122. Also see memorandum to Mr. Taft, Mar. 23, 1945, box 13, Notter Records; and Minutes of the Joint Meeting of the Committee on Trade Agreements and Committee on Trade Barriers, Feb. 6, 1945, box 101, LF 57D-284.

49. "Multilateral vs. Multilateral-Bilateral Action Background Statement," Nov. 1944, 12-13, box 7, LF 57D-284.

50. Ibid., 14-15.

51. Ibid.; and Charles Bunn to Mr. Morin, Oct. 23, 1944, 4, box 23, LF 57D-284. A number of business groups had publicly advocated trade liberalization. The House Special Committee on Post-War Economic Policy and Planning, the Colmer Subcommittee, emphasized the need for action to reduce trade barriers. House Special Committee on Post-War Economic Policy and Planning, *General Report on Economic Problems of the Reconversion Period,* 78th Cong., 2d sess., Oct. 8, 1944, 4-5, 54-55, 62-63.

52. "Procedure for Trade and Employment Conference," May 21, 1945, 1-3, box 88, LF 57D-284.

53. Notter, *Postwar,* 359. On keeping their work under wraps, see memorandum, Dec. Nov. 1944, box 60, LF 57D-284; Minutes of ECEFP Meeting, June 27, 1944, box 56, RG 353, LF 122; Pasvolsky memo, Apr. 7, 1945, box 6, Pasvolsky Records; and "Post-War Trade Possibilities," June 8, 1944, box 56, LF 57D-284.

54. "Procedure on Commercial Policy," Feb. 17, 1945, box 55, LF 57D-284; and "Methods and Procedures for the Expansion of International Trade" (Document SC-55), Feb. 27, 1945, box 55, LF 57D-284.

55. Charles Bunn to Mr. Morin, Oct. 25, 1944, 4, box 23, LF 57D-284; "Draft Study on Background of ITO," 29, box 3, LF 57D-284; and Penrose, *Economic Planning for the Peace,* 94, 106-7.

56. House Committee on Ways and Means, *Hearings on H.R. 2652, Superseded by H.R. 3240,* 79th Cong., 1st sess., Apr.-May 1945. Also see Senate Committee on Finance, *Hearings on H.R. 3240: An Act to Extend the Authority of the President under Section 350 of the Tariff Act of 1930, as Amended,* 79th Cong., 1st sess., May 30-June 5, 1945; and House Committee on Ways and Means, *Foreign Trade Agreements: Report to Accompany H.R. 3240,* 79th Cong., 1st sess., May 18, 1945.

57. Senate Committee on Finance, *Hearings on H.R. 3420,* and House Committee on Ways and Means, *Hearings on H.R. 2652, Superseded by H.R. 3240.* The nine testifying for H.R. 2652 did not include Secretary Stettinius, who had to be absent and so sent a statement of support.

58. On the standard of living, see Senate Committee on Finance, *Hearings on H.R. 3240,* 191, 351, 357, 384. On the DOS cannot be trusted, see pp. 42, 397.

59. House Committee on Ways and Means, *Hearings on H.R. 2652, Superseded by H.R. 3240,* 403, 1177, 1426-27, 1472-73.

60. Senate Committee on Finance, *Hearings on H.R. 3240,* 508; and House Committee on Ways and Means, *Hearings on H.R. 2652, Superseded by H.R. 3240,* 648-49, 730, 974-75, 1426-27, 1477-1513.

61. House Committee on Ways and Means, *Hearings on H.R. 2652, Superseded by H.R. 3240,* 859; for House quotation, see *Foreign Trade Agreements,* 41.

62. Committee on Ways and Means, *Foreign Trade Agreements,* quotations on 3, 4, 12.

63. John Patterson, "Republican Attitude on International Cooperation as Reflected in Congressional Debate on the Trade Agreements Program," June 12, 1943, box 4, Pasvolsky Records; "Legislative Program on Trade Barriers," ECEFP D-19/45, Feb. 8, 1945, box 47, RG 353, LF 122; and "Outstanding Republican Leaders Support the Principles of the Trade Agreements Program," Apr. 21, 1945, box 98, LF 57D-284.

64. Chairman to Members of the Committee on Trade Agreements and Trade Barriers, Feb. 2, 1943, box 102, LF 57D-284. Acheson notes bipartisanship did not occur on trade policy. Acheson, *Present at the Creation,* 96-97, 107-8.

65. Leddy to William A. Fowler, June 23, 1945, 1-3, box 88, LF 57D-284. For

approaches proposed before the 1945 hearings, see "Implementation of Post-War Commercial Policy Objectives," Feb. 15, 1945, box 13, Notter Records; and "The Proposed Multilateral Commercial Policy Convention," n.d., 3, 24-26, box 104, LF 57D-284.

66. The nuclear approach was similar to the multilateral-bilateral approach previously rejected as inadequate. "Proposals for World Trade and Employment Conference," June 30, 1945, 30-33, box 88, LF 57D-284. Also see "The Nuclear Approach," Apr. 11, 1945, box 60, LF 57D-284. An earlier draft of this memorandum, Mar. 28, 1945, contains the quotation by John Leddy on p. 7, deleted in the final version. It is also in box 60, LF 57D-284.

67. "Views of the Executive Committee Regarding Draft Tariff Proposals for Proposed Multilateral Agreement on Commercial Policy," memorandum for ECEFP D-104/45, 1, 2, box 47, RG 353, LF 122.

68. See "Alternative Tariff Proposal for Inclusion in Proposed Multilateral Agreement on Commercial Policy," ECEFP D-101/45, July 19, 1945; Minutes of the Meeting of the ECEFP, July 21, 1945, ECEFP M-31/45; and "Draft Tariff Proposals for Proposed Multilateral Agreement on Commercial Policy," July 21, 1945, ECEFP D-104/45, all in box 57, RG 353, LF 122. For evidence that the planners had yet to decide whether the "main effort for the reduction of trade barriers should be by bilateral negotiations under the Trade Agreements Act or . . . some other pattern," see Charles Bunn to the Committee on Trade Agreements and Committee on Trade Barriers, June 28, 1945, box 51, Notter Records; and Penrose, *Economic Planning for the Peace,* 102-7. On p. 107, Penrose notes that the assistant secretaries made the decision not to seek enhanced authority to authorize horizontal cuts or to posit an alternative to the TAP that was not selective. "In retrospect, the validity of their judgement is doubtful . . . it seemed to some of us that the attempt ought to have been made even if it failed."

69. Although the Americans had not yet given up on gaining congressional authority for horizontal tariff reduction, they had become very cautious about making the TAP less selective or enlarging presidential authority for trade negotiations. A summation of where the United States stood on the proposed multilateral convention in January 1945 is in "Summary of Provisions and Statement of Underlying Considerations," box 24, LF 57D-284. Also see Gardner, *Sterling-Dollar Diplomacy,* 150-61.

70. The British and Americans met in the United States from October 1 to December 1. "Draft Study on Background of ITO," June 29, 1948, 45-46, box 3, LF 57D-284.

71. James G. Fulton and Jacob K. Javits, *The International Trade Organization* (Washington, D.C.: GPO, 1948), 4. Public issuance of the "Proposals" were delayed to be conveyed as a benefit for the British loan and the writing-off of lend-lease. Gardner notes that Britain did not cosponsor the Proposals but acknowledged agreement with their broad points. Gardner, *Sterling-Dollar Diplomacy,* 146.

4. The Planners and the Public, 1943-1946

1. Acheson, *Present at the Creation,* 87-91, 192-93.

2. *Hearing on H.R. 2652, Superseded by H.R. 3240,* 5-9.

3. Notter, *Postwar,* 360, 432-34; Hull, *Memoirs* 218-21, 1214-17, 1656-58, 1714-19; Acheson, *Present at the Creation,* 110-20; Penrose, *Economic Planning for the Peace,* 105; and *Hearing on H.R. 2652, Superseded by H.R. 3240,* on Hawkins (239-40). On Truman's priorities in 1945, see Hinchey, "Frustration," 92, 97. Stettinius resigned on June 27, 1945, and was replaced by James Byrnes on July 3.

4. For a good understanding of the many problems senior State Department officials encountered with the end of the war, see Acheson, *Present at the Creation,* 119-28. He details the many changes in Executive Branch leadership on 109-15.

5. For a good understanding of the frequent changes in staff people working on the ITO, see "Agency Members of ECEFP and Subcommittees Who Have Worked on ITO Charter, 1944-1947," n.d., box 3, LF 57D-284.

6. Memorandum from Harry Hawkins, Apr. 8, 1944, and memorandum of first meeting, International Economic Organization, Department of State, both in box 54, LF 57D-284. Pasvolsky's staff was reorganized on Jan. 1, 1943. The economic staff was reorganized three times in this period. Notter, *Postwar,* 158-73, 209-22, 354.

7. Academics, business leaders, and government officials including judges were involved in the UN planning process. Notter, *Postwar,* 213-15; and memorandum for the Secretary, "U.S. Delegation to the United Nations Conference," Oct. 6, 1944, box 6, Pasvolsky Records.

8. For example, the UN planners worked hard to ensure that the UN was not tagged as an Administration attempt to create an international New Deal. "Informal Political Agenda Group, International Organization Discussions," IO Minutes 42, Apr. 10, 1944, box 53, LF 57D-284; and Darilek, *Loyal Opposition,* 35-37. Also see Commodities Division memorandum, Mar. 13, 1944, and Hiss to Pasvolsky, June 12, 1944, both in box 54, LF 57D-284. On the need to develop public understanding of the plans, see Emilio Collado to Hull, Mar. 20, 1944, 2, 7, and memorandum, June 30, 1944, both in box 2, Pasvolsky Records; and Schairer and Brown, "Commercial Policy Implications of the White Plan," box 82, Notter Records.

9. Executive Committee on Economic Foreign Policy, Minutes of the First Meeting, 1, 4, box 56, RG 353, LF 122; and "The Development of the Charter for an International Trade Organization," 12, 13, box 3, LF 57D-284.

10. "Agency Members of ECEFP and Subcommittees Who Have Worked on ITO Charter, 1944-1947," n.d., box 3, LF 57D-284.

11. State's approach resembled that described in corporatist histories of foreign economic policy in the period 1890 to 1930. For example, William H. Becker, *The Dynamics of Business-Government Relations: Industry and Exports, 1893-1921* (Chicago: Univ. of Chicago Press); and Michael J. Hogan, *Informal Entente: The Private Structure of Cooperation in Anglo-American Economic Diplomacy, 1918-1928* (Columbia: Univ. of Missouri Press, 1977).

12. The ECEFP took the place of the Taylor Committee as the top interdepartmental economic planning and clearing committee. The initial membership of the ECEFP included Acheson and Hawkins of State, White of Treasury, Wheeler of Agriculture, Taylor of Commerce, Ryder of the Tariff Commission, Currie of the Foreign Economic Administration, and Hinrichs of the Labor Department. Robert Carr of State directed the staff work. The ECEFP did not directly contribute to the preparatory work for general international organization under Pasvolsky, "which included provision for international economic cooperation." Notter, *Postwar,* 218-20.

13. Commodities Division memorandum, Mar. 13, 1994, box 54, LF 57D-284; and Hiss to Pasvolsky, June 12, 1944, box 54, LF 57D-284. On July 10, 1944, the Informal Agenda group was formed to discuss what organizations would be crucial to the postwar plans. Notter, *Postwar,* 170-73, 182; and "Records of Interdepartment and Top-Level Departmental Economic Policy Committees, 1939-1944," Apr. 12, 1946, box 32, Notter Records.

14. Minutes of the Executive Committee on Economic Foreign Policy, M-3/44, May 12, 1944, 3, box 56, RG 353, LF 122. For example, the State Department would support changes to agricultural legislation requested by the Department of Agriculture. Winthrop Brown to Willard Thorp, Aug. 29, 1945, box 102, LF 57D-284.

15. "Views Regarding the ECEFP," Mar. 5, 1945, 2, box 43, RG 353, LF 122; and Mr. S.S. Sheppard to Walter H.C. Laves, July 29, 1944, box 32, Notter Records.

16. The ECEFP was considered effective at resolving interagency disputes. "The Development of the Charter for an International Trade Organization," 14-26, box 3, LF 57D-284. The Department of Agriculture dissented with the decision to include commodity agreements under the proposed ITO; agricultural officials had hoped that there would be a separate international commodity commission. Memorandum, Oct. 28, 1943, box 5, Pasvolsky Records; Minutes of the Executive Committee on Economic Foreign Policy, ECEFP M-15/45, Apr. 3, 1945, box 57, RG 353, LF 122; and "Committee on Specialized International Economic Organizations," IO D-10/45, Mar. 7, 1945, box 54, LF 57D-284. Other interagency disputes were discussed in Courtney Brown to Mr. Fowler, Sept. 24, 1944, box 100, LF 57D-284; and Notter, *Postwar*, 182. Jesse Jones, Cordell Hull, and Henry Wallace also had a dispute over control of the economic warfare program. Finally, State and Treasury often disagreed on the relationship of commercial and financial policies; Treasury frequently won the battles in this period.

17. During the Depression, the administration enacted a system of production controls and price-support schemes for various commodities. Agricultural commodities were supported at prices well above those prevailing in the world market, leading to a two-price system, and American policy was inconsistent. Wilcox, *Charter*, 129; and Gardner, *Sterling-Dollar Diplomacy*, 21, 149.

18. I am basing my analysis here on Alfred D. Chandler's observations of corporate officials. Chandler noted that "the failure to develop a new internal structure, like the failure to respond to new external opportunities and needs, was a consequence of overconcentration on operational activities by the executives responsible for the destiny of their enterprises, or from their inability, because of past training . . . and present position, to develop an entrepreneurial outlook." Alfred D. Chandler Jr., *Strategy and Structure: Chapters in the History of the American Industrial Enterprise* (Cambridge: MIT Press, 1962), 15-16.

19. Although interdivisional and intergovernmental committees were established, "primary authority for policy" remained in the Department of State. Notter, *Postwar*, 208, 215-22, quotation on p. 222.

20. State Department officials may have been biased because of their experience on what one termed "the highly successful trade agreements program." "Draft Study on Background of ITO," June 29, 1948, 12, box 3, LF 57D-284; "Division of Commercial Policy," 99, 151-52, Notter Records; and Acheson, *Present at the Creation*, 93.

21. "Commercial Policy Panel," Mar. 8, 1944, box 13, Notter Records; "Memorandum re Presentation of Views by Private Interests," Sept. 1, 1944; and "Presentation of Views of Private Interests to ECEFP," Sept. 12, 1944, both in box 8, RG 353, LF 122.

22. Brown to Taft, Oct. 2, 1944, box 8, RG 353, LF 122; and Merchant to Taft, Oct. 5, 1944, box 8, RG 353, LF 122. Amos Taylor of Commerce suggested bringing the Commerce Department industry advisory committee into the development of trade policy. Woodbury Willoughby noted, "Frequently the public interest does not coincide with the desires of a particular industry group." Willoughby to Haley, Feb. 9, 1945, 1, box 8, RG 353, LF 122; and R.R. Townsend, memorandum, Mar. 28-Apr. 4, 1945, box 8, RG 353, LF 122, quotation, p. 3.

23. The Proposals "parallel . . . comprehensive programs . . . presented by such bodies" as the Committee on Economic Development, the Carnegie Endowment, the National Foreign Trade Council, the Twentieth Century Fund, and the House Special Committee on Postwar Economic Policy and Planning, as well as the work of academics such as Percy Bidwell, J.B. Condliffe, Herbert Feis, Alvin Hansen, and Michael A. Heilperin. Wilcox, *Charter*, 22-24.

24. "Reconsideration of ECEFP D-53/444 in Light of Private Business Views," ECEFP D31/45, n.d., box 47, RG 353, LF 122; Minutes of Postwar Advisory Group,

June 9, 1944, box 8, series V, acc. 1411, at HML; and "Commercial Policy Questions for Possible Informal Discussion with Representatives of the National Association of Manufacturers," June 29, 1944, box 93, LF 57D-284.

25. For example, Fowler and Haley recommended that Clayton be very general in his comments to Congress about the RTAA as the ITO's foundation. "It is as yet too early, to say what specific legislation will be needed." Cover note to Haley and cover note from Haley to Acheson, Dec. 11, 1944, box 60, LF 57D-284; and Acheson, *Present at the Creation*, 92-93.

26. Acheson, *Present at the Creation*, 96-97; 106-7.

27. House Committee on Ways and Means, *Hearings on H.R. 2652, Superseded by H.R. 3240*, 132-33, 191-92, 227, 237-49. For example, Congressman Jenkins noted he had a concern for the workingman and the businessman whereas Mr. Clayton was not connected to them (191). In this hearing, Congressman Kean wondered whether those who decide the feasibility of making trade agreements and specific tariffs to be reduced had any business experience, or were they just statisticians or career men (238). This criticism was heard frequently on Capitol Hill.

28. For an overview of congressional and special-interest concerns on lend-lease see George Cyril Herring Jr., "Experiment in Foreign Aid: Lend-Lease, 1941-1945" (Ph.D. diss., University of Virginia, 1965). He cites the following examples of congressional concern about lend-lease: the master agreements are not binding on the Senate (401); lend-lease is a global extension of the boondoggling of the WPA (401); and lend-lease should not be used to promote projects of postwar use (409). Also see Darilek, *Loyal Opposition*, 66-67; Walter S. Poole, "The Quest for a Republican Foreign Policy, 1941-1951," (Ph.D. diss., University of Pennsylvania, 1968).

29. House Special Committee on Post-war Economic Policy and Planning, *Eighth Report Pursuant to H.R. 60: A Resolution Authorizing the Continuation of the Special Committee on Post-war Economic Policy and Planning, Economic Reconstruction in Europe*, 79th Cong., Nov. 12, 1945, 3, 9.

30. Ibid., *Eighth Report*, 14-15. This was originally in H.R. 541, 79th Cong., 37-38.

31. It was reported in *New York Times*, "Asks a Conference to Cut Trade Curbs," May 9, 1946, box 83, LF 57D-284.

32. House Special Committee, *Eighth Report*, 30.

33. *Wall Street Journal*, "Outlook for 1946," Jan. 3, 1946; and *Wall Street Journal*, "Review and Outlook," Dec. 14, 1945, both in box 83, LF 57D-284.

34. Senate Joint Resolution 120, introduced Mar. 7, 1944, called for a foreign economic commission. Similar resolutions included House Joint Resolutions 247 and 249. Secretary Henry Morgenthau to Harold Smith, Director of the Budget, Mar. 23, 1944, 2, box 43, RG 353, LF 122. Also see John Leddy to Mr. Hiss and Mr. Hawkins, Apr. 21, 1944, 3, box 3, LF 57D284; and "Justification of the Appropriation Requested for the Advisory Council on Post-War Foreign Policy," n.d., box 6, Pasvolsky Records.

35. Hull, *Memoirs*, 1314-15; memorandum on NBC radio show, Dec. 13, 1943, box 5, Pasvolsky Records; and "The Department of State Speaks," Dec. 19, 1943, *New York Herald Tribune*, box 5, Pasvolsky Records. The transcripts of some radio shows are in this box.

36. This office was directed by John Dickey and, after Dec. 20, 1944, Archibald MacLeish at the assistant secretary level. Notter, *Postwar*, 379; Thomas A. Bailey, *The Man in the Street* (New York: Macmillan, 1948), 5; Acheson, *Present at the Creation*, 101; "Prospects for a Congressional Resolution Favoring United States Participation in Post-War International Cooperation for Peace," Nov. 14, 1943, box 11, Notter Records; "Recent Indications of Republican Thinking on Post-War Foreign Policy," June 12, 1943, box 4, Pasvolsky Records; Dickey to Hull, Oct. 25, 1943, box 4, Pasvolsky Records;

and "Public Attitudes on Commercial Policy in the United States and Great Britain: A Summary," Nov. 14, 1944, box 101, LF 57D-284.

37. Raymond Vernon described the situation from his vantage point at the State Department. During the war years, there was a "remarkably high degree of centrism . . . .There was a willingness to collect power centrally . . . that didn't exist before and since. When you are threatened from outside you close ranks." In the executive branch, there was a "sense of self-confidence generated from . . . the coopting of business and labor into the bureaucracy . . . .It was destined not to last." Raymond Vernon, interview with author, Feb. 22, 1991. Also see Darilek, *Loyal Opposition,* 6; and Young, *Congressional Politics,* 180-83.

38. For a good overview of the mood and concerns of Americans in 1945-1946, see Goldman, *Crucial Decade,* 3-33; and Susan M. Hartmann, *Truman and the 80th Congress* (Columbia: Univ. of Missouri Press, 1971), 1-11.

39. As an example of this new attitude, see the *Fortune* poll of business executives in October 1943, in which 72 percent said most Americans would demand relief from government if there were a depression after the war. The National Opinion Research Center (NORC) polled the public on Aug. 21, 1942, asking if the government had too much control or not enough control over our way of doing business in this country. Responses were 19 percent, too much; 34 percent, about right; 33 percent, not enough; and 14 percent, don't know. In response to the same question in September 1945, 42 percent called for more government control over business; 22 percent, the same; 20 percent, less control; and 16 percent, don't know. The polls indicated that a growing percentage of Americans were satisfied or wanted more government control over business. All in Cantril, ed., *Public Opinion,* 348-50.

40. The National Association of Manufacturers reported that "people in general are looking to the government for the solution of the unemployment problem." In October, the Opinion Research Corporation polled 1,873 people as to the greatest problems this country will face after the war. Forty-two percent of those polled worried about jobs, 23 percent about employment for ex-servicemen, and 10 percent about labor. "Digest of Findings of Public Opinion Polls on the Subject of Post-War Problems and Planning," box 842, accession 1411, HML. Two excellent histories of how government struggled to find an appropriate role in moderating the economy and unemployment are Patrick George Brady, "Toward Security: Postwar Economic and Social Planning in the Executive Office, 1939-1946" (Ph.D. diss., Rutgers University, 1975), 246-47; and Alonzo L. Hamby, "Sixty Million Jobs and the People's Revolution: The Liberals, The New Deal, and World War II," *Historian* 30 (Aug. 1968): 586-98.

41. Hartmann, *Truman and the 80th Congress,* quotation on p. 8.

42. Patrick George Brady offers a good analysis of how attitudes toward the postwar planning changed as the war wound down. Brady, "Toward Security," 246-48. Also see Hartmann, *Truman and the 80th Congress,* 1-11.

43. On January 18, 1944, the American Institute of Public Opinion reported that 62 percent of Americans said they would like to see the United States increase its foreign trade over what it was before the war, 10 percent said they wanted no increase, and 28 percent said they didn't know. In August 1945, the *New York Herald Tribune* reported that 74.7 percent of those polled said that it would be a good idea to build up our foreign trade, 9.7 percent said it was not a good idea, and 15.6 percent said they didn't know. Cantril, *Public Opinion,* 126, 128.

In August 1943, the NORC found 59 percent of those polled supported planning now for the peace, 38 percent said to wait until after the war, and 3 percent were undecided. They also found 64 percent of those polled supported American membership in a world organization in September 1944, whereas 26 percent said to stay out.

NORC, "Public Opinion on World Organization up to the San Francisco Conference," Rpt. 25 (University of Denver, 1945), 3-5. These figures were repeated in a poll asking the same questions in March 1945. An April 1944 poll found that 76 percent of those polled favored giving a union of nations the power to make laws about problems that may come up between countries, 13 percent said not to give this power, and 11 percent were undecided. NORC, "The Public Looks at World Organization, Report no. 19," (Denver: University of Denver, 1944), 11.

44. A May 1944 *Fortune* poll asked, "How do you regard the prospects for a large increase in U.S. foreign trade after the war if there is no one international organization to keep the peace and if there is one?" The responses were 30.9 percent, good prospects for trade without an international organization, and 49.9 percent, dubious prospects without an international organization. But 67.7 percent said they foresaw good prospects for trade with an international organization to keep the peace. See Cantril, *Public Opinion,* 126. In September 1943, the NORC asked if it was a good idea for nations to get together in a union of nations to decide how trade should be handled. Sixty-five percent said countries should get together in such a union of nations, 29 percent said each country should handle trade any way it wanted, and 6 percent were undecided. NORC, "Public Opinion on World Organization," 22-23. For polls that reveal a changing understanding of trade, economic growth and jobs, see NORC, "Public Looks at World Organization," 25, in which 64 percent of the public stated they would be willing to pay more taxes to support a new international organization. A NORC poll in April 1945 asked if the government continued to send lend-lease, would this mean more or fewer jobs for most Americans? Responses were 57 percent, more jobs; 10 percent, fewer jobs; 18 percent, it would make no difference; and 15 percent, they didn't know. Cantril, *Public Opinion,* 414. The NORC said that these polls showed Americans were more willing to make concessions to help achieve world union and that growing numbers of Americans believed they would benefit from such concessions.

45. It is important to note that these changes meant that trade policy was becoming an increasingly salient political issue, but they do not indicate how voters viewed trade as compared to other economic issues such as unemployment. I gained a good understanding of how to use polls on trade from my discussions with Dr. Ruy Teixeira of the Brookings Institution and the Department of Agriculture and Dr. John Benson of the Roper Center for Public Opinion Research.

46. N.A., "Background Statement on Employment Prospects in the United States," Oct. 8, 1946, box 119, LF 57D-284; "British Opinion on the American Trade Proposals," 8, 9, Oct. 3, 1946, box 98 LF 57D-284; and "Preliminary Analysis of Foreign Reactions to U.S. 'Proposals,'" box 88, LF 57D-284. On the history of "full employment" legislation in the United States, see Stephen Kemp Bailey, *Congress Makes a Law: The Story behind the Employment Act of 1946,* (New York: Columbia Univ. Press, 1950), 35, 105, 179-87; and Collins, *Business Response,* 99-110, Eric Johnston's quotation on the slave state is on p. 101.

47. For a good overview of changing American opinion on internationalism, see National Opinion Research Center, "Cincinnati Looks at the United Nations," Rpt. 37 (University of Chicago, 1947), 5; and Survey Research Center, "Public Attitudes Toward American Foreign Policy: A Nation-wide Survey," (Ann Arbor: University of Michigan, 1947). Also see Almond, *American People and Foreign Policy,* 78-86; and Goldman, *Crucial Decade,* 3-33.

48. "Current Popular Opinion on Foreign Trade Issues," Oct. 21, 1946, 1, 2, 5, box 4/M, Acheson/Thorp Papers, HSTL. The full employment issue was especially unpopular with business groupings and business publications. See "U.S. Opinion on Foreign Trade Trends," Rpt. 6, Nov. 18, 1946, 3, box 119, LF 57D-284.

49. The National Opinion Research Center, "The Public Looks at Trade and Tariff Problems" (University of Chicago, 1947), 5-14. The sample polls were taken in March 1946 (1,285 interviews) and August 1946 (2,504 interviews).

50. "Current Popular Opinion on Foreign Trade Issues," Oct. 21, 1946, 1, 2, 5, box 4/M, Acheson/Thorp Papers, HSTL.

51. The National Opinion Research Center, "The Public Looks at Trade and Tariff Problems," 16, 36. NORC asked, "Do you take a good deal of interest, a little, or no interest at all in the subject of our trade?" Thirty-nine percent answered a good deal of interest; 34 percent, only a little; 21 percent, none at all; 6 percent, don't know. NORC pollsters reported that 39 percent was an inflated percentage because "the public tends to give verbal support to plausible generalities."

52. NORC, "Cincinnati Looks at the United Nations," 7.

53. "Proposed Radio Program on Labor's Interest in Foreign Trade," June 2, 1944, box 56, LF 57D-284, shows how the planners rejected an offer to participate with labor groups on this issue. Memorandum, Feb. 8, 1944, box 13, LF 57D-284; "International Conference on PostWar Commercial Policy," Oct. 25, 1944, box 23, LF 57D-284; "UPI Story on Proposed International Multilateral Convention on Trade," Oct. 16, 1944, box 55, LF 57D-284; and "Proposed World Trade Conference," Oct. 30, 1945, box 97, LF 57D-284, show how they provided the public with only broad information and not specifics.

54. For complaints about departmental secrecy, see Philip Brown to Pasvolsky, Jan. 12, 1944, box 5, Pasvolsky Records; and memorandum to Harley Notter, on the meeting of the Political Sub-Committee, Apr. 26, 1843, 1, 3, 4, box 53, Notter Records. According to Henry Wallace, Roosevelt believed that it was the duty of the administration to keep the public informed, but Hull disagreed. John Morton Blum, ed., *The Price of Vision: The Diary of Henry A. Wallace, 1942-1946* (Boston: Houghton Mifflin, 1973), 241.

5. Public Response to the ITO, 1946-1947

1. Wilcox, *Charter,* 24.

2. N.a., "Draft Procedure for the Reduction of Trade Barriers," Sept. 6, 1945, box 98, LF 57D-284; and letter to Harry Hawkins, Apr. 9, 1946, box 41, LF 57D-284.

3. William Adams Brown Jr., *The United States and the Restoration of World Trade* (Washington, D.C.: Brookings Institution, 1950), 57-59; and Wilcox, *Charter,* 40. The nations on the Preparatory Committee were the U.S. original invitees: Australia, Belgium, Luxembourg, Brazil, Canada, China, Czechoslovakia, France, India, the Netherlands, New Zealand, South Africa, the Soviet Union, the United Kingdom, and the United States. The ECOSOC added Chile, Norway, and Lebanon.

4. "Preparations for Preliminary International Meeting on Trade and Employment," Feb. 6, 1946, 1-5, 9-10, box 25, LF 57D-284; and Brown, *U.S. and Restoration,* 61.

5. "Preparations for Preliminary International Meeting on Trade and Employment," Feb. 6, 1946, 4-5, 9-10, box 25, LF 57D-284.

6. N.a., "Draft Procedure for the Reduction of Trade Barriers," Sept. 6, 1945, box 98, LF 57D-284; Penrose, *Economic Planning for the Peace,* 349-51; and Goldman, *Crucial Decade,* 1934. The planners actively surveyed foreign reaction to the Proposals and the Suggested Draft Charter. See boxes 37 and 88, LF 57D-284.

7. An excellent history of the loan is in Randall Bennett Woods, *A Changing of the Guard: Anglo-American Relations, 1941-1946* (Chapel Hill: University of North Carolina, 1990).

8. Clair Wilcox to Will Clayton, "Timing the British Loan and the Trade Con-

ference," Feb. 11, 1946, box 3, LF 57D-284; and Oral History interview with Joseph D. Coppock, July 29, 1974, 64-68, at HSTL. According to Coppock,the ITO might have been created if "the original schedule had been adhered to . . . . Continuation of lend-lease aid would have made this schedule possible."

9. "All loans should be made contingent upon the willingness of England to remove the temporary restrictions on imports." House Special Committee, *Eighth Report,* 3. According to one historian of the loan, congressional views were "actually represented" in the negotiations by Treasury Secretary Fred Vinson. Vinson worked hard to inform the congressmen of the progress of the loan. When it was finally approved, the loan provided Britain with a line of credit of $3.75 billion, much less than it needed. Richard P. Hedlund, "Congress and the British Loan, 1945-1946: A Congressional Study" (Ph.D. diss., University of Kentucky, 1976), 21-22, 24, 36-37.

10. Leonard S. Cottrell Jr. and Sylvia Eberhardt, *American Opinion on World Affairs in the Atomic Age* (Princeton: Princeton Univ. Press, 1948), 130. The trade policy planners were well aware of public opinion on the loan. N.a., "Information Program on United States Financial-Commercial Relations with Great Britain," Oct. 5, 1945, box 3, LF 57D-284.

11. Hedlund, "Congress and the British Loan," 21-23, 50, 58; and Gardner, *Sterling-Dollar Diplomacy,* pp. 237-42. Anglophobia and anger over British actions in Palestine also affected support for the loan.

12. Historians disagree as to the reasons for the loan's passage. To Richard Gardner, the loan benefited from the growing anticommunist sentiment in the United States. Gardner, *Sterling-Dollar Diplomacy,* 248-53. To Richard Hedlund, a key factor in the passage of the measure was the leadership of Senate Majority Leader Alben Barkley. Hedlund also notes that anticommunism was a factor in getting support for the loan, but he stresses the reluctance of administration officials, except for Vinson, to rely on this approach. Hedlund, "Congress and the British Loan," 125, 132, 135, 141, 143, 176-83.

13. House Committee on Banking and Currency, *Anglo-American Finanacial Agreement Hearings on H.J. Res. 311 and S. J. Res. 138: A Joint Resolution to Further Implement the Purposes of the Bretton Woods Agreements Act by Authorizing the Secretary of the Treasury to Carry Out an Agreement with the United Kingdom, and for Other Purposes,* 79th Cong., 2d sess., May 14-June 7, 1946, 255, 261. For example, several congressmen called Clayton to task on the loan because they had been told there would be no more loans after the Bank and Fund had been approved.

14. For example, Congressman Brown asked Clayton, "Then England has agreed to do away with the sterling pool and the bilateral contracts if this loan is ratified?" Clayton replied, "Yes, she has agreed to do it." When Representative Barry asked Secretary Clayton, "You mean it breaks up the sterling block?" Clayton again replied, "Yes." Yet when Representative Wolcott asked if there was a connection between the loan and the reduction of British tariffs, Clayton replied, "No." Clair Wilcox wrote to Clayton, "Everyone agrees that the greatest benefit we get from the British loan is the opportunity . . . to put across our trade proposals." House Committee on Banking and Currency, *Anglo-American Financial Agreement,* 3, 41, 192-97, 202-5, 274. For dialogue between Clayton and Brown, see p. 196; Clayton and Barry p. 207; and Clayton and Wolcott, p. 670. Also see Clair Wilcox to Will Clayton, "Timing the British Loan and the Trade Conferences," Feb. 11, 1946, box 3, LF 57D-284.

15. At the Senate hearing, when asked if the purpose of the loan was to increase British exports, Acheson replied, "You would deceive the ordinary person if you said the purpose of this loan is to increase exports . . . . The purpose of this loan is to enable the British to import." When he was questioned about preferences, he replied, "The empire preference matters are dealt with in the proposals." Senate Committee on Bank-

ing and Currency, *Anglo-American Financial Agreement,* 79th Cong., 2d sess., Mar. 5-20, 1946; quotations from Acheson's discussions with Senators Murdock and Barkley are on p. 325; Acheson's remarks on preferences are on pp. 339-41.

16. Representative Wolcott asked about the relationship between the international trade conference and the reciprocal trade agreements. Clayton replied in frustration, "It has a very definite relationship . . . . We will not . . . make any multilateral, across the board, reductions in the tariffs in the world trade conference . . . . Any reductions . . . will be made in a separate agreement . . . in exact accordance with the provisions of the Reciprocal Trade Agreements Act." Ibid., 203, 674, 275; quotations by Clayton and Wolcott are on pp. 671-74. The Department of State issued speeches and fact sheets on the relationship of the loan and the proposals. See "Fifty Facts on the Proposed British Loan," "Our Foreign Commercial Policy," and "International Trade and the British Loan," all in box 3, LF 57D-284.

17. See House Committee on Banking and Currency, *Report to Accompany S. J. 138: Implementation of the Financial Agreement between the United States and the United Kingdom,* 79th Cong., 1946, 2d sess., H.R. 2289, 23-27. On the House side, 219 voted for the loan, 155 against. Hedlund, "Congress and the British Loan," 171-73.

18. N.a., "Information Program on United States Financial Commercial Relations toward Great Britain," Oct. 5, 1945, box 3, LF 57D-284.

19. Wilcox to Clayton, "Preparations for Trade Program," July 15, 1946, box 98, LF 57D-284; and Wilcox to Clayton, "Timing the British Loan and the Trade Conferences," Feb. 11, 1946, box 3, LF 57D-284.

20. As an example of taking public opinion for granted, see "Proposals for World Trade and Employment," 6, 19, 1945, box 88, LF 57D-284; the author believed the National Association of Manufacturers would support the ITO.

21. Clayton to Secretary Byrnes, "Date of Proposed Tariff Negotiations," Apr. 11, 1946; and Wilcox to Clayton, Sept. 26, 1946, both in box 98, LF 57D-284.

22. Wilcox to Clayton, Sept. 26, 1946, box 98, LF 57D-284. On the list, see Charles L. Aulette to Winthrop Brown, Aug. 6, 1946; and Mr. Brown to Mr. Smith, "Published List," Aug. 15, 1946, both in box 57, LF 57D-284.

23. Personal Letter, Harry Hawkins to Will Clayton, Mar. 6, 1946, box 98, LF 57D-284.

24. N.a., "Public and Business Attitudes," n.d., box 98, LF 57D-284.

25. "U.S. Opinion on Foreign Trade Trends," Oct. 16, 1946; "Group Differences in Opinion about World Trade," n.d., both in box 119, LF 57D-284; and "Current Popular Opinion on Foreign Trade Issues," box 4/M, Acheson/Thorp Papers, HSTL.

26. Memorandum to Nitze and Clayton, Nov. 3, 1946, box 40, LF 57D-284. Congress was sent copies of the Suggested Draft Charter in the summer. Will Clayton to Representative Sam Rayburn, July 23, 1946, box 12, LF 57D-284. U.S. Department of State, *Suggested Charter for an International Trade Organization,* September 1946, said very little about the GATT. See its Article 56, on p. 37.

27. V.L. Phelps to W.G. Brown, "Tariff Negotiating Teams for the Preliminary Conference," Aug. 29, 1946, box 87, LF 57D-284.

28. "Memorandum for the President, Public Notice of Intention to Negotiate under the Trade Agreements Act," Nov. 8, 1946, HST Confidential File, HSTL.

29. Memorandum for the President, "Procedure for Handling Requests for Commitments against Tariff Concessions on Particular Products in Forthcoming Trade-Agreement Negotiations," Nov. 8, 1946, HST Confidential File, HSTL.

30. Department of State, Press Release, Nov. 9, 1946, box 11, LF 57D-284; and Wilkinson, *Politics and Trade Policy* (Washington, D.C.: Public Affairs Press, 1960), 38.

31. Wilcox to Clayton, Oct. 26, 1946; Wilcox to Willard Thorp, Nov. 3, 1946;

Clair Wilcox to Clayton, Nov. 9, 1946; and Wilcox to Clayton, Nov. 23, 1946, all in box 119, LF 57D-284. Also see Brown, *U.S. and Restoration,* 62-63; and Gardner, *Sterling-Dollar Diplomacy,* 270-86. The work on the draft charter was incomplete and would require a drafting committee to meet in Lake Success, New York, in January-February 1947, to further revise the chapters and to prepare a draft text for a GATT.

32. Personal Letter, Harry Hawkins to Clair Wilcox, Mar. 14, 1946, box 98, LF 57D-284.

33. Brown, *U.S. and Restoration,* 61-62; and n.a., memorandum to Clayton and Nitze, Nov. 5, 1946, box 40, LF 57D-284.

34. Dean Acheson to Senator Eugene Millikin, Apr. 3, 1946, in House Committee on Ways and Means, *Hearings on the Operation of the Trade Agreements Act and the Proposed International Trade Organization,* 80th Cong., 1st sess., Mar. 26-May 9, 1947, 1536.

35. Hartmann, *Truman and the 80th Congress,* 8-9; Goldman, *Crucial Decade,* 44-45; and Congressional Quarterly, *Politics in America, 1945-1966* (Washington, D.C.: Congressional Quarterly Service, 1967), 3.

36. Hartmann, *Truman and the 80th Congress,* 8-14; Congressional Quarterly, *Politics in America,* 3; and Will Clayton to Senator Hugh Butler, Jan. 16, 1947, box 100, LF 57D-284. Clayton believed there was no evidence that the RTAA was repudiated by the election.

37. Their discussions focused on ways to modify the RTAA so that domestic producers would not suffer severely from foreign competition in imports. Wilkinson, *Politics and Trade Policy,* 38-39; and "Weekly Summary Report," Jan. 13, 1947, 6, box 90, LF 57D-284.

38. Senator Hugh Butler to Will Clayton, Dec. 19, 1946, box 4, LF 57D-284; Will Clayton to Senator Butler, Jan. 16, 1947, box 100, LF 57D-284; and "Weekly Summary Report," Feb. 10, 1947, 5-6, box 90, LF 57D-284.

39. Winthrop Brown to Will Clayton and Clair Wilcox, Jan. 18, 1947, box 40, LF 57D-284; "Weekly Summary Report," Jan. 20, 1947, 6-7; and "Weekly Summary Report," Feb. 24, 1947, 7, both in box 90, LF 57D-284. The executive order and the press release outlining the order are in box 11, LF 57D-284. Also see Gardner, *Sterling Dollar Diplomacy,* 352.

40. The Department prepared an analysis of the implications of the election and how they could resist protectionist tactics. "The 1946 Election," box 119, LF 57D-284. Also see Office of Public Affairs, "Principal Areas of Leadership Support and Opposition to the U.S. Foreign Trade Program (1943-1946)," box 41, LF 57D-284; Harley Notter to Dean Acheson, "Consultation for Non-Partisan Foreign Policy," Apr. 8, 1947; and Notter to the Secretary of State, Jan. 9, 1947, both in box 10, Notter Records. The negotiators at Lake Success worked to ensure that the New York draft did not make commitments on employment that the Congress could not accept. John Leddy to Clair Wilcox, "Summary Report on the Work of the Interim Drafting Committee of the Preparatory Committee of the International Conference on Trade and Employment," Mar. 7, 1947, box 41, LF 57D-284.

41. F.W. Martin, "Agreement between Administration and Republican Leaders on Trade Agreement," Feb. 10, 1947, FO 371/62280; and R.B. Stevens to J.C. Helmore, Jan. 27, 1947, FO 371/62281.

42. "Memorandum of the Press and Radio News Conference," Nov. 8, 1946, no. 63, box 11, LF 57D-284. In this period, the Department actively surveyed congressional, public, and editorial opinion. "Weekly Summary Report," box 90, LF 57D-284.

43. NBC Broadcast, "Our Trade Policy—Expanded Trade or Economic Warfare," Nov. 22, 1946, 2, box 11, LF 57D-284; and Winthrop Brown to Clair Wilcox and Will Clayton, Jan. 18, 1947, 3, box 40, LF 57D-284.

44. S. Shepard Jones to Winthrop Brown, Nov. 7, 1946, 2, box 98, LF 57D-284.

45. "U.S. Opinion on Foreign Trade Trends," Rpt. 6, Nov. 18, 1946, 2, box 119, LF 57D-284. Also see n.a., "Representative Stephen Pace," Dec. 12, 1946, box 40, LF 57D-284; n.a., memorandum to Nitze and Clayton, Nov. 5, 1946, box 40, LF 57D-284; "Weekly Summary Report," Feb. 10, 1947, 5; and "Weekly Summary Report," Mar. 17, 1947, 7, both in box 90, LF 57D-284.

46. "Memorandum of the Press and Radio News Conference," no. 63, Nov. 8, 1946, 3, box 11, LF 57D-284.

47. Harley Notter to Secretary George Marshall, Jan. 9, 1947, box 100, Notter Records. In contrast, the Commerce Department did try to gain "advice and counsel" from traders, exporters, and trade groups. "Press Release," T-81, Aug. 12, 1946, box 46, LF 57D-284.

48. This was also true of other postwar planning efforts. Robert A. Divine, *Second Chance: The Triumph of Internationalism in America during World War II* (New York: Atheneum, 1967), 253.

49. These groups included the Chamber of Commerce, the National Foreign Trade Committee, and the National Association of Manufacturers (NAM). As examples, see Minutes of Advisory Group to International Economic Relations Committee, NAM, Apr. 17, 1946, box 10, acc. 1411, HML; and "Comments on the Revised Charter for an ITO in Terms of Foreign Economic Policy," Feb. 27, 1947, box 7, LF 57D-284.

50. These discussions began before the election and were held throughout 1945-1947. The most important example of how the ITO was changed by discussions with corporate leaders was in the area of investment (see chapter 6.) Also see "Carroll Report on Charter," Dec. 10, 1946, box 60, LF 57D-284; "Drafting Instructions Based on a Conference with the NAM," Jan. 31, 1946, box 4, LF 57D-284; and Ness to Young, "International Chamber of Commerce Proposals on Investment," Mar. 13, 1947, box 55, LF 57D-284. On preparing briefs, see Winthrop G. Brown to Will Clayton, "Committee for Reciprocity Information Hearings," Dec. 19, 1946; and Winthrop G. Brown to Alfred E. Mallon, Dec. 16, 1946, both in box 44, LF 57D-284. These officials also rejected business suggestions on the ITO. E.F. Thomas to Will Clayton, Mar. 26, 1946, box 59, LF 57D-284; "Proposed Meeting on Use of Bargaining Power in Connection with Treaty and Trade-Agreement Negotiations: Nuclear Negotiations," Mar. 28, 1946, box 59, LF 57D-284; and memorandum of conversation, Apr. 8, 1946, box 4/M, Acheson/Thorp papers, HSTL.

51. Robert Schaetzel to Clair Wilcox, "WFTU and the U.S. Trade Proposals," July 22, 1946, box 98, LF 57D-284; and "United States Proposals for Expansion of World Trade and Employment," Aug. 7, 1946, box 98, LF 57D-284.

52. Report of U.S. Associates of the International Chamber of Commerce on "Proposals for Expansion of World Trade and Employment," box 16, acc. 1411, HML; and "U.S. Opinion on Foreign Trade Trends," Oct. 2-14, 1946, box 119, LF 57D-284.

53. NBC Broadcast, "Our Trade Policy," Nov. 22, 1946, 1-3, 6, box 11, LF 57D-284; memorandum of the Press and Radio News Conference, Nov. 8, 1946, no. 63, 2-4; and S. Shepard Jones to Winthrop Brown, Nov. 7, 1946, 3, 7, 9, 11, box 98, LF 57D-284.

54. "U.S. Opinion on Foreign Trade Trends," Oct. 16, 1946, 1, box 119, LF 57D-284; and S. Shepard Jones to Winthrop Brown, Nov. 7, 1946, 5, 8-12, box 98, LF 57D-284.

55. Winthrop G. Brown to Will Clayton, "Committee for Reciprocity Information Hearings," Dec. 19, 1946, box 44, LF 57D-284; "Tool and Fine Steel Industry Files Brief Relating to Reciprocal Trade Agreements," Jan. 3, 1946, *American Metal Market,* box 146, Papers of Lammot Du Pont, HML.

56. Winthrop Brown to Clayton, "CRI Hearings," Feb. 4, 1947, box 44, LF 57D-284; "Report on Informal Hearings on Proposed Charter for an International Trade Organization," ECEFP D-64/47, Apr. 16, 1947, box 45, LF 57D-284; and John H. Shan-

non to Nathan Ostroff, Feb. 11, 1947, box 44, LF 57D-284. The preparations for the hearings in Boston provide a good example of this process. See Irwin Tobin to Clair Wilcox, Feb. 10, 1947, box 41, LF 57D-284. The panels included government officials from all ECEFP agencies.

57. "Probable Supporters of U.S. Trade Program in Cities Where ITO Hearings Are to be Held," Jan. 10, 1947; "Proposed ITO Hearings Procedure," Feb. 14, 1947; and "Questions and Answers for Hearings," n.d., all in box 47, LF 57D-284.

58. "Reaction to Holding Public Hearings on Charter," Sept. 20, 1946, box 12, LF 57D-284; and "Suggestions for Changes in Proposed Charter for an International Trade Organization (Based on Testimony Presented at Public Hearings, Briefs, and Correspondence)," Apr. 3, 1947, ECEFP D-57/47, box 8, LF 57D-284. For suggestions made by individuals, consumer groups, and community groups, see pp. 19 (Albert Lee), 21 (Women's International League for Peace and Freedom), 26 (National Association of Consumers), 35 (Catholic War Veterans), and 36 (San Francisco Bay Area Council).

59. "Report on Informal Hearings on Proposed Charter," Apr. 16, 1947, 2-3, 5-9, box 45, LF 57D-284. There were 107 business and farm groups, 24 individual enterprises, 41 civic organizations, 11 religious organizations, 17 labor organizations, 6 consumer organizations, 2 veterans organizations, and 13 miscellaneous groups. The bulk of those testifying were business and professional organizations, but other presentations were made by a mayor, students, and Port Authority representatives. Witnesses appeared on behalf of 50 national organizations, 27 of which were business and farm organizations, and 23 were civic, labor, consumer, and other groups. Witnesses were drawn from twenty states and the District of Columbia.

60. "Report on Informal Hearings," Apr. 16, 1947, 3, 7; and "Report on ITO Charter Hearings," Mar. 26, 1947, 2, both in box 45, LF 57D-284.

61. Cleon O. Swayzee to F.H. McConnell, "Report on ITO Charter Hearings," Mar. 26, 1947, 2, box 45, LF 57D-284.

62. Their perspectives were counterbalanced by those business, farmer, academic, labor and other groups traditionally heard at Washington hearings. "Report on Informal Hearings," Apr. 16, 1947, 2; and Willis Armstrong, n.t., n.d., 6, both in box 45, LF 57D-284.

63. Diebold, "The End of the ITO," 14; "Report on Informal Hearings," Apr. 16, 1947, 2, 12-13, box 45, LF 57D-284; and "Suggestions for Changes," Apr. 3, 1947, box 8, LF 57D-284.

64. "Report on Informal Hearings," Apr. 16, 1947, 5, 12, 13, box 45, LF 57D-284. On business fears of planned economies, see Elvin Kilheffer to Herbert Schell, Oct. 10, 1946, box 855.3, acc. 1411, HML.

65. This point was made by Willis Armstrong in his overview of the Charter hearing in Chicago. Willis Armstrong, n.t., n.d., 6, box 45, LF 57D-284.

66. On the Trade Agreements Program, see ibid. On desire for representation on the official U.S. delegation to the ITO, see "Suggestions for Changes," Apr. 3, 1947, 35, box 8, LF 57D-284. Among those requesting representation on the ITO were the New England Shoe and Leather Association, Schenley International, Consumers Association, and Fishermen's Union. See "Consultative Status for Farm Organizations on ECOSOC and Related Matters," Oct. 29, 1946, 3, box 4/M, Acheson/Thorp Papers, HSTL. The suggestion that the Department of State needed business negotiators was made at the New York Hearing, p. 239, box 42, LF 57D-284. It would be repeated at the congressional hearings.

67. Eleanor Dennison to Willard Thorp, Mar. 5, 1947, box 3, LF 57D-284. It is important to note that most questions focused on the London Draft of the ITO Charter, but some questions were updated by referral to the New York Draft.

68. Clair Wilcox to Paul Nitze, "Material Requested by Senator Millikin," Mar. 31, 1947, box 4, LF 57D-284; Representative Harold Knutson to Will Clayton, Feb. 17, 1947; and Will Clayton to Representative Harold Knutson, Feb. 21, 1947, both in box 3, LF 57D-284.

69. Millikin's posture as the good cop surprised me. Many of the people that I interviewed, including John Leddy, Leonard Weiss, and Raymond Vernon, remembered him as a formidable opponent of the ITO. Senate Committee on Finance, *Hearings on Trade Agreements System and Proposed International Trade Organization Charter,* 80th Cong., 1st sess., Mar. 20-Apr. 3, 1947, 254.

70. Ibid. On Congress taking greater control over trade law and confusion over what authority, see pp. 33, 36, 71, 167-69, 173, 252-55, 351-57, 358-60. On distrust of the Department of State, see pp. 26-28, 42, 231-33, 600.

71. These perceptions stemmed from the London Draft Charter's sections on employment, balance of payments, and economic development. Senate Committee on Finance, *Hearings on Trade,* 100-105.

72. Ibid. For arguments on standard of living and slave labor, see p. 119; on negotiators jeopardizing U.S. industry, see pp. 28-30; on compromises and contradictions, see pp. 383-86, 475; and on exceptions, see p. 500.

73. Elvin Kilheffer to Lammot Du Pont, Apr. 2, 1947, box 77, Du Pont Company Papers (acc. 1662), HML; and Noel Sargent to Mr. Weisenburger, "Position on the Tariff," Feb. 25, 1947, box 853.3, acc. 1411, HML. The NAM received its inside information from Ways and Means Committee staff. On the determination to affect Geneva GATT negotiations, see Representative Harold Knutson to Oscar Ryder, Jan. 11, 1947, box 41, LF 57D-284.

74. House Committee on Ways and Means, *Hearings on the Operation of the RTAA.* For traditional protectionist arguments, see pp. 309, 436, 491, 760-61, 799, 1164-65, 1377. For arguments that the State Department is unfair, see pp. 331, 816, 1381, 1662; that the zeal to cultivate foreign relations hurts U.S. industry, see pp. 843, 922, 1665. On distrust of the State Department, see pp. 748, 768-69, 817, 1348, 1377; on fears that tariffs will be decided by a foreign organization rather than Congress, see pp. 507-9, 513-15; and on the need to restore to Congress the right to determine tariffs, see pp. 507, 843, 1192, 1212.

75. Ibid. For the argument that freer trade benefits high-tech industries, hurts agriculture, see pp. 713-14, 1057, 1202, 1249, 1349; that it hurts small business, see p. 890, 1017, 1349. On perfectionist arguments, see pp. 313, 315, 689, 736. The discussion with Mr. Reed is on pp. 710-14.

76. Ibid. For the argument that the United States would have to cartelize trade, see p. 1441; that other nations regiment trade or are nationalized or subsidized, see pp. 310-11, 868, 911, 1384-86.

77. Ibid., 461-63, 1338-39, 1419, 1684.

78. Other analysts and even some of the participants perceived the planners and their implements as rooted in the past rather than responsive to rapidly changing realities. Gardner, *Sterling-Dollar Diplomacy,* 4-5, 8-9; Joseph M. Jones, *The Fifteen Weeks: February 21-June 5, 1947* (New York: Vintage, 1955), 93-97; and Penrose, *Economic Planning for the Peace,* 18, 349-51.

6. The ITO, the GATT and U.S. Trade Policy, 1947-1948

1. "Verbatim Record, Meetings of Economic Consultants," Dec. 3, 1948, box 29, LF 57D-284, Viner's quotation is on p. 10.

2. Dean Acheson, "Memorandum for the President," Apr. 2, 1947, HST Con-

fidential File, no box, HSTL; and "Memorandum of Conversation," Apr. 3, 1947, box 91, LF 57D-284, quotations on pp. 2-3. Winthrop Brown was director of the Division of Commercial Policy.

3. The Geneva draft had an amendment forbidding the use of export subsidies without the prior approval of the trade organization. "Status of Negotiations," Aug. 2, 1947, box 150, LF 57D-284; and Wilcox, *Charter,* 44-46. Other nations had problems with the Geneva draft Charter. See n.a., "Turkish Questions on ITO," Mar. 18, 1947, box 4M, Acheson/Thorp Papers, HSTL; and n.a., "Finality of Monetary Fund," July 14, 1947, box 15, LF 57D-284.

4. The Brookings Institution, *Major Problems of United States Foreign Policy 1948: A Study Guide* (Washington, D.C.: Brookings Institution, 1948), 98-99; and Brown, *U.S. and Restoration,* 22-28, 39-42, 51-54. Agricultural protection remains a difficult issue for the GATT.

5. On Australia and the ITO, see Winthrop G. Brown, chairman, Committee on Trade Agreements, "Memorandum to the President," July 30, 1947, HST Confidential File, HSTL; and Coppock to Nitze, May 29, 1947, box 3, LF 57D-284. Also see Brown, *U.S. and Restoration,* 26-27.

6. H.C. Coombs to Will Clayton, May 3, 1947; Willoughby to Wood, July 26, 1947; and Nitze to Clayton and Wilcox, Telegram #794, June 30, 1947; all in box 108, LF 57D-284. The Department of Agriculture dissented from this recommendation.

7. Cordell Hull to Secretary of State George C. Marshall, June 4, 1947; Henry L. Stimson to Secretary Marshall, June 4, 1947; and Secretary George C. Marshall to Senator Aiken, June 4, 1947; all in box 1, RG 53D-444, Records of the Executive Secretariat (Records of Dean Acheson), NA. The quotation from Truman's veto statement is in *FRUS 1947,* 1:957. On Truman administration support, see Oral History interview with Winthrop G. Brown, May 25, 1947, 14, 19, HSTL; and Frederick C. Dobney, *Selected Papers of Will Clayton* (Baltimore: Johns Hopkins Univ. Press, 1971), 205.

8. Winthrop G. Brown, "Memorandum for the President," July 30, 1947, box 108, LF 57D-284.

9. Secretary of State George C. Marshall to President Truman, July 30, 1947, HST Confidential Files, HSTL; Charles E. Bohlen to Senator Hugh Butler, May 4, 1948, box 26; and Thorp to Lovett, Dec. 22, 1948, box 59, both in LF 57D-284.

10. U.S. Tariff Commission, *Operation of the Trade Agreements Program,* 2d report, Apr. 1948-Mar. 3, 1949 (Washington, D.C.: GPO, 1950), 20 n 4. By July 31, 1948, all the participating nations had brought the agreement into effect under the Protocol of Provisional Application. No nation has brought the GATT into full effect.

11. Brown, *U.S. and Restoration,* 134; and Tariff Commission, *Operation of the Trade Agreements Program,* 2d report, 3, 12, 19-21. The GATT was built on bilateral negotiations. Most countries negotiated only with their principal past or anticipated supplier of imports of that commodity. The understandings reached in these bilateral negotiations were combined to form the schedules of concessions set forth in the GATT. Because these bilateral concessions were then generalized to all the participating nations, the GATT was not a multilateral treaty or a "formal" international organization whose charter or budget would be submitted to Congress.

12. U.S. Tariff Commission, *Operation of the Trade Agreements Program,* 2d report, 19-21, 20 n 4; and U.S. Tariff Commission, *Report on the Havana Charter for an ITO* (Washington, D.C.: GPO, 5, 1949), 7. Also see Carl Corse to John Leddy, n.d., box 57, LF 57D-284; Oral History interview with John M. Leddy, June 15, 1973, 52-63; and Oral History interview with Winthrop Brown, May 25, 1973, 43, both at HSTL. Brown attributed the craftsmanship of the GATT to John Leddy, who participated in the GATT and ITO negotiations at Havana and Geneva.

13. Notter to Acheson, "Consultation for Non-Partisan Foreign Policy," Apr. 8, 1947; and Notter to Rusk, "Conversation with Mr. Francis Wilcox," Mar. 25, 1948; both in box 10, Notter Papers.

14. Acheson, *Present at the Creation,* quotation on 219; and William L. Clayton, "GATT, the Marshall Plan, and OECD," *Political Science Quarterly* 78 (Dec. 1963): 493-503.

15. General Marshall became secretary of state on January 21, 1947, replacing James Byrnes. Acheson, *Present at the Creation,* 213; and Dobney, *Selected Papers of Will Clayton,* 211-29. The successful efforts on the part of State Department officials to galvanize public, business, and congressional support for emergency aid to Europe contrasts dramatically with their efforts to build support for the ITO and GATT. However, it is much easier to build public support to meet a crisis situation (even if it entails continued shortages and high prices) than one directed toward the more amorphous objective of expanding trade and employment. See Lincoln Gordon and Paul Nitze, "Memorandum to the President," Sept. 20, 1947; and n.a., "Popular Opinion on Aiding Europe," n.d., both in Acheson Papers, HSTL. This later survey reported that "large majorities of the American people favor the idea of sending aid to Europe, but the people appear to be evenly split on supporting the aid . . . if these are to entail shortages and high prices."

16. The ECEFP made changes to the ITO in response to criticisms presented at the three sets of hearings. The bulk of these suggestions were made by the National Association of Manufacturers and other business groups. I saw no memos on changes made in response to suggestions from labor, agriculture, or civic groups, although these groups made several suggestions. See "Suggestions for Changes in Proposed Charter for an International Trade Organization," ECEFP D-57/47, Apr. 3, 1947; n.a., n.t., Apr. 13, 1950, both in box 8; and "Memorandum of Conference," Jan. 30, 1947, box 4, all in LF 57D-284. On responding to suggestions by Congress, see "Amendments Proposed by U.S. Delegation re Chapter VIII (Organization)," June 10, 1947, box 3, LF 57D-284. On handling special interests, see Clair Wilcox, "Contacts with Representatives of the Press and of Special Interest Groups," Oct. 29, 1947, box 59, LF 57D-284.

17. Quotations in Coppock to Wilcox, Apr. 25, 1947, box 55, LF 57D-284. Joseph Coppock was economic advisor to the director, Office of International Trade Policy. Woodbury Willoughby worked in the Division of Commercial Policy, eventually becoming its chief.

18. Willoughby to Ness, "Some Problems Relating to Article on Investment for Inclusion in the ITO Charter," Apr. 16, 1947; and Coppock to Nitze, "Proposed Investment Provisions in ITO Charter," Apr. 7, 1947, both in box 55, LF 57D-284.

19. Quotations in Coppock to Wilcox, Apr. 25, 1947, and Willoughby to Ness, Apr. 16, 1947, both in box 55, LF 57D-284.

20. Quotation in E. Kellogg to Kotschnig, Apr. 2, 1947, box 41; and Coppock to Nitze, Apr. 7, 1947, box 55, both in LF 57D-284.

The Treasury Department and the International Monetary Fund also objected to the Geneva draft's investment provisions. The Treasury Department noted that the State Department had contravened its own procedures by negotiating this issue at Geneva before gaining ECEFP approval. Young to Clayton, "Investment Provisions in Charter," June 16, 1947, LF 57D-284; and Telegram from Ansel Luxford, July 30, 1947, both in box 14, LF 57D-284. This issue had earlier been the subject of a turf battle between Treasury and State and between the ECEFP and another interagency committee, the National Advisory Committee (NAC), which was directed by the Treasury Department. Robert Carr to Willard Thorp, Oct. 16, 1945; and Luthringer to Clayton, June 12, 1946, both in box 31, LF 57D-284.

21. On problems at Geneva on investment see Wilcox to Paul, July 12, 1947, box

150, LF 57D-284. While the negotiations proceeded, the ECEFP approved a different approach that included the perspectives of many of these business groups; there were several provisions in the ECEFP document that were not in the Geneva proposals, and vice versa. Young to Clayton, "Investment Provisions in Charter," June 16, 1947, box 14, LF 57D-284. The National Association of Manufacturers called a meeting of seven major trade organizations on foreign investment: the American Bankers Association, the Chamber of Commerce, the Foreign Bondholders Protective Council, the Investment Bankers Association, the NAM, the National Foreign Trade Council, and the United States Associates of the International Chamber of Commerce. A compilation of their views was cabled to the U.S. Delegation at Geneva. Industrial Relations Committee Meeting, National Association of Manufacturers, Aug. 17, 1948, box unknown, acc. 1411, HML.

22. Wilcox to Clayton, "Matters for Action," n.d., box 146; and Wilcox to Bohlen, Oct. 9, 1947, box 47, both in LF 57D-284. The Committee for the Marshall Plan was composed of prominent Americans working to gain public support for the ERP. For a good overview see Michael J. Hogan, *The Marshall Plan: America, Britain, and the Reconstruction of Western Europe, 1949-1952* (Cambridge: Cambridge Univ. Press, 1987), 97-100.

23. Clayton to Wilcox, June 17, 1947, 955; Wood to Clayton, Aug. 2, 1947, Telegram #944, Aug. 2, 1947, 973; and Wood to Clayton, Telegram #943, Aug. 2, 1947, 973; all in *FRUS 1947,* vol. 1. Also see Dobney, *Selected Papers of Will Clayton,* 15; Oral History interview with Willard L. Thorp, July 10, 1971, 34-35, 120-21; and Oral History interview with Raymond Vernon, 7, 19, 1973, 24, both at HSTL.

24. As noted in chapter 3, such a strategy had paid off in the marketing of the United Nations and the Bretton Woods Institutions. Clayton to Nitze, "Delegation to the Havana Conference," n.d.; Clark L. Willard to Robert Schaetzel, "Determination of Composition of United States Delegation to First Assembly of the ITO, Havana, November 21, 1947," Aug. 13, 1947; E.I. Mullins, "Congressional Delegates to Havana Conference," Aug. 29, 1947; Telegram, Wilcox to Schaetzel, n.d.; and Schaetzel to Wilcox, Aug. 30, 1947; all in box 146, LF 57D-284.

25. Schaetzel to Wilcox, Aug. 30, 1947; Robert Lovett to Will Clayton, Aug. 15, 1947, and Senator Millikin to Will Clayton, Oct. 25, 1947, both in box 146, LF 57D-284. Also see "Meeting of the American Delegation to the Havana ITO," Nov. 17, 1947, C-7, box 147; and Wilcox to Bohlen, Oct. 9, 1947, box 47, both in LF 57D-284; and Fulton and Javits, *International Trade Organization,* v, 7. I could find no evidence that Senator Robertson or any Republican senator attended the conference.

26. Schaetzel to Wilcox, "Non-Governmental Representation at the ITO Conference," Aug. 24, 1947; and Russell to Nitze, "ITP Delegation to Havana," Aug. 13, 1947, both in box 146, LF 57D-284.

27. Russell, *UN Charter,* 594-95.

28. Representing business groups were John Abbink, past chairman, National Foreign Trade Council; H.W. Balgooyen, representing NAM, from the American Power and Light Company; Elvin Killheffer, representing the U.S. Chamber of Commerce from Du Pont; Wilbert Ward, representing the Bankers Association for Foreign Trade from National City Bank; and Victor Schoepperle, also representing the Bankers Association for Foreign Trade. Representing agriculture were Kenzie S. Bagshaw, chairman, National Grange; John J. Riggle, assistant secretary, National Council of Farmers Cooperatives; and H.L. Wingate, president, Georgia Farm Bureau, American Farm Bureau Federation. Representing labor were Lee Minton, president, Glass Bottle Blowers Association, American Federation of Labor; and John Brophy, director, Industrial Union Councils, Congress of Industrial Organizations. Representing academia and women's groups were John Dickey, former State Department official and president, Dartmouth

College; and Mildred Northrop, associate professor of economics, Bryn Mawr College. Fulton and Javits, *International Trade Organization,* 7-8.

29. Russell, *UN Charter,* 590-94.

30. Dr. Elvin Kilheffer to Du Pont staff, Jan. 15, 1948, quotations on pp. 1, 2, in Walter S. Carpenter Papers, HML.

31. "Meeting of the American Delegation to the Havana ITO," Nov. 17, 1947, box 147, LF 57D-284. The meeting revealed how even these well-informed Americans misunderstood the ITO.

32. Russell, *UN Charter,* 592-93.

33. "Meeting of the American Delegation," Nov. 17, 1947, B-2, box 147, LF 57D-284.

34. "Meeting of the American Delegation," Nov. 18, 1947, D-18-D-19, box 147; and letter, Clair Wilcox to Eugene P. Thomas, president, National Foreign Trade Council, Jan. 8, 1948, box 14; both in LF 57D-284. Wilcox here noted that "we will continue to fight for the sort of investment provisions which the Council seeks, even though some of our friends may be unwilling to admit that we are doing so." Wilcox later described the continued ambivalence about including investment in the Charter in "Verbatim Record, Meeting of Economic Consultants," Dec. 2, 1948, 6-7, box 29, LF 57D-284.

35. Wilcox to Clayton, "Issues at Havana Conference," Sept. 30, 1947, box 146; C.W. Nichols, "Relationship of the Draft ITO Charter to United States Cotton Policies and Programs," 3, 19, 1947, box 17, and Charles M. Bohlen to Senator Hugh Butler, Apr. 23, 1948, box 55, all in LF 57D-284. On the conflict between agricultural programs and U.S. foreign economic policy, see Thorp to Lovett, Dec. 22, 1948; and Brown to Thorp, Dec. 22, 1948, both in box 59, LF 57D-284.

36. B. Capella, "United Nations Conference on Trade and Employment," box 6, LF 57D-284.

37. H.W. Balgooyen to Hawkins and Rubin, Dec. 8, 1948, box 14, LF 57D-284; and Seymour J. Rubin, interview with author, May 14, 1992. Rubin was the chief negotiator on investment issues at Havana. Balgooyen was the secretary of the American and Foreign Power Company. Also see H.W. Balgooyen to Clair Wilcox, Mar. 29, 1948, box 29, LF 57D-284.

38. Dr. Elvin Kilheffer to Du Pont staff, Jan. 15, 1948, quotations on pp. 1, 2, in Walter S. Carpenter Papers, HML.

39. Statement by Clair Wilcox before Heads of Delegations at Havana, Dec. 24, 1947, box 94, LF 57D-284; Wilcox, *Charter,* 47-49; and Brown, *U.S. and Restoration,* 135-37. The delegates weighed four broad questions regarding the rules of conduct for members, the exceptions to these rules, the scope of these exceptions, and the need for ITO approval of these exceptions to the rules.

40. Winthrop Brown to Clair Wilcox, Nov. 28, 1947, box 30, LF 57D-284; and Brown, *U.S. and Restoration,* 135-37, 141-42, 148-49. Other issues of concern to the United States included balance of payments restrictions, the use of quantitative restrictions to encourage economic development, treatment of nonmembers, preferences, restrictive business practices (cartels), and foreign investment.

41. Wilcox to Brown, Nov. 25, 1947, box 144; and Wilcox to Brown, Feb. 25, 1948, box 104, both in LF 57D-284.

42. Other governments also found hypocrisy in the U.S. position. Leonard Weiss, memorandum of conversation, Dec. 30, 1947, in *FRUS 1948,* vol. 1, pt. 2, 819-23; Fulton and Javits, *International Trade Organization,* 45, 52; and Wilcox, *Charter,* 188-202.

43. As other analysts have detailed the objections of various groups toward the Charter's articles on commodity agreements, business practices, and full employment, I have not focused on their concerns.

44. James Z. Fawcett to R.C. Cox, Treaty Department, n.d., FO 371/68874.

45. E.P. Thomas to William L. Clayton, Dec. 17, 1947, box 142; and Clair Wilcox to E.P. Thomas, Jan. 3, 1948, box 147; both in LF 57D-284. Also see Fulton and Javits, *International Trade Organization,* 53-56; Diebold, "The End of the ITO," 18-20; and Willard Thorp to E.O. Shreve, president, Chamber of Commerce of the United States, Apr. 20, 1948, box 27, LF 57D-284. The Charter set out no greater or lesser right to compensation on expropriation than the U.S. Constitution.

46. Diebold, "The End of the ITO," 16; and *FRUS 1948,* vol. 1, pt. 2, 895-900.

47. Wilcox to Bohlen, "Congressional Action on ITO Charter and Trade Agreements," Oct. 8, 1947, box 147, LF 57D-284. The Act had been extended for three-year periods, except in 1945. U.S. Tariff Commission, *Operation of Trade Agreements Program,* 2d report, 9-13.

48. Wilcox to Brown, Feb. 12, 1948, 859; Brown to Clayton, Dec. 30, 1947, 824; and Coppock to Brown, Dec. 30, 1947, 825-26, all in *FRUS 1948,* vol. 1, pt. 2.

49. Coppock to Brown, Dec. 30, 1947, *FRUS 1948,* vol. 1, pt. 2, 825-26; and Wilcox to Clayton, "Renewal of the Trade Agreements Act," Dec. 29, 1947, box 55, LF 57D-284.

50. Wilcox to Bohlen, "Congressional Action on ITO Charter and Trade Agreements," Oct. 8, 1947; and Gross and Wilcox to the undersecretary, "Congressional Action on ITO Charter and Trade Agreements Act", both in box 147, LF 57D-284. Also see Winthrop Brown, "The Habana Conference, The ITO Charter and the Trade Agreements Act," Jan. 5, 1948; and telegram, Jan. 1, 1948; both in *FRUS 1948,* vol. 1, pt. 2, 829-30. On the failed consultation with Congress, see Brown to Wilcox, Feb. 5, 1948, box 55, LF 57D-284.

51. Brown to Clayton, Dec. 29, 1947, box 144; Wilcox to Clayton, Dec. 29, 1947, box 55; and Brown to Clayton, Dec. 30, 1947, box 148, all in LF 57D-284. The decision to present the Charter as a treaty was not finalized. It would be reexamined after the presidential election. N.a., "The Charter for an International Trade Organization," Nov. 26, 1948, box 45, LF 57D-284.

52. John C. Campbell et al., *The United States in World Affairs, 1948-1949* (New York: Harper and Brother for the Council on Foreign Relations, 1949), viii, ix; Winthrop Brown, "The Habana Conference," Jan. 5, 1948, and Brown to Wilcox, Feb. 5, 1948, both in box 55, LF 57D-284.

53. Clayton quotation in *FRUS 1948,* vol. 1, pt. 2, 900; Brown to Clayton, Dec. 29, 1947, box 144, and Wilcox to Brown, Feb. 12, 1948, box 148, both in LF 57D-284; Wilcox, *Charter,* 199; and Diebold, "End of the ITO," 14-16.

54. Havana to Foreign Office, telegram #43, Jan. 8, 1948, and Washington to Foreign Office, Jan. 9, 1948, both in FO 371/68874.

55. Clayton to Lovett, Jan. 23, 1948, box 144; Brown to Clayton, "Possibility of President Truman Visiting ITO Conference," Feb. 9, 1948, box 146; and Brown to Clayton, Dec. 29, 1947, box 144; all in LF 57D-284; Oral History interview with John M. Leddy, June 15, 1973, 74-76 at HSTL; and Marshall quote in *FRUS 1948,* vol. 1, pt. 2, 948.

56. Oral History interview with Raymond Vernon, July 19, 1973, 24-25; and Oral History interview with Winthrop Brown, May 25, 1973, 28, both at HSTL. Vernon noted the ITO languished on the Hill, with nobody high enough "willing to expend any time, effort, or bargaining power to jimmy it out of Committee."

57. Memorandum by H.J.B. Lintott, Oct. 11, 1947, in the Board of Trade files (hereafter BT) 11/3544, in the Public Records Office at Kew Gardens, London.

58. Havana to Foreign Office, telegram #343, Mar. 3, 1948 and Foreign Office to Havana, Mar. 5, 1948, in FO 371/68902.

59. Brown to Wilcox, Feb. 17, 1948, box 148; and Wilcox in "Verbatim Record, Meetings of Economic Consultants," Dec. 2, 1948, 1-2, box 29, both in LF 57D-284.

60. But this strategy did not assuage Clair Wilcox. Winthrop Brown wrote to reassure him that "the Charter has not been abandoned in favor of the Trade Agreements Act." Wilcox to Brown, Nov. 25, 1947, box 144; Brown to Wilcox, Feb. 5, 1948, box 55; Brown to Wilcox Feb. 17, 1948, box 148; and J. Robert Schaetzel, "Presentation of Charter to Congress," n.d., box 45, all in LF 57D-284.

61. "The Charter of the International Trade Organization," Sept. 1947; and Wilcox to Clayton, "Renewal of Trade Agreements Act," Dec. 29, 1947, both in box 55, LF 57D-284; Wilcox to Clayton and Brown, Jan. 1, 1948, *FRUS 1948,* vol. 1, pt. 2, 828; and Campbell et al., *U.S. in World Affairs,* 215-16.

62. Officials wanted to postpone changing the GATT to fit the ITO "pending expression of opinion by the . . . public and the Congress on the merits of the ITO Charter." *FRUS 1948,* vol. 1, pt. 2, 901, 903, 928-29; and Pritchard, "Will Clayton: A Study," 387 n 75.

63. Nitze to Millikin, n.d., box 57; Wilcox to Brown, Nov. 25, 1947, box 144; Coppock to Brown, "Mr. Thorp's Staff Meeting of May 3," May 3, 1948, box 59; and Edward W. Kelly to Clair Wilcox, Dec. 12, 1947, box 142; all in LF 57D-284. Some participants believed that the ITO would have become a reality if Clayton had remained as a full-time official at State. This perspective had some merit. With his full attention, Clayton might have been able to convince more of his many friends in business and banking to give the ITO a chance. See Pritchard, "Will Clayton: A Study," 346-47, 380; and Oral History interview with John M. Leddy, June 15, 1973, 74, at HSTL. On the designation of Terrill, see Brown to Thorp, "Coordinating the ITO Program," Apr. 13, 1948, box 144, LF 57D-284.

64. Brown, *U.S. and Restoration,* 237-38, 261. There is no evidence to show that administration officials deliberately abandoned the ITO in 1948. This was corroborated in my interviews with John Leddy, Leonard Weiss, and William Diebold.

65. N.a., "Proposals for Mobilizing Effective Support for RTA and ITO," n.d., 2, box 59, LF 57D-284.

7. Congressional Challenges and Public Apathy toward Trade, 1948-1949

1. As the National Opinion Research Center (NORC) reported, "The sheer bigness and complexity of international issues lead to the apathetic conviction that there is nothing an ordinary individual can do about them anyway." National Opinion Research Center, "Cincinnati Looks Again," Rpt. 37A (University of Chicago, 1948), 2 n 1, 4; Stebbins et al., *U.S. in World Affairs,* 1-11; and David McCullough, *Truman* (New York: Simon and Schuster, 1992), 468-85.

2. For a good overview, see Almond, *American People and Foreign Policy,* 48-68, polling data on 73-78; and Stebbins et al., *U.S. in World Affairs,* 12-30.

3. These numbers were consistent with 1947 figures. In September 1947, 92 percent identified the costs of living, 54 percent U.S. relations with Russia, and 23 percent our trade with other countries. NORC, "Cincinnati Looks Again," 6. NORC sampled some 745 adults in September 1947, a subsample of 592 of these were reinterviewed in March 1948, and a new sample of 758 adults in March 1948 to get a representative sample of all adults in Greater Cincinnati.

4. Survey Research Center, "America's Role in World Affairs: Patterns of Citizen Opinion, 1949-1950" (Ann Arbor: Survey Research Center, May 1952), 4, 6, 20.

5. For example, in 1946, only 35 percent thought they would be better off if

the United States exported more, and 30 percent, if the United States imported more. NORC, "Public Attitudes Toward Foreign Trade," Survey 243 (University of Chicago, 1946), 1-2, 3-4, 13, 20-21, 145-46.

6. NORC, "American Programs of Foreign Aid," Occasional Report Series FA no. 4 (University of Chicago, 1957), 5-8, 23. NORC sampled some 1,300 members of the civilian noninstitutional population. For a good explanation of public understanding of the ERP, see NORC, "The 1947 Election Situation" (University of Chicago, 1947), 10-12. For a good analysis of elite understanding of the ERP, see Joseph Barber, ed., *The Marshall Plan as American Policy: A Report on the Views of Community Leaders in Twenty-one Cities* (New York: Council on Foreign Relations, 1948), 1-6, 33-35; and Harold L. Hitchens "Influences on the Congressional Decision to Pass the Marshall Plan," *Western Political Quarterly* 21 (Mar. 1968): 51-54.

7. This Gallup poll of 1,482 adults taken in November and December 1947 was also listed as AIPO 408K, question 12c at RC.

8. NORC.480156.R21, 3, 1948, RC; and Survey Research Center, "America's Role in World Affairs," 42.

9. U.S. NORC. 490167.R17 and .R18, RC. This poll of some 1,284 adults nationwide was taken in June 1949.

10. On GATT, see Gallup 122647.RK12A, Dec. 28, 1947; on Trade Agreements Act, see NORC.480156.R20, 3, 1948, poll of 1,289 national adults; and on reciprocal trade treaties see Apr. 23-28, 1948 Gallup poll (this poll was not numbered), all at RC.

11. NORC, "Public Attitudes toward Foreign Trade," 17-20; and NORC 480161.R12 and .R13, poll of some 1,258 adults in October 1948, RC.

12. Almond, *American People and Foreign Policy,* 79-80, 100-106; and NORC, "Public Attitudes toward Foreign Trade," 3, 19, explanation on p. 20.

13. Such an approach had been attempted in selling the Marshall Plan. The plan's supporters were able to combine a humanitarian rationale (the need to help U.S. friends in Europe) with an economic rationale (the potential of economic benefits) to make a case to average Americans. But the Marshall Plan promised immediate jobs and overseas sales through direct government procurement. The ITO's benefits were more indirect, so it was harder to make an economic case for it. NORC, "Public Attitudes toward Foreign Trade," 9-17. On selling the Marshall Plan, see William F. Sanford Jr., *The American Business Community and the European Recovery Program, 1947-1952* (New York: Garland, 1987), 96-97, 319-20; and Hitchens, "Influences on the Congressional Decision," 52-68.

14. W.H. Baldwin to William Clayton, Dec. 15, 1947, and attached memorandum, "Proposals for Mobilizing Effective Support for RTA and ITO," both in box 59, LF 57D-284.

15. Interview with J. Robert Schaetzel, Aug. 12, 1992, Bethesda, Md. Schaetzel had joined the department from the Bureau of the Budget; he had good contacts at the White House and used them to help maintain Truman administration support for the ITO.

16. William C. Clayton, "GATT, the Marshall Plan, and OECD," 498, 503.

17. William O. Chittick, *The State Department, Press, and Pressure Groups: A Role Analysis* (New York: Wiley, 1970), 24-25; and Oral History interview with Francis Russell, July 13, 1973, 5-11, 16, 22, 25-29, 40-41, HSTL.

18. Office of Public Affairs, "Press and Radio Reaction to Congressional Changes in the Trade Agreements Act," June 15-25, 1948, box 55; W.G. Brown, "Trade Agreements and ITO," Jan. 13, 1949, box 55; S. Shepard Jones to E. Dennison, Apr. 25, 1949, box 3; and "Weekly Opinion Summary," Apr. 29, 1950, box 45, all in LF 57D-284.

19. "Information Program on the Habana Conference and the ITO," Apr. 5, 1948,

box 145; "Tentative Plan of ITO Reference Book," Dec. 23, 1948, box 90; "Outline of ITO Program," May 4, 1948, box 83; Brown to Clayton, n.d., box 148; "Background Information," NAM Meeting June 9," May 25, 1948, box 84; Clayton to Phillip Reed, Aug. 25, 1948, box 90; Clayton to Morris S. Rosenthal, Oct. 13, 1948, box 94; and Speech by Norman Burns to the National Farm Institute, "The American Farmer and the ITO Charter," Feb. 18-19, 1949, box 3, all in LF 57D-284.

20. The World Bank was concerned that taking a position on the Charter might affect the Bank's ability to sell its securities. Young to Terrill, July 6, 1948, box 84, LF 57D-284.

21. "Questions Likely to Be Asked and Proposed Answers," box 6, RG 43; Office of Public Affairs, "Foreign Affairs Background Summary: Expanding World Trade," 3, 1949; Office of Public Affairs, "Twenty-five Questions and Answers on the Proposed International Trade Organization," and Brown to Batt, Feb. 24, 1949, all in box 76, Clayton Papers, HSTL.

22. In 1949, the Hoover Commission examined government functions and organization, including the organization of foreign policy. As a result of the Hoover Commission's recommendations as well as congressional legislation, the department was again reorganized. The economics staff was pared down; Joseph Coppock believed it had lost some two-thirds of its staff. Many of its functions were returned to State's regional divisions and/or other departments. However, while the staff was dwindling, its responsibilities were expanding. Stebbins et al., *U.S. in World Affairs,* 69-72; and Oral History interview with Joseph D. Coppock, 31-33. At the same time, the ECEFP, by which the department spurred governmentwide consensus on foreign policy, was terminated in 1949. Increasingly, the National Advisory Council on International Monetary and Financial Problems (NAC), established by statute and headed by Treasury, took the initiative on foreign economic policy issues. These changes left the State Department staff discouraged.

23. Gardner, *Sterling-Dollar Diplomacy,* 372-73.

24. Advocates argued, for example, that the benefits of the ITO to world trade were "priceless." Office of Public Affairs, "The Place of the ITO in Our Foreign Economic Policy," Dec. 29, 1949; *Department of State Bulletin,* Jan. 16, 1949, 79; Feb. 6, 1949, 168-70; and May 8, 1949, 601-5; and Terrill to Wilcox, Mar. 2, 1948, box 6, LF 57D-284.

25. Pritchard, "Will Clayton: A Study," 346-47, 374-86.

26. W.L. Batt to Herbert S. Marks, July 31, 1945, box 141, LF 57D-284; W.R. Herod to Clayton, Dec. 28, 1948; Baldwin to Clayton, Jan. 21, 1949; Cortney to Clayton; Feb. 8, 1949; W. H. Harrison to Clayton, Mar. 1, 1949; and Gardner Cowles to Clayton, Mar. 17, 1949; all in box 76, Clayton Papers, HSTL. This box is full of letters to business leaders asking for their support of the ITO.

27. "Committee for the International Trade Organization," Clayton Papers, HSTL; Brown, "ITO Charter" Oct. 20, 1948, box 4; and Wilcox to Clayton, "Position of U.S. Chamber of Commerce on ITO Charter," box 84, both in LF 57D-284. It is important to note, however, that although these groups opposed the ITO, many business executives in these groups supported it. The ITO also attracted support from business executives working in firms doing little foreign trade, such as Georgia Power.

28. Pritchard, "Will Clayton: A Study," 381-84. I have decided not to describe in detail the response of associations to the Charter's specifics. William Diebold has eloquently done so in "The End of the ITO."

29. W.H. Baldwin to Batt, Aug. 2, 1949, box 76 Clayton Papers, HSTL; and discussion Meeting Report, "The Prospects for Multilateral Trade," 6th Meeting, Jan. 27, 1947, Council on Foreign Relations Archives, (hereafter CFR). The bulk of the Commit-

tee for the ITO's members were business executives. "Committee for the International Trade Organization," box 76, Clayton Papers, HSTL.

30. In 1947-48, Republican priorities included tax and budget reduction, the use of economic foreign aid to contain communism, local control over governmental programs, and exposure of alleged communists in government. There was great diversity of opinion on these issues, but most Republicans saw containing communism as crucial. For a good overview of these issues, see Pritchard, "Will Clayton: A Study," 357-58; Thomas G. Paterson, "The Quest for Peace and Prosperity: International Trade, Communism, and the Marshall Plan," in *Politics and Policies of the Truman Administration,* ed. Barton J. Bernstein (Chicago: Quadrangle, 1970), 8-9, 92-97; Hitchens, "Influences on the Congressional Decision to Pass the Marshall Plan," 58 n 25; and Hartmann, *Truman and the 80th Congress,* 5-52, 102-6, 117-21, 127, 131, 179-85, 203.

31. "Material on the ITO and Trade Agreement Negotiations in Geneva for Congressmen Javits and Fulton," Aug. 18, 1947, box 4M, Acheson/Thorp Papers, HSTL; Brown to Wilcox, Nov. 20, 1947; Brown, "Renewal of Trade Agreements Act," Mar. 10, 1948; and Schaetzel to Clayton, 3, 19, 1948; all in box 148, LF 57D-284.

32. Brown to Wilcox, Nov. 20, 1947, box 148, LF 57D-284; and Winthrop Brown, "Renewal of Trade Agreements Act," Mar. 10, 1948, box 148, LF 57D-284.

33. Pritchard, "Will Clayton: A Study," 359-61.

34. Coppock to Brown, "Mr. Thorp's Staff Meeting of May 3," May 3, 1948, box 59, LF 57D-284. This suggestion was a precursor of today's fast-track authority for the GATT negotiations.

35. Senate Finance Committee, *Extending Authority to Negotiate Trade Agreements: Hearings on H.R. 6566, An Act to Extend the Authority of the President under Section 350 of the Tariff Act of 1930, As Amended, and for Other Purposes,* June 1-5, 1948, 80th Cong., 2d sess., 1-16.

36. Wallace Judson Parks, *United States Administration of Its International Economic Affairs* (Westport, Conn.: Greenwood Press, 1968), 14-17, 43-47, 71. State early on accepted the rationale of a separate organization to administer the ERP. Hogan, *Marshall Plan:,* 101-10.

37. House Committee on Ways and Means, *Testimony before the Subcommittee on Tariffs and Foreign Trade of the Committee on Ways and Means, on the Operation of the Trade Agreements Program,* 80th Cong., 2d sess., May 3-8, 1948, 2-3, 69, 521; and Pritchard, "Will Clayton: A Study," 362-64. At the House hearings, fourteen experts testified in favor of H.R. 6566; eleven witnesses, including Secretary of State George Marshall, were opposed to the bill and testified in favor of the requested three year extension. At the Senate hearing, twelve witnesses testified in favor of H.R. 6566; thirteen opposed the bill.

38. House Committee on Ways and Means, *Testimony.* On tariff as a pawn, see 59, 118, 141, 357; on State abdicating its responsibilities to Americans, see 8, 81, 96, 100, 118, 357; and on distrust of the Department, see 69, 156-57, 241, 247.

39. Senate Committee on Finance, *Extending Authority,* June 1-5, 1948. On the lack of businessmen at Geneva on delegation, see 60-76, 87, 89; on the Department of State hiding information and on justifying closed House hearing, see 236.

40. House Committee on Ways and Means, *Testimony.* On linkage of support of free trade with communism, see 89, 457. On how efforts to contain communism will be aided by renewal, see 192.

41. Ibid. On the allegation that big business grew fat on protection, see 200-201, 235, 304, 319; on protecting agriculture, see 106, 109; and on restoring the balance, see 20, 58, 116, 357.

42. Ibid. On the ITO being a permanent trade agreements program (TAP) and on

RTAA committing the United States to the ITO, see 30, 131; on the GATT as a little ITO, see 130, 376-77, 503-4; and on the fact that the ITO is ready, why not present it, see 131-32, 154, 318-19, 503-6.

43. Senate Committee on Finance, *Extending Authority*. On the relationship of ERP to TAP, see 149, 162, 214, 217-18; on "implied" authority for GATT under the RTAA, see 467-70.

44. House Committee on Ways and Means, *Testimony*. On the logical relationship of TAP and ERP, see 173-74, 196, 206, 239, 314, 319, 389, 432; on furthering free enterprise by encouraging private enterprise, 238-39; and on the argument that without U.S. leadership, the world would return to autarky, 459-60. Senate Committee on Finance, *Extending Authority*. On autarky, see 43, 85; on statism, see 203-4.

45. House Committee on Ways and Means, *Testimony*. On consumer arguments, see 296, 372-73; on worker arguments, see 193, 315-17.

46. Senate Committee on Finance, *Extending Authority*. On viewing the RTAA as unimportant and State Department procrastination, see 147, 188, 471-72; on Clayton's being forced to describe departmental actions to extend the TAP, see 471-72; on poor management by the State Department, see 37, 257, 444-45.

47. Ibid. For Clayton quotations in Senate hearing, see 18, 486; also see 26, 27, 167, 177, 486; and on interagency process, see 190, 192.

48. U.S. Tariff Commission, *Operation of the Trade Agreements Program,* 2d report, 12-14; Senate Committee on Finance, *Hearings on H.R. 6566,* 1-4; and Hartmann, *Truman and the 80th Congress,* 182-84.

49. Pritchard, "Will Clayton: A Study," 366-77.

8. Dead on Arrival: The Fate of the ITO, 1948-1951

1. Winthrop Brown, "ITO Charter," Oct. 20, 1948, box 4, LF 57D-284.

2. U.S. Tariff Commission, *Operation of the Trade Agreements Program,* June 1934-Apr. 1948, part 2, 42; and U.S. Tariff Commission, *Operation of the Trade Agreements Program,* 5th report, July 1951-June 1952 (Washington, D.C.: GPO, 1954), 4, 13-16.

3. U.S. Tariff Commission, *Operation of the Trade Agreements Program,* 3d report, Apr. 1949-June 1950 (Washington, D.C.: GPO, 1951), 27-29; and Stebbins et al., *U.S. in World Affairs* (New York: Harper and Brothers, 1950), 66-67, 73.

4. Diebold, "The End of the ITO," 16-24.

5. Congressional Quarterly, *Politics in America,* 1; and Carl March, "Memorandum for the Acting Secretary," Aug. 14, 1947, box 20, RG 59, Records of the Office of Congressional Relations.

6. Hiss was chairman of the Executive Committee of the Citizens Committee for the Extension of World Trade and at the time of these accusations was the president of the Carnegie Endowment for World Peace.

7. Goldman, *Crucial Decade,* 101-12; and Congressional Quarterly, *Politics in America,* 4-11, quotations on pp. 9, 11. A majority of Americans polled both by Gallup and the American Institute of Public Opinion reported that they believed Congress should continue these investigations and that they were not purely political. NORC, "Opinion News," Oct. 1, 1948, vol. 11, no. 7, p. 8.

8. Stebbins et al., *U.S. in World Affairs,* 68-75; Chittick, *State Department, Press, and Pressure Groups,* 16-21, 37-38; and Lester Markel et al., *Public Opinion and Foreign Policy* (New York: Harper and Brother for the Council on Foreign Relations, 1949), 80.

9. Colton Hand, "Trade Agreements, ITO, and Congress," Dec. 27, 1948, box 45; and Robert A. Lovett, "Memorandum for the President," Dec. 27, 1948, box 30, both in LF 57D-284.

10. Robert A. Lovett, memorandum for the President, May 21, 1948; George M. Elsey, memorandum for Mr. Clifford, May 26, 1948, both in Clifford Papers, HSTL; J.R. Schaetzel, "White House Reaction to Department's Proposal for Submission of ITO Charter to Congress in the New Session," June 8, 1948, box 55; and Coppock to Martin, "ECA Review Group for ITO Charter," Nov. 10, 1948, box 45, both in LF 57D-284.

11. N.a., "Problems in Connection with Presentation of ITO Charter," n.d.; Brown to Bohlen, "Precedent for Presenting ITO as Joint Resolution," Dec. 27, 1948; W.G. Brown, "Trade Agreement and ITO Legislation," Jan. 12, 1949, all in box 45, LF 57D-284; and "Brief on Constitutionality of Approval by Joint Resolution," box 6, LF 57D-284.

12. N.a., "The Charter for an International Trade Organization," Nov. 26, 1948, box 45; Schaetzel to Brown, "ITO Backstop," Dec. 4, 1948, box 3; and Norman Burns, "Preliminary Plan for Congressional Hearings on the Charter," Dec. 17, 1948, box 13, all in LF 57D-284.

13. Coppock to Brown and Martin, "Preparations for Transmitting ITO Charter to Congress," Nov. 17, 1948, box 45, LF 57D-284.

14. Acheson, *Present at the Creation,* 251-53; Oral History interview with Leroy Stinebower, June 9, 1974, 14, 38-40; and Oral History interview with John S. Dickey, 7, 19, 1947, 5-9, both at HSTL. General Marshall resigned January 7, 1949.

15. Wilkinson, *Politics and Trade Policy,* 52-53.

16. Dean Acheson, memorandum, Feb. 7, 1949, Item 3, RG 53D-444.

17. Dean Acheson, "Big Four Discussion on Legislative Program," Mar. 28, 1949, Acheson Papers, HSTL; and W.G. Brown, "Presentation of ITO Charter to the Congress," Apr. 15, 1949, box 45, LF 57D-284.

18. The bill was signed by the president on September 26, 1949. It repealed the Trade Agreements Extension Act of 1948. U.S. Tariff Commission, *Operation of the Trade Agreements Program,* 3d report, 24. The House bill passed by a vote of 319-69; the Senate passed it by 62-19. The pressure of other legislation and the illness of Senator Walter F. George caused this delay.

19. On the House side, thirty-nine witnesses, including nine members of Congress, testified against a three-year extension and revision of the 1948 bill. Eighteen witnesses, including one senator, testified in support of these changes. House Committee on Ways and Means, *Extension of the Reciprocal Trade Agreements Act: Hearings on H.R. 1211, A Bill to Extend the Authority of the President under Section 350 of the Tariff Act of 1930, As Amended and for Other Purposes,* 81st Cong., 1st sess., Jan. 24-Feb. 1, 1949; on Thorp, see 38-39. On the Senate side, thirty-one witnesses, including three senators, testified against a three-year extension; twenty-one witnesses, including one senator, testified for the bill. Senate Committee on Finance, *Hearings on H.R. 1211, An Act to Extend the Authority of the President Under Section 350 of the Tariff Act of 1930, as Amended and for Other Purposes,* 81st Cong., 1st sess., Feb. 17-Mar. 8, 1949.

20. House Committee on Ways and Means, *Hearings on H.R. 1211.* On low-wage labor, 3056, 315-16, 344-45, 369, 403, 419, 460; on condemning the Department's policies, 411-12, 495, 539, 551, 584-85, 771; and on GATT as a little ITO, 255. Senate Committee on Finance, *Hearings on H.R. 1211.* On low-wage labor, 217, 436, 645, 871, 878, 887; condemning the department's policies, 8, 11, 23, 57-58, 541, 875, 1082; on GATT as a little ITO, 21, 56-58.

21. Senate Committee on Finance, *Hearings on H.R. 1211.* On escape clause as worthless, 89, 183, 387; on U.S. government subsidizing competitors, 423-24. House Committee on Ways and Means, *Hearings on H.R. 1211.* On subsidizing the competition, 282, 306-8, 312, 314-15, 338.

22. James Webb, "Memorandum for the President," Feb. 23, 1949, Confidential

File, Truman Papers, HSTL; and House Committee on Ways and Means, *Hearings on H.R. 1211,* 13-15, 91, 134-35.

23. Senate Committee on Finance, *Hearings on H.R. 1211.* Malone quotes, 869-875.

24. Ibid., 54-55, 75, 407-8, 549-50, 984, 1065-91. Millikin's examination of Brown on the GATT and the ITO, 896-1442; Judas goat quotation on 1071; moral and legal connection quotation on p. 1069.

25. Senate Committee on Finance, *Hearings on H.R. 1211.* On being a tail to the ITO dog, 1075; on Brown's concession on the ITO, 1071, 1093-94; on Millikin's misunderstanding of State's strategy, 1094.

26. Some witnesses argued that high tariffs were necessary to keep full employment, preserve free enterprise, and prevent the growth of statism in the United States! Representative Curtis claimed that free trade encouraged economic concentration overseas because the rich got richer, which would encourage world communism. House Committee on Ways and Means, *Hearings on H.R. 1211,* 333, 481; on free trade encouraging communism, 369, 375. Senate Committee on Finance, *Hearings on H.R. 1211,* 180-81, 869-75 (comments of Senator Malone).

Perfectionist opponents of the ITO would soon fine-tune this way of thinking to condemn the ITO, arguing that free trade with controlled economies is an illusion. Proponents of what I call the "becoming the enemy argument" believed socialism, capitalism, and internationalism could not be reconciled without undermining the free enterprise system. Thus, they condemned the ITO for attempting such a reconciliation. Rubber Manufacturers Association, "Pros and Cons," 12-13, 22-23, 26.

27. House Committee on Ways and Means, *Hearings on H.R. 1211,* 365-68, 393-94, 397, 435-38, 447, 460, 476, 485. Senate Finance Committee, *Hearings on H.R. 1211.* On the conditional support of free trade, 189-91, 275, 329, 410, 591; on defense rationale for protection, 437, 616-17.

28. Clark M. Clifford, memorandum for the President, Apr. 26, 1949, Clifford Papers, HSTL.

29. The Charter is designed to do two things: to establish a code of international conduct . . . and to create an agency, within the framework of the United Nations, to help implement this code . . . . It does provide a practical, realistic method for progressive action toward the goal of expanding world trade." Harry S. Truman, "President's Message to the Congress of the United States," Apr. 28, 1949, Papers of Charles S. Murphy (hereafter Murphy Papers), HSTL.

30. Russell, *UN Charter,* 935.

31. H.J. Res. 236, "Providing for Membership and Participation by the United States in the International Trade Organization and Authorizing an Appropriation Therefor," 81st Cong., 1st sess., Elsey Papers, HSTL; L.D. Battle to Humelsine, Apr. 19, 1949; and L.D. Battle to S/S, Apr. 31, 1949, box 8, RG 53D-444.

32. N.a., *Hearings Held in Executive Session before the Committee on Foreign Relations, United States Senate, on the World Situation,* 81st Cong., 1st and 2d sess., Executive Hearings, May 19, 1949-Dec. 22, 1950 (Washington, D.C.: GPO, 1974), quotations on pp. 195, 196; and Pritchard, "Will Clayton: A Study," 387.

33. Winthrop Brown to Eric Wyndham White, July 26, 1949, box 153, LF 57D-284; Batt to Clayton, June 17, 1949, box 76 Clayton Papers, HSTL; and Pritchard, "Will Clayton: A Study," 384-87.

34. Willoughby to Brown, "Agricultural Exception and *Charter* Hearings," Jan. 29, 1949, box 14, LF 57D-284; n.a., "Meeting of the Strategy Board on ITO," Nov. 29, 1949; and n.a., "Meeting of the Strategy Board on ITO," Dec. 8, 1949, both in box 45, LF 57D-284.

35. Undersecretary's Meeting, Nov. 23, 1949, box 94, LF 57D-284. Gross to

Webb, "Status of State Department Legislative Program," June 2, 1949; Brown, "State Department's Legislative Program and the Schedule of Legislation by the Foreign Relations Committee," Dec. 14, 1949; and "Legislative Items for This Session," Jan. 4, 1950, all in box 13, Records of the Office of Congressional Relations, 1948-1951, LF 53D-17, RG 59, at NA, hereafter LF 53D-17.

36. Department of State, *FRUS 1949* (Washington, D.C.: GPO, 1976), 1:657; and Winthrop Brown to Eric Wyndham White, July 26, 1949, box 153, LF 57D-284.

37. At the end of 1948, the British government remained in balance of payments difficulties. But under the Anglo-American Financial Agreement, the British were not allowed to practice discriminatory trade. In contrast, the ITO and GATT had provisions to permit such practices, and U.S. officials wanted to encourage recourse under the GATT and eventually the ITO. But if the United States encouraged the British to utilize the "Havana Option," ITO provisions setting rules for such discrimination, U.S. negotiators could be perceived as bringing the ITO into effect before congressional approval. In 1949, the United States imposed export controls on certain exports to Czechoslovakia, and justified them as being in the interest of national security. But Czechoslovakia, a contracting party to the GATT, alleged that the United States was abandoning trade liberalization principles for political profit. Chairman to Members of TAC, Dec. 9, 1948, box 55; Len Weiss, "Reply to British Request for Understanding with Regard to the Interpretation of Paragraph 1(c) of Article 23 of the ITO Charter," Dec. 13, 1948, box 3, both in LF 57D-284; and *FRUS 1949,* 1:661-63, 709-15.

38. Stevens to Helmore, Feb. 6, 1947, Economics file no. 37, FO 371/66283.

39. Michael L. Hoffman, "U.S. Embarrassed at Tariff Parley," *New York Times,* Aug. 1, 1949, Clayton Papers, HSTL.

40. Woodbury Willoughby, "Action by UK on ITO Charter," July 20, 1949, box 55, LF 57D-284; and *FRUS 1949,* 1:716, 725-26.

41. Woodbury Willoughby, "Action by UK on ITO Charter," July 20, 1949, box 55, LF 57D-284; and Department of State, *FRUS 1949,* 1:696-97.

42. N.a., "Meeting of the Strategy Board on ITO," Nov. 29, 1949, box 45, LF 57D-284.

43. Stebbins et al., *U.S. in World Affairs,* 89-91.

44. Winthrop G. Brown, "ITO Hearings," Jan. 12, 1950; "ITO," Jan. 24, 1950, both in box 45, LF 57D-284; and Kotschnig to Brown, Jan. 25, 1950, box 91, LF 57D-284.

45. Mr. Campbell also used the opportunity to criticize administration trade strategy, expressing "regret that Mr. Kilheffer's feelings had been hurt during the Havana Conference and that his advice had not been solicited . . . . Mr. Campbell implied that this was a slam against the Chamber." Corse to Brown, "ITO Hearings," Jan. 17, 1950, box 45, LF 57D-284; Office of Public Affairs, "The Place of the ITO in Our Foreign Economic Policy," Clifford Papers, HSTL; and Rubber Manufacturers Association, "Pros and Cons," 111, 114-15.

46. Elsey, "Memorandum for Mr. Murphy," Jan. 27, 1950, Elsey Papers; and Dean Acheson, "Meeting with the President," Feb. 9, 1950, box 646, Acheson Papers, both at HSTL.

47. Brown, "ITO Hearings," Feb. 2, 1950, box 45, LF 57D-284; "ITO Ratification," Mar. 13, 1950; "ITO Ratification," Mar. 24, 1950; and V.E. Bundy, "U.S. Commercial Foreign Policy," Apr. 5, 1950 all in box 12, LF 57D-284.

48. Brown, "ITO: Speeches on Imports," Mar. 27, 1950, box 10, LF 57D-284.

49. Elsey to Murphy, Apr. 12, 1950, Elsey Papers, HSTL.

50. Memorandum for the President, May 3, 1950, box 4; and "Matters to be discussed with Senator Connally," Apr. 26, 1950, box 3, both in RG 53D-444; James E.

Webb, "Meeting with the President," May 22, 1950, box 9; and Brown, "Republican Strategy in Senate on ITO," May 2, 1950, box 45, both in LF 57D-444. Also see "World Trade Unit Plea by Acheson Draws G.O.P. Fire," *St. Louis Post-Dispatch,* Apr. 22, 1950; Charles E. Egan, "Acheson Accused of Ignoring G.O.P.," *New York Times,* Apr. 22, 1950; and Joseph A. Fox, "Truman Warns against Trade 'Isolationism,'" *Washington Star,* May 14, 1950. On the constitutionality of the joint resolution, see "Brief on Constitutionality of Approval by Joint Resolution," box 6, LF 57D-284.

51. Melvin J. Fox to Charles R. Weaver, "Progress Report and Future Programs: Committee for the ITO," n.d., box 76, Clayton Papers, HSTL.

52. House Committee on Foreign Affairs, *United States in the International Trade Organization, Hearings on H.J. Res. 236: A Joint Resolution Providing for Membership and Participation by the United States in the International Trade Organization and Authorizing an Appropriation Therefor,* 81st Cong., 2d sess., Apr. 19-May 12, 1950. Examples of the efforts of Fulton and Javits, 498, 509, 518, 576-77, 581, 588. The State Department kept close track of the hearings. See n.a., "Hearings before the House Foreign Affairs Committee on the ITO Charter for May 9, 1950," n.d., box 45, LF 57D-284. On Ways and Means support, see "Ways and Means Democrats Favor American Membership in International Trade Organization," Apr. 28, 1950, box 108, LF 57D-284. Also see "The ITO Charter Couldn't Even Bring Out the Committee," *Baltimore Sun,* May 14, 1950; and Pritchard, "Will Clayton: A Study," 387-92. Clayton could not appear due to family illness. Eighteen witnesses testified for the ITO, nine against.

53. Department staff spent a lot of time analyzing the views of prominent ITO opponents. "Literature Opposing the ITO," box 8; "List of Organizations Opposing the ITO," box 45; and n.a., "What Kind of Charter Do the Opponents of the ITO Propose," box 45, all in LF 57D-284.

54. Boxes 8 and 30 of LF 57D-284 are full of documents rebutting criticisms of the ITO Charter. Here is a good example. Why do we want an ITO Charter? Why not go along with bilateral agreements? Countries resort to war when they are unable to work out concerted action. The ITO will facilitate concerted action, speed up recovery abroad, and improve economic conditions of other countries, thereby lessening their need for governmental controls. The argument seems indirect. House Committee on Foreign Affairs, *Hearings on H.J. Res. 236,* 76-83.

55. Ibid., 485-99.

56. Ibid. Positive arguments, 78-79, 102-3, 112-24, 464-66; on surrender of sovereignty, 161, 259, 300-303, 367, 378, 486-89, 502. Also see "Principal Criticisms of the ITO Charter," Feb. 23, 1949, 4-5, box 45, LF 57D-284; and Brown, *U.S. and Restoration,* 370-71.

57. Ibid. Arguments that the ITO is consistent with U.S. economic practice, 271, 274, 330-31, 350-58, 644-45; arguments that it is inconsistent with U.S. economic practice, 261-62, 271, 295-96, 426-27, 502-3, 598-601.

58. Ibid. Proponents' arguments on full employment, 92-93, 272-73; and opponents' arguments, 161, 259, 367. Also see Diebold, "The End of the ITO," 17; and Oral History interview with Leroy Stinebower, June 9, 1974, 66-71. On full employment (Article 56) in United Nations Charter see Russell, *UN Charter,* 784-88.

59. Ibid. On state trading, 263, 617-18; and on linking the ITO to state intervention, big bureaucracies, and communism, 297-98, 367, 427, 502-4, 567, 573-74, 583, 599-600.

60. Ibid. Examples of Charter's hypocrisy, 260-62, 265, 383, 428-29. Also see Javits and Fulton, *International Trade Organization,* 34-44; and Rubber Manufacturers Association, "Pros and Cons," 23, 26, 31.

61. Pritchard, "Will Clayton: A Study," 392.

62. Elsey, "Memorandum for Mr. Spingarn," May 27, 1950, Elsey Papers, HSTL; and Pritchard, "Will Clayton: A Study," 388-92.

63. Judge John Kee to Harry S Truman, Aug. 10, 1950; and Harry S. Truman to Congressman Kee, Aug. 14, 1950, both in Elsey Papers, HSTL; Office of Public Affairs, "The Place of the ITO in Our Foreign Economic Policy," Dec. 29, 1949, 5, Clifford Papers, HSTL; and Pritchard, "Will Clayton: A Study," 393-95.

64. Draft, "Memorandum for the President," Nov. 10, 1950; Leddy to Elsey and Bell, Nov. 10, 1950, both in Elsey Papers, HSTL; and Acheson, "Cabinet Notes," Nov. 21, 1950, box 65, Acheson Papers, HSTL.

65. Len Weiss, "ITO Charter," May 24, 1950, box 45; and Eric Wyndham White to Winthrop Brown, Feb. 7, 1950, box 153, both in LF 57D-284.

66. Weiss to Leddy, "ITO Prospects," Aug. 12, 1950, box 12, LF 57D-284.

67. N.a., "Secretary's Comments on Draft of Economic Speech," Mar. 7, 1950, box 9; memorandum for the President, Mar. 8, 1950, box 3, both in RG 53D-444; and Pritchard, "Will Clayton: A Study," 393-94.

68. Department of State, Press Release, no. 1221, Dec. 6, 1950. In the next few years, some of these officials would attempt to reshape the GATT to be more like the ITO. Ingram to Brown, "Cost Estimates of ITO," May 17, 1950, box 50; and Kusick to Hunt, June 18, 1953, box 153, both in LF 57D-284.

69. Roger Makins, "Record of Conversation," Nov. 28, 1950; and A. McCall-Judson, "Minutes," Dec. 21, 1950, both in FO 371/82947.

70. Roger Makins, "Record of Conversation," Nov. 28, 1950; and A. McCall-Wilson, "Minutes," Dec. 21, 1950, both in FO 371/82947; P. Mennell, "Minutes, Aug. 23, 1950, FO 371/82970. Also see Thompson-McCausland, "Future of GATT, Minutes," Oct. 20, 1951, FO 371-91962 and "The Sixth Session and the Future of the General Agreement on Tariffs and Trade," FO 371/91962; and "Tariffs (International Discussions)" Feb. 15, 1951, FO 371/91962.

9. The Rise and Erosion of the Freer Trade Consensus and the Debate over NAFTA, 1949-1994

1. In a 1957 report, President Eisenhower delineated the three objectives of U.S. foreign economic policy: to promote the economic strength of the United States, to promote the economic strength of the rest of the free world, and to build and maintain cohesion in the free world. Office of the President, "Foreign Economic Policy and the Trade Agreements Program," in Committee on Ways and Means, *Foreign Trade Policy: Compendium of Papers on United States Foreign Trade Policy* (Washington, D.C.: GPO, 1957), 5-8. Although international trade was and is an engine of growth for the U.S. economy, neither exports nor imports comprised more than 12 percent of GNP throughout the postwar period through today. Paul Krugman, "Competitiveness: A Dangerous Obsession," *Foreign Affairs* 73 (Mar./Apr. 1994): 28-30.

2. Robert Griffith, "Dwight D. Eisenhower and the Corporate Commonwealth," *American Historical Review* 87 (Feb. 1982): 97; and Bauer, de Sola Pool, and Dexter, *American Business and Public Policy,* 86-91.

3. In the early postwar period as well as today, polling data reveals a correlation between higher levels of education and income with support for freer trade. On levels of education, see NBC News/Wall Street Journal Survey, July 24-27, 1993; and Yankelovich Clancy Shulman Poll for Reuters, Aug. 24-Sept. 9, 1992, both reported in Karlyn Bowman and Everett Carl Ladd, "Public Opinion and Demographic Report," *American Enterprise,* (Sept./Oct. 1993): 83, 85. Also see Gwen Ifil, "Americans Are Split on Trade Accord, Poll Finds," *New York Times,* Nov. 16, 1993, A1; and *Times Mirror,*

"The People, The Press and Politics: Public Opinion About Economic Issues," Mar. 1989, 1, 7, 8, 37, 38, 91. For comparative historical data, see Bauer, de Sola Pool, and Dexter, *American Business and Public Policy,* 86-91.

4. For example, between 1965 and 1990, inflation-adjusted exports grew by 439 percent, while world production rose 136 percent. Council of Economic Advisers, *Economic Report of the President, February 1993* (Washington, D.C.: GPO, 1993), 280.

5. Nations could adhere to GATT without accepting all of these codes. United States Trade Representative, *A Preface to Trade,* 5-10.

6. Robert E. Hudec, *Enforcing International Trade Law: The Evolution of the Modern GATT Legal System* (Salem, N.H.: Butterworth Legal, 1993), 9, 193, 357; John H. Jackson, *The World Trading System: Law and Policy of International Economic Relations* (Cambridge: MIT Press, 1989), 35-51; Executive Office of the President, U.S. Trade Representative, *A Preface to Trade* (Washington, D.C.: GPO, 1982), 5; and Department of State, Bureau of Intelligence and Research, "The Developing Institutional Character of the GATT," Unclassified Report no. 562, Aug. 16, 1976, i-iii, 1-3.

7. Wilkinson, *Politics and Trade Policy,* 65. Robert Hudec notes that the GATT disclaimer was included in the 1953, 1954, 1955 and 1958 trade agreements legislation. It was omitted in the 1962 act and returned in the Trade Act of 1974. Hudec, *GATT Legal System,* 356 n 3.

8. Hudec, *Enforcing International Trade Law,* 45-46, 203; Hudec, *GATT Legal System,* 63, 355, 356 n 17; and Dam, *GATT,* 337-38.

9. For example, on the eve of the GATT/WTO vote (November 29, 1994) a *USA Today*/CNN/Gallup poll of 1,020 adults found 53 percent of those polled saw trade as an "opportunity," whereas 38 percent saw trade as a "threat." Reported in Elys A. McLean, "Most Unclear on GATT," *USA Today,* 4A.

10. Carol Sullivan, "*Newsweek* Poll: More Than Half of Americans Blame Japan's Unfair Trade Policies for America's Trade Deficit," July 3, 1993, 3.

11. *Newsweek* Poll, June 30-July 1, 1993 and the Yankelovich Partners Survey for *Time* and CNN, both reported in Bowman and Ladd, "Public Opinion," 84.

12. Voter Research and Surveys Poll conducted Nov. 3, 1992, reported in Bowman and Ladd, "Public Opinion and Demographic," 84; and Princeton Survey Research Poll for Times Mirror, Mood of America, Apr. 06, 1994, obtained from file 485, of the Roper Center for Public Opinion Research, on America Online.

13. N.a., *The Polling Report,* vol. 8, no. 3, Feb. 10, 1992, 8.

14. Kevin Anderson, "Consumers: Quality Still Comes First," *USA Today,* Mar. 9, 1992, 1A, 1B; and Princeton Survey Research Associates Poll, for *Newsweek,* cited in Bowman and Ladd, "Public Opinion," 84.

15. Yankelovich, "Foreign Policy After the Election," 2-12.

16. Public Agenda Foundation, "Cross-talk," 18-19; and Rosita Thomas, "Public Opinion on Trade," *CRS Review* (Feb./Mar. 1992): 17. Thomas cites a *New York Times*/CBS News Poll of June 1991 and a CBS News/Tokyo Broadcasting News poll of May 1988. Also see Galen and Vamous, "Portrait of An Anxious Public," 80. On letting market forces determine U.S. competitiveness see a survey of 1,255 adults conducted Jan. 7-Jan. 10, 1994. Press release, *Business Week*/Harris Poll, Jan. 24, 1994, 3.

17. Saad, "GATT Still a Mystery," 1. This was also true for NAFTA. Sharon Warden and Jefferson Morley, "NAFTA, a Class Issue," *Washington Post,* Nov. 14, 1993, C3.

18. Daniel Yankelovich, "Foreign Policy after the Election," *Foreign Affairs* 71 (fall 1992): 2-12; and Jim Hoagland, "A Turn Inward," *Washington Post,* Jan. 10, 1995.

19. The Council on Competitiveness, "Looking for Leadership: The Public, Competitiveness, and Campaign '92," Sept. 1991, 3, 5, 6; and Galen and Vamos, "Portrait of an Anxious Public," Mar. 13, 1995, 80.

20. Times Mirror Center for the People and the Press, "The New Political Landscape: The People, the Press, and Politics," Oct. 1994, 25-29, section on "Economic Attitudes and Faith in America;" Galen and Vamos, "Portrait of An Anxious Public," Mar. 13, 1995, 80; and n.a., "We're #1 and It Hurts," *Time,* Oct. 24, 1994, 50-56.

21. Times Mirror Center, "America's Place in the World," Nov. 1993, 90. When Americans were asked which long-range foreign policy goals should be a top priority, 85 percent chose protecting the jobs of U.S. workers; 55 percent chose reducing our trade deficit; and 27 percent chose aiding the interests of U.S. business abroad. In short, protecting U.S. jobs was the number one foreign policy goal. Also see "Statement by the AFL-CIO Executive Council on *The Uruguay Round Trade Agreement,*" May 11, 1994; and Dr. Gregory Woodhead, "Statement before the House Committee on Small Business on the Uruguay Round of Multilateral Trade Negotiations," Apr. 26, 1994. Dr. Woodhead, an economist for the AFL-CIO, provided me with these documents.

22. See the theme shared by Curtis H. Barnette, CEO, Bethlehem Steel, testifying on behalf of the American Iron and Steel Institute and Steven R. Appleton, CEO, Micron Technology, on behalf of the Semiconductor Industry Association, Senate Committee on Finance, *Results of the Uruguay Round Trade Negotiations Hearings,* 103d Cong., 2d sess., Feb. 8-Mar. 23, 1994, 108-13.

23. Hufbauer, ed., *Free Trade Debate,* table 3.2, "Cases Involving Countervailing Duties," 184; Destler, *American Trade Politics,* 2d ed., 153-56; and Robert Keatley, "World Economy: Congress Inserts Rules in GATT Treaty that Make It Harder to Trade Globally," *Wall Street Journal,* Aug. 19, 1994, A6.

24. Daniel P. Moynihan, "The United States Should Retaliate Against Unfair Trade Partners," in *Trade: Opposing Viewpoints,* ed. Wiliam Dudley (San Diego: Greenhaven Press, 1991), 102-5. For an example of Richard Gephardt's views see David S. Broder, "Gephardt Warns against Trade Pact With Chile," *Washington Post,* Mar. 14, 1995, D2.

25. According to a Princeton Survey Research Associates poll of 744 adults on June 30-July 1, 1993, some 56 percent of those polled blamed Japan's unfair trade policies for the U.S. trade deficit. Carol Sullivan, "*Newsweek* Poll: More than Half of Americans Blame Japan's Unfair Trade Policies for America's Trade Deficit," July 3, 1993, 1.

26. For recent evidence as to how this has affected government officials see James K. Jackson, *Foreign Direct Investment in the United States,* Apr. 14, 1993, Congressional Research Service, Library of Congress, 4, 10; and U.S. General Accounting Office, *Technology Transfer: Foreign Participation in R&D at Federal Labs,* GAO/RCED 88-203BR, 11. For evidence of its influence on corporations see the nonpartisan Council on Competitiveness, *Roadmap for Results: Trade Policy, Technology and American Competitiveness,* (Washington, D.C.: Council on Competitiveness, 1993), 1, 2, 5-20; and "IIE Urges Administration Not to Cite Foreign Barriers under Super 301," *Inside U.S. Trade,* Sept. 23, 1994, 12.

27. Tyson, *Who's Bashing Whom: Trade Conflict in High Technology Industries,* especially 116. Although Dr. Tyson has not renounced cautious activism, she has been a strong supporter of multilateralism since she has joined the Clinton administration. At this writing, Laura D'Andrea Tyson is chair of the National Economic Council and former chair of the Council of Economic Advisers to the President. Also see Pat Choate and J.K. Linger, *The High-Flex Society* (New York: Knopf, 1988), 63-77; and Clyde Prestowitz, chair of the Economic Strategy Institute, *Trading Places: How We Are Giving Our Future to Japan and How to Reclaim It* (New York: Basic Books, 1988).

28. Hufbauer, *Free Trade Debate;* and "U.S. International Transactions, 1946-1992," Council of Economic Advisers *Annual Report 1993,* 462 (table B-100).

29. For example, *Economic Report of the President, February 1995,* 21-23; 249-53; and *Economic Report of the President, February 1994,* 212-14.

30. For two very different views on wage stagnation and trade, see Krugman, *Peddling Prosperity,* 58, 146-50; and Bluestone, "The Inequality." Also see upcoming works by Susan Collins, Brookings Institution, "Imports, Exports, and the American Worker," and William R. Cline, Institute for International Economics, "Trade, Jobs, and Income Distribution," 1996.

In 1992, the Clinton campaign put out a book detailing their plans if elected. On trade, the campaign noted "to win in global markets, America needs an economic growth plan . . . a trade policy that puts people first by investing in ourselves." The campaign promised to promote world growth, ensure that the Uruguay Round of GATT raises rather than lowers standards for health, safety, and the environment, and stands up for American workers. Bill Clinton and Albert Gore, *Putting People First: How We Can All Change America* (New York: Times Books, 1992), 155-60.

31. Lee Walczak, "The New Populism," *Business Week,* Mar. 13, 1995, 73-80; Alfred E. Eckes Jr., "Trading American Interests," *Foreign Affairs* 71 (fall 1992): 154; and telephone discussion with Brian Little of the United States Business and Industrial Council, June 29, 1994. Also see William R. Hawkins, "The Anti-History of Free Trade Ideology," in John P. Creagan, ed. *America Asleep: The Free Trade Syndrome and the Global Economic Challenge* (Washington, D.C.: U.S. Industrial Council Educational Foundation, 1991), 65.

32. Telephone interview with Roger Conner, executive director of the American Alliance for Rights and Responsibilities, Mar. 7, 1995. Also see Luttwak, "Will Success Spoil America?" C1; Lind, "Spheres of Affluence," 91-99; Sir James Goldsmith, "Global Free Trade and GATT," extract from the book *Le Piege,* 1994; and Tom Dunkel, "Not in His Right Mind," *Washington Post,* Aug. 6, 1995, F1.

33. Interview with Lori Wallach, director, Citizens' Trade Campaign, Apr. 6, 1995; Committee on Finance, *Results,* testimony of Ralph Nader on 85-88; and Citizens' Trade Campaign, "Our Jobs, Our Environment, Our Future," 1993.

34. Citizens' Trade Campaign (CTC), press release, "CTC Launches Media Campaign to Postpone GATT Consideration," June 9, 1994. Among the CTC supporters are the International Ladies' Garment Workers Union, Friends of the Earth, Greenpeace, United Methodist Board of Church and Society, and the National Farmers Union.

35. See Times Mirror Database: Public Attentiveness to Major News Stories (1986-1995), in Times Mirror Center, "Strong Support for Minimum Wage Hike and Preserving Entitlements," Feb. 17, 1995, 44-53.

36. Destler, *American Trade Politics: System under Stress,* 3d ed. (Washington, D.C.: Institute for International Economics, 1995), 96-103

37. Saad, "GATT Still a Mystery," 3.

38. The State Department began to lose control over U.S. trade policy in the 1950s. In 1962, House Ways and Means Chairman Wilbur D. Mills helped create a special representative for Trade Negotiations in the White House. This office was made statutory in 1974 and given cabinet rank. An Office of the United States Trade Representative was established in 1980. Today the United States trade representative is charged with advising the president, working with Congress, and leading and coordinating the U.S. government on international trade negotiations. Destler, *American Trade Politics,* 3d ed., 19-20, 105-6, 322, 444.

39. Telephone interview with Lori Wallach, director, Citizen's Trade Campaign, Apr. 5, 1995.

40. For a good overview of the debate over NAFTA, see Destler, *American Trade Politics,* ed ed., 98-101, 222-28. Also telephone interview with David Marchick, who

worked in the White House War Room on NAFTA, Jan. 11, 1995; and interview with Ambassador Rufus Xerxa, Jan. 5, 1995.

41. Walczak, "The New Populism," 73.

42. I participated in one talk show, National Public Radio's *Talk of the Nation,* to explain how the GATT affected average Americans on Nov. 29, 1994. The lines were jammed. Kevin Kearns, president of the U.S. Business and Industrial Council, noted that he had done fifty callin shows in 1994 on this topic. Free trader and Heritage Foundation economist Joe Cobb participated in thirty-three TV and radio debates and interviews on GATT or trade policy. Cobb, "Log of Activities," May 4, 1995, in possession of author. Telephone interview with Kevin Kaerns, Oct. 13, 1994. Ralph Nader, Chris McGinn, and Lori Wallach participated also participated in some twenty radio talk shows about the GATT. Interview with Lori Wallach, Mar. 21, 1995, and Apr. 5, 1995, and Chris McGinn to Susan Aaronson, "A small sampling of some of the radio shows Lori and I have been on:" in possession of the author.

43. For a good overview of how the media covers trade, see Center for Media and Public Affairs, *Media Monitor,* vol. 6, no. 4, 1993, pp. 4-5; and vol. 7, no. 1, p. 2. Also see Kohut and Toth, "Trade and the Public," 1. For recent examples, see Steven Pearlstein, "Dollar's Slide Mirrors Growing U.S. Dependence on Other Nations," *Washington Post,* June 28, 1994, A23; and Nancy Dunne, "Fears over 'Gattzilla the Trade Monster,'" *Financial Times,* Jan. 30, 1992.

10. Present at the Creation of the WTO, 1986-1994

This brief history of the WTO was written some four months after the Uruguay Round passed the Congress. With the benefit of time, I presume other analysts will provide a broader perspective. I am grateful to Congressman Bill Frenzel of the Brookings Institution, Dan Gardner of the Department of Commerce, Kimberly Ann Elliott of the Institute for International Economics, and Lori Wallach of Public Citizen for their help and corrections.

1. President William Jefferson Clinton, "Remarks by the President at American University Centennial Celebration," Feb. 26, 1993.

2. Yankelovich, "Foreign Policy After the Election," 2-12; Daniel Yankelovich is quoted in Jim Hoagland, "A Turn Inward," *Washington Post,* Jan. 10, 1995; Times Mirror Center for the People and the Press, *America's Place in the Cold War World,* Nov. 1, 1993, 1-3, 20, 33-36; Lind, "Spheres of Affluence," 91-99; and Greenberger, "Cold Shoulder," Oct. 28, 1993.

3. GATT Secretariat, "Final Act Embodying the Results of the Uruguay Round of Multilateral Trade Negotiations," Dec. 15, 1993, Annex IV, 91. Also see Organization for Economic Cooperation and Development, *Industrial Policy in OECD Countries: Annual Review 1992* (Paris, 1993), 11; and U.S. International Trade Commission, *The Year in Trade: Operation of the Trade Agreements Program, 1991* (Washington, D.C.: GPO, 1992), 13.

4. The ITO was much more comprehensive. Senate Committee on Finance, *Hearings on the Results of the Uruguay Round Trade Negotiations,* 103d Cong. 2d sess., Feb. 8-Mar. 23, 1994, Feb. 8; Mar. 9-23, 1994, 114-16.

5. Susan Aaronson, "The WTO: We've Been There Before," *Journal of Commerce,* June 17, 1994, 10A.

6. N.a., "GOP Leaders Warn Against GATT Campaign Promises," *Inside U.S. Trade,* Oct. 14, 1994, 1, 15; and President of the United States, "Message Transmitting the Uruguay Round Trade Agreements, Texts of Agreements Implementing Bill, Statement of Administrative Action and Required Supporting Statements," Aug. 27, 1994.

I.M. Destler believes the delay in writing the implementing bill was due to the Administration's strategy. Destler, *American Trade Politics,* 238-53.

7. Senate Committee on Finance, *Results of the Uruguay Round,* testimony of John H. Jackson, 114-16; John H. Jackson, "The World Trade Organization, Dispute Settlement, and Codes of Conduct," in Collins and Bosworth, eds., *The New GATT: Implications for the United States*(Washington, D.C.: Brookings Institution, 1994), 66-71.

8. Julius L. Katz, deputy U.S. trade representative, in Collins and Bosworth, *The New GATT,* 66-68; telephone discussion with Mark Silbergeld, director, Washington office, Consumers' Union, May 31, 1994; and interview with Lori Wallach, Mar. 21, 1995 and Apr. 5, 1995.

9. Alan Riding, "Months of Risk, Moments of Isolation, Now Boasts of Triumph," *New York Times,* Dec. 15, 1993, D19; and Council of Economic Advisors, *Economic Report of the President, February 1995,* 205-14.

10. Council of Economic Advisors, *Economic Report of the President, February 1995,* 212-13.

11. Telephone interview with Catherine Fields, Office of the General Counsel, USTR, May 1, 1994; and Omnibus Trade and Competitiveness Act of 1988, P.L. no. 100-418. The first trade negotiating objective for the U.S. in the Act was "to provide for more effective and expeditious dispute settlement mechanisms and procedures." Also see President Bill Clinton, "Memorandum for the United States Trade Representative, "Subject: Trade Agreements Resulting from the Uruguay Round of Multilateral Trade Negotiations," *Federal Register,* Dec. 15, 1994, 26.

12. Committee on Finance, *Results of the Uruguay Round,* written statement of John H. Jackson, 197; and Jackson, "The World Trade Organization," in Collins and Bosworth, eds., *New GATT,* 65-69.

13. Mark Ritchie and Karen Lehman, Institute for Agriculture and Trade Policy, "GATT Facts: Sustainable Agriculture"; Edmund G. Brown Jr., "Free Trade's Huge Costs," *New York Times,* May 2, 1993, E19; Citizens' Trade Campaign, "GATT Media Packet—The World Trade Organization's National Policy Prerogatives," June 1994; Senate Committee on Foreign Relations, transcript, Hearings on the World Trade Organization and U.S. Sovereignty, June 14, 1994, 29-30.

14. Mark Ritchie and Karen Lehman, "GATT Facts: Sustainable Agriculture."

15. Collins and Bosworth, eds., *New GATT,* 78-79.

16. See Save Our Sovereignty press release, June 13, 1994.

17. Judith H. Bello and Alan F. Holmer, "Dispute Resolution in the New World Trade Organization: Concerns and Net Benefits," *International Lawyer* 28 (1994), 5, 8; and Robert Keatley, "World Economy: Congress Inserts Rules in GATT Treaty That Make It Harder to Trade Globally," *Wall Street Journal,* Aug. 19, 1994, A6.

18. Congressman Lane Evans and fifty-four other members to President William Jefferson Clinton, Apr. 28, 1994; Statement of Kevin L. Kearns, President, United States Business and Industrial Council, June 13, 1994; Statement of Senator Larry Pressler, *Congressional Record,* Apr. 6, 1994, S5344-46; and *Inside U.S. Trade,* May 6, 1994, 12-13.

19. "Clinton Urges Bipartisan Support for GATT amid Conflicting GOP Signals," *Inside U.S. Trade,* Nov. 11, 1994, 17.

20. Ibid.

21. "Survey Shows Congress Still Concerned over WTO, Other Issues in GATT Bill," BNA, *Regulation, Economics and Law* 121 (June 27, 1994): A-13; and "Gingrich Lays Out Conditions for Republican Support of GATT Bill," *Inside U.S. Trade,* July 1, 1994, 1, 20-21. To understand how the financing provisions were included in the implementing legislation and the separate Senate vote see U.S. Senate, *Uruguay Round*

Agreements Act: Joint Report of the Committee on Finance; Committee on Agriculture, Nutrition, and Forestry; and Committee on Governmental Affairs to Accompany S. 2467, 103d Cong., 2d sess., Nov. 22, 1994, S.R. 103-412, Title VII, 134-35 n 1-5.

22. Bob Davis, "Economy: Lawmakers Set to Finish Work on Trade Pact: New Provisions Are Added to Protect U.S. Firms; October Vote is Planned," *Wall Street Journal,* Aug. 20, 1994, A2.

23. As I.M. Destler notes, the draft legislation was also delayed by the administration's position on obtaining a broad fast track authority for future trade negotiations that would include labor and environmental issues. Destler, *American Trade Politics,* 3d ed., 238-51.

24. On policymakers' needs to listen to the public, see R.W. Apple Jr., "Challenges from a Headstrong Public," *New York Times,* Jan. 29, 1993, A1. On the sovereignty issue and middle America, interview with Mickey Kantor, on The Diane Rehm Show, WAMU Washington, June 29, 1994; and the comments of Mickey Kantor, "The Emerging Debate about GATT," conference at the Heritage Foundation, May 25, 1994.

25. President Bill Clinton to the Honorable Thomas S. Foley, May 3, 1994; U.S. Department of Commerce, "First Look at the Uruguay Round, Flash Report" Dec. 16, 1993; U.S. trade representative,"Sector-Specific Fact Sheets for Goods," Dec. 17, 1993; U.S. Department of Commerce, "Uruguay Round Opportunities," n.d., and "Inside U.S. Trade," May 6, 1994, 17.

26. For example, William Jefferson Clinton, "Remarks by the President at American University Centennial Celebration," Feb. 26, 1993; and "Remarks by the President at NAFTA Products Event," Oct. 20, 1993.

27. Interview with John K. Boidock, vice president, Texas Instruments, Nov. 4, 1994; and n.a., "Roundtable to Raise Funds for Trade Pact Campaign," *Wall Street Journal,* Nov. 3, 1994, A4.

28. I have left these issues to others to examine. The 1994 hearings on the Round included those held in January, February, and June by the House Ways and Means; March and April hearings by the House Agriculture Committee; and February, March, and June hearings by the House Foreign Affairs Committee. On the Senate side, the Senate Finance Committee held hearings in February and March; the Senate Commerce Committee held hearings in October and November; and the Senate Foreign Relations Committee held hearings in June.

29. The Senate Foreign Relations Committee held hearings under the request of Senators Helms and Pressler. Letter to Senator Claiborne Pell, Chair, Senate Foreign Relations Committee, from Senator Jesse Helms and Senator Larry Pressler, May 4, 1994. Some of the Senate Commerce Committee hearings were held after the election, while Congress was in recess.

30. Committee on Ways and Means, *World Trade Organization Hearings,* 103d Cong., 2d sess., June 10, 1994, testimony of Ambassador Kantor 9, 38, 44.

31. Joe Cobb, unpublished memorandum circulated to trade staff of Republican members, Apr. 14-15; and "The Real Threat to U.S. Sovereignty," *Heritage Lectures,* no. 497, Aug. 1, 1994. Also interview with Joe Cobb, Aug. 13, 1994; and editor, "Pass GATT," *Washington Times,* Oct. 5, 1994.

32. *Inside U.S. Trade,* May 6, 1994, 17-21; Jack Anderson and Michael Binstein, "Bork to the Rescue," *Washington Post,* June 5, 1994; Joe Cobb, John M. Olin Senior Fellow in Economics to Trade Legislative Assistants, "The Issue of U.S. Sovereignty under the New GATT Agreement," Apr. 14-15, 1994; and Michael Kantor to members of Congress, Apr. 28, 1994.

33. Committee on Ways and Means, *World Trade Organization Hearings,* 38-43.

34. Collins and Bosworth, *New GATT,* 66, 73-75, 76-80; Helene Cooper, "Wash-

ington Insight: U.S.'s Slow Action on World Trade Pact Mirrors Treatment of Failed '49 Accord," *Wall Street Journal,* Aug. 29, 1994, A6. Also see Adam Zagorin, "Battered and Bruised," *Time,* Aug. 15, 1994, 28; and Destler, *American Trade Politics,* 37.

35. Remarks of Mr. Underwood and Mr. Engel, *Congressional Record,* Nov. 29, 1994, H11495.

36. Senate Commerce Committee, *GATT Implementing Legislation Hearings, S. 2467,* 103d Cong., 2d sess., Oct. 4-Nov. 15, 1994, testimony of Lawrence Tribe, 286-312; testimony of Claire Reade, co-chair, Section on International Law and Practice, Committee on International Trade, American Bar Association, 339-49. Reade's view was echoed by Professor Bruce Ackerman, 312-39.

37. For arguments that the GATT/WTO would lead to job loss see Senate Commerce Committee, *GATT Implementing Legislation Hearings,* statement of Kevin Kearns, head of Save Our Sovereignty, 127; Charles McMillion, president, MBG Information; 93-113; and Thomas R. Donahue, secretary/treasurer, AFL-CIO, 159-67. For arguments it would create high wage jobs, see testimony of Hon. Michael Kantor, 33-53; and testimony and discussion of Felix Rohatyn, senior partner, Lazard-Freres, 463-83.

38. Committee on Ways and Means, *World Trade Organization Hearings,* 70-71; and David E. Sanger, "Senate Approves Pact to Ease Trade Curbs," *New York Times,* A1.

39. Telephone discussion with Lori Wallach, Mar. 17, 1995; on better coordination of domestic and foreign economic policies see Clyde Prestowitz in Collins and Bosworth, eds., *New GATT,* 78-80, 82; and Council on Competitiveness, *Roadmap for Results,* 5-20, 73-90.

40. Environmentalists were also divided; some wanted an international organization to cover the environment.

41. Committee on Ways and Means, *World Trade Organization Hearings,* 28-32; "U.S. Drops Plan to Monitor Compliance with China Business Principles," *Inside U.S. Trade,* Nov. 11, 1994; Michael Bergsman, "ACTPN to Call for Short-Term Focus in APEC," and "House Letter on Indonesia Worker Rights," both in *Inside U.S. Trade,* Oct. 28, 1994, 23-24; and David E. Sanger, "Trade Agreement Ends Long Debate but Not Conflicts," *New York Times* Dec. 4, 1994, A1.

42. Council of Economic Advisors, *Economic Report of the President, 1995,* 249-50.

43. Collins and Bosworth, eds., *New GATT,* 76-77, 81.

44. Senate Commerce, *Committee Hearings on S. 2467,* opening statement of Senator Hollings, 1-3, 173-96.

45. Charles McMillion, "GATT Claims/The Facts," fact sheet, Nov. 29, 1994, and telephone interview, Mar. 22, 1995.

46. Bureau of National Affairs, "State Officials to Ask Clinton for Trade Consultation Summit," *Daily Report for Executives,* June 24, 1994, A121; and *Inside U.S. Trade,* July 1, 1994, 11.

47. Patti Goldman, "The Democratization of the Development of United States Trade Policy," *Cornell International Law Journal* 27, no. 3, 1994; Patti Goldman, "Resolving the Trade and Environment Debate: In Search of a Neutral Forum and Neutral Principles," *Washington and Lee Law Review* 49, no. 4 (fall 1992): 1279; and telephone discussion with Goldman, June 29, 1994.

48. Thomas L. Friedman, "Dole Explains Trade Treaty Stand," *New York Times,* Aug. 13, 1994, D2; "Administration Weighing Dole Proposal for Review of WTO Decisions," *Inside U.S. Trade,* Nov. 18, 1994, 1, 22, 23; and U.S. Senate, *Uruguay Round Agreements Act: Joint Report 103-412 of the Committee on Finance, Committee on Agriculture, Nutrition, and Forestry, and Committee of Governmental Affairs, to Accompany S. 2467,* Title I, Subtitle C, Sections 123-30, Nov. 22, 1994, 20-27. A threat of a U.S. pullout might encourage the WTO to "modify or correct the flaws in the dispute settlement

rules." In the 1995 104th Congress, the Dole Bill was introduced as S. 16. I am grateful to Rolf Lundgren of Senator Dole's staff for sending it to me.

49. Gingrich was quoted on the NBC program *Meet the Press*. John Maggs, "Sovereignty Issue Threatens Trade Pact, as Fears of 'World Government' Voiced," *Journal of Commerce,* Apr. 26, 1994; and Senate Commerce Committee, *Hearings on S2467,* 4-32.

50. U.S. Senate, *Joint Report 103-412,* Report of the Committee on Governmental Affairs, 221-23.

51. Alliance for GATT Now, "Statement of Purpose," "Pro-GATT Editorials," "America's Leading Economists Endorse Uruguay Round," "Governors Voice Support to GATT Trade Pact," "Alliance for GATT Now Membership," and "Voices in Support of the Uruguay Round," and letter Michael E. Carpenter, attorney general of Maine to Honorable Michael Kantor, July 27, 1994. Also see fact sheets "Senate Budget Waiver," "The Costs of Delay," and "Why Pass the Uruguay Round Implementing Bill This Year." All of these documents were provided to me by Paula Collins of the Alliance for GATT NOW. I am grateful for her assistance.

52. "Green Group Calls on Administration to Back Reform of GATT Rules," and letter from Defenders of Wildlife, *Inside U.S. Trade,* Oct. 28, 1994, 15-17.

53. Interview with Lori Wallach, Mar. 21, 1995.

54. Remarks of Senator Ernest Hollings, *Congressional Record,* unofficial version, S214746-214747, Oct. 7, 1994, includes Sept. 14, 1994, letter to President Bill Clinton; and Catherine S. Manegold, "In Loud Political Week, Talk Radio Makes Itself Heard," *New York Times,* Jan. 30, 1995, A13.

55. Sierra Club ad, "Jeopardized by GATT," *New York Times,* June 27, 1994, A15. Also see Mike Mills, "Post Criticized on GATT Editorial," *Washington Post,* Oct. 4, 1994, C3; editorial, "The Trade Bill and the Post," *Washington Post,* Oct. 5, 1994, A22; and ad, Pacific Telesis Group,"Here's Another Reason the *Washington Post* Wants Congress to Pass GATT Right Away," *Washington Post,* A7.

56. Destler, *American Trade Politics,* 3d. ed., 250; and "Gibbons, Archer Criticize Administration for Allowing Senate Delay," *Inside U.S. Trade,* Oct. 7, 1994, 17, 19, and Oct. 14, 1994, 1, 15. On p. 21, *Inside U.S. Trade* printed the letter from members urging a delay until the 104th Congress.

57. N.a., *Public Citizen,* 1-2, 1995.

58. "Senate Letter on GATT Delay, *Inside U.S. Trade,* Nov. 18, 1994, 20.

59. "Clinton Urges," and "Moynihan Says Latest Count Shows 41 Senators Behind GATT Waiver," *Inside U.S. Trade,* Nov. 18, 1994, 1, 16, 19; and "Administration Offers to Support WTO Review Body in Deal With Dole," *Inside U.S. Trade,* Nov. 25, 1994, 1, 22.

60. "Clinton Urges Bipartisan Support for GATT amid Conflicting GOP Signals," *Inside U.S. Trade,* Nov. 11, 1994, 1, 16.

61. David E. Sanger, "Trade Agreement Ends Long Debate but Not Conflicts," *New York Times,* Dec. 4, 1994, A1.

62. Andrew Kohut and Robert C. Toth, "Trade and the Public," Times Mirror Center for the People and the Press, Dec. 13, 1994, 4-5; and David S. Broder, "Gephardt Warns," *Washington Post,* Mar. 14, 1995, D2.

63. A survey by Princeton Survey Research Associates, October 6-9, found that only 26 percent of 1,513 polled by phone followed the GATT news stories; 72 percent did not follow it closely or at all. On November 8 and 9, a telephone poll of 1,250 voters found that 41 percent thought trade should be a top priority, 33 percent mid-list and only 21 percent near the bottom. Greenberg Research for the Democratic Leadership Council. On November 28-29, the Gallup Organization polled some 1,020 Americans by telephone and found that 41 percent followed the GATT treaty closely; whereas 59

percent did not follow it closely or at all. All from the Roper Center for Public Opinion Research, Dialogue File 468.

64. Princeton Survey Research Associates poll of 3,800 July 12-25, 1994, and a follow-up poll of 1,511 adults December 1-4, 1994, from Roper Center for Public Opinion Research, Dialogue File 468.

65. Editor, "Washington Wire," *Wall Street Journal,* Dec. 16, 1994, A1.

Conclusion: Democracy and Economic Interdependence

1. Bob Packwood, chairman, and Daniel Patrick Moynihan, ranking member, Senate Finance Committee to the President, in *Inside U.S. Trade,* Apr. 7, 1995, 19.

2. Key officials including Treasury Secretary Robert Rubin and Trade Representative Michael Kantor also believe Americans must get a better grasp of how global markets will affect their lives. Interview with Ambassador Michael Kantor, Jan. 13, 1995; Walckzak, "The New Populism," 74-78; Clay Chandler, "The Reluctant Warrior," *Washington Post,* A1; and "Packwood, Moynihan Letter," 19.

3. The National Opinion Research Center (NORC), Confidential Survey 156 du-1 (University of Chicago, Mar. 25, 1948), 1, 4.

4. NORC, Confidential Survey 167, DU-1 (University of Chicago, June 30, 1949), 1, 7. The next largest percentage, 11 percent of those polled, wanted more information about the U.S. relationship with Russia.

5. House Committee on Foreign Affairs, *Hearings on H.J. Res. 236,* 429-30, 435; Rubber Manufacturers Association, "Pros and Cons," 114-15, 122; and McCullogh, *Truman,* 611.

6. Remarks of Congressmen Hunter, *Congressional Record,* Nov. 29, 1994, H11495.

7. See Robert Wright, "TRB from Washington, Doleful Cynicism" *New Republic* Oct. 10, 1994, 6.

8. Galen and Vamos, "Portrait of an Anxious Public," 80; and telephone interview with Chris McGinn, *Public Citizen,* Mar. 25, 1995.

9. Remarks of Senator Barbara Mikulski, *Congressional Record,* Nov. 30, 1994, S15102.

10. Peter Behr, "Trade Cases Pose Threat to Environmental Law, GATT," *Washington Post,* June 10, 1994, F1; and editors, "Sovereignty and Trade," *Washington Post,* June 13, 1994.

11. Harlan Cleveland, "The Informatization of World Affairs," keynote address at "Bretton Woods Revisited," Oct. 16, 1994.

12. Otis L. Graham Jr., "The Uses and Misuses of History: Roles in Policymaking," *Public Historian* 5 (spring 1983): 5-19.

13. I take this language from a letter written to me by Dr. Proctor Reed of the Program Office, National Academy of Engineering.

14. David S. Broder, "Global Trade Treaty Bill in Danger," *Washington Post,* Apr. 10, 1994; and *Inside U.S. Trade,* May 6, 1994, 17-18.

15. "Nominations for the Trade and Environment Policy Advisory Committee," *Federal Registry,* May 10, 1994, 24213. Until May 1994, neither consumers nor the general public were represented on the three-tier advisory system that advises trade policymakers. The President of the United States, *1993 Trade Policy Agenda and 1992 Annual Report of the President of the United States on the Trade Agreements Program* (Washington, D.C.: GPO, 1993), 115-18, esp. 116-17 on private sector advisory committee system.

16. "USTR Proposal for Opening Advisory Committee Meetings Draws Fire," *Inside U.S. Trade,* Oct. 7, 1994, 1, 2 and telephone interview with Clayton Parker, di-

rector of Intergovernmental Affairs, USTR, Oct. 14, 1994. Under President Clinton, the Advisory Committee for Trade Policy Negotiations was chaired by Susan Hammer, mayor of San Jose, California. Of the thirteen new members appointed, nine were business leaders, one was president of Consumers' Union, another was the CEO of the World Wildlife Fund, two were minorities, and four were women. "New Appointees Give ACTPN Its Full Complement of Advisors," *Inside U.S. Trade,* Oct. 14, 1994, 7. According to Clayton Parker, director of Intergovernmental Affairs at USTR, these steps will make the advisory committee "more like America" and the process more responsive and credible.

17. N.a., "Dole WTO Bill Opens Door to Private Participation in Dispute Panels," *Inside U.S. Trade,* Jan. 13, 1995, 10-11; and Jagdish N. Bhagwati, "Dole's GATT GAFFE," *Wall Street Journal,* Nov. 23, 1994, A23.

18. In late 1994, the Clinton administration called on the GATT/WTO to adopt new rules allowing more public access to the GATT's deliberation. They also pushed to allow nongovernmental organizations to gain observer status in the WTO's new Committee on Trade and the Environment. In the face of opposition and stalling tactics by other member nations, the administration announced that the United States had given up "for now" at making the WTO more democratic. "U.S. Calls for New GATT Rules to Make Public Most Documents," *Inside U.S. Trade,* Oct. 7, 1994, 13; "WTO Environment Panel Likely to Allow Public Access to Some Papers," *Inside U.S. Trade,* Dec. 2, 1994, 23; and U.S. Gives Up on NGO Seats in WTO Trade-Environment Committee," *Inside U.S. Trade,* Dec. 9, 1994, 13.

19. In this regard, see the recommendations of Patti Goldman, " Democraticization," 84-120; and Steve Charnovitz, "Environmental and Labour Standards in Trade," *The World Economy* 14 (May, 1992): 353-55. Deputy Trade Representative Rufus Yerxa said he will work to make the WTO more open. Senate Foreign Relations Committee, transcript, Hearings on the World Trade Organization, testimony of Rufus Yerxa, 29-30.

20. These Americans include corporate officials, environmentalists, members of the United Nations Association, and the Bretton Woods Committee.

21. Jo-Marie Griesgraber, "Multilateral Democracy, a Think-Piece," unpublished paper for the Multilateralism and Democracy Project, Jan. 1995. Griesgraber is project director, Rethinking Bretton Woods.

22. Senate Committee on Foreign Relations, transcript, Hearings on the World Trade Organization, testimony of Ralph Nader on the Uruguay Round, June 14, 1994, 12.

23. In 1994-95, several organizations sponsored conferences and projects to reexamine ways to make the multilateral institutions more democratic. In October 1994, the Institute for Agriculture and Trade Policy, a Minneapolis think-tank, sponsored a conference at the Mount Washington Hotel in Bretton Woods New Hampshire, site of the final negotiations on the World Bank and the International Monetary Fund. This conference brought together young leaders and the living architects of multilateralism in the hope that they could develop workable tactics to improve the openness and operations of the international organizations and make them more responsive to concerns of groups within their member states. The conference also attempted to bridge individuals of the right and left from around the world. Author's observations, "Bretton Woods Revisited," Oct. 15-17, 1994. The Bretton Woods Committee, an international organization of economists, bankers, and world leaders, and the United Nations Association also proposed major changes to the international organizations. Global Policy Project of the United Nations Association, *A Consensus for Change: Transforming the United Nation's Role in Global Economics* (New York: UNA, 1994); Bretton Woods Committee, *Bretton Woods, Looking to the Future* (Washington, D.C.: Bretton Woods Committee, 1994).

Bibliography

PRIMARY SOURCES

Archival Sources
National Archives

RG 43, International Conferences and Expositions
RG 53D-444, Records of the Executive Secretariat (Dean Acheson, 1944-53)
RG 59, General Records of the Department of State
RG 59, Lot File (LF 57D-284), International Trade Files, Boxes 1-122
RG 59, Records of Leo Pasvolsky
RG 59, Records of Harley Notter
RG 59, Records of Assistant Secretary Dean Acheson
RG 59, Lot File 53D-17, Records of the Office of Congressional Relations, 1948-51
RG 353, Lot File 122, Inter- and Intradepartmental Committees of the Department
    of State

Public Records Office, Kew Gardens, England

FO 371, Foreign Office Records
BT 11, Board of Trade Files

Hagley Museum and Library

American Iron and Steel Institute Papers
Walter S. Carpenter Papers (Du Pont Company)
Chamber of Commerce of the United States Papers
Du Pont Company Papers
Lammot Du Pont Papers
National Association of Manufacturers Papers
National Industrial Conference Board Papers
Philip D. Reed Papers (includes documents related to General Electric Company,
    the International Chamber of Commerce, and the Committee for Economic
    Development).

Harry S Truman Library Institute

Dean Acheson Papers
Thomas C. Blaisdell Papers

William L. Clayton Papers
George M. Elsey Papers
Willard Thorp Papers
Confidential Files, Harry S Truman Papers
Official Files, Harry S Truman Papers

Oral History Interviews
Dean Acheson
Willis C. Armstrong
Thomas C. Blaisdell
Winthrop G. Brown
Joseph D. Coppock
John S. Dickey
John M. Leddy
Francis Russell
Leroy Stinebower
Raymond Vernon
Willard Thorp

At the Council on Foreign Relations

Committee papers

The Brookings Institution

Papers of Leo Pasvolsky

U.S. Government Publications

Clinton, William Jefferson. "Memorandum for the United States Trade Representative, Subject: Trade Agreements Resulting from the Uruguay Round of Multilateral Trade Negotiations." *Federal Register.* Dec. 15, 1993.
Council of Economic Advisers. *Economic Report of the President.* Washington, D.C., 1985-95.
Notter, Harley. *Postwar Foreign Policy Preparation, 1939-1945.* Washington, D.C., Department of State, 1949.
President of the United States. *1993 Trade Policy Agenda and 1992 Annual Report of the President of the United States on the Trade Agreements Program.* Washington, D.C., 1993.
U.S. Department of Commerce. *Historical Statistics of the United States: Colonial Times to 1957.* Washington, D.C., 1960.
U.S. Department of State. *Commercial Policy Series.* Nos. 11-22. Washington, D.C., 1936.
————. *Commercial Policy Series.* Nos. 37-55. Washington, D.C., 1938.
————. *Foreign Affairs Background Summary: Expanding World Trade, U.S. Policy and Program.* Washington, D.C., Mar. 1949.
Foreign Relations of the United States. Annual vols. 1940-50. Washington, D.C., 1959-76.
————. "Growing Institutional Character of the GATT." Report no. 562. Aug. 16, 1976. Unpublished and unclassified.
————. *Proceedings and Documents of United Nations Monetary and Financial Conference.* Vol. 1. Washington, D.C., 1948.
————. *Reciprocal Trade Agreements Program of the United States.* Washington, D.C., 1938.

———. *The State Department Policy Planning Staff Papers.* New York, 1983.
———. *Suggested Charter for An International Trade Organization.* Washington, D.C., 1946.
U.S. International Trade Commission. *The Year in Trade: Operations of the Trade Agreements Program 1991.* Washington, D.C., 1992.
U.S. Tariff Commission. *Operation of the Trade Agreements Program.* Annual reports 1934-52. Washington, D.C., 1948-54.
———. *Report on the Havana Charter for an ITO.* Washington, D.C., 1949.
U.S. Trade Representative. *A Preface to Trade.* Washington, D.C., 1982.

International Organization Publications

GATT Secretariat. "Draft Final Act Embodying the Results of the Uruguay Round of Multilateral Trade Negotiations." Geneva, 1991.
Organization for Economic Cooperation and Development, *Industrial Policy in OECD Countries: Annual Review 1992.* Paris, 1993.

Congressional Bills, Hearings, and Reports
Hearings and Reports on the ITO

Fulton, Honorable James G., and Honorable Jacob K. Javits. *The International Trade Organization.* Washington, D.C., 1948.
House Committee on Foreign Affairs. *United States in the International Trade Organization: Hearings on H.J. Res. 236, A Joint Resolution Providing for Membership and Participation by the United States in the International Trade Organization and Authorizing an Appropriation Therefor.* 81st Cong., 2d sess. Apr. 19-May 12, 1950.
H.J. Res. 236: A Joint Resolution Providing for Membership and Participation by the United States in the International Trade Organization and Authorizing an Appropriation Therefor.

Hearings Held as the ITO Was Drafted

House Committee on Ways and Means. *Reciprocal Trade Agreements Program: Hearings on the Operation of the Reciprocal Trade Agreements Act and the Proposed International Trade Organization.* 80th Cong., 1st sess. Mar. 26-May 8, 1947.
Senate Committee on Finance. *International Trade Organization: Hearings on Trade Agreements System and the Proposed International Trade Organization Charter.* 80th Cong., 1st sess. Mar. 20-Apr. 3, 1947.

Hearings and Reports on Foreign Economic Policy Issues

House Committee on Banking and Currency. *Report to Accompany S. J. 138: Implementation of the Financial Agreement Between the United States and the United Kingdom.* Report no. 2289. 79th Cong., 2d sess. 1946.
———. *Anglo-American Financial Agreement: Hearings on H.J. Res. 311 and S. J. Res. 138, A Joint Resolution to Further Implement the Purposes of the Bretton Woods Agreements Act by Authorizing the Secretary of the Treasury to Carry Out an Agreement with the United Kingdom and for Other Purposes.* 79th Cong., 2d sess. May 14-June 7, 1946.
House Committee on Ways and Means. *Extending the Authority of the President*

under Section 350 of the Tariff Act of 1930, as Amended: Report no. 1594. 76th Cong., 3d sess. Feb. 14, 1940

———. *Extension of Reciprocal Trade Agreements Act: Hearings On H.J. Res. 311, A Joint Resolution to Extend the Authority of the President Under Section 350 of the Tariff Act of 1930, as Amended.* 78th Cong., 1st sess. Apr. 12-23, 1943.

———. *Hearings on H.R. 2652, Superseded by H.R. 3240: An Act to Extend the Authority of the President under Section 350 of the Tariff Act of 1930, as Amended.* 79th Cong., 1st sess. Apr. 1945-May 1945.

———. *Foreign Trade Agreements: Report to Accompany H.R. 3240.* 79th Cong., 1st sess. May 18, 1945.

———. *Trade Agreements Program: Testimony before the Subcommittee on Tariffs and Foreign Trade of the Committee on Ways and Means on the Operation of the Trade Agreements Program.* 80th Cong., 2d sess. May 3-May 8, 1948.

———. *1949 Extension of the Reciprocal Trade Agreements Act: Hearings on H.R. 1211, a Bill to Extend the Authority of the President Under Section 350 of the Tariff Act of 1930, as Amended and for other Purposes.* 81st Cong., 1st sess. Jan. 24-Feb. 1, 1949.

———. *Foreign Trade Policy: Compendium of Papers on United States Foreign Policy.* 1957.

House Special Committee on Post-War Economic Policy and Planning. *General Report on Economic Problems of the Reconversion Period.* 78th Cong., 2d sess. Oct. 8, 1944.

———. *Report Pursuant to H.R. 60, a Resolution Authorizing the Continuation of the Special Committee on Post War Economic Policy and Planning.* Nov. 12, 1945.

Jackson, James K. Congressional Research Service, Library of Congress. *Foreign Direct Investment in the United States.* Washington, D.C., Apr. 14, 1993.

Senate Committee on Banking and Currency. *Anglo-American Financial Agreement: A Joint Resolution to Implement Further the Purposes of the Bretton Woods Agreements Act by Authorizing the Secretary of the Treasury to Carry Out an Agreement with the United Kingdom and for Other Purposes.* 79th Cong., 2d sess. Mar. 5-20, 1946.

Senate Committee on Finance. *1945 Extension of the Reciprocal Trade Agreements Act: Hearings on H.R. 3240, An Act to Extend the Authority of the President Under Section 350 of the Tariff Act of 1930, as Amended.* 79th Cong., 1st sess. May 30-June 5, 1945.

———. *Extending Authority to Negotiate Trade Agreements: Hearings on H.R. 6566, an Act to Extend the Authority of the President Under Section 350 of the Trade Agreements Act of 1930, As Amended and for Other Purposes.* 80th Cong., 2d sess. June 1-5, 1948.

———. *Report to Accompany H.R. 6566, Extending the Authority of the President Under Section 350 of the Tariff Act of 1930, As Amended.* 80th Cong., 2d sess. June 8, 1948.

———. *Extension of Reciptocal Trade Agreements Act: Hearings on H.R. 1211, An Act to Extend the Authority of the President Under Section 350 of the Tariff Act of 1934, As Amended and for Other Purposes.* 81st Cong., 1st sess. Feb. 17-Mar. 8, 1949.

Senate Committee on Foreign Relations. *Hearings Held in Executive Session on the World Situation.* 81 Cong., 1st and 2d sess. May 19-Dec. 22, 1950.

———. Presented by Mr. Sparkman, *Review of Bipartisan Foreign Policy Consultations since World War II.* 82d Cong., 1st sess. Washington, D.C., 1952.

U.S. General Accounting Office. *Technology Transfer: Foreign Participation in R&D at Federal Labs.* GAO/RCED 88-203BR. Washington, D.C., 1988.

Hearings and Reports on the Uruguay Round and the World Trade Organization

House Committee on Ways and Means. *Trade Agreements Resulting From the Uruguay Round of Multilateral Trade Negotiations, Hearings.* 103rd Cong., 2d sess. Jan. 26-Feb. 22, 1994.
———. *The World Trade Organization, Hearing.* 103rd Cong., 2d sess. June 10, 1994.
President of the United States. *Message Transmitting the Uruguay Round Trade Agreements, Texts of Agreements, Implementing Bill, Statement of Administrative Action, and Required Supporting Statements.* 103rd Cong., 2d sess., House Document 103-316. Sept. 27, 1994.
Senate Committee on Commerce, Science, and Transportation. *S.2467, GATT Implementing Legislation, Hearings.* 103rd Cong., 2d sess. Oct. 4-Nov. 15, 1994.
Senate Committee on Finance. *Uruguay Round of Multilateral Trade Negotiations Hearing.* 103rd Cong., 1st sess. Nov. 10, 1993
———. *Results of the Uruguay Round Trade Negotiations, Hearings.* 103rd Cong., 2d sess. Feb. 8-Mar. 23, 1994.
———. "Chairman's Proposal: Legislation Implementing the Uruguay Round of Multilateral Trade Negotiations." July 19, 1994.
———."Committee on Finance Action on the Uruguay Round Implementing Legislation," Aug. 5, 1994.
———. *Uruguay Round Agreements Act: Joint Report of the Committee on Finance, Committee on Agriculture, Nutrition, and Forestry, and Committee on Governmental Affairs, to Accompany S. 2467,* 103rd Cong., 2d sess., Report 103412. Nov. 22, 1994.
Senate Committee on Foreign Relations. Transcript, Hearings on the World Trade Organization and U.S. Sovereignty, June 14, 1994.

SECONDARY SOURCES

Articles

Aaronson, Susan. "A Wake-up Call from the GATT." *Journal of Commerce,* Mar. 25, 1992, 8A.
———. "How Cordell Hull and the Postwar Planners Designed a New Trade Policy." *Business and Economic History* 2d ser., 20 (1991): 171-78.
———. "The Irony of Persistence on Solving World Trade Woes." *International Economy* 4 (Aug.-Sept. 1990): 30-31.
———. "The WTO: We've Been There Before." *Journal of Commerce,* June 17, 1994, 10A.
Allen, George V. "Telling Our Side of the Story." *Department of State Bulletin,* Jan. 24, 1949, 142-43.
Balogh, Brian. "Reorganizing the Organizational Synthesis: Federal Professional Relations in Modern America." *Studies in American Political Development* 5 (spring 1991): 119-77.
Banner, James M., Jr. "The History Watch: A Proposal." *Public Historian* (winter 1993): 47-54.
Bello, Judith H., and Alan F. Holmer. "Dispute Resolution in the New World Trade Organization: Concerns and Net Benefits," *International Lawyer* 28 (1994): 1095-1104. In author's possession as United States Trade Law and Policy Series, #24.

Bergsten, C. Fred, and Edward M. Graham. "Needed: New International Rules For Foreign Direct Investment," *International Trade Journal* 7 (fall 1992): 15-43.

Bluestone, Barry. "The Inequality Express," *American Prospect* (winter 1995): 81-93.

Bonilla, Frank. "When is Petition `Pressure'?" *Public Opinion Quarterly* 20, no. 1 (spring 1956): 39-48.

Cantril, Hadley. "Opinion Trends in World War II." *Public Opinion Quarterly* 12 (spring 1948): 30-44.

Charnovitz, Steven. "Environmental and Labor Standards in Trade." *World Economy* 14 (May 1992): 350-55.

Clayton, William L. "GATT, the Marshall Plan, and OECD." *Political Science Quarterly* (Dec. 1963): 493-503.

Cleveland, Harlan. "The Management of Peace." *GAO Journal* 11 (winter 1990/91): 4-23.

Cohen, Roger. "Another Gap for Europe to Close: Leaders Got Way Ahead of the Public in the Pursuit of Unity." *New York Times,* Oct. 7, 1992, 1.

Crosbie, John. "My Plan for a World Trade Organization." *International Economy* (June/July 1990): 40-43.

Deardorff, Alan V., and Dalia Hakura, "Trade and Wages: What are the Questions?" Paper prepared for a seminar at the American Enterprise Institute, Sept. 10, 1993.

Dickey, John Sloan. "Our Treaty Procedure Versus Our Foreign Policies." *Foreign Affairs* 26 (Apr. 1947): 357-77.

Diebold, William, Jr. "The End of the I.T.O." *Essays in International Finance* 16 (Oct. 1952): 1-37.

———. "Reflections on the International Trade Organization." *Northern Illinois University Law Review* 14 (spring 1994): 335-46.

Dryden, Steve. "How Congress Let Trade Harmony Slip Away." *International Economy* (June-July 1990): 44-47.

Eckes, Alfred E. "Trading American Interests." *Foreign Affairs* 71 (fall 1992): 135-54.

Ferguson, Thomas. "From Normalcy to the New Deal: Industrial Structure, Party Competition and American Public Policy in the Great Depression." *International Organization* 38 (winter 1984): 41-94.

Gaddis, John Lewis. "The Corporatist Synthesis: A Skeptical View." *Diplomatic History* 10 (fall 1986): 357-62.

Galambos, Louis. Review of *Leadership and Innovation: A Biographical Perspective on Entrepreneurs in Government,* ed. Jameson W. Doig and Erwin C. Hargrove. *Business History Review* 62 (autumn 1988): 548-49.

———. "Technology, Political Economy and Professionalization: Central Themes of the Organizational Synthesis." *Business History Review* 57 (winter 1983): 471-93.

Goldman, Patti. "Resolving the Trade and Environment Debate: In Search of a Neutral Forum and Neutral Principles." *Washington and Lee Law Review* 49, no. 4 (fall 1992): 1279-98.

———. "The Democratization of the Development of United States Trade Policy." *Cornell International Law Journal* 27 (fall 1994): 631-97.

Goldsmith, Sir James. "Global Free Trade and GATT." Excerpt from *Le Piege,* 1994.

Graham, Otis L., Jr. "The Stunted Career of Policy History: A Critique and an Agenda." *Public Historian* 15 (spring 1993): 15-37.

———. "The Uses and Misuses of History: Roles in Policymaking." *Public Historian* 5 (spring 1983): 5-19.

Greenwald, Matthew, and Ruy Teixeira. "Storm Warnings on the Trade Front." *JAMA Forum* 5: 14-23.

————. "Trade Talks: Public Attitudes About Protection." *Public Opinion* (Sept./ Oct. 1986): 50-51.

Griffith, Robert. "Dwight D. Eisenhower and the Corporate Commonwealth." *American Historical Review* 87 (Feb. 1982): 87-122.

Hamby, Alonzo. "Sixty Million Jobs and the Peoples' Revolution: The Liberals, the New Deal, and World War II." *Historian* 30 (Aug. 1968): 586-98.

Hawley, Ellis W. "The Discovery and Study of a 'Corporate Liberalism'." *Business History Review* 52 (autumn 1978): 309-20.

Heilperin, Michael. "How the U.S. Lost the ITO Conferences." *Fortune* 40 (Sept. 1949): 80-82.

Heymann, Heinz. "The G.A.T.T. at Crossroads." *Scandinaviska Banken,* July 1951, 58-64.

Hitchens, Harold L. "Influences on the Congressional Decision to Pass the Marshall Plan." *Western Political Quarterly* 21, no. 1 (Mar. 1968): 51-68.

Hogan, Michael J. "Corporatism, a Positive Appraisal." *Diplomatic History* 10 (fall 1986): 363-72.

Ikenberry, G. John. "The World Economy Restored: Expert Consensus and the Anglo-American Postwar Settlement." *International Organization* 46, no. 1 (winter 1992): 289-321.

Kaygay, Michael R., with Janet Elder. "Numbers Are No Problem for Pollsters, Words Are." *New York Times,* Aug. 9, 1992, 5.

Kelly, Robert. "The Idea of Policy History." *Public Historian* 10 (winter: 1988), 35-49.

Kindleberger, Charles P. "U.S. Foreign Economic Policy, 1776-1976." *Foreign Affairs* 55 (Jan. 1977): 395-417.

Lawrence, Robert Z., and Matthew J. Slaughter, "International Trade and American Wages in the 1980s: Giant Sucking Sound or Small Hiccup?" *Brookings Papers on Economic Activity, Microeconomics* 2 (1993): 161-223.

Lind, Michael. "Spheres of Affluence." *American Prospect* (winter 1994): 91-99.

Lively, Robert A. "The American System: A Review Article." *Business History Review* 29 (Mar. 1955): 81-95.

Livesay, Harold C. "Entrepreneurial Dominance in Businesses Large and Small, Past and Present." *Business History Review* 63 (spring 1989): 1-21.

Logomasini, Angela. "Free Trade and Economic Growth: Opportunities for Environmental Improvements." *CSE Economic Perspective.* Washington, D.C., Feb. 24, 1993.

McCormick, Thomas J. "Drift or Mastery? A Corporatist Synthesis for American Diplomatic History." *Reviews in American History* 10 (Dec. 1982): 318-30.

McKillen, Beth. "The Corporatist Model, World War I, and the Public Debate Over the League of Nations." *Diplomatic History* 15 (spring 1991): 171-97.

Mead, Walter Russell. "Bushism, Found." *Harpers* 285 (Sept. 1992): 37-45.

Odell, John S. "Understanding International Trade Policies: An Emerging Synthesis." *World Politics* 43 (Oct. 1990): 139-67.

Pastor, Robert. "Congress and U.S. Foreign Policy: Comparative Advantage or Disadvantage." *Washington Quarterly* 14 (autumn 1991): 101-14.

Putnam, Robert D. "Bowling Alone: America's Declining Social Capital," *Journal of Democracy* 6 (Jan. 1995), 65-78.

Shuman, Michael. "Democracy vs. Gattzilla." *Bulletin of Municipal Foreign Policy* 4 (autumn 1994): 4-6.

Sweezy, Alan. "The Keynesians and Government Policy,1933-1939." *American Economic Review* 62 (May 1972): 116-24.

Thomas, Rosita. "Public Opinion on Trade." *CRS Review* (Feb.-Mar. 1992): 17.

Ullman, Owen. "A Presidential Train Wreck." *International Economy* (Nov.-Dec., 1994): 6-10.

Vernon, Raymond. "America's Foreign Trade Policy and the GATT." *Essays in International Finance* 21 (Oct. 1954): 1-25.

Walczak, Lee. "The New Populism." *Business Week,* Mar. 13, 1995, 73-80.

Werking, Richard Hume. "Bureaucrats, Businessmen, and Foreign Trade: The Origins of the U.S. Chamber of Commerce." *Business History Review* 52 (fall 1992): 2-12.

Books

Aaronson, Susan Ariel. *Trade is Everybody's Business.* Alexandria, Va., 1995.

Acheson, Dean. *Present at the Creation.* New York, 1969.

Aitken, Hugh S. *Syntony and Spark.* Princeton, N.J., 1976.

Alchon, Guy. *The Invisible Hand of Planning: Capitalism, Social Science, and the State in the 1920s.* Princeton, N.J., 1985.

Anderson, Terry H. *The United States, Great Britain, and the Cold War, 1944-1947.* Columbia, Mo., 1981.

Bailey, Stephen Kemp. *Congress Makes a Law: The Story Behind the Employment Act of 1946.* New York, 1950.

Baldwin, David A. *Economic Statecraft.* Princeton, N.J., 1985.

Baldwin, Robert E. *The Political Economy of U.S. Import Policy.* Cambridge, Mass., 1985.

Barfield Claude E., and William A. Schambra, ed. *The Politics of Industrial Policy.* Washington, D.C., 1986.

Barrie, Robert W. *Congress and the Executive: The Making of the United States Foreign Trade Policy 1789-1968.* NewYork, 1987.

Bauer, Raymond, Ithiel de Sola Pool, and Lewis Anthony Dexter. *American Business and Public Policy.* New York, 1963.

Beard, Charles A. *The Idea of National Interest: An Analytical Study in American Foreign Policy.* New York, 1934.

Becker, William H. *The Dynamics of Business-Government Relations: Industry and Exports 1893-1921.* Chicago, 1982.

Becker, William H., and Samuel F. Wells Jr., eds. *Economics and World Power.* New York, 1984.

Berelson, Bernard R., Paul F. Lazarsfeld, and William M. McPhee. *Voting: A Study of Opinion Formation in a Presidential Campaign.* Chicago, 1954.

Bernstein, Barton J., ed. *Politics and Policies of the Truman Administration.* Chicago, 1970.

Bernstein, Michael A. *The Great Depression: Delayed Recovery and Economic Change in America, 1929-1939.* Cambridge, England, 1987.

Bidwell, Percy. *A Commercial Policy for the United Nations.* New York, 1945.

Blum, John Morton, ed. *The Price of Vision: The Diary of Henry A. Wallace, 1942-1946.* Boston, 1973.

Blum, John Morton, *V Was for Victory: Politics and American Culture during World War II.* New York. 1976.

The Brookings Institution. *Major Problems of United States Foreign Policy 1947: A Study Guide.* Washington, D.C., 1947.

———. *Major Problems of United States Foreign Policy 1948: A Study Guide.* Washington, D.C., 1948.

Brown, William Adams, Jr. *The United States and the Restoration of World Trade.* Washington, D.C., 1950.

Bucholz, Rogene A. *Essentials of Public Policy for Management.* Englewood Cliffs, N.J., 1985.

Burk, Robert F. *The Corporate State and the Broker State: The Du Ponts and American National Politics 1925-1940.* Cambridge, Mass., 1990.

Campbell, John C., and the staff of the Council on Foreign Relations. *The United States in World Affairs 1948-1949.* New York, 1949.

Chandler, Alfred D., Jr. *Scale and Scope: The Dynamics of Industrial Capitalism.* Cambridge, Mass., 1990.

———. *Strategy and Structure: Chapters in the History of the American Industrial Enterprise.* Cambridge, Mass., 1962.

Chafe, William H. *The Unfinished Journey: American Culture during World War II.* New York, 1986.

Chapman, Richard N. *Contours of Public Policy, 1939-1945.* New York, 1981.

Chittick, William O. *The State Department, Press, and Pressure Groups: A Role Analysis.* New York, 1970.

Choate, Pat, and J.K. Linger, *The High-Flex Society.* New York, 1988.

Clearing Committee for Organizations Supporting Reciprocal Trade. *Grass Root Opinion on International Trade.* Washington, D.C., 1947.

Clinton, Bill, and Albert Gore Jr. *Putting People First: How We Can All Change America.* New York, 1992.

Cohen, Bernard C. *The Influence of Non-Governmental Groups on Foreign Policy-Making.* Boston, 1959.

Cohen, Stephen D. *The Making of United States International Economic Policy.* New York, 1977.

Collins, Robert M. *The Business Response to Keynes, 1929-1964.* New York, 1981.

Collins, Susan M., and Barry P. Bosworth, eds. *The New GATT: Implications for the United States.* Washington, D.C., 1994.

Congressional Quarterly. *Politics in America, 1945-1966.* Washington, D.C., 1967.

Cortney, Philip. *The Economic Munich.* New York, 1949.

Council on Competitiveness. *Roadmap for Results: Trade Policy, Technology, and American Competitiveness.* Washington, D.C., 1993.

Creagan, John P., ed. *America Asleep: The Free Trade Syndrome and the Global Economic Challenge.* New York, 1991.

Critchlow, Donald T. and Ellis W. Hawley. *Federal Social Policy: The Historical Dimension.* University Park, 1988.

Cuff, Robert D. *The War Industries Board: Business-Government Relations during World War I.* Baltimore, 1973.

Dallek, Robert M. *Franklin D. Roosevelt and American Foreign Policy, 1932-1945.* New York, 1979.

Dam, Kenneth W. *The GATT: Law and International Economic Organization.* Chicago, 1970.

Darilek, Richard E. *A Loyal Opposition in Time of War.* New York, 1976.

Destler, I.M. *American Trade Politics: System under Stress.* 2d ed. Washington, D.C., 1992. 3d ed., 1995.

Destler, I.M., and John S. Odell. *Antiprotection: Changing Forces in United States Trade Politics.* Washington, D.C., 1987.

Diebold, William, Jr. *New Directions in Our Trade Policy.* New York, 1941.

———. *The United States and the Industrial World.* New York, 1972.

Divine, Robert A. *Foreign Policy and U.S. Presidential Elections, 1940-1948.* New York, 1974.

————. *Second Chance: The Triumph of Internationalism in America during World War II.* New York, 1967.

Dobney, Frederick C., ed. *Selected Papers of Will Clayton.* Baltimore, 1971.

Dobson, John M. *Two Centuries of Tariffs: The Background and Emergence of the U.S. Iternational Trade Commission.* Washington, D.C., 1976.

Doig, Jameson W., and Erwin C. Hargrove, eds. *Leadership and Innovation: A Biographical Perspective on Entrepreneurs in Government.* Baltimore, 1987.

Dudley, William, ed. *Trade: Opposing Viewpoints.* San Diego, 1991.

Eckes, Alfred E., Jr. *A Search for Solvency: Bretton Woods and the International Monetary System, 1941-1971.* Austin, Tex., 1975.

————. *Opening America's Markets: U.S. Foreign Trade Policy Since 1776.* Chapel Hill, 1995.

Edelman, Murray. *Political Language: Words that Succeed and Policies That Fail.* New York, 1977.

Evans, Peter B., Dietrich Rueschemeyer, and Theda Skocpol, eds. *Bringing the State Back In.* Cambridge, England, 1985.

Fossedal, Gregory A. *Our Finest Hour: Will Clayton, the Marshall Plan and the Triumph of Democracy.* Stanford, Calif., 1993.

Fraser, Steve, and Gary Gerstle, eds. *The Rise and Fall of the New Deal Order, 1930-1980.* Princeton, N.J., 1989.

Galambos, Louis. *America at Middle Age.* New York, 1983.

————. *Competition and Cooperation: The Emergence of a National Trade Association.* Baltimore, 1966.

————. *The New American State: Bureaucracies and Policies Since World War II.* Baltimore, 1987.

Galambos, Louis, and Joseph Pratt. *The Rise of the Corporte Commonwealth.* New York, 1988.

Galbraith, John Kenneth. *Economics, Peace and Laughter.* Boston, 1971.

Gallup, George, and the American Institute of Public Opinion Staff. *The Political Almanac, 1952.* New York, 1952.

Gardner, Lloyd. *Economic Aspects of New Deal Diplomacy.* Madison, Wisc., 1964.

Gardner, Richard N. *Sterling-Dollar Diplomacy in Current Perspective.* New York, 1980.

Gilpin, Robert. *The Political Economy of International Relations.* Princeton, N.J., 1987.

Goldman, Eric F. *The Crucial Decade—and After: America, 1945-1960.* New York, 1960.

Goodrich, Carter. *Government Promotion of American Canals and Railroads.* New York, 1960.

Goodrich, Leland M., ed. *Documents on American Foreign Relations.* 4 vols. Boston, 1942.

Graebner, Norman A., ed. *An Uncertain Tradition: American Secretaries of State in the Twentieth Century.* New York, 1961.

Graham, Otis L., Jr. *Losing Time: The Industrial Policy Debate.* Cambridge, Mass., 1992.

————. *Toward a Planned Society.* New York, 1976.

Hamouda, Omar F., and John N. Smithin, eds. *Keynes and Public Policy after Fifty Years.* Vol. I. New York, 1990.

Hansen, Alvin H. *A Guide to Keynes.* New York, 1953.

————. *America's Role in the World Economy.* New York, 1945.

Hartmann, Susan M. *Truman and the 80th Congress.* Columbia, Mo., 1971.

Hartz, Louis. *The Liberal Tradition in America.* San Diego, 1955.

Hawkins, Harry C. *Commercial Treaties and Agreements: Principles and Practice.* New York, 1951.

Hawley, Ellis. *The New Deal and the Problem of Monopoly: A Study in Economic Ambivalence.* Princeton, N.J., 1966.

Hays, Samuel P. *The Response to Industrialism.* Chicago, 1957.

Hennessey, Bernard C. *Public Opinion.* Belmont, Calif., 1965.

Hilderbrand, Robert C. *Dumbarton Oaks: The Origins of the United Nations and the Search for Postwar Security.* Chapel Hill, N.C., 1990.

Hilsman, Roger. *The Politics of Policy Making in Defense and Foreign Affairs.* New York, 1971.

Hoffman, Paul G. *Peace Can Be Won.* Garden City, Doubleday, 1951.

Hofstadter, Richard. *The Age of Reform.* New York, 1955.

Hogan, Michael J. *Informal Entente: The Private Structure of Cooperation in Anglo-American Economic Diplomacy, 1918-1928.* Columbia, Mo., 1977.

————. *The Marshall Plan: America, Britain, and the Reconstruction of Western Europe, 1947-1952.* Cambridge, England, 1987.

Holborn, Louise W., ed. *War and Peace Aims of the United Nations.* Boston, 1948.

Horowitz, David, ed. *Corporations and the Cold War.* New York, 1969.

Howson, Susan, and Donald E. Moggridge, eds. *The Wartime Diaries of Lionel Robbins and James Meade, 1943-1945.* New York, 1991.

Hudec, Robert E. *Enforcing International Trade Law: The Evolution of the Modern GATT Legal System.* Salem, N.H., 1993.

————. *The GATT Legal System and World Trade Diplomacy.* New York, 1975.

Hufbauer, Gary Clyde. *The Free Trade Debate: Reports of the Twentieth Century Fund Task Force on the Future of American Trade Policy.* New York, 1989.

Hughes, Jonathan R. T. *The Governmental Habit.* New York, 1977.

Hull, Cordell. *The Memoirs of Cordell Hull.* 2 vols. New York, 1948.

Ikenberry, G. John, David A. Lake, and Michael Mastanduno. *The State and American Foreign Economic Policy.* Ithaca, N.Y., 1988.

Jackson, John H., *The World Trading System: Law and Policy of International Relations.* Cambridge, Mass., 1989.

Jones, Joseph M. *The Fifteen Weeks: February 21-June 5, 1947.* New York, 1955.

Katzenstein, Peter J., ed. *Between Power and Plenty: Foreign Economic Policies of Advanced Industrial States.* Madison, Wisc., 1978.

Kelly, William B., Jr, ed. *Studies in United States Commercial Policy.* Chapel Hill, N.C., 1963.

Key, V.O., Jr. *Public Opinion and American Democracy.* New York, 1964.

Keynes, John Maynard. *The General Theory of Employment, Interest, and Money.* New York, 1936.

Kindelberger, Charles P. *Marshall Plan Days.* Boston, 1987.

Kock, Karin, *International Trade Policy and the GATT, 1947-1967.* Stockholm, 1969.

Kolko, Gabriel. *Railroads and Regulation: 1877-1916.* Princeton, N.J., 1965.

————. *The Triumph of Conservatism: A Reinterpretation of American History, 1890-1916.* New York, 1963.

Kolko, Gabriel, and Joyce Kolko. *The Limits of Power.* New York, 1972.

Krugman, Paul. *Peddling Prosperity: Economic Sense and Nonsense in the Age of Diminished Expectations.* New York, 1994.

————. *Strategic Trade Policy and the New International Economics.* Cambridge, Mass., 1994.

LaFeber, Walter. *America, Russia and the Cold War.* New York, 1967.

Lake, David A. *Power, Protection and Free Trade.* Ithaca, N.Y., 1988.

Larkin, John Day. *Trade Agreements: A Study in Democratic Methods.* New York, 1940.

Lasch, Christopher. *The Revolt of the Elites and the Betrayal of Democracy.* New York, 1994.

Lawrence, Paul R., and Davis Dyer. *Renewing American Industry: Organizing for Efficiency and Innovation.* New York, 1983.

Lenway, Stefanie Ann. *The Politics of U.S. International Trade.* Marshfield, Mass., 1985.

Letiche, John M. *Reciprocal Trade Agreements in the World Economy.* New York, 1948.

Lind, Michael. *The Next American Nation: The New Nationalism and the Fourth American Revolution.* New York, 1995.

Lindblom, Charles E. *Politics and Markets.* New York, 1977.

Lodge, George C., and Ezra F. Vogel. *Ideology and National Competitiveness.* Cambridge, Mass., 1987.

Loree, Robert. *Position of the National Foreign Trade Committee with Respect to the Havana Charter for an ITO.* New York, 1950.

McCormick, Thomas J. *America's Half Century.* Baltimore, 1987.

McCullough, David. *Truman.* New York, 1992.

Mann, Thomas E., and Gary R. Orren, eds. *Media Polls in American Politics.* Washington, D.C., 1992.

Markowitz, Norman D. *The Rise and Fall of the People's Century.* New York, 1973.

Martel, Leon. *Lend-Lease, Loans, and the Coming of the Cold War: A Study of the Implementation of Foreign Policy.* Boulder, Colo., 1979.

Meade, James Edward. *The Economic Basis of a Durable Peace.* New York, 1940.

Mikesell, Raymond F. *U.S. Economic Policy and International Relations.* New York, 1952.

Milward, Alan S. *War, Economy and Society.* Berkeley, Calif., 1977.

Nader, Ralph, et al. *The Case against Free Trade.* San Francisco, 1993.

Nevins, Alan. *The New Deal and World Affairs.* New Haven, 1950.

North, Douglas. *Structure and Change in Economic History.* New York, 1981.

Nourse, Edwin G. *Economics in the Public Service.* New York, 1953.

Olson, Mancur, Jr. *The Logic of Collective Action: Public Goods and the Theory of Groups.* Cambridge, Mass., 1965.

Paarlberg, Robert L. *Leadership Abroad Begins at Home: U.S. Foreign Economic Policy After the Cold War.* Washington, D.C., 1994.

Parks, Wallace Judson. *United States Administration of Its International Economic Affairs.* New York, 1968.

Pastor, Robert A. *Congress and the Politics of U.S. Foreign Economic Policy, 1929-1976.* Berkeley, Calif., 1980.

Patterson, Merril D. *Adams and Jefferson: A Revolutionary Dialogue.* Oxford, England, 1978.

Patterson, James T. *Congressional Conservatism and the New Deal.* Lexington, Ky., 1967.

——. *Mr. Republican: A Biography of Robert A. Taft.* Boston, 1972.

Pennant-Rea, Ruppert, and Bill Emmot. *Pocket Economist.* London, 1983.

Penrose, E.F. *Economic Planning for the Peace.* Princeton, N.J., 1953.

Perkins, Dexter. *The New Age of Franklin Roosevelt, 1932-1945.* Chicago, 1957.

Phillips, Kevin. *Arrogant Capital: Washington, Wall Street, and the Frustration of American Politics.* Boston, 1994.

Pollard, Robert A. *Economic Security and the Origins of the Cold War, 1945-1950.* New York, 1985.

Prestowitz, Clyde V., Jr. *Trading Places: How We Are Giving Our Future to Japan and how to Reclaim It.* New York, 1988.

Rees, David. *Harry Dexter White: A Study in Paradox.* New York, 1973.

Reich, Robert B. *The Work of Nations: Preparing Ourselves for 21st Century Capitalism.* New York, 1992.

Roberts, Russell D. *The Choice: A Fable of Free Trade and Protectionism.* Englewood Cliffs, N.J., 1994.

Russell, Ruth B. *A History of the United Nations Charter: The Role of the United States 1940-1945.* Washington, D.C., 1958.

Sanford, William F., Jr. *The American Business Community and the European Recovery Program.* New York, 1987.

Sayre, Francis Bowes. *The Way Forward: The American Trade Agreements Program.* New York, 1939.

Schattschneider, E.E. *Politics, Pressure and the Tariff.* New York, 1935.

Schott, Jeffrey J. *The Uruguay Round: An Assessment.* Washington, D.C., 1994.

Schriftgiesser, Karl. *Business and Public Policy: The Role of the Committee for Economic Development, 1942-1967.* New York, 1967.

Schulzinger, Robert M. *The Wise Men of Foreign Affairs.* New York, 1984.

Schwab, Susan C. *Trade-Offs: Negotiating the Omnibus Trade and Competitiveness Act.* Boston, 1994.

Sidelsky, Robert, ed. *The End of the Keynesian Era.* New York, 1977.

Skowronek, Stephen. *Building a New American State: The Expansion of National Administrative Capacities, 1877-1920.* Cambridge, England, 1982.

Small, Melvin, ed. *Public Opinion and Historians.* Detroit, 1970.

Smith, Gaddis. *American Diplomacy during the Second World War.* New York, 1985.
———. *Dean Acheson.* New York, 1972.

Smith, Merrit Roe. *Harpers Ferry Armory and the New Technology.* Ithaca, N.Y., 1977.

Stebbins, Richard P., and the research staff. *The United States in World Affairs, 1949.* New York, 1950.

Sutton, Francis, Seymour E. Harris, Carl Kaysen, and James Tobin. *The American Business Creed.* Cambridge, Mass., 1956.

Sylla, Richard. *The American Capital Market, 1846-1914: A Study of the Effects of Public Policy on Economic Development.* New York, 1975.

Tasca, Henry J. *The Reciprocal Trade Policy of the United States: A Study in Trade Philosophy.* Philadelphia, 1938.

Taussig, Frank W. *The Tariff History of the United States.* New York, 1931.

Thurow, Lester. *Head to Head: The Coming Economic Battle among Japan, Europe, and America.* New York, 1992.

Tractenberg, Alan. *The Incorporation of America.* New York, 1982.

Tyson, Laura D'Andrea. *Who's Bashing Whom? Trade Conflict in High-Technology Industries.* Washington, D.C., 1992.

Vandenberg, Arthur H., Jr. *The Private Papers of Senator Vandenberg.* Boston, 1952.

Van Dormael, Armand. *Bretton Woods: Birth of a Monetary System.* New York, 1978.

Verdier, Daniel. *Democracy and International Trade: Britain, France, and the United States, 1860-1990.* Princeton, 1994.

Wallace, Henry. *America Must Choose: The Advantages and Disadvantages of Nationalism, of World Trade, and of a Planned Middle Course.* New York, 1934.

Weinstein, James. *The Corporate Ideal in a Liberal State, 1890-1918.* Boston, 1969.

Wentworth, Donald R., and Kenneth E. Leonard. *Teaching Strategies: International Trade.* New York, 1994.

Wiebe, Robert. *Businessmen and Reform: A Study of the Progressive Movement.* Cambridge, Mass., 1962.

———. *The Search for Order.* New York, 1967.

Wilcox, Clair. *A Charter for World Trade.* New York, 1949.

Wilkins, Mira. *The Emergence of Multinational Enterprise: American Business abroad From the Colonial Era to 1914.* Cambridge, Mass., 1970.

———. *The Maturing of Multinational Enterprise: American Business Abroad from 1914 to 1970.* Cambridge, Mass., 1974.

Wilkinson, Joe R. *Politics and Trade Policy.* Washington, D.C., 1960.

Woods, Randall Bennett. *A Changing of the Guard: Anglo-American Relations, 1941-1946.* Chapel Hill, 1990.

Yankelovich, Daniel. *Coming to Public Judgment: Making Democracy Work in a Complex World.* Syracuse, N.Y., 1991.

Young, Roland N. *Congressional Politics in the Second World War.* New York, 1956.

Zeiler, Thomas W. *American Trade and Power in the 1960s.* New York, 1992.

Public Opinion Polls and Books on Public Opinion

Almond, Gabriel A. *The American People and Foreign Policy.* New York, 1950.

Bailey, Thomas A. *The Man in the Street: The Impact of American Public Opinion on Foreign Policy.* New York, 1948.

Barber, Joseph, ed. *The Marshall Plan as American Policy: A Report on the Views of Community Leaders in Twenty-one Cities.* New York, 1948.

Bowman, Karlyn, and Everett Carl Ladd. "Public Opinion and Demographic Report." *American Enterprise,* Sept.-Oct. 1993.

Cantrill, Hadley, and research associates. *Gauging Public Opinion.* Princeton, N.J., 1947.

Cantril, Hadley. *Public Opinion, 1935-1946.* Princeton, N.J., 1951.

Cottrell, Leonard S., Jr., and Sylvia Eberhardt. *American Opinion on World Affairs in the Atomic Age.* Princeton, N.J., 1948.

Council on Competitiveness. "Looking for Leadership: The Public, Competitiveness, and Campaign 92." Washington, D.C., 1991.

Galen, Michele, and Mark N. Vamos, "Portrait of An Anxious Public," *Business Week,* Mar. 13, 1995, 80.

Gallup Poll News Service, "GATT Still a Mystery to Most Americans: Informed Public Favor Treaty." Dec. 1, 1994.

Immerwahr, John, Jean Johnson, and Adam Kernan-Schloss. "Cross-Talk: The Public, the Experts, and Competitiveness: A Research Report from the Business-Higher Education Forum and the Public Agenda Foundation." Washington, D.C., 1991.

Markel, Lester, et al. *Public Opinion and Foreign Policy.* New York, 1949.

Mosteller, Frederick, et al. *The Pre-Election Polls of 1948: Report to the Committee on Analysis of Pre-Election Polls and Forecasts.* Bulletin 60. New York, 1950.

National Opinion Research Center. "American Programs of Foreign Aid." Occasional Report Series FA. No. 4. University of Chicago, 1957.

———. "Cincinatti Looks at the United Nations." Report no. 37. Chicago, 1947.

———. "Cincinnati Looks Again." Report no. 37A. Chicago, 1948.

———. "Confidential Survey" 156, du-1 and DU-1. Mar. 25, 1948, and June 30, 1949.

———. "Lend-Lease to England." Report no. 11. Chicago, Aug. 1943.

———. "A Nation-wide Public Opinion Survey on Post-War and Current Problems." Denver, Aug. 1942.

———. "The 1947 Election Situation." Chicago, 1947.

———. "Public Attitudes toward Foreign Trade." Survey 243. Chicago, 1946.

———. "The Public Looks at Politics and Politicians." Report no. 20. Chicago, Mar. 1944.

———. "The Public Looks at Trade and Tariff Problems." Chicago, 1947.

———. "The Public Looks at World Organization." Report no. 19. Denver, 1944.

———. "Public Opinion on World Organization up to the San Francisco Conference." Report no. 25. University of Denver, 1945.

Polling data

     Princeton Survey Research Associates

     Gallup

     Greenberg Reseach/Democratic Leadership Council

     Business Week

     New York Times

     Washington Post

     Wall Street Journal

     USA Today

Social Science Research Council. "Public Reaction to the Atomic Bomb and World
Affairs." Parts 1 and 2, "Findings of the Extensive Surveys." Ithaca, N.Y., 1947.

Survey Research Center. "America's Role in World Affairs: Patterns of Citizen Opinion, 1949-1950." Ann Arbor, Mich., May 1952.

———. "Public Attitudes toward American Foreign Policy: A Nation-wide Survey," Ann Arbor, Mich., May 1947.

———. "Patterns of Attitudes Toward American Foreign Policy." Ann Arbor,
Mich., May 1947.

Times Mirror Center for the People and the Press. Robert C. Toth. "America's Place
in the Post–Cold War World." Washington, D.C., Nov. 1993.

———. "The New Political Landscape: The People, the Press and Politics," Washington, D.C., Oct. 1994.

———. "Public Expects GOP Miracles." Washington, D.C., Dec. 8, 1994.

———. "The People, the Press and Politics: Public Opinion About Economic Issues." Washington, D.C., Mar. 1989.

———. Andrew Kohut and Robert C. Toth. "Trade and the Public." Washington,
D.C., Dec. 13, 1994.

———. "Strong Support for Minimum Wage Hike and Preserving Entitlements."
Washington, D.C., Feb. 17, 1995.

Dissertations

Beddow, James Bellamy. "Economic Nationalism or Internationalism: Upper Midwestern Response to New Deal Tariff Policy." Ph.D. diss. University of Oklahoma, 1969.

Brady, Patrick George. "Toward Security: Postwar Economic and Social Planning
in the Executive Office, 1939-1946." Ph.D. diss. Rutgers University, 1975.

Graham, Charles John. "Republican Foreign Policy, 1939-1952." Ph.D. diss. University of Illinois, 1955.

Hedlund, Richard P. "Congress and the British Loan, 1945-1946: A Congressional
Study." Ph.D. diss. University of Kentucky, 1976.

Herring, George Cyril Jr. "Experiment in Foreign Aid: Lend-Lease, 1941-1945."
Ph.D. diss. University of Virginia, 1965.

Hinchey, Mary Hedge. "The Frustration of the New Deal Revival, 1944-1946." Ph.D. diss. University of Missouri, 1965.

Poole, Walter S. "The Quest for a Republican Foreign Policy, 1941-1951." Ph.D. diss. University of Pennsylvania, 1968.

Pritchard, Ross Joseph. "Will Clayton: A Study of Business-Statesmanship in the Formulation of United States Economic Policy." Ph.D. diss. Fletcher School of Law and Diplomacy, Tufts University, 1955.

Tilman, Lee Rickels. "The American Business Community and the Death of the New Deal." Ph.D. diss. University of Arizona, 1966.

Interviews by the Author

ITO/GATT

Armstrong, Willis C. Washington, D.C., Mar. 14, 1991.
Diebold, William, Jr. New York, July 12, 1990.
Hand, J.M. Colton. McLean, Va., May 8, 1991.
Leddy, John M., and Margaret Leddy. McLean, Va., Oct. 5, 1990.
Norwood, Bernard, and Janet Norwood. Washington, D.C., June 9, 1994.
Rubin, Seymour. Washington, D.C., May 12, 1992.
Schaetzel, Imogen, and J. Robert Schaetzel. Bethesda, Md., Aug. 9, 1992.
Thorp, Clarice, and Willard Thorp. Amherst, Mass., Feb. 24, 1991.
Tresize, Phillip. Washington, D.C., Feb. 4, 1991.
Vernon, Raymond. Boston, Mass., Feb. 23, 1991.
Weiss, Leonard. Arlington, Va., May 22, 1991.

GATT/WTO

Boidock, John. Lobbyist, Texas Instruments, and organizer, Alliance for GATT NOW. Washington D.C., Oct. 27, 1994, Nov. 3, 1994, and Jan. 3, 1995.

Cobb, Joe. John M. Olin Fellow in International Economics, Heritage Foundation. Washington, D.C., Aug. 13, 1994 and Oct. 22, 1994.

Collins, Paula. Business Roundtable. Washington, D.C., Feb. 14, 1995.

Connor, Roger. Executive director, American Alliance for Rights and Responsibilities. Telephone interview, Mar. 7, 1995.

Danowitz, Jane. Citizens' Trade Campaign. Telephone interview, Nov. 14, 1994.

Eder, Ann. Special assistant to the deputy director for public liaison, White House. Telephone interview, Feb. 22, 1995.

Fields, Catherine. Office of the general counsel, USTR, Washington, D.C. Telephone interview, May 1, 1994.

Gardner, Daniel. Office of Multilateral Affairs, Department of Commerce. Washington, D.C., Feb. 22, 1995.

Goldman, Patti. Lawyer, Citizens' Trade Campaign and Sierra Club. Telephone interview, June 29, 1994

Heine, Robert. Lobbyist, Du Pont Company. Telephone interview, Dec. 30, 1994.

Jontz, Jim. Consultant, Citizens' Trade Campaign. Telephone interview, Feb. 21, 1995.

Kantor, Ambassador Mickey. United States trade representative. Washington, D.C., Jan. 13, 1995.

Kearns, Kevin. President, U.S. Business and Industrial Council and "Save Our Sovereignty." Telephone interview, Feb. 22, 1995.

Kohut, Andrew. Director, Times Mirror Center for the People and the Press. Washington, D.C., Mar. 8, 1995.

Luzzato, Ann. Assistant United States trade representative for public affairs. Telephone interview, Feb. 11, 1995.

Marchick, David. Office of the United States trade representative. Telephone interview, Jan. 17, 1995.

McMillion, Dr. Charles. Telephone interview, Mar. 22, 1995.

Mitchell, Larry. National Farmers Union. Telephone interview, Feb. 22, 1995.

Parker, Clayton. Director of intergovernmental affairs, United States trade representative. Washington, D.C., Oct. 14, 1994.

Seligman, Dan. Senior trade fellow, Sierra Club. Telephone interviews, Feb. 22, 1995 and Mar. 3, 1995.

Silbergeld, Mark. Director, Washington Office, Consumers Union. Telephone interview, May 13, 1994.

Xerxa, Ambassador Rufus. Deputy United States trade representative. Washington, D.C., Jan. 5, 1995.

Wallach, Lori. Director, Citizens' Trade Campaign. Washington, D.C., Mar. 17 and 21, 1995, and Apr. 5, 1995.

Index

Abbink, John, 88, 213 n 28
Acheson, Dean, 4, 42, 116, 178 n 7
  proposed compromises with Republican congress on TAP, 69-70, 207 n 36
  role in ITO, 44-45, 52, 80, 95, 199 n 12; as Secretary of State, 117, 118, 123, 125, 126, 130
  role in 1939-42 postwar planning, 26, 27, 30, 32, 38
  testimony on proposed loan to Britain, 65, 205 n 15
Advisory Committee (1942), on postwar trade policies, 32, 192 n 68
Advisory Committee on Problems of Foreign Relations (1941), 24
AFL-CIO, concern with job security, 136
Agricultural Adjustment Act, 185 n 31; and proposed ITO, 54, 80-81, 200 n 17
agriculture, American: growing need for foreign markets, 15; protectionist policies of the 1920s-30s, 16, 18; subsidy programs and ITO debates, 54, 76, 80-81, 200 n 17
AIPO (American Institute of Public Opinion): 1938 poll on tariff policies, 21-22; poll on government postwar planning, 202 n 43
Alliance for GATT NOW, 150
American Association of Retired People, 182 n 44
American Bar Association, 152
American Enterprise Institute, 138
American Institute of Public Opinion (AIPO): 1938 poll on tariff policies,

21-22; poll on government postwar planning, 202 n 43
Anglo-American Financial Settlement, 223 n 37
Annecy (France) Round, of GATT negotiations, 96, 117, 124
anticommunism. *See* communism
Appleby, Paul, 192 nn 68, 71
Archer, Bill, 151
Armstrong, Hamilton Fish, 192 n 68
Article VII, Atlantic Charter, 54; American/British compromise negotiations, 30-31, 191 n 56; effect on lend-lease legislation, 25-29, 30, 36-37, 187 nn 15, 17; effects of revised compromise draft, 31-33, 191 n 62
Atlantic Charter, influence on postwar trade policies, 28-29, 31, 189 n 39
Australia, controversy with U.S. over wool tariffs, 81-82

balance-of-payment, as trade problem, 75-76, 80, 223 n 37
Baldwin, W.H., 100-101, 103
Balgooyen, H.W., 88, 89, 213 n 28
Barfield, Claude, 153-54
Barkley, Alben, 92, 118, 205 n 12
Barnes, Albert, 128
Batt, William, 103, 113, 123, 126
Bean, Louis H., 192 n 69
Bell, David, 116-17
Bentley, Elizabeth, 115
Bidwell, Percy, 192 n 69